S0-EGG-762

NOT WITHOUT CAUSE

NOT WITHOUT CAUSE

DAVID PETERSON'S
FALL FROM GRACE

GEORGETTE GAGNON
DAN RATH

HarperCollins*PublishersLtd*

NOT WITHOUT CAUSE

Copyright © 1991 by Georgette Gagnon and Dan Rath. All rights reserved. No part of this book may be used or reproduced in any manner whatsoever without prior written permission except in the case of brief quotations embodied in reviews. For information address HarperCollins Publishers Ltd, Suite 2900, 55 Avenue Road, Toronto, Canada M5R 3L2.

First Edition

Canadian Cataloguing in Publication Data

Gagnon, Georgette
Not without cause

ISBN 0-00-215842-6

1. Ontario — Politics and government — 1985- .*
2. Peterson, David, 1943- . 3. Ontario Liberal Party.
I. Rath, Dan. II. Title.

FC3076.2.G34 1991   971.3'04   C91-094595-0
F1058.G34 1991
91 92 93 94 95 RRD 5 4 3 2 1

For our families

Contents

You all did love him once,
not without cause

–William Shakespeare
Julius Caesar

PROLOGUE

Seeking A Comfort Level

The phone calls came on Friday, July 27.

"We're meeting Sunday morning at Gossage's," was the cryptic message from Kathy Robinson, chair of the Ontario Liberal Party's 1990 election campaign. "Be there." No more needed to be said, when the word was put out to the members of the Liberal campaign's strategy committee: Premier David Peterson was ready to call an election and they were being summoned for a final, critical session to prepare him for the campaign kickoff.

A partner in a respected law firm and former president of the Ontario Liberal Party, Robinson left her home northwest of Toronto early Sunday as the heat began to build. With her convertible's top down, she cruised purposefully downtown to the meeting that would cap a year of pre-election buildup. Tall, auburn-haired, often pursed-lipped with determination, Robinson wanted a no-nonsense, productive session this morning at the office of Patrick Gossage, a former press secretary to Pierre Trudeau. Assembled in a media training room when Robinson came striding in were the members of the Liberal strategy committee: a group of experts that could run a campaign blindfolded.

Some of them would claim later that was exactly what they were asked to do.

Sharply dressed pollster Martin Goldfarb, his fringe of longish hair in its typical wild disarray, was dropping a binder and notes into a chair. Hershell Ezrin, David MacNaughton, Senator Michael Kirby and Dan Gagnier were studying one another's feet as Robinson arrived. All were shod in identical brown Topsiders.

"This must mean something," Ezrin laughed. "Do you think we're all yuppies?" It was Ezrin's third campaign with Peterson since he became the fledgling Liberal leader's chief of staff in 1982, a position he held for six years until moving on to the private sector. Returning to the Liberal strategy committee in 1990, Ezrin would concentrate on preparing Peterson for the televised leaders' debate. In the 1985 and 1987 elections Ezrin had been one of a tiny core of full-time campaign strategists. This time he was sharing those duties as a member of a larger group of volunteers.

MacNaughton, a friend of Peterson and president of the giant government relations firm Public Affairs International, had co-chaired the Liberals' majority-winning 1987 election campaign. Kirby, the federal Liberals' dean of propaganda since running the Canadian Unity Information Office during the patriation period, divided his time between the Senate and a vice-presidency at Goldfarb's polling firm. Gagnier, a career public servant who had worked with both Kirby and Ezrin as the senior bureaucrat in the unity office, had moved chameleon-like through a series of top federal and provincial government positions before accepting the job of Peterson's principal secretary on secondment. Gagnier was an experienced problem solver; it was his fluency in the lingo of constitutional reform that in 1990 made him an asset to Peterson.

"Can we get started, please?" Robinson called out. Caught up in small talk, no one was listening; the air-conditioning was blasting out cold air to battle the mid-morning sun lancing a wall of windows. "Excuse me," Robinson tried again.

Campaign director Beth Webster arrived and positioned herself in a far corner to get a hawk's-eye view, keeping an eye on the strategists and a handful of campaign staff. Married to John Webster, campaign director for John Turner's Liberals in the 1988 federal election, Webster was a sharp, demanding manager taken on by Peterson as executive coordinator of his office. Walking in behind her was strategist David Morton, the chair of the Liberals' volunteer campaign advertising coalition, Red Trillium.

The steely profile of an Ontario Provincial Police bodyguard poked through the doorway. "Where there's smoke," a campaign staffer observed, "there's fire," and Peterson breezed in, wearing sandals and sweatpants, fresh off the beach of his rented cottage at Grand Bend near London, his tan deep and ruddy from the Lake Huron sun.

Peterson had tried to recharge during an on-and-off three-week vacation. Early Friday he had given the final nod to Robinson and Webster—not on whether an election would be called, but on his choice for the date. For more than a month, since the collapse of the Meech Lake Accord, Peterson had been certain he would call a fall election. But he had been anguishing over the decision for weeks.

Since the previous summer the Liberal party had been preparing for an election to give Peterson the flexibility to send Ontario voters to the polls in 1990, only three years into a mandate that could run for five. Bob Rae's New Democrats, dispirited after years of failing to score points against Peterson and make inroads with voters, appeared to pose little threat. The Tories, emerging from a divisive leadership process, were shackled with debt, their organization a shambles and their new leader Mike Harris almost unknown.

Girding the Liberals with the confidence that they could win an early election was an array of public opinion research and analysis provided to the strategy committee by Goldfarb in May. A campaign strategy paper based on broad provincewide polling had Peterson poised to win another fat majority. For months the Liberals' popularity among decided voters had hovered at about 50 percent. Across Ontario other pollsters were making similar findings and predicting re-election for the Liberals.

Backing up Goldfarb's strategic document was a pivotal analysis of Peterson's public image drawn from "focus group" interview sessions. It concluded that Ontarians liked Peterson and most of what he represented. Both reports tantalized, encouraged and reassured the Liberal strategists; both cautioned of potential landmines they believed could be managed and overcome.

"Good morning, David, we're just about to get going," said Robinson as Peterson poured himself coffee and then straddled a chair in the middle of the room. "I want to start," she announced, "by summarizing where we are and setting out the parameters of what we want to do today. We've all agreed that there has to be a clear rationale in terms of the statement and the call, in terms of why the premier has made the decision to issue the writ. We have to sketch out in broad terms what the issues are that we feel are important and will be addressed during the course of the campaign.

"There has to be," she raised her voice for emphasis, "a level of comfort that there has been a wide consultation on all of these issues and a real focusing and a broad consensus about what is important."

"Could we sort of go around and get a sense of what the thinking is?" Peterson suggested. "Hershell, Marty: Waddya think?"

"Well, anxieties in many different areas are very strong for people right now," Ezrin began, "and that has to be addressed right off the top in the statement."

"Yes!" piped up Goldfarb. The longtime Liberal pulse-taker jumped in. "People with families, especially the middle class, are extremely concerned about the erosion of their prosperity. We have to be seen to be protecting the interests of the middle class and that means we have to reassure them. That's your role."

Peterson looked to the back of the room where the campaign staffers had gathered. "Waddya think, guys?"

One aide had anticipated the premier's favorite question. "I think," he said slowly, "that you're gonna get your nuts cut off if you don't have a good reason for going and that you have to state it very clearly and stick to it."

"Exactly," said Ezrin. "The rationale has to be right up front."

Peterson nodded grimly in agreement. He had listened to the same concern expressed for weeks, in somewhat more diplomatic language, in meetings of the Liberal cabinet and caucus.

"Look, we're all in agreement on that and it's in the statement," said Robinson.

"And how's the press gallery going to feel?" Peterson explored further.

"It'll be a very tough sell this time," Ezrin cautioned. As Peterson's chief of staff and principal secretary, he had been an accomplished "spin doctor," an artful interweaver of policy and communications who could predict how issues and decisions would play and then massage the Liberals' messages for optimum impact.

"Unbelievably tough," an aide added. "Some of them hate your guts, some are just bored, some don't think you care. A lot of them see themselves as the real 'official opposition,' and they say they're going to make you 'earn' re-election."

"Well, I think we're ready for that," replied Peterson with confidence. "Vince will be on the bus." As he spoke, Vince Borg walked in, sweating, swarthy and unshaven; he had raced back from his cottage, where he had planned to spend the next week. One of Peterson's closest personal advisors and confidantes for a decade, Borg would spend five weeks in lockstep with Peterson on the Liberal campaign bus. Good with reporters, Borg could also be counted on to pay constant attention to Peterson's "comfort level."

"You know, it's freezing in here," Peterson said. "Are you guys cold?" The air-conditioning had won its battle with the sun. Borg peeled his rugby shirt off over his T-shirt and handed it to the premier.

"I believe we have the draft of a statement ready and that we're going to go over it now," Robinson said, urging the meeting back on track.

"David, would you please go behind the podium and we can run through this," Robinson directed. "Do one read-through and we'll all listen and change it as we go. Then questions and answers."

Peterson placed one hand on the front of the podium, leaning slightly forward. Even in sweats and baggy shirt, his familiar speech-making stance could be discerned: "Ladies and gentlemen, I've just spoken to His Honor the Lieutenant-Governor and I've informed the leaders of the opposition parties that on September 6, 1990, an election will take place in Ontario." Peterson marked his script for pauses and emphasis as he read.

"Choosing the most appropriate time for an election is never an easy decision to make and over the past few weeks I've given this matter a great deal of thought and consideration. I've reviewed the issues and challenges that lie ahead of us, and having weighed the alternatives, I've concluded that an election is appropriate at this time. In the three years since Ontarians last went to the polls, we've experienced many dramatic economic and political changes. Ontario industries are facing increasingly tough competition from the United States and around the world. Our workers are struggling to keep up with new technologies and the demand for higher skills.

"You know," Peterson looked up. "What I'd like to put in here is something about '85 percent of the technology that we'll have in the year 2000 has not even been invented yet.' That stuff from the Premier's Council." Heads nodded as aides scribbled down the additions.

"Federal policies such as free trade, a high dollar and high interest rates and the GST have each created a very difficult climate for growth and imposed many personal hardships. People are anxious about the future—about the security of their jobs and homes—about their ability to continue providing a high standard of living for themselves and their children—about the future stability of our country."

"Oh, that's very good," Goldfarb murmured.

"In making this decision, I've considered the fact that elections cost money, now or a year from now," Peterson read. "Hmm," he paused, glancing up. "Does that belong in there?"

"The Tories are going to keep on this unnecessary election issue," Borg pointed out. "They've got those ads out about a $40-million election."

"We could say that's the price of democracy," an aide volunteered, "and $40 million works out to a dollar per person per year over four years in Ontario."

"Let's leave the whole thing for the question-and-answers," Ezrin spoke up. "We can't let it cut into the main message."

"It's out, then," Robinson concluded.

"Over the next few weeks," Peterson resumed, "I'll be seeking the confidence of the people to proceed with an agenda for building a stronger economy, protecting our environment, and preserving safe, healthy and caring communities. A strong economy is the key to creating and protecting jobs at home, competing and succeeding abroad, and moving forward with our program of social reforms."

"That's the clip right there," an aide interrupted. "We can tighten it up and then it's all in the delivery."

"Ye-e-es!" exclaimed Goldfarb, wheeling in his chair, his finger piercing the air. "I think that we could still omit that reference to the social welfare agenda. Our constituency is more concerned about maintaining their standard of living and we don't need to mix the messages."

"Well, we've agreed, Marty, that has to stay," ruled Robinson, "to balance the economic agenda."

"Okay, let's keep going," said Peterson. "What do you suggest there—the wording?"

"Let's say," proposed a staffer, "'I am setting out today to seek the confidence of the people to proceed with an agenda to build a stronger economy,' just to make it flow better. This is supposed to be about finding a comfort level for you, so you should sound at ease with the words explaining the reason. That clip makes every newscast, and we want it to resonate over and over again."

"Ye-e-es!" Goldfarb spun in his chair again, finger jabbing excitedly. He leaned over to the staffers keeping track of the amendments. "Why don't we say at that point, 'We've worked hard in Ontario to earn our standard of living and now we have to work hard to maintain it,'" he whispered. "Our strategy has to define the middle class who voted us in."

"Well, then, is everyone satisfied on the reason?" Robinson looked around, anxious that the meeting keep moving.

"The emphasis really has to be not on the when," Ezrin offered, "but on the what and the why." Other strategists murmured in agreement. To keep the statement tight and simple, they agreed, no more elaborate explanation of the reason would be added.

"How about," Borg offered glibly, "'I'm calling this election because I think I can win'?"

"The reason's in there," came a chorus of impatient voices. "It's in, it's clear, it's fine."

"Well, let's keep going, can we, please," Robinson insisted. Peterson scanned the script and again found his place.

"In the days ahead," he read, "I will be outlining a series of proposals to———"

"Too weak," came several voices. "How about, 'I will put forward detailed policy initiatives to———'"

"—assist our workforce," Peterson continued, "in improving their skill levels, create new opportunities for training and upgrading, provide new support for entrepreneurship and export development, and expand our scientific and technological capacity."

"Mm, that really sounds like just more of the same," an aide cautioned. "You might talk more about exactly what we're doing."

"The announcements will come out in the campaign," Robinson called out and turned back to Peterson.

"I will also be introducing proposals," he read on, "to ensure that we can protect Ontario's economic interests regardless of any changes that may take place in the structure of federal-provincial relations in the years ahead. Together, we will ensure that Ontario's economic future and standard of living will not be jeopardized as a result of bilateral discussions between the federal government and other provinces or regions." Peterson stopped abruptly and looked up, gazing into the distance. The room fell cautiously silent as the premier began to ponder a question on national unity, his most heartfelt concern—and the key to his personal motive for wanting an election. But dwelling on Canada's post-Meech problems, the strategists had agreed, would be "off-strategy" for the campaign.

"That's not it; it's not right. Let's do something with those two paragraphs. Right here is where I want to say this, get this down," and he savored each word like a caramel: "'In a changing political environment in Canada, it is imperative to protect Ontario's economic and political interests. To this end, I will be putting forward in the near future a process for involving our people in a broad consultation with respect to our interests.'"

"We can work on that," said Robinson. "Let's keep going."

"Since 1985 the Ontario economy has grown at a faster rate than that of any major country in the industrialized world and we've created 714,000 jobs. Our unemployment rate is down to 5.2 percent—the lowest rate of any province in Canada." Peterson stopped again. "What I'd like to add here is," and again he seemed to relish each word: "'But we cannot take our good fortune for granted.' Got it?" Peterson read on, rhyming off a dozen of his government's top accomplishments.

"Ladies and gentlemen, we all take a great deal of pride in Ontario," Peterson intoned. "Ontario is a good place to live, a good place to work and a good place in which to raise a family."

"Geez!" Borg interjected. "That sounds like Bill Davis!"

"Ontario didn't become that way by accident," Peterson read with a smile, "and it won't stay that way through inactivity. It will only stay that way through a clear and meaningful agenda for the '90s. The time has come to chart our course for the decade ahead. Thank you."

"No, no, no!" burst out Ezrin, leaping to his feet. "That's not the way to end it. This is where you have to close the deal!"

"Ye-e-e-es!" exhorted Goldfarb.

"And the way to do it is very simple," Ezrin continued excitedly, his arms circling like a conductor urging an orchestra to a crescendo. "To close the deal you say, 'I am asking the people of Ontario for their support!'"

Twice more Peterson read patiently through; each time, a tape of the performance was replayed and studied. By Peterson's third take the session began to bog down in detail: Should "the" or "a" be used in a certain sentence? During one sequence, with some in the room ready to nod off, Borg sprang up and pointed frantically out the window at a neighboring rooftop that was shimmering in the afternoon heat.

"There's Boris Spremo from the Toronto *Star* and he's taking our picture!" he shouted. Peterson and a dozen others jumped, looked and then all laughed at once. Borg had succeeded in breaking the tension in the room, knowing Peterson would appreciate a time-out from the grind.

Kirby relieved himself of the drudgery by checking out early to play golf. A staffer convinced Borg to hand over his Visa card and used it to order $42 worth of pizza for lunch.

With the statement worked out, the group subjected Peterson to a grueling two-hour session of questions and answers, aimed at testing and perfecting his responses to the darts that members of the media would fire the next morning. After poring over his briefing books at the beach, Peterson had absorbed thousands of facts and figures. He answered each question in detail, often dropping his tone to the near-mumble he was accustomed to using in response to tough questions when scrummed by reporters.

"You didn't stop free trade like you said you would, premier, and now we're facing plant closures and layoffs and you haven't done anything about retraining," Ezrin taunted.

"Well, that is completely unfounded," Peterson responded indignantly. "You know, let me tell you something," he continued, his voice picking up conviction. "We've done something in this province that's never been done before. We are getting people to come together as they never have, from business, from management, from labor, at the Premier's Council and elsewhere. We're bringing people together around the table to talk these things out and work on them, people who used to spill blood across the table. That's a change I can tell you has the most far-reaching implications for how we plan for the future in this province and it's one in which I take a great deal of pride." Second to his offerings on national unity, the soliloquy was

Peterson's most passionate contribution to the day, a response in which he exhibited spontaneity and emotion.

"Premier Peterson," Borg burst in, "Patti Starr is here now and she'd like to come up and say a few words."

Peterson grimaced at the mention of the former Liberal fund-raiser who was facing criminal charges and charges under the Election Finances Act in the wake of a scandal that had tainted his government.

"Oh, hell, I don't know, what do I say?" he scowled. "She's not going to show up or anything like that, is she?"

"Well, I don't think so," said Borg. "But the key on those answers is the tone. You can't sound at all defensive." Peterson listened sullenly; he was tired of the Starr affair, resigned that the fund-raising scandal would re-emerge at the election call, frustrated he would have to deal with it again. But he acquiesced to a long rehearsal of answers until the group was satisfied he was responding without rancor.

"Mr. Premier," said MacNaughton, trying a different topic. "We represent the local residents of our community and we don't want Toronto's garbage in our back yard. We————"

"Oh come on now, look, reasonable people would agree ————" Peterson snapped, his impatience showing at an issue he knew could be a source of troublesome protests during the campaign.

"No, no," MacNaughton broke in. "These guys, these environmentalists have a lot of credibility and you've got to sympathize with the cause. You've got to sort of hug the tree-huggers."

"You have to resist the urge to bash them around," Borg added. "You have to separate the environmentalists from the nuts. The polling stats show they're credible as interest groups and that governments don't match up in credibility." Peterson nodded. The grilling continued; outside the room, Borg and Webster touched base.

"So, Vince," queried Webster, "what's all this shit about a 'comfort level'?"

"That's the buzzword of the day, eh?" said Borg. "The big bugaboo."

"Yeah, but what's going on?" asked Webster. "Are we going through this to get his comfort level up or are we trying to make ourselves comfortable that he's got all the answers?"

"I don't know," said Borg. "I thought you would."

They looked at one another with uncertainty and went back into the room.

"Is that it, then?" Peterson scanned the faces. A few heads nodded. There was little enthusiasm left in the group. Minds were drifting ahead to the events of the coming days, to the demands of a five-week campaign; there was nothing left, they believed, to talk about. Finally, all the months of planning, all the behind-the-scenes machinations, were about to transform into the reality of an election campaign. There was no turning back.

Peterson's campaign kickoff statement was passable; it seemed to get across the reasons for the early-election call and sketch out the Liberal agenda. But there were second thoughts.

"There was not, particularly with the premier himself, but even among a lot of the people in that room, a determination that they should actually be proceeding with this election," said one aide. "Nor was there a strong comfort that the reasons were sufficiently well-crafted and I would say that there was still a lot of unease and discomfort there."

There were nagging worries: there would be some protesters along the way, Peterson still seemed inclined to talk about national unity when voters were believed to be tired of it, the specter of recession was creeping closer. But while these aches and pains were recognized, they were dulled by a cooling anesthetic: Peterson's image, the group had determined, was positive, strong and resilient enough to overcome potential glitches and a mid-July poll showed Liberal support still topping 50 percent, leaving room for a little slippage.

Confident they knew what Ontarians were thinking in the summer of 1990, the Liberal strategists gave no thought to the possibility Peterson might actually be defeated in the election he was about to call. Like most Ontarians, they never dreamed that forces were about to be unleashed that would bring down one of the most popular governments in Canada.

1

It Just Sort of Happened

Life in politics is timing.

–DAVID PETERSON

On election night, September 10, 1987, David and Shelley Peterson embraced onstage, warmed by the twin glow of television lights and public adulation. Blessed by the province's voters with an overwhelming 95-seat majority and a solid 47 percent of the popular vote, the premier, young, fit and prosperous, represented all that was good and right about Ontario. As Liberals stood shoulder to shoulder in London's Centennial Hall and cheered, Peterson vowed to respect the confidence Ontarians had shown in his party. "We must earn the people's trust every single day," he said.

Beaten down to 26 percent of the popular vote and trimmed back to 19 seats from 23, Bob Rae and the NDP could take solace only in their return to official opposition status. After winning his Toronto seat by a slim 240 votes, Rae promised a watchdog role over the mighty Liberal majority. "As long as I have breath to breathe, there will be no abuses of power," he pledged. The tired Tories collapsed from 50 seats to 16, and 25 percent of the popular vote; leader Larry Grossman lost his downtown Toronto seat and resigned.

"It's wonderful," Peterson told reporters. "Nobody has been more lucky or more blessed than I." In September 1987, setting out to govern with a majority, Peterson was cautiously optimistic. "We will make mistakes but we will be judged on how we handle those," he predicted. As Liberals congratulated one another on their success, Peterson played down their expectations with a dose of realism, saying he doubted Ontario would ever "see a government reign for 42 years again."

*   *   *

"We were skiing and he broke his leg," recalled Clarence Peterson of the second of his three sons, David. "He was about Grade 10 and he followed Jimmy—always following the older brother— and he got his leg twisted and had a bad break. He's gutsy. He can take chances that maybe he shouldn't take physically. He probably goes on higher hills than he should."

Born in Toronto in December 1943, four months after the Progressive Conservative party began a 42-year dynasty at the Ontario legislature, David Peterson was nurtured on Liberal politics. By 1946 Clarence, once a youthful supporter of the Co-operative Commonwealth Federation and witness to the birth of its founding Regina Manifesto, was a Liberal businessman in conservative London. When Clarence ran as an alderman, winning seven straight terms, David handed out leaflets door to door. "It was a very rich life for me," said Clarence. "And I think it enriched the life of my family, because we discussed politics all the time around the table."

Love of country was a given for the Petersons; belief in its perpetual unity unquestioned. "I am naive enough," said Clarence, "to think that the country should stay united, that we give and take like you try and keep a family together with a little give and take." The family seemed to personify what David would come to call "the Liberal view of generosity and kindness." "We always just put on the table, 'Well, here's our money, what do you need?'" said Clarence. "I don't think they ever asked for something that was unreasonable. They just got what they needed and shared what we had." Marie Peterson saw the traits of a peacemaker in David: "Anytime there was a problem or difference of opinion he'd know how to neutralize it, and he was like that all the time."

Experiences through young adulthood shaped Peterson's character. A bachelor of arts degree in philosophy from the University of Western Ontario in hand, he entered the University of Toronto's law school in 1964, where he acquired a nickname: the Squire. Boxing filled his spare time—a workout and a confidence-builder for a passable young light-heavyweight. Self-enrichment filled his summers, including an experience with Frontier College in the western provinces, where he worked out of a boxcar, driving spikes during the day, teaching English to railway workers at night. Interest in his lessons lagged when workers showed a preference for drinking at hotels: Peterson once arranged with an innkeeper to provide free beer for his wayward students and won full attendance thereafter. One summer, Europe beckoned; at a French school, he began picking up the language. Another summer brought another try at French in Trois-Pistoles, Quebec, where he became immersed in the language and culture.

Peterson articled in Toronto and was called to the bar in 1969. He returned to London but not to practice law full-time: Clarence persuaded his son to enter the family business, an electronics firm, where Peterson demonstrated managerial acumen, expanding sales six times.

Watching Canadian politics, the young lawyer-businessman Peterson was impressed by London Tory John Robarts, the powerful Ontario premier whose quest to strengthen national unity led him to call the Confederation of Tomorrow conference in 1967. "John was a big guy and I liked him a lot," said Peterson.

"John was never small. What I liked about Robarts was a certain generosity, a magnanimity, a vision and instincts. When they're confronted with a tough situation, some people do the generous, kind thing, other people do the small, weasely thing. John did the big thing. John's vision of the country didn't come so much out of his profound understanding of Quebec nationalism or the history of Quebec or a personal affinity with Quebecers or their lifestyle, as it did out of a personal magnanimity and a personal generosity."

The influence lingered. Peterson saw a strength of will and leadership in Robarts he would emulate: "When you get down to some very tough decisions, you get everybody on all sides of the issues and everybody's giving advice, a million political calculations. But ultimately, the judgment is one guy's and that depends on your own personal vision or your own personal instincts. Robarts very much controlled that, something I admired very much about him. If there was any sort of model for me, it was him."

In 1974, the year he married actress Shelley Matthews, daughter of London developer Don Matthews, Peterson heard Ontario Liberal Leader Bob Nixon speak in London about Liberal principles of fairness and equal opportunity and his interest in politics was rekindled. Boyhood chum Ted McGrath, a top criminal lawyer, urged Peterson to run for the Liberal nomination in London Centre for the 1975 provincial election. No burning issue or passionate ideology drew Peterson into seeking a provincial seat. "I had never had any grand plan to get into politics and it wasn't as if it was sort of a magic thing that I wanted to do. I wouldn't have planned my life that way. It just sort of happened. I had been sort of political and there were an awful lot of things that I was not very happy about with the current administration at that point in time."

It was the first of many critical decisions Peterson would, in his words, "fall into," but he would win the nomination, then a seat at Queen's Park facing the well-entrenched Tories of Premier Bill Davis. The election was a Liberal setback; Nixon led the party to a third-place finish and resigned, putting the Liberal helm up for grabs. At the leadership convention in 1976 Peterson was convinced by friends to run. But a badly delivered campaign speech helped knock Peterson out of the race and he lost to Stuart Smith.

As an opposition MPP, Peterson extended his contacts outside Ontario. In 1977, invited to the annual convention of the Quebec Liberal party, he met Opposition Leader Robert Bourassa and struck up a lasting friendship. An economist, Bourassa was a source of intellectual conversation and camaraderie. "I'm very fond of him," said Peterson. "His personal persona is much different than his public persona, which is dry and calculating. He's really very warm and charming and enormously funny, a self-deprecating and a kind guy with a lot of experience. A very shrewd man." The two would remain close and mutually supportive, even in the early 1980s when Bourassa would express displeasure with Peterson for not backing the enshrinement of official bilingualism in the Constitution.

As a credible veteran, Peterson was poised for a second shot at the leadership in 1982, after Smith failed to make gains with the party in elections in 1977 and 1981. To prepare him to give a better speech than in 1976 and look more "leaderly," image consultant Gabor Apor appeared behind the scenes, recommended by Senator Keith Davey. Well supported by the Liberal caucus, better backed and with a broader base in the party than his competitors, Peterson fought off a late rush by Sheila Copps and emerged as the leader of a Liberal party in trouble.

The 1981 election left the Liberals with a $1.5 million debt; its strategic planning, fund-raising and communications were dismal. "We didn't have any policies, we didn't have any organization, we didn't have any candidates, and no hope either," said Peterson. The new leader at least had a clean slate to work with. But he needed a brilliant mind in his office as chief of staff.

"I phoned Keith Davey and asked, 'What am I going to do?'" said Peterson. "He said, 'I've got this guy Hershell Ezrin; he's working for the Canadian Unity Information Office, and he might be interested.' Hershell came down to see me. We talked for five minutes and I offered him the job. I was impressed with him— bright, creative and energetic: all of the things that I desperately needed and I wasn't. Then I phoned a friend of mine who worked in the foreign service with him and I asked, 'Do you know this guy Ezrin?' He said, 'That guy can sell anything.' I said, 'That's exactly what I want.'"

Ezrin, schooled in the reading, managing and interconnecting of public opinion and public policy, began structuring Peterson's office, enhancing the Liberals' research, policy and communications functions. Determined to use the best techniques available to win support for his product, Ezrin's commitment to public opinion research brought the Liberals a modern, scientific approach to developing and conveying policy. Ezrin's practices put him at odds with his leader's stated beliefs on polling—although his skills would be to Peterson's enormous benefit over the years.

"Hershell has a very different view of polls than I do," said Peterson. "I think polls corrupt the bloody system and I think politics would be better without polls, if you want to know the truth. I have a very low view of them as a way to govern or as a way to confirm your own judgment. There's nothing about polls that you can't figure out yourself. I didn't read the damn things. I think it's an abomination. Hershell would read the goddamned things from the top to the bottom. His views and his interpretations did not always square with mine."

Peterson made his first speech as leader to the party's 1982 annual meeting in Sudbury. After promising to unify the party and use "hardball politics to evict the tired and drifting Tory government," he decried the Davis government's well-known use of public opinion polls to guide its actions: "The tragedy is that Tory rule has been reduced to public manipulation by polls," he said. Ten days later, a Leader's Advisory Committee met at Queen's Park to decide on a summer work plan. Set up by Ezrin and Ross McGregor, a veteran Liberal who worked on Peterson's leadership campaign, the committee's number two agenda item, after "strategy," was "polling." Throughout his opposition years Peterson often reminded the Tories that "polls turn leaders into followers," while his advisors, limited only by the funds available to them, worked to help the Liberals learn the fine political art of leading from the rear.

Ezrin's fascination with polling would have to wait to be put into play. With its deficit, the party had no budget for detailed public opinion research. From his federal days Ezrin was familiar with the work of Prime Minister Pierre Trudeau's pollster, Martin Goldfarb. But Goldfarb was working in Ontario for the Davis Tories and his advice would stay out of reach of the Peterson Liberals for years.

Opposition Leader Peterson led the Liberal charge in the legislature, tilting against the Tory majority's windmill. Jockeying against Bob Rae, the highly rated NDP leader elected within months of his own emergence as Liberal leader, Peterson was widely expected to be outrun. At first uncomfortable with the attack role of opposition, Peterson resigned himself to understanding what he had to do to dent the Tory armor and win media attention. "My definition of opposition is to criticize," said Peterson. "Only the criticisms get any publicity; it's never the policy stuff. They say, 'Oh, we don't care about your policy view because you're never going to get a chance to do it anyway.' What's interesting is the blood, the guts, the glory, the confrontation, the mistakes. It's not the good stuff that you do. It was only the big hits that scored. You slap the government around, the press goes after them and beats the hell out of them and you try to chip away at their credibility." In later years Peterson would know the receiving end.

Building his own credibility was Peterson's greatest challenge in opposition. Opportunity came gift-wrapped in late 1982 as details began to surface of a massive, highly suspect real estate deal that became known as the "trust company scandal"—an issue that allowed Peterson to attack the government over a financial and economic issue in which he could take a real interest. Legal and bureaucratic contacts kept his attacks one step ahead of the Tories' defenses; he pummeled Davis' ministers for failing to protect investors and tenants and rode the scandal to headlines, a public persona as a hard-hitter on issues and a profile that rivaled Rae's.

Backing up Peterson's attacks was the growing reputation of the Liberal policy research unit as a credible source of information and alternatives that filled the party's policy-making gap. Peterson took firm positions on tough issues, although some, such as ending extra billing by Ontario doctors, required pressure from caucus. Habits emerged: staff found him difficult to brief in detail; he often waved off all but broad-strokes information on issues in which he had no strong interest.

The process of building up the Liberal party was not kind to Peterson. In the summer of 1983, young aide Vince Borg rented a motor home, and Peterson, Shelley and their three young children, Ben, Chloe and Adam, piled in to tour northern Ontario to galvanize Liberals. The first problem was finding them. Meetings of remote riding associations might draw two or three members, Peterson and Borg. The family's working holiday turned into a horror show.

"We did the tour up to North Bay and we had little picnics along the way in Cochrane, got bitten by every black-fly in Hearst," grimaced Peterson. "The Winnebago didn't work and the water didn't work. Adam had to sleep in the can; we left the lid open and it rained all over him. We came into Sault Ste. Marie and Adam fell out of the Winnebago and cracked his head open, so we rushed him to hospital. We were sitting around there for about three hours. Then Shelley's grandmother died and so we got on a plane and got the hell out, and left the Winnebago with Vince."

Borg and Peterson persisted; there were Liberals to be tracked down and support for the party to be built up. In eastern Ontario on a long, low-budget road trip, when a cheap motel room offered them no towels, they showered and then dried off on the drapes.

The ignominious demands of building a party from nearly nothing did not pay off in 1984. Caucus members began defecting to what appeared to be greener pastures: one to the Tories, four to the federal cause to run for John Turner, two more left politics. Peterson took each blow and did not shrink in the face of the abandonments. But he called the time "the worst summer of my life."

*   *   *

Since his arrival Ezrin had been developing themes for attacking the Tories in the next election. By the end of 1983 ideas were starting to gell on how to position the Peterson Liberals as an alternative. In the year before the 1985 election Ezrin searched for Tory soft spots Peterson could poke. Still lacking the party funds for full-blown polling, he turned to focus groups with voters to probe their views. Ezrin attended the sessions, watching and prompting as researchers tested his themes.

At the same time Peterson continued to hone his media skills. Liberal relations with the media improved under George Hutchison, a London *Free Press* reporter who gave Peterson a credible link to the Queen's Park press gallery. Peterson began to emerge as a creature of television, comfortable in politics' key medium. A local cable show he launched as an MPP went provincewide: "The Peterson Report" became "David Peterson's Ontario." Gabor Apor returned to offer advice as Peterson began to improve his personal appearance and image.

A flashy television producer of Hungarian origin, Apor set out to craft Peterson's image by accentuating the positives and burying the negatives, to create a leader's persona Ontarians would find appealing. "The very first thing that talks about you before you open your mouth is how you look," believed Apor. Through 20 years of making television commercials, Apor had perfected his eye for casting. He found a new challenge in trying to mold Peterson into the role of the politician of the 1980s: an attractive and convincing deliverer of messages on television, representative of how Ontarians viewed themselves.

Peterson was not oozing telegenic qualities but Apor had high hopes. "David always had the charm, whether he wore thick glasses or whether his hair was cut with sideburns. We literally took hours and hours in front of the camera, repeating and dealing with speech delivery, interview techniques, how you use your eyes, where do you look." Peterson was transformed into a top-notch communicator—a politician capable, in Apor's eyes, of doing his job better: "If someone decides to dedicate his or her life to the public good, it is a big enough undertaking without also the assumption that he knows how best to communicate. You have to learn how to communicate best what you decided to dedicate your life to doing, and learning it doesn't take any real value or sincerity away from your actions."

Apor wanted a trademark for his prize pupil. "I was always intrigued with Trudeau's trademark of the red rose and I thought, maybe I'll go a step farther. If we could introduce one element that's consistent, that is a tie." Within a week, people were noticing, and soon a red tie identified Peterson. Apor and Shelley encouraged the Liberal leader to relegate his corduroy jackets to the back of his closet and spring for blue two-piece suits. Actress Shelley taught her husband to relax and control his breathing, enabling him to read and speak with control and confidence. Peterson took up jogging and shed 20 pounds.

With his style massaged, Peterson's staff filled gaps in substance to complete the packaging of the new product. The best available niche combined Peterson's business bent with social policy ideas, and a few sexy campaign promises, to plant Peterson in the center of the political spectrum.

*   *   *

The door to Ontario's political center was thrown open on Thanksgiving Day 1984, when Davis shocked the province by announcing his retirement from politics instead of calling an election; after a divisive leadership contest, he was succeeded by right-wing Treasurer Frank Miller, who called an election for May 2, 1985. For six months the Liberals had been refining their strategy for a campaign that would offer Peterson as an alternative. But they were still playing catch-up: only half of the Liberals' debt had been paid off in three years, new plans for fund-raising were in their infancy and provincewide organization remained chaotic and unfocused.

But John Turner's election loss in 1984 had freed up federal Liberal talent and some of it was placed at Peterson's disposal.

Senator Keith Davey attended a handful of strategy sessions headed by Ezrin; months before the election, he recommended organizer Gordon Ashworth to Peterson. Campaign director for Trudeau in 1979 and 1980, Ashworth was an accomplished fixer who could get people and systems working and solve problems. Introduced quietly as campaign coordinator, Ashworth kept a low profile as he worked with campaign communications chief Ezrin and campaign chair McGregor on election strategy.

With big-league pre-election polling still out of his reach, Ezrin continued to rely on focus groups and asked Senator Michael Kirby, his old boss at the Canadian Unity Information Office, to conduct them. A vice-president at Goldfarb's firm, Kirby was in demand for his ability to read public attitudes from focus groups. Ezrin ordered up fourteen groups in five cities in the month before the election call. A new pollster, Michael Marzolini, told Ezrin that Peterson's name recognition was incredibly low: unprompted, only 14 percent of Ontarians could identify him as Liberal leader.

Homing in on perceptions of the leaders' images, Kirby found Peterson lacked the sharp edge needed to make an impression. Miller, widely seen as another laid-back Tory manager, was poised to win a reduced majority; Rae had carved out a working-class constituency by reinforcing traditional NDP support. Kirby advised Peterson to get out in front on social issues, build on his appeal to the middle class, make a few striking promises to get noticed and go after disaffected Tories and others, especially women, youth, minorities and urban Ontarians who were searching for a party that would represent their interests. Pre-election polls showed the Tories holding an awesome lead at 55 percent of the popular vote, while the NDP stayed a few points ahead of the Liberals in the mid-20 percent range. But Peterson's team believed, through their research, that Miller's broad support was "a mile wide and an inch deep."

Weeks before the election call Peterson began aggressively announcing a bold new Liberal platform: a ban on extra billing, employment programs for young people and retraining for older workers, an end to health insurance premiums, equal pay for work of equal value, free dental care for children and seniors, subsidized child care, more affordable housing and fairer taxation. Armed with these carefully chosen policies, Peterson's artfully sculpted persona was turned loose on an Ontario public—and the media—eager for a product that was fresh and different.

"We were trying to be the new broom," said advertising consultant Ken Tilley, part of Ezrin's communications committee. "Peterson looked like the new broom and Miller looked especially like the antiquated broom." Sensing many Queen's Park reporters were tired and bored with the Tories, the Liberals aimed to convince these key members of the media that their party was a real alternative; the message, they believed, would then be passed along to voters. "Virtually all of our activity was directed at this tiny group of people who would be the tone-setters and filters through which the Ontario electorate would view us," said Tilley.

Kirby's research showed potential Liberal voters—women, youth, minorities—did not feel part of their province in 1985. They felt disenfranchised by the Tories, left out of the new opportunities and spreading wealth in Ontario after the recession of the early 1980s. "These were people who had their noses against the bakery window, who could smell the aroma of all the goodies in the shop, but who were never invited inside," said Tilley. Ezrin's group translated that feeling into an "umbrella" theme, the gist of the Liberal campaign: "Vote for Your Ontario."

Peterson stole the show on the day of the election call. He attacked "the darker side of Miller's Ontario" and closed-shop Tory practices. "The Ontario Liberal Party is the only party that is not in the back pocket of any special-interest group," said Peterson. "I'm asking you, the people of Ontario, to vote yourselves a better future. To vote for your Ontario." Using that theme, the Liberal strategy was simple: Peterson would identify an issue, describe the situation under the Tories and ask people to change the status quo.

A slick, well-organized Liberal campaign tour bolted away from Queen's Park within hours of the election call, directed by

Doug Kirkpatrick, another Turner refugee; Hutchison ministered to reporters on the Liberal bus. Peterson made every campaign announcement in front of a vivid new Liberal backdrop, a rising red sun. Centrally generated campaign materials were sent out for distribution by Liberal candidates, pumping out a propagandist's dream: visually consistent messages with standardized content. Liberal headquarters was located in a rundown building in downtown Toronto; the campaign drew an unprecedented response from Liberals who showed up, volunteering to help. Ashworth, emerging quickly as the brains of the campaign, focused on the tour and providing assistance to the Liberals' poorly organized ridings. Ezrin worked to give maximum exposure to sexy campaign announcements, including a promise to make it possible for Ontarians to buy Canadian beer and wine in independently owned grocery and variety stores.

In the first week of the campaign, Ezrin tried his hand at playing pollster, with dismal results. He asked a data collection service to take a poll for the Liberals based on a questionnaire he had designed. The survey, which cost the campaign $60,000, was intended to help the Liberals plan their strategy. But the findings were not processed and delivered to Ezrin until the last week of the campaign—in the form of a mountain of computer printouts no one could decipher. It was Ezrin's first and last attempt to be his own pollster.

As the Liberals crystallized as a credible, timely alternative to the Tories, Rae and the NDP, linked to the interests of labor by their opponents and the media, failed to present a leading-edge platform or mount an effective attack. The Tories, still infighting and with a leader becoming widely disliked, watched their sweeping support collapse. Alienated special-interest groups and voters from a broad range of constituencies sought refuge with the Liberals.

On May 2 Peterson was placed on the verge of power when voters gave the Liberals 37.9 percent of the popular vote; the Tories crumbled to 37 percent and Rae held the balance with 23.8 percent. Vote splits gave the Tories 52 seats, the Liberals 48 and the NDP 25. Negotiated into power through a two-year accord with the NDP, Peterson became Ontario's twentieth premier on June 26, 1985, forming a Liberal government that ended the Tory dynasty. Before 5,000 well-wishers at a symbolic open-air swearing-in ceremony on the lawn of the legislature, Peterson promised to deliver "the kind of government to which Ontario is entitled: a government without walls or barriers." To underscore his promise, Peterson threw open the doors of the premier's office and cabinet room and allowed guests to wander through the once-sacrosanct corridors of power.

Like that warm, sunny summer day, Peterson's words were a breath of fresh air to Ontarians: they promised a new age heralded by a different kind of government that vowed to break away from the traditions of the past and solve problems. "We face many pressing needs," Peterson said in his first statement to the legislature. "One that touches upon all others is the need to make Ontario's government open, compassionate and competent, like its people. People can only achieve the changes they want and need if they are allowed to put their hands on the levers of power and shift gears when necessary."

Above all, Peterson promised, the Liberals would adhere to an unprecedented code of honesty and integrity in government. "I want to change the process," he said. "I want to make everyone feel they own us, we don't own them. That no one is beholden to me, that I am beholden to them. We've got to take the lid off this place, take the lid off cronyism, take the lid off a system that has been closed and regressive. I think we can change the cynicism that has come from blatant patronage." It was a tall order that fueled expectations the Liberals were serious about change, keeping their promises and being a different kind of government.

The Liberals' program was enormously ambitious but reforms outlined in the Liberal-NDP accord were long overdue: freedom of information laws, environmental action, a ban on extra billing, equal pay for work of equal value for women, extended rent review, protection for workers, better child care and affordable housing. "The accord agenda provided a shopping list of things Ontarians, by and large, thought should have been addressed in the previous 10 years but weren't," said Toronto MPP Ian Scott, named Peterson's attorney general. "That agenda was an agenda we would have come to on our own, even if the NDP hadn't discussed it with us. They were the obvious, easy things to do." While Liberals maintained the accord matched their campaign promises, New Democrats believed only their pressure put major changes on the new government's agenda.

Peterson turned to the job of cabinet-making. He heeded Davis' advice that the crucial seats at the cabinet table were treasurer and attorney general, with their broad financial and legal roles. Peterson picked veteran Nixon and newcomer Scott for the hot seats. Nixon, a hard-nosed farmer from a long line of Ontario Liberals, combined a pay-as-you-go fiscal attitude with a commitment to reform. Scott, a sharp-minded and sharp-tongued litigation lawyer, approached his role in cabinet as an advocate for change and individual rights. Peterson's cabinet ministers considered themselves true reformers, committed to a philosophy of openness, aggressive change, social progressivism, fiscal responsibility and ready to try new ways to solve problems. Peterson was adamant: "We weren't going there just to manage the joint, we were going to do it our way, from our philosophy."

Once in power the Liberals studied options for running the premier's office and cabinet, the political side of the government, and for its relationship to the bureaucracy, the nonpolitical, nonpartisan side. Two different systems were proposed. One, a decentralized model used by former prime minister Lester Pearson, allowed ministers great liberty to initiate policy, while reporting to the premier and cabinet. It gave individual ministers substantial power and influence, with responsibility to bring ideas forward while leaving ultimate decision-making authority and accountability in the premier's office. The second was a highly centralized model in the style of the Trudeau government: the leader and the head of the bureaucracy, the secretary of cabinet, had control and authority as both originators of policy and key decision makers. Cabinet ministers played a less significant role.

Peterson accepted the recommendation of a Liberal transition team to adopt the Pearson model; it would let the strong personalities in his cabinet thrive and was better suited to his character and approach to decision making. Peterson believed Davis had run too centralized a shop, relying too heavily on cabinet secretary Ed Stewart, who controlled the flow of information to and from the premier and was involved in all major decisions. Peterson told his ministers to consider all views and options in arriving at their policies. To develop a decision-making process that supported the approach he preferred, he urged his ministers to work out their differences in cabinet and reach consensus whenever possible, allowing him to be a mediator instead of an authoritarian who called every shot.

"I ran a unique system, a multiple-access system," Peterson explained. "I was always worried about only getting one point of view or a particular bias. I wanted to hear all sides of the argument because I wanted to make sure I knew as much as I could know from people. My theory was, when you're making a tough decision, you get the eight smartest people, the most knowledgeable people on the issue, in the room and fight about it, and if anything, at least exhaust all the possibilities. I had a rule: if any deputy minister or caucus member wanted to see me, they all had easy access to my office. You try to keep an easy flow of communications. My office was like A&P on a Friday night, as opposed to the solemn, decorous place that it used to be." The decentralized operation promised to turn the exercise of power in Ontario into an inspired process with plenty of give and take, but had a serious downside: the system could get out of control if central planning and coordination lapsed.

The Liberals set up a new working relationship between the bureaucracy and the premier's office. Peterson wanted a nonpartisan, apolitical public service. "The premier had a perception that the secretary of cabinet had become a little too closely involved with the Conservative party," said Bob Carman, who replaced Stewart. Peterson gave many of Stewart's functions to political staff, creating an office in which three people reported to him directly: Ezrin, heading up policy and communications as principal secretary; Ashworth, running the political side and managing the office as executive director; and Carman, in charge of the public service as cabinet secretary. This three-legged stool, which some Liberals would come to describe as a "three-headed monster," could work, said Carman, as long as "those three people would communicate amongst one another in a really superlative sort of way—and that's a pretty big challenge."

A diligent bureaucrat renowned for his plain brown suits and 12-hour workdays, Carman became the key link between the Liberals and the province's 105,000-member bureaucracy and also undertook a long-overdue overhaul of the planning, development and management of the public service. Carman was an anchor of stability and knowledge for Peterson who brought common sense to the often-panicky hothouse of decision making in the young Liberal government. Ashworth gave Peterson administrative expertise, business, political and fund-raising contacts, and kept the wheels of the premier's office turning in his role as a fixer of problems. He served as liaison with the party and kept an ear to the ground for political trouble. Ezrin consumed each policy initiative, applied communications spin, sparked ministers and their staff and often performed "mind-melds" with Peterson to fill his head with advice or crank him up for a performance. Closest to Peterson was Borg, his executive assistant, who served as gatekeeper. A trusted friend of the premier, Borg was often the cushion on the three-legged stool.

On the hunt for better and more strategically useful gauges of public opinion, Ezrin turned to pollster Martin Goldfarb. In government, Ezrin finally had the funds for comprehensive research. He began using Goldfarb's polling data, analysis and strategic recommendations, along with the findings of other pollsters, to refine and target initiatives to maximize positive play in the media and make the best impression on voters. Ezrin displayed a rare talent for interpreting polling data and applying it to the nuances of complicated issues. "Hershell was plumbing depths deeper than any of us could see," said Hutchison. "His greatest value was his ability to take a number of disparate positions and tell Peterson how things would unfold far down the line." Ezrin commissioned more research by Goldfarb to work up a strategy for the next election.

Ezrin worked relentlessly to inculcate the new government with practices that would milk announcements for the best possible returns. Ministers were prompted to devise marketing and communications strategies for their policies, which Ezrin would furiously revise. Ezrin urged ministers to perfect their presentation skills, often under Apor's tutelage; over the life of the government, Peterson's image-shaper would counsel 17 Peterson ministers. Rather than try to create Peterson clones, Apor concentrated on teaching ministers and their staffs to work on their own strengths and tailor their messages for television. "Any government's prime ambition must be not only to do good, but to tell the largest amount of people what they've done," Apor advised.

Good relations with the Queen's Park press gallery and the province's media gave the Liberals a lengthy honeymoon. With Hutchison as press secretary, Peterson stayed accessible and on good terms with the media, knowing his ability to project a positive, re-electable image depended on how his personality and activities were reported to voters. Many reporters who had felt frustrated covering the tight-lipped, inactive Tories enjoyed the active and colorful Liberals.

Between Ezrin and Ashworth, a highly charged and often ferociously competitive relationship emerged. Over time, the staff of Peterson's office became divided into "Hershellites" and "Ashworthites." Many Liberals were convinced the two aides despised one another but their interplay usually served Peterson well. "A very healthy tension was created in the office," Ezrin believed. "The press gallery would write or speculate about how Ashworth and I didn't get along. We would have one hell of a row on tons of things because we had two very different perspectives, but that's what you wanted." Ezrin's policy and communications group would argue the merits of a position; Ashworth's political group would view it through a political prism and outline the consequences with special-interest groups and different levels of government. "The two of them there fighting it out was important," said Ezrin. "That's the right brain-left brain syndrome. It's a syndrome a politician's got to have."

Peterson sorted out the arguments and made final decisions. Ezrin ensured each choice was properly "spun" to the media and public; Ashworth ensured it was "smoothed in" with key interest groups and other levels of government. "Part of this exercise is not just making a good decision," said Ezrin. "A good decision doesn't stop at Queen's Park. What Ashworth valued more than anything was his network across the whole country and talking to different people. He would start the process of selling things politically with the internal troops, who were then going to be the organization and workers selling things out-side." The balancing act entertained other staff. "Sometimes Gordon's advice would be taken, sometimes Hershell's," said Borg. "Hershell tended to have more zany ideas. He'd have eleven ideas, nine of which were completely zany, dangerous, complete miscalculations and two of them were great. Gordon was far more steady-as-she-goes; he was a very calm, cool and collected guy who'd been through a lot of stuff."

With their decentralized system in place the Liberals went to work. Ministers and their deputies were expected to bring for-ward new policies in the process of making reforms happen. "It wasn't all being run out of the premier's office and cabinet office," said Carman. "The premier said to the ministers, 'It's up to you people to bring the stuff up through the policy commit-tees; we're not driving everything from the center, but I will be driving certain things.'"

Peterson had three broad economic, educational and social goals outside the accord through which policies and allocation of resources were given priority; ministers and the bureaucracy were urged to tie their initiatives into the government's goals. Peterson wanted to restructure Ontario's industrial base to meet high-tech competition on world markets, plan for an aging soci-ety and check rising health care costs without reducing the qual-ity of care and improve the education system to produce the highly skilled workers needed in a postindustrial society. Action on environment and housing was ensured by the accord with the NDP.

While much policy formulation and day-to-day ministry business were farmed out to ministers, critical decision making stayed clearly in the premier's office where it could be controlled and managed. Peterson became accustomed to absorbing the advice of Ezrin, Ashworth and Carman, seeking more from a small circle of ministers and broadening the discussion in cabinet. The Liberal caucus often served as a large focus group, a sounding board Peterson could go to for perspectives on how plans were likely to be received. Even in a decentralized system Peterson was unmistakably in charge and accountable, a pattern of top-level decision making that would be maintained through the life of the government. "Real changes were made because of a conversation that usually occurred in the little office next to the premier's office with the premier present, the treasurer present, the minister present and a few other people, depending on what the issue was," said a senior deputy minister. "That's where the choices were made."

As the Liberals notched successes with their reforms, Peterson became the chief beneficiary, identified by Ontarians as a reform-minded leader making needed changes. Within months of moving into the premier's office, his recognition level and personal popularity soared. But that focus on Peterson, like the decentralized system, had potential dangers. It depended on the fragile balance of personalities at the top to work well. And if the decisions made alienated individuals, special-interest groups or voters, Peterson would be positioned to take the fall.

*   *   *

While winning public support, many items in the accord's reform agenda put the Liberals at odds with a wide range of powerful special-interest groups. The ban on extra billing, passed by the Liberals in June 1986, provoked strikes by doctors that capped their inability to dislodge the government from its course. The embittered Ontario Medical Association would never forgive the Liberals. Ontario lawyers were incensed by Scott's move to abolish the Queen's Counsel title, a Tory-vintage honor for lawyers. Teachers and public school boards were unhappy with the climbing costs of extending funding to senior separate school grades. Members of the Ontario Public Service Employees Union became impatient as the Liberals failed to move on the accord's promise to expand political rights for public servants. The Liberals' commitments to pay equity and NDP-prompted worker-protection and pro-union laws were turning off the business community.

But on the increasingly high-profile environment front, the Liberals were earning a good reputation for moving on an activist agenda; Environment Minister Jim Bradley was becoming known as an advocate for environmental groups. Similar advances were marked in housing and the Liberals moved ahead on hospital capital funding, help for farmers and a massive northern development fund, with slower progress on child care, the elimination of OHIP premiums, tax reform and denticare.

Under Ezrin the Liberals cultivated endorsements of their policies to get extra mileage from their announcements. Properly reinforced, even a policy that was not unanimously popular could become positive on balance for the government, Ezrin believed, if it was made to "resonate" with the media and voters through external support. "Third-party validation" was orchestrated for pay equity and freedom of information legislation, early environmental action and a program to move government jobs to northern Ontario. The Liberals found that third-party groups, when consulted in the development of policies or well briefed before announcements, could provide valuable help when it came time to sell the finished product. In later years the practice would dwindle, leaving the Liberals to speak without the benefit of supportive echoes.

To draw together the support of both business and labor, two constituencies uncomfortable with the new government, Peterson announced in 1986 a Premier's Council on Technology. Chaired by Peterson, it united often-warring factions to provide strategic direction for the Ontario economy and helped guide a $1-billion fund to encourage high-tech research and development. Peterson held up the group, and another premier's council on health, as evidence of an "open and accessible" government, although they were often criticized as elitist and few of their ideas implemented. Among the critics were provincial bureaucrats who felt excluded from the creation of the plans they were expected to act on.

The Liberals opened new doors as they abandoned the tradition of a strictly partisan patronage system. Tory deputies and other high-level appointees were assured they would be kept on their merits; patronage jobs for New Democrats and Tories were announced. Peterson's sister-in-law, Heather Peterson, married to his brother Jim, was placed in charge of appointments to government agencies, boards and commissions, with a mandate to spread patronage beyond Liberal boundaries and include more women and minorities. Meant to be a symbol of the Liberals' will to change, the new process was still criticized: by the opposition and the media because it did not subject appointments to review by an all-party committee of MPPs as promised, and by party faithful because it failed to make the most of access to the spoils of power for Liberals.

In his first two years Peterson dealt inconsistently with scandal: harshly when he believed he had been betrayed or a trust broken, gently when he believed no slight had been intended or felt the perpetrator too valuable to dismiss. Shortly after Peterson took office, 1985 campaign manager Ross McGregor's consulting firm sent clients a letter touting its government ties; Peterson exorcised McGregor from his office and the party. A Liberal closer to Peterson provided greater embarrassment: Don Smith, president of London construction empire Ellis-Don, who became president of the Ontario Liberals in 1984. To pull in money for the 1987 election, Smith invited business leaders to buy $1,000 memberships in a Liberal Economic Advisory Forum that promised access to Peterson and cabinet. He also helped Health Minister Murray Elston organize a paid-access fund-raising event for health officials and doctors at $150 a ticket. But

Smith, a longtime Peterson friend and husband of rookie London MPP Joan Smith, received no public rebuke from the premier and orders went out instead to the party that greater discretion should be the rule in future fund-raising endeavors.

Peterson came down harder in two cases that threatened to cast aspersions on his government's integrity. He accepted the resignation of Elinor Caplan, chair of cabinet's management board, while a legislative committee probed conflict-of-interest allegations against her. Caplan's husband had been tied to a firm that received government loans for high-tech development. The committee cleared Caplan, but Peterson kept her out of cabinet as a push for further inquiries came from Rae and Larry Grossman, who had replaced Miller as Tory leader. The Tories kept rumors in circulation about more serious wrongdoing, although secret Ontario Provincial Police and Ontario Securities Commission investigations revealed no improprieties. Peterson told Caplan he was convinced she had done no wrong but, concerned about appearances, he refused to return her to cabinet until after the next election.

The Liberals' sole northern Ontario minister, René Fontaine, was also turfed from cabinet while another committee checked his failure to disclose ownership of shares in a mining company; he too would be returned only after redeeming himself with voters. Peterson's tough stand on most threats to perceptions of Liberal honesty and integrity was guided by a simple rule, laid out by Ezrin: governments are expected to have scandals and are judged not on the problems themselves but on how they are dealt with.

*   *   *

Although minority parliament made heavy demands on his time, Peterson worked to contribute to national unity. He began to build personal relationships with other premiers and restore bonds between Ontario and other provinces. "I was determined that one of the things that I would really try to do was use whatever strength I had available to me to keep the country as together as possible," he said. Peterson was Ontario's first premier with a strong command of French and he looked for opportunities to forge ties with Quebec.

In December of 1985, six months after Peterson was negotiated into power, Robert Bourassa's Liberals defeated Pierre-Marc Johnson and the Parti Québécois. Bourassa's first public meeting, within days of his election, was a dinner with Peterson at the Beaver Club in Quebec City. "It was a very dramatic statement that, after this 10-year binge of separatism, they wanted back in, we were going to re-establish our links," Peterson felt. "It was highly symbolic and extremely important at that time just to say, look, we're back in, we're open for business, we're going to work together, we're going to build a strong country together, and he was saying, 'I'm a federalist.'"

Many regional tensions between Quebec and Ontario had been left to fester under Davis and Miller; Peterson saw a chance for positive change: "I thought we had a moment in history, we were coming out of separatism, when you had a federalist premier in Quebec, and we had to seize this opportunity because they don't come very often, and life in politics is timing."

To show leadership on minority rights in their own backyard, the Liberals moved quickly to enshrine in Ontario law the right to provincial government services in French for the province's 500,000 francophones in designated areas of the province, where numbers warranted. Bill 8, the Liberals' French Language Services Act, was passed in November 1986, with a three-year phase-in.

Peterson's early efforts at nation-building extended to the west, where he found an ally in Tory Premier Don Getty. Cooling out the war between Ontario and Alberta over energy came first; Peterson and Getty removed the acrimony from talks between the two provinces.

As Canada moved toward new constitutional talks in 1987, Peterson was accumulating goodwill among colleagues, including Prime Minister Brian Mulroney. To Peterson, Mulroney "had an enormous amount of will to do the right thing at that time and to try and make the country work." While prepared to work with Mulroney on national unity, Peterson demonstrated a willingness to take on the prime minister as other issues required. At his debut at a First Ministers' Conference in Halifax in November 1985, Peterson proved a vehement spokesman for Ontario, ready to challenge and rebuke Mulroney if necessary, as he did in a televised confrontation over reduced federal transfer payments.

In June 1987 the first ministers signed the Meech Lake Accord, which recognized Quebec as a distinct society within Canada and an English-speaking minority in Quebec and French-speaking minorities outside Quebec as fundamental characteristics of Canada. Provincial legislatures had three years to ratify the deal, designed to bring Quebec into the Constitution, or it would die.

*　　*　　*

Organization for the 1987 election began in earnest inside the Liberal party early in 1986. In April, Peterson's office threw support into a by-election in the Toronto riding of York East. Against strong contenders the effort earned a seat for Liberal Christine Hart in a long-held Tory riding.

A new figure surfaced on the Liberal scene in the by-election. Hart's campaign received a call from Peterson's office asking staff to find a role for a woman named Patti Starr. "She'll raise the money, she'll come in and work in the office or whatever," the campaign was told. When Starr called to find how she could help, she was asked to supply stakes for Hart lawn signs. "Not even half a day later the stakes arrived," said the campaign manager. "The stakes, though, instead of being four feet long, were two feet." The enthusiastic newcomer had not realized that part of the stakes had to go below ground. But Starr would have many more opportunities to help out the Liberals in the future.

After the by-election Peterson announced the appointment of campaign co-chairs: his sister-in-law Debbie Nash, a popular organizer, and longtime Liberal David MacNaughton, who was plugged in to Liberals across the country, well known to business and fluent with polling and strategizing. A strategy group took shape: MacNaughton, Ezrin, Ashworth and pollster Goldfarb.

Using polling and focus group research, Goldfarb recommended that the Liberal campaign target a broad-based constituency spanning the voting population. He believed the incredible popularity of Peterson and the government provided an opportunity to go after nearly every type of voter, with little regard for demographic or regional patterns or even previous voting behavior. The greatest source of new Liberals, he predicted, would be disaffected Tories. Only hard-core Tory and NDP voters were not likely to be drawn to the Liberal camp.

The objective of the campaign, linked to Peterson's strong personal appeal and positive image, was simple: "To build, strengthen and solidify the resonance between David Peterson and the Ontario voter." Goldfarb found Peterson's personal support extremely high—a strength based not on policy or government accomplishments but on Peterson's image—his "personal characteristics of honesty, sincerity or frankness and his leadership ability."

Goldfarb and Ezrin believed since Ontarians already felt good about Peterson, the campaign had to connect those good feelings with the values and aspirations of voters. To do that, substance, it was clear, could take a backseat to style in a campaign designed as a showpiece for Peterson, not Liberal policy: "The role of policy is to add credibility to Peterson," the strategy stated. "It is not necessarily meant to gain votes in its own right. Caution is to be exercised before making specific promises which appear momentarily popular unless there is a clear commitment that the government will in fact deliver. One of our greatest strengths is Peterson's credibility, which can't be put at risk."

Three strategic directions were devised to connect Peterson with voters: conveying that Peterson could be trusted to keep his promises, defend Ontario's interests and understand people's values and aspirations; demonstrating that a Liberal government would help people fulfill those aspirations; and supporting those directions with just enough policy. "Research suggests that while policy and programs do have a role to play, it is not the major one, and the record puts the campaign in the past, not the future," read the Liberal strategy.

With economic growth, consumer confidence and prospects for the future at their highest level of the decade in mid-1987, Goldfarb and Ezrin were confident the Liberal campaign could succeed with a "feel-good" tone. The campaign had to be "active, upbeat, positive and optimistic, looking to the future, not the past," read their strategy. "It should have the 'look of the leader,' dealing with our strengths and agenda, not attacking the other parties or their leaders. Peterson's friendliness, sincerity and approachability should be emphasized. He should appear spontaneous. Communications should play to his strengths, not attempt to overcome his minor weaknesses. (For example, we should not spend an inordinate amount of time trying to make him appear compassionate)."

As the accord with the NDP expired in June 1987, the Peterson Liberals enjoyed an astonishing level of public support. "It was the best damn government that Ontarians ever saw, could ever remember," said pollster Michael Marzolini. "They couldn't have thought higher of a government than the one they had between '85 and '87. They saw it as proactive. They were rating that government as between good and excellent. They thought the world of the premier, of the government and what was being done."

Locked into the time-limited agenda of the accord, the Liberals were effective, if sudden, reformers; the long-overdue changes won them support from a broad spectrum of voters. The NDP failed to get a share of the credit, make inroads with voters or win new battles on behalf of its traditional constituencies; the Tories under Grossman were disorganized, indebted and caught up in internal warfare.

Kept at the center of the Liberal efforts, Peterson emerged as the focus of Ontarians' positive feelings about their government. The Liberals had demonstrated they could undertake reform while maintaining fiscal responsibility, aided by the return of prosperity in Ontario. The good times brought a climate of public self-perception that made Peterson representative of what many Ontarians wanted to be in 1987—a successful, attractive yuppie with a great future. The Liberal machine was ready to roll, and after a two-year test drive, Ontarians were ready to decide whether they wanted to buy the vehicle.

*   *   *

Peterson called the election on July 31, 1987. "Ontarians are entitled to pass judgment on the leadership we have provided for the past two years and on the directions we believe are necessary for the years to come," he told reporters. "Ontario's government has caught up with its people. It has been a good beginning but there's more to do."

Peterson offered up what he called the Liberals' "agenda for tomorrow," a vague agenda, heavy on rhetoric: "We have begun to restore quality education. Now we must guarantee that our children get the skills and knowledge they need. We've taken action to increase the supply of affordable housing. Now we must ensure that every Ontarian has a decent place to live." Such broad initial statements set up the Liberal campaign to emphasize Peterson over policy. "We have done what we said we would do," Peterson proclaimed. "But there is more to do and with the people of Ontario's support, we will get it done."

At the kickoff of the campaign, Peterson revisited a theme he had raised more than two years earlier, on the day of the 1985 election call. "We are not the puppets of any special interest," he told Ontarians. "We are committed to the interests of all the people of Ontario."

The Liberal campaign floated off dreamlike across the province, barely touching ground for 40 days. Recalling their 1985 success the Liberals again launched a strong visual campaign with a simple theme, "Leadership that's Working," and used bold red sunrise graphics to spread their message. The Liberal tour, headed again by wagon master Doug Kirkpatrick, used local events and audiences as props for the staging of daily 30-second news clips. Press secretary George Hutchison kept reporters busy with ready-made stories and amused them with buttons, frisbees, coffee mugs and sweatshirts emblazoned with "Premier Tour '87," a phrase both bilingual and ambiguous.

A finicky attention to "optics" by the Liberals surfaced on their 1987 tour. An advance man arranged a visit by Peterson to a dairy farm near Woodstock, between London and Toronto. Peterson was to enter a barn and walk past a row of cows waiting to be milked. At the end of the line, he was to attach an automatic milking machine to a waiting Bessie. The advance man worried about the long walk, dangerously close to the tail-ends of several dozen cows. "Can you make sure every one of those cows does its thing before the premier gets here?" he asked the old farmer. Yes, the dairy man answered solemnly, he would be sure to give each cow an enema that morning.

When the fateful morning arrived, Peterson, wearing a bright white shirt, strode into the barn surrounded by reporters and television cameras. His advance crew confidently guided him down the row of cows, toward patient Bessie. Partway, Peterson stopped to make a few comments to reporters. From behind him came a loud rumble and the premier flinched as something bounced off his arm and thudded to the ground. As the red-faced advance man scurried behind Peterson to wipe off the shirt with a towel, he was amazed at what he found: almost nothing had stuck. Peterson kept walking and smiling and slapped the milking device on grateful Bessie. The Liberal tour was charmed in 1987 and the spell spilled over into local Liberal campaigns across the province.

Organizational problems were washed away for most Liberal candidates by a tide of volunteers eager to canvass, drawn by the success and appeal of the new cause and the prospect of being part of a winning team. On doorsteps across Ontario they dispensed centrally generated campaign materials, repeating another 1985 campaign lesson. Demoralized and in organizational limbo, the Tories were slow off the mark in their ridings and on Grossman's tour. NDP organizers struggled to keep workers interested in a campaign the Liberals seemed ready to run away with: Rae's tour grimly pounded away at the theme that only the NDP stood for the interests of "ordinary people" and "working families."

Peterson had two "black hats" he played off against in the 1987 election. He pointed to the extra billing battle against the Ontario Medical Association as an example of a principle for which he had fought on behalf of Ontarians, saying the practice had represented a barrier to health care services for those who could not afford to pay. And he took part in the popular provincial pastime of Fed-bashing, with free trade the issue.

Before the campaign Peterson made statements on free trade with a patriotic ring, but reporters pointed out they lacked substance. Peterson talked about fighting anything but "the right deal" for Canada but failed to lay out conditions or suggest what mechanism he might use to shut down a "wrong deal." On the day before a speech in Windsor early in the campaign, the Liberal strategists met in Toronto to deal with the problem of a popular leader who was starting to sound like a free trade "wimp." They agreed a strong statement was needed to cool out media criticism and allow Peterson to deal decisively with the issue.

"Have you ever seen that commercial on television where the woman says, 'Whole grain rice in five minutes'?" MacNaughton asked. "What we've got to do is have some conditions for accepting free trade, five conditions. Through the rest of the campaign, if anybody asks him about it, he could hold up his hand and say, 'Look, I've given my five conditions.'" Ezrin dashed off to write the speech. Late that night he called MacNaughton.

"It's great, it's wonderful, I'm sending a copy over to you and it will work really well," said Ezrin. "There's only one problem. There's six conditions, not five."

The next day, Peterson's stand was revealed. "We're not prepared to accept any free trade deal under which Canadian policies are dictated by U.S. interests rather than decided by the Canadian people," he declared. Six conditions were laid out that would have to be met to make a deal acceptable to Ontario. Within days Goldfarb and other pollsters began to notice an upward swing in Liberal support. Throughout the campaign, as

Peterson's personal rating with voters climbed, overall Liberal fortunes followed.

After convincing Ontarians to sample their new wares in 1985 the Liberal campaign communicators found they suddenly had a product in high demand. "It was as good as it could get," said ad expert Tilley. "He was pretty, his wife was pretty, his kids were pretty, his dog even. Here was the premier with his white shirts and the sleeves rolled up. He must have bought the shirts with the sleeves pressed and sewn that way, but it was good stuff." With their leader's image perfect for the times, the group concentrated on conveying Peterson as more statesmanlike and sophisticated. The campaign poster delivered: a close-up of Peterson, looking firm and leaderlike, gazing into the distance.

The Liberals' reliance on Ezrin continued to deepen during the 1987 campaign as he managed and interpreted Goldfarb's appraisals of Peterson's image and the pollster's strategic recommendations with absolute authority. "If Hershell said, 'Print that David Peterson's got hemorrhoids,' we'd print it—hey, nobody'd even ask," said Tilley. Ezrin insisted every component of the campaign's communications, from its poster to its brochures, be subjected to rigorous focus group testing by Goldfarb.

Ezrin's energy was also channeled into the campaign platform. "Hershell would plan the day's policy announcement the day before, write up the 42-page pieces or get somebody else to do it," said MacNaughton. "You'd say, 'Hershell, we need something on this issue,' and by eight or nine that night we had the document." That life-on-the-edge approach to campaign policy was a product of the zoolike demands of running a minority parliament. Political staff had little time to think up policy for the next election; the public service had few ideas on the shelf of interest to the Liberals. The accord with the NDP, with its instant agenda, had masked that problem for two years. Created on the fly, the 1987 Liberal platform tried to continue the reform-minded thinking of the previous two years, with the help of strategic recommendations Goldfarb had drawn from his research.

As the campaign progressed Peterson's image came more sharply into focus as the key to the Liberals' success. "Knowingly or unknowingly, he was campaigning as the antithesis of a politician," said MacNaughton. "He was just overwhelmingly different and open. A good guy. If you were male, you'd probably want to be like David Peterson. If you were female, you'd probably want to be married to somebody like David Peterson or you'd want your kid to grow up like that." Pollsters struggled for superlatives that could capture the blossoming relationship between Peterson and voters. "Canadians like to feel optimistic and idealistic about government," said Winnipeg pollster Angus Reid. "Peterson was able to touch that feeling." As he traveled the province, Peterson galvanized and excited Ontarians.

"It was not unlike campaigning with Alan Alda," said Global Television reporter Robert Fisher. "He was like being around a movie star, a rock star on a bus rolling across Ontario." Peterson's imagery was made for television but print reporters were equally impressed with his star quality. "It was like the second coming," observed Toronto *Star* reporter Matt Maychak. "There would be a flood of people following him, trying to touch the border of his Roots sweatshirt. Liberals would hold up babies for him to kiss. It was quite an event."

2

Tales from the Pink Palace

I've never seen a government age so quickly.

–*Dan Gagnier,*
Principal secretary to the premier

Boom times: that term, in 1987, spoke of full employment, big raises and great job prospects, consumer confidence, bullish stock markets, rising real estate values, a spend-spend-spend retail sector and a provincial treasury fattening up on the proceeds. Bust time: it began five weeks after the Peterson Liberals were elected. On October 19 the Dow Jones industrial average fell 508 points in New York, with an estimated loss of $503 billion. The Toronto stock exchange plummeted 407.2 points, erasing $37 billion from the value of Canadian stocks. An economic downturn began that would spiral into recession in the summer of 1990. In Ontario the impact would be felt slowly: provincial revenues and expenditures would continue to increase in 1988 and 1989. But combined with the impact of free trade, federal policies of a high dollar and high interest rates, the cycling down would bring fundamental change to the province's economic climate. Within three years the success and bright prospects of 1987, epitomized by the province's premier, would be bitter memories.

*   *   *

The government caucus room was stuffed with bodies. Smiling, laughing, newly elected, the 94 Liberals poured in under the gleaming brass chandeliers and milled about in front of the old oil paintings. It was the first time many had been inside the Pink Palace, as the legislative building was often called. When every chair was taken they sat on tables; when the tables were filled they stood at the back. A door opened and Peterson walked in through a halo of white television lights; the caucus stood as one and applauded lustily. Peterson sat behind a long table at the front and surveyed the troops. "Surf fishing" had brought a lot of them here, he knew: helpful splits in many ridings had landed more seats than most Liberals had dreamed possible. "Lots of people whom you never expect to be elected in 1987 were," he observed. "Lots of people who weren't particularly familiar with politics, who hadn't been active with the party, who hadn't done a lot of the years of step-work that comes with working your way through. They don't always get the sense about very difficult politics."

The room grew quiet. "Look, that was the easiest one you're ever going to have," Peterson cautioned his exuberant MPPs. "Now is the time to make sure that you get elected the next time." And he offered some prophetic advice: "Just as I was a big asset this time around, there's no guarantee that I'll be an asset whenever the next election is. You've got to secure your own base." That meant communicating with constituents, serving them well and earning re-election as individuals. The premierial coattails were long, he told them, but they could not be counted on to last.

The Liberals had promised change without the pressures of the accord and the NDP looking over their shoulders. Internally, they were determined to deliver. "We have ownership of the type of activism that characterized that two-year agenda," cabinet's new management board chair Murray Elston told ministers' staff at a training session. "We'll have a report card issued every three or four or five years whether we like it or not." Gordon Ashworth issued a call for political astuteness and long-term planning. "We have to paint a face on this government that reflects the message of the last election and prepares for the next one," he said. Cabinet secretary Bob Carman, committed to help improve the government's effectiveness, supported the Liberals' consensus-building approach and Peterson's own "multiple-access system": "My observation is that you get a better solution by fighting it out, by working it out, than through a backroom approach," he told the group.

As the implementation of the accord wound up, the Liberals found charting their own course difficult and frustrating. Designed to deal with long-standing problems around which there was consensus, the accord focused on an agenda of cleanup and repair. The Liberals now had to come up with a proactive agenda of reform that would demonstrate the sense of visionary leadership and commitment to change Ontarians had voted for—or settle for just reacting to problems and managing the system. The Liberals believed their four- or five-year mandate gave them time for a longer-term agenda that delivered solutions to deep-rooted problems. That meant taking on complicated issues, including fundamental reform of the government's largest institutions and services.

During the accord period, the NDP had agreed to let the Liberals carry on with the government's business and act on the items of consensus. The Liberals had the distinct advantage of having their hard choices made at the outset, with the NDP opposition in basic agreement about what was being done. The accord provided the government with a scorecard; each item acted on could be pointed to clearly by the Liberals as a promise kept. As a majority after the accord period, the

Liberals encountered dramatic differences: they had to confront tough decision-making on their own for the first time
with full-blown criticism close at hand every day. They became
a government like most others—one with relentless opposition
to its actions and choices. And their longer-term agenda of
reform made it harder for the Liberals to demonstrate in scorecard style the commitments they were acting on.

To make the decentralized government work in the post-
accord era, Peterson's inner circle believed it was up to the
premier's office to drive the system, to replace the sense of
urgency and pressure that had been provided by the accord,
with its time limit. Prompted by Hershell Ezrin and backed up
by Martin Goldfarb's continuing research, Peterson urged
ministers to develop bold, sweeping strategic plans that would
capture the public's attention. "Vision" was the watchword of
the day. Most ministers complied, working with their political
staff and top bureaucrats to plan their moves; some looked to
Goldfarb for advice on which initiatives in their jurisdiction
were priorities for Ontarians.

Ministers scurried off to fight a multitude of battles as the
premier's office struggled to coordinate. "There's an overwhelming push to be activist all the time," Peterson said,
although he recognized not every plan could be accommodat-
ed: "There's a limited capacity of the system to absorb change."
Setting priorities became the new challenge for the Liberals.
"Having got most of the accord behind you, you then have the
problem of saying, 'Okay, what's next?'" said Ian Scott. "And
about that there was no consensus."

As a result, priority setting and policy making for the Liberals tended to become a protracted process. Without the built-in
agreements of the accord, the primary objective was often to
achieve consensus. When there was a difference of opinion
among strong ministers or other forces inside or outside the
government, Peterson seemed reluctant to proceed unless an
urgent and compelling reason demanded a decision—usually a
thick black headline in a newspaper that suddenly identified a
long-recognized problem as a crisis.

In November 1987 the Liberals unveiled their first majority government Throne Speech, criticized widely for just rehashing campaign promises and failing to produce an agenda consistent with a striking majority and economic prosperity. There appeared to be little substance in the talk about "long-term solutions to long-standing problems." "Lack of vision" and "no government agenda" began to surface as criticisms that would stick to the Liberals—and to Peterson.

*   *   *

Over the winter of 1987-88 an all-party committee announced by Peterson reviewed the Meech Lake Accord. The MPPs recommended that the legislature approve the deal; it would be ratified in June 1988. Peterson was riding high in his role as a nation-builder.

But some Ontario Liberals took issue with the substance of Meech, and at the same time, with the leadership of Peterson. At the party's annual general meeting in Ottawa in May 1988, a group of party members opposed to Meech attempted to call for amendments to the Accord. They wanted to give the Charter of Rights and Freedoms precedence over the deal's recognition of Quebec as a distinct society.

The proposal was angrily debated, treating reporters to the sight of Liberals screaming at one another across the floor. Fast organizing gathered enough pro-Meech Liberals to narrowly defeat the motion, but the dissidents found recourse in a routine vote on a leadership convention, a vote of confidence in the leader. The anti-Meech rumblings translated into a personal rebuke for Peterson as 116 Liberals questioned his leadership, 1 in 6 who voted—a signal that not all party faithful shared the premier's support for the substance of Meech. "I don't think the party's split at all," Peterson told reporters. "There's different points of view on this issue but I think the party's strongly united." Yet the discord would simmer among Liberal ranks: anti-Meech feelings would join a list of factors causing disenchantment among party members.

"Meech was terribly hard on our party," Peterson would later admit. "Really hard on the federal Liberal party; to some extent, our own party as well. There's no question: there is an issue that I, in a sense, imposed my will. The leader has the prerogatives, right or wrong, and this is an area where I exercised my prerogatives and fought like hell for it. But there's no question, not everybody felt as strongly as I did about this issue."

While Peterson focused his attention on Meech, portraying himself as an ally of Mulroney and Bourassa in the quest for national unity, an anti-French backlash was growing in Ontario. In some areas the phenomenon was prompted by ignorance and fear over the Liberals' French Language Services Act (Bill 8). Much of the backlash was provoked by the Alliance for the Preservation of English in Canada (APEC), a league whose activities capitalized on racist and anti-French sentiments in small-town Ontario. "APECkers," as they were often called by their critics, spread misinformation about the impact of Bill 8, telling municipalities the Liberal law would force them to offer services in French and require them to raise taxes. APEC urged municipalities to declare themselves unilingual and support an Ontario referendum on official bilingualism.

Quietly at first, starting in May 1987, towns across the province declared themselves unilingual; by 1990, 70 municipalities would fall victim to the APEC campaign. In January 1990, Sault Ste. Marie declared English its only official language, the largest municipality to do so, and the trend began to receive national attention. The message: an anti-French and anti-Quebec feeling seemed to be rampant in Ontario, partly in reaction to the policies of the Peterson Liberals and their pro-French, pro-Quebec leanings.

*   *   *

A bid to make up for shortfalls in substance perceived in the Liberals' first majority Throne Speech came in Nixon's first majority budget in April 1988. In spite of the stock market collapse, the treasury continued to overflow with the fruits of

Ontario's prosperity. Nixon offered up $2 billion for affordable housing, $900 million over three years to build schools and provided research and development write-offs for business. A tax-cutting plan got rid of income tax for 350,000 low-income Ontarians. The largesse came at a price: overall Ontario income tax was raised by a percentage point to offset federal cuts and the retail sales tax was hiked from 7 percent to 8. Still, times were good and complaints were muted.

As the majority government trudged on, the delicate balancing act between Ezrin and Ashworth continued. The setup that worked well in a minority situation began to show cracks as the pressures eased. "That period of two years was only functional because it was a short time span," said Vince Borg. "There was a higher objective than personal ambition, ego or anything else. Gordon would park his ego when he knew Hershell's needed to be massaged." But with political survival no longer on the line, co-existence became a problem. "They became more interested in their own futures within," said David MacNaughton. "There was a lot of jockeying and I think it led to the absence of a policy agenda." Other Liberals offered harsher criticism of Peterson's top aides, especially Ezrin. Many felt he had excelled at crisis management and communications during the accord period but fell down when it came to planning and communicating a longer-term agenda. As problems in those areas emerged, many Liberals traced the roots to a reliance by the government on Ezrin's crisis-management style, which they believed was no longer adequate or appropriate.

Compounding the problem, members of Peterson's inner circle began to leave. Borg departed after the election to work at Decima Research, the polling firm run by Allan Gregg, MacNaughton's business partner. A year later, Ezrin left for the private sector to head corporate and public affairs at Molson Industries. Ezrin's exit meant trouble: it depleted the Liberal idea bank and weakened the government's corporate communications—and he had not groomed a successor to fill the void left by his departure and, to some Liberals, his shortcomings.

As the familiar structures in Peterson's office started to decay, so did central direction and planning. Without a clear agenda and set of priorities emanating from the hub, the government evolved into a series of competing fiefdoms lorded over by individual ministers. Most ministers were off on their own in pursuit of "vision"; the government was moving in many different directions at once, some mutually exclusive, as ministers tried to counter the criticism that the Liberals had no agenda. The downside of the decentralized model began to be realized. Policies were announced that did not seem to amount to anything because they were not tied to a central theme. With ministers doing their own thing, the Liberals often appeared to be doing nothing.

The full effect of the breakdown would emerge before the 1990 election, when polling would reveal most Ontarians could not name an achievement of the Peterson government. "One of our problems was we did so goddamned much stuff, I think we were almost too activist a regime," said Peterson. "On almost every front we were into major reforms. I always figured you had to do more than one thing at a time and lots of problems had to be attacked. But we weren't particularly identified with any one."

In many areas, however, the Liberals were closely identified with the issues—by groups that opposed their actions. By making change, the Liberals were bound to make enemies. Peterson was often the target of those who opposed Liberal action. "This whole system is coalesced around one person and it's so hard to break out of that," he said.

The late Dalton McGuinty, a philosophical MPP for Ottawa South, became famous among Peterson Liberals for coining the phrase "Operation Alienation" to describe the government's growing pattern of turning off special-interest groups through either inaction or action. Some groups, and many Liberals, saw the Liberals' consensus-building process as consultation gone mad.

"If I had one word to describe this government it would be 'consultation,'" said a top bureaucrat in 1988. "We are so busy consulting that no one is noticing that nothing is happening." The head of the province's public service union, Jim Clancy, agreed: "They were long on consultation and short on action. They'd always try and look for the halfway house if they had two competing interests. You didn't quite please these people and you didn't really satisfy anyone else. When you try and walk down the middle on the issues, that's deadly for leadership."

But to some powerful interests unhappy with Liberal decisions, no amount of consultation could suffice. Doctors, lawyers, teachers, municipal leaders and other groups accused the Liberals of alienating them irrevocably by making decisions that affected them without genuine consultation or with no consultation at all. The reformers in Peterson's cabinet defended their actions. "There is no good way of taking on these changes without upsetting people, none," said Scott. "We may have made the wrong choices or made the wrong decisions about what the policy could be, but our government didn't fail to take on the tough battles." Said Health Minister Elinor Caplan, "I never believed in Dalton McGuinty's Operation Alienation. If you're a reformer, you shake up the status quo, you make changes. That's what you're there to do. Someone once said to me, 'You'll know when you're making progress if you get a reaction.' Much of the reaction that we got from all of those groups were reactions to positive and progressive change. They tried to portray themselves as defenders of the public interest, but in fact we were acting in the public interest or tried to find the balance."

Housing Minister Chaviva Hosek told party members in 1989 not to be surprised or offended by criticism from the opposition, special interests and media. "Some would have you believe that we've lost our way, but these are the people whose job it is to criticize," she said. "The best way to avoid criticism is not to get up in the morning and to do nothing." Being elected to govern meant being asked to choose between competing interests, she explained. "When you choose, you create heat. And there is plenty of heat."

"I've never figured out the difference between making tough decisions and being arrogant," said Peterson. "I think I know the difference now: if you make the tough decisions, your supporters will say you're a strong leader and the people that disagree with you will say you're arrogant. So it really applies to whether they agree or disagree with the tough decision."

*   *   *

Issue management for the Liberal majority was a panoply of stark contrasts, with brilliant successes pitted against staggering failures. Moving ahead in some areas the Liberals showed a strong will to solve problems with welfare reform, court reform and environmental protection, and to water the arid deserts of education and health care funding.

After banning extra billing, the Liberals had a tough act to follow in the health care field as a majority government. They decided on a long-term approach to health care reform targeted at illness prevention, a balance of institutional and community-based care, better specialty services and a stronger orientation toward customer service, while increasing funding. But the plan left Health Minister Caplan vulnerable to a case-study strategy of criticism by the NDP and Tories in the legislature, which used examples of failures of the system to build an impression that the government was not solving problems. Even when the Liberals fulfilled their election promise to eliminate health insurance premiums for Ontarians, the political cost was high: the change required employers to pay a health tax for workers, turning many small business operators against the government.

The Liberals' drive to reform Ontario's $3-billion-a-year social assistance system won them wide initial accolades—but the reforms would be slowed by declining revenues and their positive publicity undercut by other events. The Liberals appointed a Social Assistance Review Committee (SARC) chaired by Judge George Thomson to come up with strategies for overhauling the system; his committee devised a consultation process to incorporate the views of special-interest groups from the outset. The result: the SARC report was warmly received and "validated" by third parties.

Few issues caused as many problems for the Liberals as Sunday shopping. In 1987 an all-party select committee had recommended keeping a common pause day in Ontario, turning down wide-open Sundays. But bowing to concerns about abuses the majority Liberals decided to change the decade-old Retail Business Holidays Act and opened a Pandora's box that would trouble them for years, adding to the impression they were incapable of solving problems. The Liberals created a "municipal option" that gave Ontario's cities and towns the power to regulate Sunday and holiday shopping by adapting the provincial law to local needs. Companion labor legislation was also brought in to protect retail workers who refused to work Sundays.

The Liberals' solution, born of their belief that a compromise could satisfy everyone, proved instead to satisfy no one. Labor and retail groups lined up to protest. Municipal councils, complaining they had not been adequately consulted, rebelled at having tough decision making passed down to their level. Sunday shopping would become a popular example of what critics called the Liberals' practice of "downloading" problems or costs, rather than dealing with them by making the decisions themselves or paying for solutions out of provincial revenues. Similar charges of downloading would be levied by municipalities over the costs of improved court security, pay equity and pollution controls on sewage treatment.

With Sunday shopping the Liberals had hoped to prove they could take on the biggest of problems: that the government had not traded its reformist bent for majority complacency. They chose Sunday shopping to make a mark and paid a high price for picking an issue over which they could not hope to satisfy all sides. As interest groups on all sides protested, the issue dominated a full session of the legislature, knocking the government off-course. Court challenges further muddied the waters and led the government to suspend efforts to enforce the Sunday law. "I think what we did was right and sensible and practical but it consumed too much energy," said Scott. "It was not worth expending that much energy on what was a triviality."

Scott's reforms in his own jurisdiction also came at a high price. After consulting with judges and lawyers on a 1987 report on the judicial system, he embarked on sweeping court reforms to regionalize the court structure, create a single trial court and improve efficiency. The goals were simple: lower costs and better service to improve access to justice, principles that were widely praised. But putting the changes in place was a process to be measured in years, not months, and lengthy court delays and backlogs built up. Scott stuck to his belief that improved local management of the courts would solve the problems and refused to opt solely for the quick solution of appointing more judges and spending more money on the system. Many lawyers and judges disagreed and joined the growing list of groups unhappy with the Liberals' way of doing business.

Prominent on that list were teachers and public servants. Ontario teachers and their powerful, politically active unions were eager to work with the Liberals to improve education; educators were pleased to be drawn into such processes as renewing curriculum and improving teacher training. They praised the Liberals for spending unprecedented sums to build new schools but joined the chorus of complaints that Peterson was failing to meet a promise to raise the province's share of the ongoing costs of education. A bitter dispute over the pensions of teachers and public servants would create a rift between the two groups and the Liberals—and return to confront Peterson in the next election.

*   *   *

Ezrin's departure left Peterson without a principal secretary. To fill the big vacancy, Peterson called on Borg to come back, who agreed but was dismayed at what he found. "When I walked back in there, it was dead, completely dead," Borg said. He faced the task of having to jump-start both policy and communications to get the Liberals in gear. Many Peterson staff were tired or moving on, and a fresh injection of brains was overdue.

Law professor Patrick Monahan, policy advisor to Scott, and welfare reformer Patrick Johnson, co-author of the successful SARC report, were brought into the premier's policy unit. To fight Operation Alienation, Borg pushed ministers to solve problems with interest groups. Goldfarb was commissioned to help several ministers find policy with public appeal. A new focus on corporate communications was planned to replace Ezrin's one-man-band approach, using the caucus and better planning to sell Liberal ideas to Ontarians.

On April 25, 1989, the Liberal agenda got back on track. After months of preparation, a Throne Speech set out six priority areas for continued reform: economic development through improved training programs and pursuit of new markets, education initiatives including junior kindergarten, action on SARC reforms, promotion of safe and secure communities and healthy lifestyles were stressed. More environmental protection measures were promised. The new activist agenda was followed up with a big-spending budget to pay for the promises. But the Liberals' fresh start was blown out of the water by something far more attention-grabbing: scandal.

Just as a series of Throne Speech follow-up announcements began, the legislature learned that Solicitor General Joan Smith went to an Ontario Provincial Police (OPP) detachment in Lucan, outside London, to inquire about the son of a family friend who had been arrested for causing a disturbance. Claiming a serious error in judgment had been made, the opposition howled for Smith's resignation, accusing her of political interference in the judicial process. Smith refused to resign, never admitting to wrongdoing. Peterson, loyal to his friend, the wife of Liberal party fund-raising chair Don Smith, resisted advice to ask for her resignation. After weeks of hammering by the opposition that dominated the news, Peterson asked Smith to step down to enable the government to carry on with its new reform agenda. It was a bad time for the Liberals but the worst was still to come.

*   *   *

The Liberals' attempts to solve Ontario's housing problems tracked, for two years, the stormy career in government of Chaviva Hosek. Attracted like many other activists by the chance to be part of a reform-minded government, the widely respected feminist, former president of the National Action Committee on the Status of Women, was made housing minister in Peterson's first majority cabinet. "What I saw was openness, curiosity, a willingness to try new things, to hear people, to be uncomfortable while we figured out what to do," she said. "The sleepy administrative haze of the Tories had disappeared and there was room for intelligence, energy and organizational change." But Hosek discovered consensus-building in housing under the Liberals had become a mess: developers and tenants, brought together to help write a new rent review law, had produced chaos. "That was absolutely unworkable because it had no core," she said. "It was a treaty between two groups that fundamentally and deeply distrusted each other. There was a lot of openness and creativity and goodwill on the part of the government, but not enough wisdom," she believed.

Hosek was confronted with a housing crisis in Ontario, brought into prominence by a middle-class housing crunch in Toronto. For the star rookie, expectations were high. "Nobody gave me any time," she said. "Everybody assumed, or treated me, as though I thought I was a hotshot and had the answers, when what I really did was come in and say, 'I don't know enough about this, let me think about it.' Then they'd kill me for thinking about it instead of having a magic answer. When I said I didn't have the answers yet, it was treated as if I didn't care." Hosek ran into structural problems as she tried to get her ministry in order. Powers she needed to make changes resided in other ministries: land development levers were in municipal affairs; government land resources were in another ministry. Conflicting priorities threw up roadblocks and slowed Hosek's plans.

Pressured by the media and Peterson's office to show results, Hosek announced a massive nonprofit housing program, and won commitments from cabinet to free up government land holdings and arm-twist municipalities on land-use approvals. Developers opposed the land-related initiatives, claiming they would flood the market with low-priced government land. "We had people coming to us from developers saying, 'Don't do this, you're going to bankrupt us, you're going to blow the market,'" said Hosek, "to which my response was basically, 'We're doing it. We've got this land, we've got people who have no place to live, people in despair.'" True to her words, Hosek was feeling the heat that comes from making choices. Her efforts were further undercut as opposition critics and media found her an easy target whose preachy speaking style came across as arrogant.

As part of the follow-up to the 1989 budget and the new reform agenda, Hosek announced a plan to spur affordable market housing. It met the Liberals' commitment to require that 25 percent of new housing construction be affordable to people of low-to-moderate income, demanded that municipalities set aside land for housing, promised to streamline the land-use planning process and pledged to make better use of existing buildings through housing intensification. But the plan did not help Hosek. She and the Liberals were up to their necks in scandal.

*　　*　　*

The undoing of Hosek's political career—and the beginning of a series of events that would shake the Liberals to their foundations—was precipitated by her experiences with John Sewell, the former Toronto mayor appointed by the Liberals in 1986 as chair of the Metro Toronto Housing Authority (MTHA). A tough and uncompromising reformer, Sewell wanted to improve the security, maintenance and appearance of the 110 projects operated by the $200-million-a-year public housing agency. Sewell was a zealous chair but Hosek believed he was behaving improperly by trying to run the organization single-handedly. Hosek told Peterson that Sewell was skirting her authority by dealing on his own with the federal housing ministry; she felt he made far-fetched commitments to MTHA clients that would disrupt the delicate balance between low-income housing projects and surrounding neighborhoods.

"Sewell did the cardinal sin of community development," said Hosek. "He went to the tenants of MTHA, some of the most vulnerable people in this whole society, and he made them promises which he was incapable of fulfilling. I agreed with John's analysis but he was going out there and making promises to tenants about changes he could not deliver on. In some of the housing developments, the conflict between the surrounding community and the people in the housing development, which was partly racially based, wasn't strong, and he was throwing hand grenades into a place where, if your constants were not properly managed, you could end up having racial warfare."

A consultant's study found Sewell too involved in MTHA's day-to-day business, straying from his mandate of overall policy development. Hosek told Sewell she did not want his contract renewed—and bought herself serious trouble.

"If people want to say that I'm impatient, I am," Sewell told a reporter. "I want to change things. I don't think that's a fault." He told another, "Any time you push for change in a large organization, you tend to develop tension. But I don't think I've been pushing too hard." Housing activists and tenants launched a campaign to support Sewell as word spread that Hosek wanted him out.

"Chaviva was having the most terrible time with him," said Scott, when Hosek brought her problem to the attorney general for advice. "He wouldn't meet with her and wouldn't tell her what he was doing, and he was announcing plans for buildings for which he had no money, and he was driving her crazy."

"Look, I know John Sewell better than you do," Scott told her. "He's an icon, that means a little gold-tinted god, and you don't screw around with them. This is John Sewell; just keep him there and make him king if you have to, but don't fire him."

"No, I can't," Hosek maintained. "I can't run my ministry properly with this guy in charge. It's impossible. He's got to go." The problem ended up in the premier's office.

"It would be a mistake to fire him," Scott told Peterson. "He has all kinds of credibility, nobody knows exactly why, but he has it all, and to fire John Sewell would be just terrible."

"Do you want me to be minister of housing?" Hosek asked Peterson bluntly. "You've got to allow me to run it. I can't handle John Sewell."

"Okay," Peterson decided, "if you can't live with him, he's gone. But don't say anything negative about him." Peterson wanted no public attack. "I tried very hard not to do that," he said later. "It's not fair and, in a sense, when you're governing, you have to take it, you don't give it out." Hosek agreed; she would make no negative comments about Sewell to back up the decision.

Hosek asked Peterson's problem-solver Ashworth to find Sewell another position. "I had told Gordon that we were having terrible trouble with John Sewell; could we please find a solution," she said. "We wanted to give John something, so we could ease him out. We begged and pleaded with Gordon to handle this matter. He never did." Peterson did not insist Sewell be placated, and the ex-mayor took no new government position from the Liberals. "Other things were offered to him as I understand it," Peterson said; but Sewell was furious the Liberals would not renew his contract. "In retrospect, that might have been smarter politics," said Peterson later, "but it had reached, unfortunately, sort of an intolerable position."

The decision was widely reported as a firing. Shortly after, *Globe and Mail* columnist Michael Valpy, a longtime friend of Sewell, began writing anti-Hosek columns. "Ms. Hosek fired Mr. Sewell because his public profile and manner bruised her ego," Valpy wrote. He also suggested Hosek had close ties with developers, because half her 1987 campaign contributions came from individuals and firms in the land and housing development industries, including the giant developer Tridel. Other reporters began to dig as Valpy asked questions about Liberal fund-raiser Patti Starr, head of the Toronto branch of the National Council of Jewish Women (NCJW), who was appointed chair of Ontario Place by the Liberals three months before the 1987 election and made a member of the board of directors of MTHA, where she had been critical of Sewell.

A gregarious mover and shaker who loved to be the center of attention, Starr was a former Tory supporter who switched to the Liberals before the 1985 election. An acquaintance of Peterson's MP brother Jim, she worked on his 1984 federal campaign. Starr was well known in the premier's office, dropping in frequently to "park her fur," one staffer noted, when attending meetings in the legislative building. "There's not a Liberal she hasn't touched," Peterson once exclaimed at a Starr dinner; he praised her ability to "bulldoze her way through some of the toughest doors in the province." Scott once described her as "our Patti." Starr had favorites in the premier's office, often referring to Ashworth and Ezrin as "my babies," and lunching regularly with Peterson's top staff.

As a Liberal fund-raiser helping to address the party's chronic needs, Starr received explicit direction from the premier's office advising her which candidates, MPPs and ministers required assistance; such from-the-top-down advice to a fundraiser, considered an essential practice by the Liberals, was not unfamiliar to the other parties. The top Peterson aides tended to target Starr's efforts at weaker cabinet ministers who needed help.

Although Starr had begun to make headlines at Ontario Place with a shake-up that caused some staff to quit, she became a media focal point as Valpy sparked interest in Liberal fund-raising. When Valpy alleged that developers made contributions to Hosek's 1987 campaign knowing she would be appointed housing minister, Hosek was incensed, but had agreed with Peterson not to reveal the problems with Sewell or defend herself. "I, like a stupid idiot, kept my bargain," she said. "I was absolutely stupid. What's stupid about keeping my word is that my character was crucified. Michael Valpy wrote about me for a year without ever talking to me. He never checked anything with me. Every single thing I was accused of in his column has since been proven to be absolutely untrue. There are still people who believe that garbage about me."

Hosek's supporters and friends in the government were furious. "All of that was shown to be false," said Scott. "If you want to find a victim in this whole exercise it's Chaviva, a woman who did nothing wrong, against whom the most serious allegations were made, who lost her job because of those allegations. Valpy never apologized, never admitted he was wrong, never said anything. It just passed on to another issue, and to me it's one of the biggest injustices I've ever seen."

Hosek was chafing at the bit to sue Valpy for libel but was ordered to back off by Borg. "The advice that I got from the premier's office was to leave it alone and let it die," she said. "Third-rate journalists get quite carried away with the fact that they're taking somebody down and they don't care about the consequences," said Peterson. "Should we have sued? Maybe. But then, I don't want to spend my whole life in lawsuits and I guess I believed it was just so factually inaccurate that the truth would eventually come out, and that part of the job is to take it. So I didn't fight back with every third-rate road apple."

Valpy wrote on, alleging Hosek had demonstrated Liberal links to developers by hiring developer Dino Chiesa as a special advisor, that Starr had provided inside information to Tridel when she was a member of the MTHA board and that Hosek and Starr were closely connected. Peterson charged the reports were "just innuendo"; while Chiesa had worked on Hosek's campaign, for example, he had been hired through a public service competition.

Valpy's work prompted more investigations by *Globe* and other reporters, as new stories poured out for nearly a full year. In February 1989 the *Globe* ran reports of allegations of fund-raising improprieties, focused on the 1987 election campaign, involving Starr. The scuttlebutt around Hosek alone was soon overwhelmed by broader charges. The *Globe* revealed that the Toronto NCJW, under Starr's presidency, had made political contributions, in violation of federal tax laws prohibiting political donations by charities.

The NCJW was reported to have received a $251,000 Ontario sales tax rebate for a nonprofit seniors' housing project in North York built in 1985 with Tridel; the money was to be used to reduce rents for low-income tenants. Starr ran the project's finances and part of the money was later found to have been used to make political donations through a capital fund she controlled. The NCJW distanced itself from Starr: "We are appalled at the allegations and their implications," the organization stated. "The reputation of the NCJW of Canada is being blackened. [The] Toronto section has been in existence for 93 years and until Mrs. Starr's involvement has never had a single suggestion of misuse of funds." The *Globe* stories later won a National Newspaper Award for reporter Linda McQuaig.

Valpy and the *Globe* kept digging: Starr was reported to have arranged a consulting contract for $4,950 through Ontario Place to Hosek's spouse, Alan Pearson; through the NCJW, she was reported to have provided consulting fees of $10,000 to Chiesa, which he returned, and other consulting fees to Tridel's development vice-president Mario Giampetri, a longtime Liberal. Peterson repeatedly denied any knowledge of wrongdoing by the Liberal party, his office, cabinet ministers, caucus members or government staff. He ordered MPPs and the party to scour records of campaign donations to root out and report contributions linked to Starr or the NCJW.

In February 1989, prompted by the media reports, Ontario public trustee Hugh Paisley began investigating the financial records of the NCJW, including the capital fund controlled by Starr. Politicians and organizations across the province began searching their files for evidence of improper donations from the NCJW; many came forward to proclaim their innocence of wrongdoing and promised to pay back funds.

The *Globe* and other media homed in on the Liberals' relations with developers and produced more allegations—including some that challenged Peterson's own integrity. Revelations surfaced that companies controlled by developer Marco Muzzo and two associates contributed $112,000 to the Liberals in the 1987 campaign, the largest known group of contributions to an Ontario political party. Peterson was questioned for refusing demands from ratepayers in York Region, north of Toronto, to call a public inquiry into development practices in the region, where Muzzo's companies did extensive business. Implications of impropriety also accompanied reports that a Muzzo-linked company called Envacc Resources had met with Peterson to look for advice on winning a $1-billion contract to dispose of garbage from the Greater Toronto Area; other stories suggested Peterson's father-in-law, London developer Don Matthews, had been offered an opportunity to buy into Envacc.

Still more reports pointed out that Muzzo was connected to Avinda Video Incorporated, a Mississauga company that purchased the Peterson family business, C. M. Peterson Company Limited, in 1987 for $9.6 million in cash and Avinda shares. Muzzo was chairman of the board of Consolidated HCI Holdings Corporation, which purchased some Peterson company properties directly, and was the majority shareholder in Avinda. Muzzo was reported to have signed bank loan guarantees for the purchase along with Liberal pollster Martin Goldfarb and his brother Stanley. Peterson's one-third share in the family business had been placed in a blind trust when he became premier and the sale was negotiated by his brothers, who avowed no knowledge of Muzzo's links to Avinda.*

Demonstrating ties between Starr, Peterson and the Liberals, and Tridel's president, Elvio Del Zotto, became a subject of intense fascination for some reporters and members of the opposition. A sinister hook was found for stories about Del Zotto in a 15-year-old report by county court judge Harry Waisberg, who conducted a royal commission into violence in the province's construction industry in 1974. Waisberg heard testimony from Elvio and Angelo Del Zotto who, along with their

---

* Many of the allegations regarding the Liberals' relations with developers reported in the *Globe* and other media over a period of months remained only that: allegations. Many of the implications of wrongdoing were left unresolved. They are repeated here for the purpose of accurately reconstructing the political and media climate of the period. The question of the truthfulness of any of the allegations would prove less critical to the political fortunes of the Liberals than the effect of their repeated publication and broadcast: the creation of a climate of broad public perception that associated the Liberals with impropriety involving the development industry.

brother Leo, owned Del Zotto Enterprises, the forerunner of Tridel. While he found no evidence of wrongdoing by the Del Zottos and no charges were laid against them, the judge directed disparaging comments their way: "A reasonable inference from the evidence is that they knew a great deal more than they were prepared to tell," he wrote.

Waisberg's references had been resurrected by reporters when Elvio Del Zotto ran successfully for the presidency of the Ontario wing of the federal Liberal party in 1988. A prodigious developer with a long-standing commitment to community service, Del Zotto wanted to help rebuild the federal party by contributing his fund-raising expertise. Publicity-shy, he suggested in rare interviews that he was a victim of racially motivated smears. "If you suffer from prejudice, you know what it's like," he said. Del Zotto worked hard at a wide range of charitable and community causes. "I'll stand up for anyone who's an underdog," he said.

Accounts of Starr's activities often referred to her friendship with Del Zotto and his wife. Stories included denials by Starr of rumors she lobbied the ministry of housing on behalf of Tridel-related companies. More linkages were drawn as the fund-raising scandal unfolded: an internal probe by an NCJW lawyer revealed a $14,400 contribution by a Tridel-related company to the charity in 1987; the money had been used to pay for both charitable and political contributions.

In May the Commission on Election Finances notified the Ontario Provincial Police that officials of the 1987 election campaign of Citizenship Minister Lily Oddie Munro had made personal use of campaign funds. Two of the three contributions were made on behalf of the NCJW by Starr. Within days, Starr took a leave of absence from her post at Ontario Place, then resigned. The revelations continued: Munro admitted to the legislature that her mother had accepted $5,000 from Starr to do campaign-related mailing work. By the end of June 1989, the public trustee's office had discovered that 126 questionable contributions had been made through the NCJW, totalling more than $85,000.

By the standards of other political scandals, the amount of money involved was small—pocket change in U.S. political fund-raising and far less than the payoffs involved in Ontario's highway scandals of the 1950s and subsequent Tory scandals. But in Ontario in 1989 the appearance and principle of widespread wrongdoing was big news, especially when it involved a government that vowed, as Peterson had in 1987, "We are not the puppets of any special interest."

The improper contributions discovered by the public trustee dated back to 1985 with the federal Conservative party. But most went to provincial Liberal cabinet ministers, their aides and relatives, and Liberal MPPs and candidates in the 1987 election. Federal and provincial candidates of every stripe were touched, along with many municipal politicians. Funds were also provided to Del Zotto during his campaign in the federal Liberal party. Starr told reporters she had received instructions from a senior member of Peterson's cabinet on how to make political contributions. More investigations began: the provincial auditor found bad management and questionable business practices at Ontario Place. Overpayments to the NCJW were discovered in audits of the ministries of community and social services and citizenship.

With the scandal spreading like wildfire the government asked the OPP to probe the allegations about political contributions going back to 1985 and government grants to the NCJW. Critics attacked a police probe as too narrow and demanded a public inquiry.

Partway through the revelations, a longtime Davis aide told one Liberal minister the government's approach to the problem was naive. "What you stupid idiots decided was that implementing your bills and policies was more important than dealing with this issue," the Tory said. "Davis and Robarts and Frost, who confronted issues that were much more challenging than this, would have simply prorogued the legislature, sent them home, and called it back eight months later. If there's no question period, there's no symbiotic relationship with the press and the thing can't be played quite the way it was played." Determined to tough it out, the Liberals would not hear of adjourning the house.

Ten days after the police investigation was announced, the scandal hit closer to home than Liberals imagined possible: Ashworth resigned. Ashworth had authority over Starr's appointment to Ontario Place and had kept up a working relationship with Starr; he and his wife had also become personal friends with Starr. A release from Peterson's office stated Ashworth had wrongfully accepted favors, including a refrigerator and paint job for his house, arranged by Starr through a company related to Tridel, which denied involvement. In a statement, Ashworth claimed no knowledge of the incidents: "These renovations were overseen by my wife Dianne who has always taken on the responsibility of the management of our household and related expenses." Ashworth confirmed no invoice had been received for either item. "My wife and I have no hesitation in discussing these matters with all official investigative authorities," he wrote.

"I feel like I've been kicked in the head," Peterson muttered darkly to reporters who gathered outside his office late that evening. "You think you're doing things well, and something like this comes along, and you look at yourself and say, 'What have I done wrong? What did I miss? How did all this happen?'" Pale and morose, Peterson told reporters he felt "betrayed." Some reporters were unimpressed and unsympathetic. "Somebody said, 'Go out there, undo the tie and look distraught,' and then you have the puppy-dog look like somebody's taken your Alpo away," said Global TV's Queen's Park bureau chief Robert Fisher.

The next day, after meeting with advisors including Ezrin, back to help deal with the crisis, Peterson announced a public inquiry. He told reporters he knew "of no special relationship between our government and the development industry, but that is not what the appearance tends to be and we've got to get to the root of it." He pledged to ensure that "all public officials, whether elected or appointed, are people of integrity and I insist that the democratic system depends on the public trust and faith in the integrity of their public officials." Ezrin's rule that governments are not rated by their scandals but by how they respond to them was followed again. "Heads will roll," promised Peterson, if it was proved that any minister, MPP or official acted improperly. It was almost four years to the day since he was first sworn in as premier.

As he announced the inquiry, knowing Tridel would be involved, Peterson said he would ask Del Zotto to resign if he was president of the Ontario Liberal party rather than the Ontario wing of the federal party. Intended to suggest that he wanted to clear the air while the probe was conducted, Peterson's comment instead fueled speculation about hidden problems. Reporters and the opposition continued to produce new allegations. A three-year-old story was revived that embarrassed the Liberals and provoked a damaging reaction by Peterson: Del Zotto had been rejected by the Liberals in May 1986 as a candidate for appointment to the Ontario Police Commission. "The attorney general and I agreed it was not the appropriate appointment in the circumstances," Peterson said. Other stories revealed that Del Zotto had been recommended for the appointment by Starr in a letter to Scott.

Peterson instructed Borg to demand a series of resignations: Del Zotto, from the board of directors of the Ontario Arts Council; his wife Marlene, from the board of TV Ontario; his brother Angelo, from the board of trustees of Toronto's Sunnybrook Medical Centre. "The sense was it would be the prudent thing to do, because there is a full judicial inquiry going on," Peterson said. "The sense was just to save embarrassment."

But opposition members charged that Peterson had gone overboard, creating "guilt by association" that maligned members of the Del Zotto family. Elvio Del Zotto resigned from the Arts Council while the others ignored the requests. But the damage was done: Peterson's order caused resentment in Toronto's huge Italian community, where fund-raising and organizing for the Peterson Liberals would never be the same. "It was an overreaction," Peterson would later admit. "In retrospect, I wish it hadn't happened."

On July 6 Scott announced details of the inquiry. Ontario Court of Appeal Justice Lloyd Houlden was appointed to look into the relationship between Starr and Tridel, and all MPPs, cabinet ministers, municipal politicians and unelected public officials. Houlden was asked to determine "whether a benefit, advantage or reward of any kind was conferred upon any elected or unelected public official or any member of his or her family." Backing up the Houlden Commission was a massive joint-forces police investigation that combined the efforts of eighteen Metro Toronto police officers and five OPP investigators. Within months, the Toronto force would set up a parallel criminal investigation.

Critics charged the inquiry was too narrow to restore public confidence. "The government seems intent upon limiting this judicial inquiry to the narrow focus of the Patti Starr-Tridel-Gordon Ashworth triangle," said interim Tory Leader Andy Brandt. The Tories insisted, to no avail, that the inquiry look into the awarding of contracts by organizations, including Ontario Place; the approval of development projects by the government; the possibility that influence had been exerted on elected and appointed officials; the appointments process that put Starr at Ontario Place; any contraventions of the Election Finances Act and the Conflict of Interest Act; and the appropriateness of ministers' fund-raising practices. Rae echoed the demands.

Peterson's dismay over the scandal was clear and genuine, but his office had nurtured the climate in which Starr worked as a fund-raiser. The Liberals' openness to fund-raising help was linked to the party's chronic fund-raising troubles. Liberal staff, including executive and political assistants to ministers, were schooled in encouraging individuals and organizations who were doing (or who might do) business with the government to attend fund-raising events for ministers and make contributions to the party. Each Peterson cabinet minister was expected to raise a minimum of $15,000 each year for the party and was provided with advice on how to organize fund-raising events. Peterson, like many of his senior ministers, was a popular attraction at such fund-raisers. In the gray area of ethical conduct in the relations between the government and potential clients, where the law extended only to disclosure and limits on donations, Peterson's participation condoned the Liberals' practices.

"No question, I encouraged people to raise money, to be well financed and ready for the next campaign all the time," said Peterson. But he insisted the Liberals were not for sale. "I defy anybody to find one case where somebody got treated differently because they contributed to the party. No minister that I was ever aware of said I will do something special for somebody because they gave a donation to the party."

The Liberals were little different from other parties in their fund-raising practices. Like the other parties they operated within existing legislation; as the party in power, they received the attentions of Starr more generously than the opposition. But the Liberals' flaw was their failure to exercise the discretion and diligence needed to adhere strictly to the high expectations of ethical conduct created by their promises. Many Ontarians would come to perceive the Liberals were corrupt; with perception the reality in politics, the Liberals would pay the price for appearing to let Ontarians down.

*   *   *

The political costs to the Liberals were not immediately evident in their summer of scandal. A July 12 poll by Toronto's Environics Research showed the furor had not changed the pattern of support for the three parties. The Liberals were backed by 45 percent of decided voters, up one point since Environics' last poll four months earlier. The Tories stood at 29 percent, the NDP at 25. But, Environics warned, "the public is not oblivious to the so-called scandals": confidence in the honesty and integrity of the government was waning. "These things take time," said Rae. "It takes time to bring down a government."

In August, reports surfaced that police investigators had broadened their focus to include the sale of the Peterson family business; Peterson had refused opposition demands to add that clause to the terms of reference of the Houlden inquiry, adamant he had not been involved in the sale. In September the inquiry began; by October an Angus Reid poll showed the Liberals regaining support—an election would get them the backing of 48 percent of decided voters, while the NDP climbed back into second place with 25 percent and the Tories slumped to 24. A growing number of voters were becoming concerned about the honesty of the Liberals: 51 percent said they were not impressed with the government's record at providing honest, open government. But the Liberals took solace in the finding that Peterson's personal approval rating stayed above the fray, hovering over 60 percent. Days later an Environics poll echoed the findings and even showed general approval of Peterson's handling of the Starr affair.

By January 1990, however, support for the Liberals was wavering, according to Environics. A new poll showed the government clinging to the support required to form a majority, with 42 percent of decided voters; the Tories had rebounded to 30 percent and the NDP had drifted down to 26. But Environics also said Peterson's personal popularity had dropped to its lowest point as premier—39 percent, compared with 46 percent in September 1989.

The Houlden inquiry was scuttled abruptly by the Supreme Court of Canada in April 1990 at the request of Starr's lawyers. In a six-to-one decision, the court ruled the terms of reference of the inquiry invalid, calling the probe unconstitutional because it in effect served as a substitute police investigation and was in substance a matter falling within parliament's exclusive criminal power, without giving the claimant opportunity to defend herself. Starr filed a civil suit against Peterson, Scott and Borg that she would later drop. The police probe supporting the inquiry was discontinued but the criminal investigation carried on.

By summer 1990 Starr would be charged with 11 criminal offenses, including fraud and uttering forged documents, and 34 violations of the Election Finances Act. No charges would be laid against Ashworth. In March 1991 Starr would be found guilty of four charges of violating the election laws. "Starr showed a deliberate intent to make contributions with no regard for the legal limits," the trial judge would say. In June 1991, Starr would plead guilty to a charge of criminal breach of trust related to the NCJW capital fund and a fraud charge related to a provincial grant for renovations to NCJW headquarters. She would be sentenced to six months in jail.

A perception of widespread corruption in the Peterson government helped undermine its credibility, creating an impression that Liberals were using their public office for private gain. "I don't know whether Ashworth received a refrigerator, but assuming he did, the interesting thing was the number of people that thought I got a fridge, if not better," said Scott. "The allegation breeds the sense that the allegation is true. People in my riding who read that Ashworth got a refrigerator began to wonder what I got, and I don't blame them for that."

Knowing the power of those perceptions, the NDP and Tories would keep the Starr scandal in the spotlight through the first half of 1990, maintaining their attacks on the honesty and integrity of the Liberals. Rae raised the public inquiry issue repeatedly with Peterson in the legislature. "What is it that is stopping him from holding a broader inquiry into the question of how such a degree of outside influence could have been exercised on his government, and what is precisely the relationship between the Liberal party and the development industry?" he would ask in April.

The Tories also kept the heat turned on. In May, Tory justice critic Norm Sterling would call the fund-raising scandal "a shameful chapter in the history of this administration, because the Starr inquiry was the check on the issue of accountability and credibility of this government."

*   *   *

In August 1989 Peterson and his core of advisors huddled to remake the Liberal cabinet and put a new face on the government. Peterson used the shuffle to remove a handful of aging ministers and bring up new members expected to form the backbone that would carry the party into the next election. Five ministers were dropped who had been touched by Starr, Hosek and Munro among them. Three new cabinet committees were set up, the most important an agenda committee: composed of cabinet's policy committee chairs, it was designed to set government priorities, make better use of cabinet's time and ensure all policies and programs were part of a coordinated agenda.

The new cabinet held its first meeting in Brantford. Peterson had put out the word: sound judgment and discretion would prevail from now on. But naivety emerged immediately. As reporters, ministers and locals gathered on the morning of the meeting, a government car pulled up containing Christine Hart, the new minister of culture and communications. As Liberals gasped in disbelief and onlookers snickered, Hart's black driver, wearing white gloves, jumped out and smartly opened the door for his smiling boss in a scene that seemed the epitome of bad judgment. Borg rebuked the rookie minister; the driver stayed, the white gloves were trashed and Hart learned to open her own doors.

Over the summer, as the Houlden inquiry geared up, Peterson took other steps to restore order. Toronto lawyer Steve Goudge was asked to conduct an internal investigation, talking to ministers and staffers to determine if the Liberals were in for any more Starr-related trouble. He reported back with an all-clear signal. At the same time, the organizational chaos wrought by the outbreak of the scandal was taken on by a new addition to the premier's office, Dan Gagnier.

Ezrin and Peterson had brought Gagnier, a constitutional expert, from Ottawa to Queen's Park as deputy minister of energy. Gagnier was transferred to Peterson's intergovernmental affairs ministry to advise him on Meech Lake. When Ashworth resigned, Gagnier was made a special advisor to cabinet and assisted with Goudge's investigation while evaluating the organization of the premier's office and consulting with Peterson on the escalating Meech problems.

In September 1989 Peterson made a staffing change that reflected his personal priorities. He moved Borg out as principal secretary and replaced him with Gagnier, who came aboard on secondment from the public service. "Vince was at a certain point that he just got tired of it, the 24-hour-a-day job," said Peterson. Borg, who had been reluctant to return, had been spread too thin and no longer wanted the job.

"I think what drew the premier to ask me to come into his office was a comfort level with me in terms of taking on and managing the office, quieting it down," said Gagnier. "It had gone through a serious set of shocks with Hershell departing and Ashworth's resignation. The roles inside of it had become fuzzy and people were wondering where it was going to go, who was going to arbitrate between the various players in the premier's office, ensure that liaison was consistently undertaken with cabinet office. The three-legged stool they had set up on transition, secretary of cabinet, principal secretary and executive director, had broken down." Earlier in the year, cabinet secretary Carman had retired to take a private sector job and was replaced by another public servant, Peter Barnes.

But the Starr affair stuck with the Liberals. Not only did the scandal help derail the new reform agenda outlined in the 1989 Throne Speech and dismember the premier's office, it overwhelmed the Liberals for months. A sense of drift and helplessness floated through the halls of the legislature, much of it emanating from Peterson's office, which seemed mesmerized by the Starr affair. Ashworth's fall shocked those around him because he was felt to be, in Carman's words, "the conscience of the Liberal party."

While polls continued to show support for the Liberals, the fund-raising scandal helped contribute to an impression that the government had no agenda, was indecisive and was not solving problems. The Liberals resumed their drive for reform in the fall of 1989, pushing through new legislation and meeting campaign, Throne Speech and budget promises. But to the media and most Ontarians the government's agenda was overshadowed by the Starr affair—and then by the unfolding constitutional crisis.

* * *

The specter of scandal did not seem to spook Operation Alienation, which marched on as the reforms continued. Lawyers were one of many groups that opposed the Liberals' push for a no-fault auto insurance system. Since the early 1980s insurance costs in Ontario had been shooting upward, driven chiefly by higher claims and court settlements. Availability of insurance also emerged as a problem. In 1986 a Liberal-appointed task force recommended insurance industry reforms, including changes to the tort system and some form of private sector no-fault system; another task force looked more closely at no-fault plans. Escalating rates were big news in 1987: pressed for answers on the campaign trail, Peterson claimed the Liberals had a plan to reduce rates, when a comprehensive scheme was actually far off. In September 1989 the government produced the Ontario Motorist Protection Plan, which promised to solve cost and availability problems.

The plan raised the minimum level of benefits for accident victims but limited their right to sue except in cases of serious and permanent injury. Premium hikes would be kept to a provincewide average of 4 percent in the first year of the plan, far below the 35 percent increase predicted without the changes. But outrage over the plan broke out. Victims' groups pushed for higher guaranteed benefits than the Liberals proposed and the benefits were boosted. Litigation lawyers across the province could not be as easily appeased. The plan's limits on the right to sue hit them hard in the pocketbook: $500 million in claims payments in 1989-90 went to pay legal costs for victims.

The plan provoked a massive antigovernment campaign by a group called Fair Action for Insurance Reform (FAIR). Ironically, FAIR had been created by 1987 Liberal campaign chair David MacNaughton's government relations firm PAI, drawing in 39 groups concerned about no-fault's impact on victims.

MacNaughton urged them to negotiate with the Liberals to find compromises. When that route failed, FAIR dropped PAI.

"When the government decided to charge off on their own particular scheme, the FAIR committee came to the conclusion I was not the best person to develop a war strategy to beat the shit out of the government," said MacNaughton. "So they dropped our account and hired [longtime Tory strategist] Hugh Segal to develop the baseball bat approach." Spearheaded by angry lawyers, FAIR slammed the Liberals with an ad campaign that listed scores of groups purportedly opposing the no-fault plan—though some, including the Canadian Federation of Independent Business and the Consumers' Association of Canada, supported it.

The no-fault push was to be sold through the most detailed communications strategy the Liberals cooked up to try to sell a policy to Ontarians. The scheme used research from 15 focus groups held provincewide and aimed its messages at the general public, anti-impaired driving, disabled and victims' groups, litigation lawyers and others. By spring 1990 a million-dollar ad blitz was ready—but was scrubbed by Liberals planning the coming provincial election who felt the pitches were badly conceived and ill-timed. At the same time, loopholes in the new house rules agreed to by the Liberals in 1989 permitted delays in the passage of the no-fault legislation. The auto insurance turmoil gave a back seat to the question of whether the Liberal plan represented a valid response to a difficult and complex problem. Instead, it helped give Ontarians the impression that the Liberals were accumulating more enemies.

*   *   *

Liberal hyperactivity on environmental protection as a minority was prodded by the accord with the NDP, but Environment Minister Jim Bradley went beyond the deal and earned a reputation as an ally of the environment movement. Cuts in acid rain-causing sulphur dioxide were ordered against the province's four largest industrial air polluters; water pollution was attacked through a

Municipal-Industrial Strategy for Abatement (MISA); soft drink container regulations were improved and Blue Box municipal recycling started; fines were stiffened to make polluters pay cleanup costs. The Liberals entered the 1987 election perceived as authors of real change on the environment and promised more: a beaches cleanup, pesticide controls, more pollution inspection and enforcement, better water and sewage works.

Bradley met the promises, but by 1989, many environment groups were questioning his ability to win battles. The enemies, they believed, were a Tory-dominated bureaucracy resisting change and the antienvironment interests of developers, represented by the ministries of municipal affairs and housing, and of business, represented by others in cabinet. A slowdown in environmental action was also blamed on Treasurer Nixon, dubbed by some environmentalists as "Tyrannosaurus Nix." "We doubled the money in five years [for the ministry of the environment's budget]," said Nixon, "but it didn't come anywhere near what they would like to have had. I felt we had to be coming up with solutions rather than identifying problems." Nixon's views frustrated environment activists: "When the last tree is cut, when the last river is polluted, when the last acre of land dries up and blows away, you can't eat the money, Bob," said one.

The Liberals' slowdown on the environment coincided with the explosion of environmentalism among Ontarians, matched by the growth of the organized environmental movement. Greenpeace in Toronto, for example, burgeoned from a motley group of rebels in 1985 to the headquarters of a national organization claiming 350,000 members in 1990. Unity grew at the same time in the environmental community as Pollution Probe, Greenpeace, Friends of the Earth and other groups worked toward common goals, often against incumbent governments. Alliances emerged with other powerful special interests, including unions and native groups.

Frustration with the Liberals among environmentalists came to a head over the implementation of MISA. Environment groups expecting an uncompromising water pollution cleanup regardless of the cost to industry were left wanting when

Bradley's ministry adopted a regulatory principle called Best Available Technology Economically Achievable (BATEA), a trade-off between cost and pollution cuts that environmental hard-liners found intolerable.

Discontent also crystallized around the Liberals' apparent support for land development at the expense of the environment. Peterson pledged in 1988 to "cut the approvals process in half" to speed development, chiefly to ease Toronto's housing shortage. In September 1989 treasury and municipal affairs officials produced Project X, a discussion paper entitled "Reforming Our Land Use and Development System" that seemed to put development ahead of the environment by cutting Bradley's power. Nixon maintained the idea was to slash red tape that raised land costs, not reduce environmental protection. But the paper was written without Bradley's knowledge or his ministry's involvement. Copies of Project X leaked out to environment groups and reporters, who attacked the report and the split in the government.

The list of beefs grew: Nixon's 1990 budget plan for a Crown corporation to manage and speed sewer and water infrastructure development prompted charges that the system would skirt environmental approvals, again to benefit developers. A $5 Ontario tax on each new tire sold was collected but not spent as promised on tire recycling; the environmental threat from stockpiled used tires became a disaster when a pile of 12 million tires in Hagersville in southern Ontario was torched by arsonists in February 1990. With the fire out, Bradley announced tire recycling measures; environment groups scoffed at the move as action after-the-fact.

Peterson's May 1990 announcement that Toronto's Rouge Valley would be preserved as a park was lauded by environmentalists, then undercut when the Liberals would not rule out a garbage dump on-site. The possibility of a dump in the Rouge was only part of the Liberals' garbage woes. By not taking decisive action to solve the problem of where to put Toronto's trash, the Liberals ensured they would enter the next election facing the wrath of both large environment groups and residents of dozens of towns determined to fight being stuck with a garbage dump. By summer 1990 environmentalists were fed up with the Liberals and called Bradley "the white shield that David Peterson hides behind."

*　　*　　*

Ezrin's departure as Liberal mastermind left corporate communications by the government in limbo; Borg tried rebuilding around the 1989 Throne Speech but was derailed by the Starr affair. Just as the government had trouble setting policy priorities, it had trouble deciding which messages it wanted to get across to Ontarians. Liberal MPPs often received fuzzy signals on what to tell constituents about what the government was doing. A caucus service bureau was bolstered to help members talk to the people who elected them. Placed in charge was veteran Peterson aide Bill Murray, an enormous Londoner with a voice like a gravel truck stuck in low gear; he hired new staff and expanded the operation. But as the government aged its corporate communications efforts received less attention and direction from Peterson's office.

Many Peterson staffers seemed to believe good policies would sell themselves, an attitude dating to the extra-billing battle when some Liberals felt the moral correctness of their cause accounted for public support for their policy. A belief grew that when communications help was needed the premier could be counted on to get the government through by sheer force of personality, which had always seemed to work in the past. Peterson appeared to agree.

Gagnier tried his hand at rebuilding the communications function in the premier's office but ran into what he called "the premier's own belief that he could handle communications with twice-a-day, a few times a day, media scrums." Gagnier ordered external reviews of the Liberals' corporate communications; when he attempted to act on the "scathing" reports, he found Peterson's support halfhearted. "Part of the reason why it was an uphill battle was the premier himself never backed it fully," said Gagnier. The result: the Liberals were doing a lot, but were failing to get their accomplishments across to Ontarians. "It was not a stagnant period," said Peterson later. "Very much the contrary. But we did not convey that. We didn't share that sense of excitement with people. We weren't able to get through."

All too often, the result was that nothing was communicated with consistency by Liberal MPPs, ministers, bureaucrats and the premier. The Liberals failed to balance a news agenda dominated by stories about Liberal indecision and inaction—a big, bloated government that could not make up its mind what to do, was not solving problems, and did not seem to care. When it came to talking to Ontarians the Liberals were often tongue-tied and convinced they had plenty of time to get their messages out. Continued support in the polls provided further assurance the Liberals were doing a good job.

The Liberals were well aware of the importance of not only talking to Ontarians but also listening to them. Their consensus-building approach depended on it. Keeping their government "open and accessible" and free of "walls or barriers" was an often-repeated maxim. But in practice, the Liberals' openness and accessibility dwindled. The community relations function in the premier's office, once reporting to Ashworth, shriveled with neglect as the staffers responsible for interacting with ethnic, linguistic, political and other third-party groups were virtually ignored by top aides.

Peterson led the slide by example: as premier, he abandoned his cable television shows, spent much less time in his constituency office and reduced his community involvement in London. The demands of the premier's office made such changes inevitable but neglect of his own backyard would catch up with Peterson.

Peterson's relations with the media, especially the Queen's Park press gallery, deteriorated painfully during the Liberal majority. Press secretary Hutchison left for a foreign posting; his successors found their role gradually reduced, to the dismay of reporters. "You never really had a lot of faith in the press office," said Global TV's Robert Fisher. "My sense was they just didn't have information. They were excluded from the process."

As familiarity and disrespect grew between Peterson and the media over the years, the relationship often turned confrontational. "He was more pleasant to deal with in 1986 than 1990," said the Toronto *Star*'s Matt Maychak. "But having said that, we were probably easier to deal with in 1986 than in 1990. The relationship changes over time because there's a certain aspect of living together in this building. You try to get along, but at some points we're adversaries too, and that wears on over time."

One incident stood as a symbol of Peterson's deteriorating relationship with the media. At a tribute dinner for Nixon in 1987 Peterson mugged and hit his head with his hand, saying Nixon looked "like a retard." The phrase was a disturbing choice of words for a premier. Fisher discovered the slip when he screened the tape later. "We ran it three times; Peterson argues we ran it more like fifteen," he said. "To this day I think he still hates me for that particular incident." Peterson apologized publicly for his "little joke," but felt slighted when his error was rerun mercilessly: "It was stupid, I shouldn't have said it," he admitted. "Fisher played that four or five times." While reporters maintained such errors by public figures were legitimate news, Peterson often complained the media tended to look for faults rather than "use their pens constructively."

Some reporters believed Peterson did not understand or care about ordinary people. "He was a rich man," felt the *Globe*'s Richard Mackie. "The language that Peterson used didn't talk about people needing jobs because they need to give themselves assurance, confidence in themselves, because it's something we owe them. It was to create a reliable work force. It was not to help people. Reporters were just aghast at this lack of understanding of human problems. You didn't see the government dealing with people who were facing hardships, single mothers, people who deal with food banks, that type of thing; there was no compassion in anything the government seemed to want to do." To Liberals such criticism confirmed a lack of "institutional memory" in the media, which they felt ignored the government's social reforms.

Peterson's acid tongue often hurt him in the game of media relations. "There's ego in politics but there isn't any less in journalism," he believed. "Why should such an unbalanced group be able to pass judgment on anybody? The only solution to the dilemma is the press being just as tough on themselves as it is on other people." Peterson's style helped aggravate reporters. He usually spoke in a murmur in media scrums, a technique that made him appear calm and controlled, gave television viewers the impression he was surrounded by shouting journalistic louts and drove reporters crazy. They often could not tell what the premier had said until they returned to their offices and listened intently to their tape recorders.

During the accord years, some Queen's Park reporters had found the Tories and NDP ineffective and began to refer to themselves as "the real opposition," a belief enhanced for many reporters when the Liberals decimated the opposition in the 1987 election. "I think there was a great feeling in the gallery that it had failed in '87, that it hadn't kept on top of things," said the *Globe*'s Mackie. "There's a public perception that it's pack journalism here, that everybody gets together in the morning at nine o'clock and does a bunch of high-fives and says, 'Let's go get Peterson,'" said Fisher. "That's not true but I think there was a sense that 'The opposition ain't going to do it; by God, we're going to take this guy on.'"

*   *   *

The Liberals learned the hard way that bad communications is bad government. The success of their long-term reform agenda depended on good communications. "We had a long-term agenda but we didn't communicate the medium-term agenda that lead to the long-term," said Borg. The Liberals did not tell Ontarians in clear and simple terms the reasons for and benefits of the changes they were making—changes that turned off so many powerful special-interests. "There was never a government in

Ontario that took on the whole range of special-interest groups, and we paid the price for it," said Scott. "We didn't sell our products as well as we should have. But it was in the public interest to do the things we did." The Liberals' record was impressive with action and long-term reforms undertaken in many areas. But, by 1990, Ontarians could get the impression the reform-minded government they thought they had elected had turned into a traditional party that was not solving the problems of the day and had lost its way. In only three years the excitement and promise of 1987 had been replaced by a sense of ennui and uninterest.

Around a leader who "fell into" politics, whose rise "just sort of happened," those impressions could easily evolve. "David could have done this job and done it very well if he had a driving goal; if he had entered public life wanting to make certain things happen, he would not have lost his bearings as he did after '87," said one minister. But Peterson did have his own honest passions and sources of motivation: national unity and international economic competitiveness. Those were diffuse goals, however, to be achieved over decades, not weeks or months, and were easily sideswiped by scandal or lost in day-to-day fire fighting. When his image proved timely, not timeless, and he emerged as a man for one season, not all, Peterson could not fall back on a vision, an agenda and goals wired to his gut—other than those too distant to strike a chord with Ontarians.

In the months before the 1990 election many of the government's problems were personified by Peterson. His morning briefings were reduced to half-hour sessions of machine-gun bursts of information from staff, who found they often had only a few moments of attention to get their points across. Cabinet and its policy and priorities board became, almost exclusively, briefing sessions for the premier. Liberals close to Peterson began to believe he no longer enjoyed his job or felt at ease with the people around him. "When Dan Gagnier and Peter Barnes arrived and took over, that was fine, except that he never really had the relationship with them," said Health Minister Caplan. "I'm not saying that he didn't trust them, I'm saying that he just didn't have the same kind of relationship that he did with Hershell and Gordon. I don't think he ever got over not having confidantes to confide in, and the events with Joan Smith had separated him and Don Smith. He was left a very lonely man."

Peterson's attention became fixated on national unity, those around him found. "If it was something with regard to the Constitution, he could do it," said MacNaughton. "But if it was something that had to do with other issues, he just didn't feel strongly enough about it to take the heat." When he raised non-Meech questions with Peterson, said MacNaughton, he was met with "the glazed eye."

Gagnier found Peterson growing increasingly dependent on his own opinion to make decisions. "Often times you'd come in with a piece of advice and he'd disagree with you," said Gagnier. "He'd say, 'Oh, no, trust the old premier.' Once you're faced with that kind of response, no matter how right or wrong your policy advice is, the door's closed; he'd made a decision."

The "old premier": the phrase became Peterson's favorite way to describe himself. An aide who knew both Bill Davis and Peterson noted that while Davis began to call himself "the old preem" after about ten years on the job, Peterson started to do the same after three years. Peterson's view of himself symbolized a Liberal problem identified by Gagnier: "I've never seen a government age so quickly," he said.

Peterson's hair turned from salt-and-pepper to silvery-white by the summer of 1990 and he began to look older. He changed and those closest to him noticed. "I know there were times when he didn't have that gleam in his eye as he left for the office," said Shelley Peterson. "David never lost sight of the importance of his job. The importance that he make good decisions. He knew that he had been entrusted with a lot. That never left him, the dedication to the job. It was just not as easy."

Early in 1990 Peterson made another lonely decision: he would not run for the federal Liberal leadership vacated by John Turner. Close friends had been split on their advice; some had been convinced he would take the plunge. In Quebec,

Bourassa publicly issued a call for Peterson to enter the race; privately, Alberta's Don Getty urged him to give it a shot.

"The reality is, I did not consider it seriously," said Peterson. "There's two reasons. First, I have only two things in life, there's politics and my kids. I know what it's like and I know the time commitment now: you multiply that by five to be a national leader. I didn't see it necessarily as the next logical progression, and I know what it takes to build a party and I'd done it. Second, I knew that the country was in horrible trouble over Meech Lake and I was very worried about that. I figured that I could be far more in a position of influence as the premier of Ontario than as the leader of the opposition nationally—if I could have won. I knew that the next year or so was going to be extremely political and I figured I should try to be there to keep it glued together."

3

Ramping-Up to the 1990 Election

Don't miss the train, get on board.

–Dan Gagnier,
Principal secretary to the premier

At first, it worked fine. As other politicians plied their trade on the rubber-chicken circuit, Peterson worked a summer picnic-and-hot-dog-barbeque circuit in Liberal Ontario. Peterson's summer strolling and schmoozing with Liberals began as a campaign tactic in 1987, when reporters all but laid palm leaves in his path and style could carry the day. The premier was a great draw and news reports from such events showcased his image and confirmed his popularity. In 1988 party officials asked Peterson to appear at a handful of picnics across the province to help Liberal ridings raise funds.

Each event was staged to evoke the feeling of a family reunion: a massive barbeque hissing with wieners, the summer air resounding with the cheers of softball, spectators and David, tanned and smiling, arm in arm with Shelley, being welcomed with handshakes and hugs. The picnics were an easygoing routine, exuding positive vibes: Peterson would arrive in his white-shirt-and-red-tie uniform, "meet and greet" folks, then serve up hot dogs or lob a few balls in the game. Peterson's tosses were often socked out of sight by someone's kid, to hearty applause.

A similar symbiosis was sometimes displayed when members of the local media lobbed easy questions at the premier; often, the visit of the celebrity premier was all the story they wanted in 1988. Even a tiny SWAT team of members of the Ontario Public Service Employees Union (OPSEU), testing a tactic for the next provincial election campaign, could generate only passing coverage as it pestered Peterson with protests at every stop.

A series of 14 more picnics was arranged late in the summer of 1989. To the province's media and especially to members of the Queen's Park press gallery, the purpose of yet another round of hot dogs and handshakes was blindingly obvious: get Peterson's smiling mug back in the papers and on television, preferably kissing a baby or serving up hot dogs. These events were too cute, reporters began to say, too deliberately designed to evade issues or deliver substantive messages, too indicative of a carefree attitude in defiance of the Starr furor still bristling in the headlines. "It was a great way to get him out," said Global Television's Robert Fisher. "It was the type of thing where he'd shine. If he didn't shine in the house, and he didn't shine in the scrums, he certainly shone in those types of settings." Reporters began to view the routine with cynicism and filed their conclusion away for future reference.

Actually, Peterson's hot dog circuit in 1989 had a purpose more serious than garnering easy publicity. He was being used as bait to build membership in the Ontario Liberal Party (OLP), in a scheme to jump-start sputtering efforts to organize its ridings. "The premier's picnics in the summer of '89 were really a membership drive," said party president Kathy Robinson. "We set out as a goal that every riding would have 400 members."

Two years into the Liberals' majority, "we were all worried about complacency," she believed, and Peterson's appearances provided "ridings that sort of a hook to join in with."

The Liberals' problem was that they had bounded into majority government without a corresponding party machine. Convinced that in the long run "OLP was fundamentally only going to be as strong as its ridings were," Robinson embarked on a three-year plan to rebuild the party's organization, communications and policy formulation. After the 1987 election, Peterson's office, party executives and Liberal riding presidents agreed that action was long overdue.

Robinson dived in and grappled with the party's structural challenges. "Looking forward to the next campaign," she said, "I felt we really had to take the sort of steps that were necessary to put the organization in shape." Robinson showed results quickly and provided the party with the leadership it needed.

Liberal party organization, communications and policy making had been weak for decades, overwhelmed by the strength of the provincial Tories. London developer Don Smith became president of the party in 1984 to help out his friend Peterson, and focused on the Liberals' chronic shortage of cash. He remained the party's fund-raising chair in 1988, when Robinson was acclaimed to replace him as president.

Smith's reliability and effectiveness as a corporate fund-raiser constituted a Liberal legend. When the party needed money he could pick up the phone and find contributions fast: in 1988 he raised a one-year record of $2.7 million for the party. But his one-man-band style had a downside. For instance, Smith balked at bringing the party into the 1980s by introducing direct-mail techniques, rapidly proving their worth for the federal Tories. Robinson found that when the Ontario Liberals tried direct-mail test runs, Smith's view was reinforced: "We'd make $5,000 and he'd say, 'I can do that in five phone calls and here you've spent all this time and effort doing it. What's the point?'" But fund-raising troubles continued to plague the Liberals in spite of the work of Smith and other party officials, keeping them dependent on corporate rather than individual donations and making them vulnerable to the Starr events.

The internal process of ratcheting the Liberal party machine up the ramp to the 1990 campaign began in earnest nearly two years in advance. Robinson found that the party's communication with its members was sporadic, so she began sending out newsletters and brochures to clue in Liberals about what their government was doing. Policy making received similar attention. Like other parties the Liberals recognized the lure that playing a role in policy development held, and it was used to encourage Liberals to come to meetings and participate. Sessions at training meetings for Liberal organizers were devoted to such topics as "using enthusiasm for policy to advance Liberal goals in the riding." Missing were reports on government actions prompted by the grass-roots policy work. While progress could be duly noted in the party's organization and communications, the flame that drew many moths to the Liberal camp burned cold. One senior minister summarized the government actions that reflected the party's policy process as "Nada, nil, nothing."

The lack of follow-through was not a product of disregard for the party's ideas or neglect, believed Peterson policy chief Jan Whitelaw: "Most of the party's policy resolutions were about things we were already doing, which spoke to a communications problem. They also tended to be more generic." But the apparent lack of responsiveness led some Liberals to believe their government was not listening to them and to feel less inclined to jump with enthusiasm into the next election campaign.

Robinson's struggle was uphill. To build what she described as "a partnership between the elected members and the volunteer sector," Robinson worked riding association meetings and events at nights and on weekends in far-flung corners of the province, impressing both premier and cabinet with her diligence and commitment. "Kathy's the kind that would drive through a snowstorm 150 miles to attend a meeting and to solve problems," said Peterson. Robinson cleaned up a long-standing organizational mess by carving the province into six regions of "political responsibility." Each was assigned to a senior cabinet minister, caucus member and party workers.

Membership in Liberal riding associations had to be shored up to do more than raise money. A large membership base was needed, the Liberals believed, to protect sitting members who might face nomination challenges in the next election. Several Liberal nominations had been nasty affairs in 1987 but the vulnerability of Liberal incumbents had been laid bare in the nomination process for the 1988 federal election. "It became acceptable to take a run at a sitting member, and up until that time that was heresy," said Robinson. "As soon as that happened and the party establishment took no steps to say, 'sitting members are off limits,' it changed the whole nature of the nomination process." After bitter debate Ontario Liberals concluded they could not shut the door on nomination challenges to incumbents and maintain both the appearance and the reality of an open party.

Four of Peterson's MPPs, including two cabinet ministers, found themselves "paying the price" for an open party in the spring of 1990. They fended off challenges to what they felt was their right to run as Liberal candidates in their ridings. The challengers came with different motives but all had a bone to pick with the Peterson government.

In his Wentworth North riding near Hamilton, Government House Leader Chris Ward was targeted by local lawyers determined to take down a cabinet minister to protest the Liberals' no-fault auto insurance legislation. The lawyers persuaded David Molnar, a local insurance broker who claimed no special interest in the insurance issue, to challenge Ward for the nomination. Under the banner of "dissatisfied Liberals," Molnar attracted local environment activists and teachers as he tried to sign up enough new Liberal members to offer Ward a serious threat. Even members of the local Tory riding association bought Liberal memberships to vote against Ward.

In April, Liberal lawyer Herman Turkstra, who backed Molnar, sent a letter of support to MPP Peter Kormos, as the New Democrat conducted a filibuster in the legislature to protest the auto insurance bill. Avowing he personally had "absolutely no economic interest" in litigation, Turkstra told Kormos, "I know that there are thousands of Liberals across this province who are deeply disappointed with their own party because of this legislation, and because of the approach taken to its enactment . . . in Ontario, everyone but the cabinet become dolts after the election, except for fund-raising."

Ward out-organized Molnar and kept the nomination but the challenge, reported as a split among Liberals that showed discontent with the Peterson government, eroded Ward's support in the riding.

West of Toronto three more Liberals faced nomination challenges. Highly organized splinter groups in the mostly Liberal Sikh community emerged to take on Solicitor General Steve Offer in Mississauga North and MPPs Linda LeBourdais in Etobicoke West and Carman McClelland in Brampton North. The challenges appeared to call into question the Peterson Liberal's much-touted relationship with ethnic communities. The challengers complained the premier had neglected Ontario's large Sikh population and had never visited a Sikh temple.

Skilled in organizing and mobilizing members of their community, Sikh leaders were able to sign up huge numbers of riding association members and bring them out to vote for the candidates of their choice. Early in 1990, their skills were demonstrated at federal Liberal leadership convention delegate selection meetings, where whole slates of Sikh-supported delegates were elected in some Toronto area ridings.

After repeated pleas by Liberals, Peterson visited several Sikh temples, where he wore a makeshift turban as required by Sikh custom, and was photographed looking awkward and uncomfortable. The belated gesture did not prevent bitter and exhausting nomination battles in the three ridings. Resentment festered in Liberal ranks at the failure of Peterson's office and the party to detect and respond to the delicate complexities of the Sikh community's internal politics. The incidents confirmed that the premier's office had neglected community relations, an important early warning system; storm warnings that did get through were greeted with indifference and a lack of motivation to understand the nuances of the issue. News reports trumpeted more Liberal infighting and concluded the party was losing support among ethnic groups.

* * *

To Peterson, the report card on Robinson was impressive. The party had been yanked out of an organizational stupor; its infrastructure was becoming more like that of a party in power. Peterson and Robinson would talk almost daily, as Robinson built a position as a trusted confidante. One Peterson aide described her move into the inner circle: "She was one of the guys. She told him what he needed to know without any bullshit or fucking around." At the same time, though, Robinson was generating criticism among party workers and ministers' political staff, who referred to her as "the imperial president" and complained that she used her links to the top to operate by edict.

By the end of 1989 Robinson was the front-running candidate for chair of the next Liberal election campaign. Most Liberals knew the case could be made that she was a "child of the party" who had worked hard to earn the job. At 40 she had more than two decades of political involvement, starting with the student Liberals at Trent University. She chaired the first-time voters committee for Trudeau in 1972 and by 1975 knew Robert Nixon well enough to become his right-hand organizational assistant for the provincial election. She co-chaired federal campaign training in 1979, served as vice-chair of the 1980 and 1984 federal campaigns in Ontario and co-chaired the Liberal's Metro Toronto campaign in 1987. Peterson believed she had the right stuff for a campaign chair: "Kathy's very conscientious and she's got good judgment and she's cool under pressure. Kathy is a good friend and I trust her completely. I thought she was the right one to glue all the elements together and I knew she was prepared to do the work." But some Liberals, including a handful of cabinet members, were uneasy about Robinson's lack of high-end campaign management experience.

Robinson was an aggressive, committed politico. In 1988, on her ascension to the party presidency, Nixon recalled her pragmatism in his 1975 campaign: "One time we were in Chatham, when the *Globe and Mail* had picked up on something I'd said the day before and written a story that was not exactly positive. She went around and bought every *Globe* in town and dumped them. The reporters who were traveling with me couldn't follow up that story." Robinson, Nixon added, had "a great future in politics." Media reports cited her "ambition to run federally or provincially" and quoted colleagues and friends as saying Robinson thought herself prime minister material.

In November 1989 Liberals gathered for a meeting of riding presidents in Peterborough. Peterson spoke eloquently on the need for national unity and tolerance for one another's differences, and ended his address by naming Robinson campaign chair. "I have asked Kathy," he said, "to assemble a sound and determined team that will encompass all aspects of campaigning." Although the announcement followed months of speculation, media reports expressed surprise that Peterson would appoint a campaign chair after only two years in office, with up to three years left in his mandate.

Privately, Peterson made his expectations clear to Robinson. "He said he wanted the party to be in a state of readiness so that was not a factor in the decision as to whether we went or we didn't go," Robinson said. "We were really taking a look at getting all of the pieces in place by late spring so we would have all of our options available, depending on what the political climate was like."

As early as fall 1989 Peterson believed the nation's political climate was changing in ways that might lead him to call an election in 1990. To justify an early election, he foresaw two rationales, one related to economic conditions, one to national unity. "Obviously it was the economic question and obviously we were going into a slowdown, there's no question about that," he felt. "You knew the GST was coming along in some form or another, you knew the effects of free trade, you knew the budgetary position of the government, you knew the pressures on the government from a thousand different groups. But the other question, the big question to me always was the state of the union and the state of confederation. This was an unstable period for Meech and the question was: Would Meech pass or wouldn't it?" Having Robinson goose the party machine for a 1990 election provided Peterson with a safety valve if the nation's economy should sour or if Meech should fall apart. Or both.

Quick to stir up activity in her new post, Robinson assembled a campaign-readiness committee of senior party officials. She turned in mid-December to the six new regional political ministers for help in finding candidates in the 37 ridings across the province not held by Liberals. The party wanted to find high-quality candidates who could flesh out the caucus' demographic weaknesses, especially women with business experience and members of visible minorities. By year's end, Liberals were reading a clear message in their political tea leaves: the train was starting to roll toward a 1990 election.

*   *   *

Weeks later, in early January, the Liberal caucus flocked north to Muskoka for an annual private retreat. The venue was the spartan quarters of the YMCA's Geneva Park conference center on Lake Couchiching, a popular getaway spot for organizations hoping to hold think tanks with no distractions. Staff were forbidden to attend, spouses were left at home. Jeans and sweats were de rigueur; suits and ties showed up only on the nerdish or forgetful.

Business came first—sessions on budget pressures and auto insurance, regional caucus meetings and a report on election readiness from Robinson and Debbie Nash, the 1987 campaign co-chair now organizing campaign training. At the end of the first day, the Liberals groaned when they were introduced to the entertainment for the evening—a debate on the subject, "Early Election: Yes or No?" Assuming the "yes" position for the exercise were MPP Steve Mahoney and Treasurer Bob Nixon; arguing "no" were Attorney General Ian Scott and

Education Minister Sean Conway. The debate began to roll, focusing on the state of the economy, speculating on the shifting sands of the political landscape. Back and forth the exchange flew, Mahoney joking, Nixon growling, Scott acerbic, Conway preachy.

Environment Minister Jim Bradley demonstrated a unique way of making his view known on election timing. "1992!" he bellowed every few minutes, waving a large handmade sign with that date on it at his colleagues. The debaters paused politely each time, then resumed.

As the debating club began to lose steam, the dinner rolls came in handy. "Bun fight!" an MPP yelled and the air was suddenly thick with baked goods, forcing the debaters to flee the stage. A brief show of hands revealed the caucus split on the early-election-call question but no one kept score.

Later, outside in the Muskoka moonlight, the Liberals assembled, plumped against the cold with layers of coats, sweaters, gloves and hats. Someone had found broomball equipment and the favorite caucus rivalry would be played out on an icy basketball court: the class of '85 versus the class of '87. Worries about an early call disappeared into the Muskoka sky with the hoots and cheers of the game. And, again, no one kept score.

*   *   *

Gathering steam early in the year, the campaign train began grinding faster as Robinson signaled the party to pull out the stops on election preparedness. "Pre-writ activities are being encouraged in each riding," she reported to the party's executive committee on January 27. "Training will be provided in regional sessions in February, there will be a training component at the annual general meeting and at the Presidents' Council in June. Trainers will be available to ridings on an individual basis. There is a lot of organizational work to do."

Nash rolled her training road show through southern Ontario in February. Hundreds of Liberals paid $20 each to attend day-long sessions on "the do's and don'ts of effective targeting, raising the Liberal profile in your community, fund-raising tips, issue and list management, membership recruitment and checklists for riding activity." By the end of March, Liberal campaign workers from every riding were primed for even more training and hyping-up at what was widely expected to be the party's last annual general meeting before an election.

As Liberal troops went through their drills in February and March, the party's campaign-readiness team agreed to come to grips with an old chestnut that had troubled Liberals for years: Was their sun rising or setting? The "sun" in question was part of the Ontario Liberal logo, created in 1984 as part of a new-look marketing plan for the party. The logo had raised some eyebrows at the time because of its resemblance to the logo of the Italian Socialist Party, but won wide acceptance among Liberals. In 1990, however, like weather forecasters torn between using "partly cloudy" or "partly sunny" to describe the same sky, some Liberals were worried about how voters were now interpreting the half-hidden sun that adorned all their literature, especially during campaigns. After six years of accumulating anti-Liberal attacks, they fretted, the public psyche might be reading "sunset" from a graphic that, in the party's happier past, had depicted sunrise.

At Robinson's request, pollster Martin Goldfarb ordered up focus groups, conducted by his vice-president Doug Hurley. Waving artboards in front of small groups of respondents, Hurley tested the old logo and nearly 20 alternatives, including a fully risen sun, no sun, and a red maple leaf similar to the federal Liberal logo. He concluded that the old logo's message had not changed: it was still the party's best option. People described the half-sun as "bold, strong and solid," with the imagery suggesting "warmth, optimism and renewal." Its doubts eased, the campaign-readiness committee decided to keep its old standard, confident the Peterson Liberals' sun remained on the ascent.

On March 22, one week before the Liberals' annual meeting, Robinson quietly lifted the party's freeze on nominations for candidates. To Peterson's senior ministers, the announcement was a collective slap in the face. They had not been consulted on an arbitrary decision that had the effect of fixing the timing of the election for later that year. One political minister challenged Robinson on the decision at the next caucus meeting. "Whose decision was it?" he demanded. "Mine," was Robinson's curt reply; the imperial-style edict let Peterson's top ministers know early on that their involvement in planning the election was not considered useful.

Robinson might as well have bolted a rocket atop the election-readiness train. The news that nominations were open shot out to Liberals, who took it as a signal that Nash's training was no drill and an early election *was* coming. Reporters caught wind of the story and helped whip up expectations as the Liberals' yearly fete approached. But already the prospect of an early election call was being tagged with the question, "How could they ever justify it?"

More than 1,200 Liberals descended on Windsor on the dismal, cold last weekend in March, the weather mirroring that border city's welcome for the Peterson clan. After five years of what it felt was neglect by the Liberals, Windsor was pulling no punches. Shepherded by local NDP organizers working tightly with activists from OPSEU and the Canadian Auto Workers, 500 people who were furious at the Liberals demonstrated outside the Cleary Auditorium as delegates arrived on Friday night. Provincewide media coverage noted the seething contempt that greeted Peterson.

Windsor's frustration was linked to the city's economic stagnation, as its industrial base felt the pinch of recession months ahead of most regions of Ontario. The area's four Liberal members were believed to lack influence in a Toronto-centered government. Many of the concerns were related to health care: the city wanted its own cardiac surgery unit, better chronic care, and expansion of four local hospitals. A focus for the protest emerged months before the Liberal meeting, in the death of a Windsor child waiting for surgery in a Toronto hospital. The incident became a local symbol for the belief that the Liberals were incompetent and uncaring managers of health care.

On Saturday hundreds of protesters massed in front of the Liberals' hotel. Peering down from her room, Health Minister Elinor Caplan decided to take a bold step. She waded through the crowd and climbed onto the stage, where antigovernment speakers were lining up at a microphone to berate her. Speaker after speaker rose to rip into Peterson's government; most also took personal slaps at Caplan. "I wanted to show the people I was there and visible and with them," she said, but the event's NDP organizers refused to let her speak. Coverage of another day of the Liberal meeting conveyed a growing theme of anti-Peterson, antigovernment venom. Still, Liberals planning for the coming election shrugged off the protests, blaming NDP organization and calling Windsor a tough town. They did not detect a pattern in the onslaught of aggressive, deeply angry protesters drawing the media's attention.

On the final day of the meeting, Peterson delivered his closing speech with a rare passion that sent Liberals back to their ridings pumped up and ready to campaign—but still in the dark on the timing of an election. Few took seriously the words of chief political minister Chris Ward, whose wrap-up speech to delegates included a grim warning: "The people of our province put us here and the people of our province could just as quickly toss us right out if we slip and let them down."

*   *   *

The nuts and bolts of Liberal campaign preparation sped up after the Windsor convention. On April 3 Robinson and Dan Gagnier nailed down the final piece of two organizational puzzles by hiring Beth Webster as executive coordinator of the premier's office—and as director of the Liberal campaign.

Webster had been promoted for months by Robinson as the best choice to fill the need for a political fixer and administrator in Peterson's office. But confusion surrounded Webster's role. She was not brought in to fill Gordon Ashworth's chair: Robinson, with her years of party work, had been trying to replace Ashworth's political links with MPPs and their ridings. Instead,

Webster was to fill the urgent need for a pre-election traffic cop. "It was a coordinating function of pulling together all the essential elements for what would become the framework for the campaign from an organizational point of view," said Webster. Plugged into Liberals across the province, well acquainted with the federal scene and equipped with managerial experience as Ward's chief of staff, Webster was capable of cracking the whip to get things done. But her hiring as campaign director infuriated more senior Liberals in Peterson's office who thought the coveted job should have been theirs; the bitterness would spill over into the Liberal campaign.

Webster kick-started regional political ministers on election readiness, organized help for the incumbents fighting nomination battles and turned to the huge task of creating a "riding services package," the chief propaganda vehicle for the campaign. The need to get working on such a package with adequate lead time was flagged by veteran Liberal advertising consultant Ken Tilley, who specialized in preparing pre-campaign and campaign brochures and print, radio and television ads for federal and provincial Liberals. Tilley had prepared printed materials for the Liberals in 1985 and 1987.

"Following is a list of the shots we will inevitably need for our campaign brochures, issues flyers, ads, etc.," Tilley wrote to Robinson four months before the election. "For each theme shot we should try and get one of the premier and theme, and one of the theme alone: New Ontarians, i.e., visible minorities, seniors, children, youth, education, statesman—premier at First Ministers' Conference or similar forum, environment (not smokestacks)," and finally, "family—David and Shelley and kids." Tilley tried in vain to avert last-minute problems by mentioning to Robinson "we will also need to begin the process of getting a new 'poster shot.'"

"It's really simple stuff," explained Tilley. "I never kid anybody that it's brain surgery." Basic as it was, Tilley's request went unanswered for weeks because the Liberals had neglected to build a photo file of Peterson in preparation for the campaign. "It surprised me they don't have it," said Tilley, shaking his head. "It's hard to believe when you hear it now but they can't get the premier half the time." The photo-file follies represented only the first time in the ramp-up to the election campaign that the Liberals suffered directly from neglect of corporate communications and record-keeping by Peterson's office.

In May, when Tilley asked for summaries of ministry initiatives to craft into pre-election brochures, he was appalled to find Peterson's office had not been compiling data on what the Liberals had accomplished. "It was scrambled, not like they could go to some binder and have it," he said. Tilley found that Robinson and Webster expected him to fabricate the material on his own. He was astonished: "You can't just say, 'Go off and give me what you think we should be saying.' That's for you to come to me and tell me that. We can massage it, we can play with it, we can express it in different ways, but the basic research has got to come from you. Unless they're going to involve us at some other point in this process, six months ago, and say, 'Crawl around every ministry and come back with a point of view.'" By June, with only weeks to go before the election call, Webster's assistants would still be trying to extract the vital data from ministers' offices.

*   *   *

In late May, just before the final week of Meech negotiations, cabinet gathered as usual on a Wednesday morning. After two hours of normal business, Robinson and Webster arrived to give Peterson's ministers a routine briefing on campaign readiness. Robinson had increased the frequency of her visits to cabinet since the beginning of the year but had offered only perfunctory summaries of the progress, light on detail and focused on process. But this visit would be anything but routine. On this day, the Liberal cabinet would be formally cut off from whatever right to greater detail on the campaign it thought it had.

"I want everyone to know," Peterson announced, as Robinson and Webster pulled heavy armchairs close to the long, leather-topped cabinet table, "that as of today, as far as I am concerned,

Kathy and Beth have dictatorial powers with regard to campaign readiness, campaign preparation and the campaign itself." Peterson turned the floor over to Robinson, who launched into another brief summary of campaign preparations.

When the meeting broke up, many ministers pushed through the cabinet room's padded doors and walked away shaking their heads. They were not sure whether Peterson had chosen the wrong words or had used hyperbole to hammer home a point about his confidence in the campaign's chair and director. Their doubts were erased less than a week later at a meeting of the government caucus, when Peterson, flanked by Robinson and Webster, repeated the same phrase. "When he said 'dictatorial powers' the second time, we knew he meant it," a senior minister realized. "The message was, 'Back off, they're in charge and I'm behind them.'"

Webster was embarrassed by Peterson's choice of words but had her own sense of what he meant. "It did not escape him that there were women going to do these jobs," she said, "and that he had to say something that was going to be supportive."

Other observers realized they were witnessing a transition of enormous decision-making power. "The secretary of cabinet knew, I knew, the ministers knew, this is it," said Gagnier. "There has been a subtle shift in terms of power and influence and delegated authority."

*　　*　　*

To go early or not to go early? Although it had been set aside without firm consensus by the Liberal caucus at its January retreat, the pivotal political question of the year in Ontario was buffeted about at each cabinet meeting from January to July of 1990. A senior minister observed that Peterson's "favorite line was, 'Waddya think?'—always, everyone he ran into in the hall, 'Waddya think?' He was plugged in right across the country for advice. One day he came into cabinet and told us he had specific advice from Bourassa that he should go. The next time it was Getty telling him to go now while the economy's still okay."

As early as March it was becoming clear to cabinet and caucus that Peterson was convinced an early election might be necessary to respond to a continued economic slide or the failure of Meech.

"It became a question of grinding everybody down," said a cabinet veteran. Peterson was prepared to go through the exercise of hearing what others had to say. While he looked high and low for opinions, many around him thought he was seeking reinforcement for his position. Over time, opponents of an early call backed off, as it became clear what they thought was irrelevant. Notably unwilling to relent were Environment Minister Jim Bradley and Consumer Minister Greg Sorbara. Both railed against an early call in cabinet and caucus at every opening—but neither could sway Peterson or those who shared his view.

Bradley's peers were accustomed to his pessimism. They knew him to be an idiosyncratic campaigner who had never deferred to the party's way of running elections. Since first winning his St. Catharines seat in 1977, he had stubbornly refused to incorporate the leader of the day into his campaigns. He even snubbed the Liberals' red-and-white lawn signs and logos. Colleagues respected Bradley's political nose but saw him as a perpetual prophet of doom. "You give him a story, he can tell you everything that's going to go wrong, everything, because he's paranoid," said one minister. Chaviva Hosek likened him to "the canaries that they used to take down in the mines: when they stopped breathing, you'd know you were dead."

Sorbara had strong views against an early call but colleagues questioned whether he was politically pragmatic: "All he talked about was the 'quality of the mandate,'" said a friend in cabinet. People looked at him and said, 'What does that mean?' But his analysis was entirely nonpolitical and very straightforward: you only go at the end of your mandate and then you get another one; you run on your record." Sorbara and other Liberals believed debate about an early election should be avoided entirely by calling an election only when a term was over.

With the exceptions of Bradley and Sorbara, Peterson's cabinet colleagues were loathe to take him on openly over the early call he was leaning toward. "Only those two had the guts," said a top minister. "When you knew what he was going to do, you didn't try to influence him or tell him what he didn't want to hear." Others close to Peterson, including Scott and Conway, expressed their strongest opposition only in private. Public self-immolation was not only foolhardy, most ministers felt, but futile. "You could always tell him exactly what you thought in private," said another minister. "The frustrating thing was that you knew he was going to do what he wanted to do anyway."

Many ministers also sat on knowledge that Peterson's positive image, long relied on as a constant the Liberals could fall back on, was not what it was cracked up to be in many ridings. "You didn't see any ground swell but you were getting it all the time in the constituency," one minister found. Across the province, cabinet members who studied the ripples of discontent with the Liberals were finding a common center: Peterson. But they were reluctant to raise that concern, some thinking the problem was limited to their own ridings, others reluctant to be personally critical of the leader who had brought them to power—especially when the polls showed he and the party remained popular. One senior minister found room to offer Peterson a personal critique, but only behind closed doors: "People were not as open as you would think about criticizing him. People had that respect for him, right to the end."

Whether they felt complacency, frustration or overconfidence, Peterson's cabinet ultimately let him down by deferring too quiescently to his will and by not telling him what they really felt about an early call or his waning popularity. When Peterson needed to be defended by fierce guard dogs on the alert for his protection, he was surrounded instead by too many meek lapdogs, who arfed politely when asked.

The Liberal caucus was equally deferential, with meager exceptions. "It was pretty clear," one caucus member observed, "that you didn't want to be the squeaky wheel on this one. If you didn't want to limit your career options, you kept your criticism to yourself." A colleague agreed: "Everyone knew he was going to make the decision to go, and the truth is that he had the support."

And it *was* true. Although the caucus was split in half in a show of hands on the early call question in January, support shifted steadily toward Peterson. As winter turned to spring at Queen's Park, Peterson entertained visits in his corner office from scores of caucus members, asking them what their local issues were and always starting and ending with his perennial, "Waddya think?" Many caucus members worried about an early election double-tracked their concerns to Gagnier, who found the Liberal MPPs "increasingly less divided as the machine got built up and moved toward an election date. Even if they were against the idea, they said, 'What choice do I have? The guy's going to call an election. I'd better be ready. You know—don't miss the train, get on board. You may as well root for the team. You're in this whether you like it or not.'"

Late in June the Liberal MPPs would gather in the government caucus room and threw the debate open again. A handful of members would offer words of caution. But when the dust settled, a show of hands would have supporters of an early call outnumbering dissidents by a ratio of seven to one.

As the election-readiness train kept charging along, realistic Liberals in Peterson's cabinet and caucus would narrow their concern about an early call down to the tougher question of coming up with the right reason. "Coming up with a plausible rationale was a major concern, far more than going early," a senior minister said. "Everybody was willing to go for political purposes. We knew there was a recession around the corner and we were going to get our asses kicked. You just have to go at the most advantageous time. We knew an early call would be a problem, and we expected that it would be dealt with in the strategy and that it would be an economic strategy. We expected there would be a strategy and a platform and an agenda to back up the rationale." Reasonable expectations. But would they be met?

4

The Liberal Strategy Team

There's always a little bit of tension in every single group.
                                                    –DAVID PETERSON

By early January the Liberals' campaign strategy committee had begun to congeal into its final election-ready form. The lineup read like an all-star team drawn from previous Liberal triumphs: Kathy Robinson as campaign chair, 1987 co-chair David Mac-Naughton as strategy committee chair, with equal-member status for Hershell Ezrin, Dan Gagnier and Senator Michael Kirby. Poll-ster Martin Goldfarb remained on the fringe in a role still to be formally defined. Like many all-star teams, the committee appeared at first blush to be unbeatable, but when the game got going, the gears had serious trouble meshing. MacNaughton, busy with his growing government relations firm, deferred to Robinson as the premier's choice to draw the players together and be responsible for getting the job done. Ezrin would be involved only part-time. Gagnier, as a seconded public servant, would be ending his formal involvement when the election was called. Even Kirby and Goldfarb, although linked through Kirby's vice-presidency in Goldfarb's firm, were known to be combatants over strategy as recently as the 1988 federal campaign. The committee had undercurrents of discord but appeared to be custom-made for Peterson's multiple-access system, his preferred method of obtaining advice from a number of different, even warring, perspectives.

But from its earliest meetings, forces far more destructive than mere personality clashes were at work inside the strategy committee. Deep, malingering feelings of distrust and competition between Goldfarb and MacNaughton oozed to the surface and began to play havoc with the group's ability to function as a team. MacNaughton and some Liberals had reservations about what they called Goldfarb's "anthropological" research techniques, the practice of polling for clues rather than solutions to problems, based on the theory that members of the public are not capable of supplying answers on their own. They wanted to avoid what MacNaughton described as Goldfarb's inclination to analyze and interpret his political polling data to produce the conclusions he believed in. "Marty is basically an activist who has a set of views about how society should work," Mac-Naughton said, "and he uses his numbers to try to persuade people of his view of society." Such accusations had been leveled at Goldfarb since the late 1970s, carrying through to his polling on free trade for the federal Liberals in 1988.

Goldfarb was accustomed to defending his methods. "We don't just analyze data," he told one interviewer, "we interpret it based on our understanding of society." To another, he said, "I know some people question the degree to which I interpret. All I can say is that to say what people think is only the beginning. Anyone can come up with statistics, good statistics. It's another thing to say why."

Goldfarb had fallen further out of favor with many Liberals during the 1988 federal election by taking part in two activities many considered inappropriate for the party's pollster during a campaign. He conducted polls for CTV and the Toronto *Star* while working for the Liberals, and released midway through the campaign a book (*Marching to a Different Drummer*, co-authored with Tom Axworthy) that many Liberals viewed as highly critical of party leader John Turner and the Meech Accord.

Top Ontario Liberals, including some Peterson ministers and staff, had been questioning since 1987 the wisdom of keeping Goldfarb as the pollster for their next campaign. That year Gold-farb resigned angrily from the Canadian Association of Market Research Organizations (a pollsters' group promoting nonbind-ing guidelines) when it began investigating complaints against him tied to conflicting polls released during the November 1985 Tory leadership contest. MacNaughton had made up his own mind after his experience as 1987 campaign co-chair. "The polling in the last campaign had not been everything that it should have been," he said. "So I started to put some ideas down on paper after that about how it might be done next time." It was time, he believed, for a change.

"There had been a lot of concern expressed about Goldfarb, about the cost of the polling in '87, about the value of Marty, whether or not he was up to date with modern polling tech-niques or campaigns," MacNaughton said. "I talked to Kathy about it and she said, 'I'm quite prepared to change,' and I said, 'Well, I don't know if you want to change or if you don't want to change, but one thing's for sure, and that is, if you're going to get the best bang for the buck you've got to change the way in which you deal with Marty. You've got to force him. We have to decide what kind of polling we need during the campaign, give it some general priorities, then give it to a couple of other firms, have them come back to us with some ideas about techniques that they would use and give us some scope and then we'll call for tenders.'"

Some Liberals, including Peterson, were willing to attribute the emerging battle to a competitive spat between Mac-Naughton and Goldfarb. "David's with Decima, but Marty's there, and Marty's with Goldfarb," Peterson said. He expected

Robinson to iron out the differences and keep everyone working together. But to MacNaughton, the dispute had nothing to do with a fight for the campaign's polling contract. The likelihood of the Liberals switching to MacNaughton's partner, Decima Research's Allan Gregg, was a nonstarter. Gregg was deeply dug in with federal and provincial Tories; he was a trusted source of strategic advice to Mulroney. Instead, MacNaughton maintained, he wanted a guarantee the Liberals would get the polling they wanted, when they wanted it, before and during the campaign, free of Goldfarb's own political views.

Robinson asked MacNaughton for a written proposal to be duly considered by the strategy committee. "I wrote a memo," said MacNaughton, "which said here's how to do it and here's how to get some creative ideas as to how the polling should be done and here's how we go about it. The principal impetus of that memo came from Kathy." Dated January 25, Mac-Naughton's memo outlined "criteria for the selection process": get a detailed description of how the polling firm planned to collect, analyze and report its quantitative or polling-based data and conduct provincewide tracking studies as well as constituency studies of swing ridings to provide the campaign's rolling polls or day-to-day results. Second, the memo called for details of the proposed qualitative research or focus groups, with a rundown on how the groups would be recruited and interviewed to give the campaign a deeper feel for what people were thinking. Get a cost estimate up front, the memo added cryptically above MacNaughton's signature.

With memo in hand, all the strategists except Kirby, who stayed away to avoid a conflict of interest, gathered in Gagnier's office early in February to hash over the advice. "The meeting sort of degenerated into considerable rancor," said Mac-Naughton. Goldfarb left in a huff, telling the group to decide if it wanted him or not.

The memo lit the fuse. After the meeting, "Marty went nuts," said MacNaughton. "Called everybody in sight, talked to the premier, talked to Hershell, talked to Kathy; Hershell talked to everybody. Marty decided that it was a competitive issue with me. I said, 'Look, I don't give a shit. If you want to deal with Marty, deal with Marty. But make sure you set up the rules so you know what it is you're getting.' I was asked to prepare something that said, 'Here's how you deal with polling,' and I did, and it got into a great fight, and I finally just said, 'Oh, piss on it. If you want to do it, do it, but don't come and ask me for advice as to how to deal with it, get me in the midst of it and then decide that you can't stand up to Marty's badgering.'"

"I wasn't sure we'd be the pollsters," said Goldfarb. "I wasn't sure they wanted me." Missing the influence and confidence he enjoyed a decade earlier as pollster and strategic advisor to Trudeau, Goldfarb was prepared to go to the wall on this one. Since Ezrin's departure, Goldfarb's access to the premier's inner circle had declined; while he had good relations with Vince Borg and Gagnier, his influence had waned as Peterson relied less on the principal secretaries who followed Ezrin. Now, he was determined to jealously guard his position close to the ear of a governing Liberal party. "The issue of business never entered into any of this for me," Goldfarb maintained. "I cared with all my heart that Liberals should be running a piece of this country."

Other members of the strategy committee believed MacNaughton had an underlying goal that Goldfarb resented. Campaign-related polling involves three phases: describing the process and objectives for collecting data, collecting it, then analyzing and interpreting it. As chair of the strategy committee, MacNaughton wanted all of its members to have open access to Goldfarb's data before the final stage, to minimize spin-doctoring by the "activist" pollster. "It's in that third, interpretive phase that MacNaughton wanted to personally deal with it—wanted the whole committee, actually, to be able to play a role," said Kirby, "as opposed to simply having one person, whether it's Marty for us or Allan Gregg for them, interpret the data."

The threat of losing or sharing his position was anathema to Goldfarb: "You can't have two or three sources of information in a campaign. All you do is have—you have instruments. It's like flying a plane across the country. Either you trust the instruments or you look down and you say, 'I think Toronto's down there.' Your instruments are the people you put in place to do the job. The wonderful thing about Trudeau was he trusted us, never questioned us, and the marvelous thing about the Trudeau team is they admired each other, they trusted each other."

Faced with internecine warfare, Robinson had on her hands by February a strategy team with all the chemistry of a cupboardful of household cleaners: used separately, any one could do a good job; mix them together and the result could blow up in one's face. "The seeds of the conflict were there because of this whole schmozzle," said MacNaughton. "It went on for like two months, March and April. It was just a goddamned zoo." To Goldfarb, it was "a perverse time." The strategists' chemistry problem did not disappear. The stench of the infighting would hang over the strategy committee—and have serious repercussions down the line.

Peterson obtained summaries of the soap opera from Robinson but, caught up in preparations for the final round of Meech talks in June, did not have time or interest to deal with it personally. "Peterson was told that he had problems with the chemistry between that group and he relied on Kathy to sort them out," said Borg, watching the storm clouds gather from his new post as Peterson's advisor on Toronto's 1996 Olympics bid. "Whereas before he would have got more involved with it in terms of sorting it out and making sure that things were melding properly, he in my view tended to say, 'Well, we've got to have this done here, and Kathy's going to sort it out.'"

"Look, I'm a big boy in the sense that I know there's always a little bit of tension in every single group," Peterson said with a shrug. "There's always different points of view, and these are strong-willed, opinionated, bright people and they're not going to agree on every bloody thing. It was all worked out; I mean, they basically assume their own views, they fight, they compromise." Although often out of the country and not involved in the strategy committee's meetings, Borg lined up with MacNaughton. "If you use Marty," he advised Robinson, "adopt a consortium kind of approach to the function of the strategic advisory group; don't take his analysis of the numbers without any question, which is what you should always do anyway."

Pressured by a majority of the members of the strategy committee and with the clock ticking, Robinson acquiesced: the committee would stick with Goldfarb. "Little by little they got chiseled away to the point that it was then agreed that Marty would be the pollster and Marty would submit the data, but that he wouldn't interpret it to the premier at any meeting that was held," said MacNaughton. "We would meet in advance, we would agree on what the interpretation of the data was, and then I would present the strategic recommendations to the premier."

*　　*　　*

In May Goldfarb stoked the engines of the accelerating campaign train with two potent new sources of fuel. He delivered to the strategists a massive polling-based paper entitled *Ontario Liberal Strategic 1990*, including 211 pages of detailed issue-related findings, followed by a 15-page focus group-based report on Peterson's image. These thick tomes of data, analysis and strategic recommendations became the key joists on which the Liberals would build their campaign strategy and platform.

Goldfarb's strategic paper was based on random in-home interviews conducted in April with 1,000 Ontarians aged 18 and over. The paper provided the strategy committee with a badly needed first draft of an election strategy.

From cover page to its accompanying questionnaire, the *Liberal Strategic* reported in exhaustive detail temperature readings on party standings, alternate voting preferences, political momentum of the parties and support for the leaders. It scrutinized the government's performance and image, identified key issues and concerns of the electorate, isolated "leverage issues" (those with the potential, on their own, to influence voting behavior), probed deeper on "hot button" areas including government spending, taxation, the economic outlook, free trade, the environment and the Meech Accord, and tested public recognition of recent government achievements.

Front and center in the overview summary were top-line numbers on party popularity with decided voters: Liberals 48 percent, NDP 31, PCs 21. The Liberals were one point higher than in September 1987 when they won their majority. Dwarfed in stature was the NDP's steady climb in popular support. It was noteworthy, Goldfarb suggested, only because it placed the NDP clearly ahead of the Tories—and not because it represented his highest rating for the NDP since the 26 percent support received on voting day in 1987. The Liberals were clearly heading for another majority.

Goldfarb's top-line findings and predictions of good fortune for the Liberals were little different from those of other pollsters in spring 1990. "I thought they'd get re-elected with some loss of seats," said Environics Research president Michael Adams. "I was quite sure this guy would win. When we compared Ontario with the other governments of the country, we had Saskatchewan, Nova Scotia, Alberta, British Columbia, where there were far lower levels of satisfaction with the overall performance of the government." Numbers closely approximating Goldfarb's findings were gathered by Decima Research for the Tories and by Winnipeg-based Viewpoints Research for the NDP.

Developed in the premier's office in Gagnier's hands and then fine-tuned by Goldfarb, the questionnaire for the poll contained no questions designed to determine voting intentions under conditions specific to the summer of 1990. Goldfarb did not ask, in particular, how voters might lean if forced to vote in an "unnecessary" or "early" election called by an "opportunistic" Peterson—although such pejoratives had been bandied about for months by Liberals, the opposition and the media, and their potential danger pondered by the strategy committee.

The question was ignored by Goldfarb in April—and by other pollsters, including those working for the opposition parties, who similarly failed to divine the critical early-election issue in advance. Environics' Adams, who did not ask an early-call question for his own *Focus Ontario* or *Focus Canada* reports, later agreed such a query would permit a government to "ask themselves a fundamental question like 'If you told your grandmother, what would she say?' She'd say, 'Well, why, dear, are you calling an election?' And maybe they should listen to Granny. Maybe Granny's smarter than my pollster."

Goldfarb's analysis of his "second choice" or alternative preference voting behavior data contended that the Liberals stood to benefit from any switching away from the NDP or the Tories, but warned that "any switching away from the Liberals would go more heavily to the NDP than to the Tories."

The strategic paper pulled no punches when it pointed out the Liberals' faults. "Ontarians have difficulty pointing to specific achievements or accomplishments of note of the Liberal government since it was re-elected in 1987," Goldfarb found. "More needs to be done to make voters aware of these and other key program initiatives." MacNaughton noted with dismay that "When you asked people what are the three things you liked most about what the government had done, they'd get stuck on number one." The legacy of the Liberals' poor corporate communications was clear. But Ontarians were quick to cite Liberal failures: increasing taxes, the no-fault insurance plan, and its handling of free trade, the GST and Meech Lake. "It is noteworthy," Goldfarb added, "that a lot of the frustration with the Liberal provincial government centers around what are essentially federal government policy creations."

Other soft spots were government image-oriented. Some felt the Liberal government was "a little bit too left of center in its orientation, too pro-social welfare, losing touch with ordinary people, becoming a little bit arrogant, and is drifting or lacking a clear agenda for where it wants to lead the province." To Goldfarb, those beliefs were "not particularly strong or well developed at this point in time," but he recommended they be swiftly countered by showing the government had compassion for the needy, although not at the expense of free enterprise; supported personal initiative, entrepreneurship and continued economic growth; had an agenda for the future and was still open, accessible and listening.

Goldfarb suggested the Liberals play from their strong suit: remind people leading up to and during the campaign about "the fact that the Ontario government inherited a large budgetary deficit and now has a balanced budget," and about the ban on extra billing, pay equity, Ontario's economic growth, Peterson's leadership and how the government treated minorities. That month, Treasurer Nixon had produced the Liberals' second straight balanced budget and the Liberals launched an intense propaganda effort, pumping out the balanced budget line. But they did not explain the critical second half of the balanced budget equation: that it provided Ontario with the financial flexibility to deal with an economic downturn. The decision to focus on a simple balanced budget message would later hurt the Liberals.

The government received its lowest confidence ratings for its handling of Sunday shopping, Meech, free trade and French language rights. Goldfarb recommended "counter strategies need to be developed to head off and blunt the effect of opposition party and media criticism of the government's record in these areas. Strategy papers need to be developed, in case they are needed during the campaign, on how to handle each of these issues."

Goldfarb assured the strategists "the overall honesty and integrity of the Liberal provincial government is not a sensitivity for most people. Most [83 percent] feel the Liberal government's standards of honesty and integrity are average [57 percent] or above average [26 percent]." But Goldfarb arrived at that conclusion without specifically asking people if they thought the Peterson Liberals were honest and had integrity. Instead, his question was worded to invite people to compare the Peterson Liberals' standards with those of other governments. The strategy paper did not sound a specific warning about public distrust and suspicion of the Liberals. Believing they could play down the issue, the Liberals would go into the campaign without a strategy to deal with attacks on their honesty and integrity. They were encouraged by Goldfarb's finding that the "political momentum" of the Starr scandal was fading, with 55 percent of those interviewed feeling the issue was losing momentum and 63 percent saying they had been paying little attention to the judicial inquiry into Starr's activities.

In unaided responses Goldfarb's interviewees listed their top issues and concerns for provincial government attention: the proposed GST, the environment, curbing taxes, car insurance rates, free trade, getting tougher on drunk drivers, fighting crime and drug abuse. Farther down the list were job creation, health care, housing, cutting government spending and Meech. The findings would be reflected in the Liberals' campaign platform.

Top leverage issues included each party's stance on honesty and integrity in government, the GST, environmental policy, free trade and each party's leadership; Goldfarb suggested these should be central to campaign strategy. Noting that two of the top five leverage issues, the GST and free trade, were federal issues, he planted the seed for a key strategic twist of the campaign: "Both of these issues present opportunities for the provincial government to take the offensive against the federal government in strengthening its own appeal. There is an opportunity here for the provincial Liberals to develop part of their strategy around running against the federal Tory government." The strategists deigned to keep that tactic on the back burner. Peterson frowned on blatant Fed-bashing. "The easiest thing for me to do would have been to bash Mulroney," he said.

In a search for potential campaign announcements, Goldfarb floated before his interviewees a skyful of trial balloons, including one that would turn out to be the Liberals' *Hindenburg*: reducing the retail sales tax from 8 percent to 7 percent. On Goldfarb's "voting appeal index," the tax cut rated at the top with 72 out of 100, on par with spending more to protect the environment and balancing the budget. That finding told Goldfarb that "offering some form of tax relief could be an extremely potent vote-getting tactic, given the current public mood and concern, particularly about the GST." But the success of the initiative, said Goldfarb, was tied to building understanding of the flexibility provided by a balanced budget and unleashing the tactic at a timely point during the campaign.

For the first time Goldfarb found most Ontarians favored "lowering taxes ahead of improving services in all but the most essential areas." They preferred tax cuts over reducing the deficit, building rental housing and transit improvements, but not at the expense of improved environmental protection, better health care and boosts for job creation and training.

Goldfarb identified "a feeling of insecurity as opposed to optimism about the economic outlook." He cited free trade as "a focal point and whipping boy for public frustration with everything that is wrong with the Ontario economy" and recommended the Liberals echo that frustration but show leadership by launching a free trade adjustment program and strategy "built around preparing Ontario to take advantage of the new free trade environment so that the Americans are not able to take unfair advantage of Ontario from a consumer, labor, business investment or trade point of view."

Using issue after issue as brush strokes, Goldfarb painted a background of discontent with the Liberals: 6 in 10 Ontarians thought Liberal environmental spending was inadequate; more than half (55 percent) opposed the auto insurance scheme; 51 percent felt the government was moving too slowly in implementing pay equity, including 54 percent of Liberals. While 60 percent supported the principle of providing services in French, 58 percent supported the English-only declarations sweeping through small-town Ontario, a problem Goldfarb warned "could be whipped up into a major campaign issue by the press."

On national unity, Goldfarb offered guidance for Ontario as Peterson geared up for the final Meech talks in June. "Ontarians clearly prefer to see the Ontario government play a leadership role in trying to build a consensus between the provinces (75 percent)," he wrote, citing "evidence of the strong nationalistic feelings of Ontario residents and willingness to put the national good ahead of the province's. This is the kind of statesmanship-type of role the premier should be perceived as playing at the national level." With 44 percent feeling Ontario was too supportive of Meech Lake and 68 percent indicating they preferred a compromise agreement over adoption of the Accord, Goldfarb counseled that "the way for the premier to handle the Meech Lake issue is to play the role of statesman in seeking a consensus, and by relating the importance of Meech Lake to the national interest, to national unity, to building a stronger country, all of which is in Ontario's best interest." Although Goldfarb was long-known as a vehement opponent of Meech, he seemed to recognize the futility of arguing against the Accord with Peterson, and settled instead for trying to shape the premier's actions to cast him as the consensus-builder Ontarians wanted.

The heart of the report was a blueprint for the campaign strategy. Peterson, Goldfarb stated adamantly, was the key to victory. "The primary focus of the campaign," he deemed, "should be on the premier—his leadership skills and the respect that he has from the public at large. The premier is the campaign." Goldfarb heralded Peterson's leadership as the third most important factor, at 6.1 on a scale of 10, in creating confidence in the government—among Liberal supporters. Making the premier the focus was Goldfarb's recommended approach in spite of less glowing reviews in data gathered from all voters—not only Liberals—that placed Peterson's "leadership style" farther down a list of 19 factors contributing to confidence in the government, with a score of 5.1 on a scale of 10, putting Peterson in a five-way tie for sixth place. When not propped up by Liberals, public opinion of Peterson's leadership style floundered among such issues as the government's handling of French language rights in Ontario.

Using Peterson's strength among Liberals to support making the premier the focus of the campaign reflected Goldfarb's belief in the existence of a Liberal core vote that the government had to concentrate on retaining. Goldfarb found "the Liberals are continuing to draw a broad-based mix of well-balanced support across the voter spectrum." It was up to Peterson's team, he suggested, to home in on "holding its existing constituency of voters together," especially the vaunted "core" of middle- to upper-income earners, ethnics, nonunion households, women, people under 25 and over 55 and "switchers to the Liberals—more young, upwardly mobile, contemporary households."

Goldfarb wanted "the issue of leadership" to be "the centerpiece of the campaign strategy because it exploits the Liberals' key strengths and the oppositions' greatest weakness." But deeper in Goldfarb's data were hints that Ontarians were not pleased with Peterson's leadership—hints that Goldfarb did not pick up on or emphasize. On closer scrutiny, Goldfarb's detailed findings revealed that when Ontarians were asked "Who would make the best premier?" Peterson came out on top with 43 percent but Rae "is a strong second choice, attracting 30 percent support." In southwestern Ontario, Rae was actually running ahead of Peterson in the critical "best premier" category, Goldfarb found, by a margin of 38 percent to 35 percent.

Also hidden in his data was a finding given only cursory attention: that nearly identical numbers of voters said they were either "very impressed" or "somewhat impressed" with Peterson (40 percent) and Rae (39 percent). Similarly, Goldfarb dismissed findings that a "significant minority" or 28 percent of voters said their impression of Peterson had changed for the worse, while only 4 percent said the same about Rae: "This is consistent with other data pointing to some slippage in the premier's performance rating in the past year," Goldfarb suggested, "but as other data shows, this slippage appears to have bottomed out" at 35 percent in July of 1989. And he assured the Liberals that "Bob Rae is not benefiting to any great extent from the government's problems of the past year, as 79 percent say their impression of him has not changed recently and only 16 percent say their impression of him has changed for the better."

Under the leadership theme, Goldfarb advised, a province-wide "umbrella campaign" strategy and supporting advertising "needs to be designed to convey and reinforce in voters' minds the qualities and characteristics voters like and admire about the premier—his strong leadership ability, his openness and frankness, his accessibility, his honesty, his family image and values, his energy and his progressive, reformist-minded approach to government. Part of the objective here should be to re-imprint in the public's mind the open, accessible style of leadership that people originally loved so much about the premier."

Next on the leadership theme came a plan to involve high-profile cabinet ministers in the campaign, inspired by federal Tory Michael Wilson's "liar" attacks on Turner in the 1988 federal campaign. Goldfarb pitched a scheme that would designate "a couple of key cabinet ministers," and give them "specific campaign responsibilities and their own organized tours around the province separate from, but coordinated with, the premier's tour." This supporting cast was meant to create an echo effect that would convey the government's record and demonstrate that Peterson had "competent, talented people behind him in government and, in the process, focus attention on the lack of support talent the opposition party leaders have behind them." It would also allow the Liberals to "use key ministers to take on campaign assignments that the premier should be a step away from—such as bashing the federal government over the GST and free trade or bashing the NDP on their policy ideas."

Lest the Liberal campaign be judged to be too shallow, Goldfarb recommended applying a little meat to the bone: "While the leadership issue should be the centerpiece of the campaign, the Liberal strategy should not rely on this one issue alone. There also needs to be some policy and substance prominent in the Liberal campaign."

While Goldfarb advised building "part of the strategy around running against the federal Tory government," the Liberals' main target fell sharply between his sights: "The party and party leader that the Liberals need to be most concerned about is the NDP and Bob Rae, not the Tories, and the Liberal campaign strategy needs to reflect this. Liberal campaign strategy should virtually ignore the Tories." In the midst of a leadership campaign to replace interim leader Andy Brandt, the Tories would help the NDP by making the election a two-horse race, Goldfarb contended, but the Tory collapse was showing signs of swinging disenchanted Liberals to the NDP. The Liberals entered the campaign knowing full well Rae was their worst enemy. Predicting more close races in ridings where the NDP finished a strong second in 1987, Goldfarb saw the need for a regionally targeted campaign in areas of NDP strength, including northern and southwestern Ontario and Hamilton-Niagara, directed against the NDP, instead of a demographically targeted strategy.

Goldfarb urged a subtle approach to deal with the threat of the NDP, one designed "to quietly and indirectly make the public uneasy about their ideas and policy orientation . . . and create concern about the free-spending ideas of the NDP, that the NDP would increase the tax burden on the already struggling middle class and that a strong showing for the NDP will scare away business investment and discourage business development in Ontario."

Goldfarb believed the Liberals had to tell middle-class voters they were the party that understood and shared their values and would govern accordingly: "The central theme around which the policy and substance dimension of the campaign should be framed is the theme of effective, open, sensitive leadership and a commitment to wealth generation for the middle class coupled with a sensitivity to social welfare programs and the needs of the disadvantaged in society. The middle class is the key voter constituency for the campaign strategy to target. They are the swing voters. They are the voters who got the Liberals elected. They vote on the basis of self-interest, not ideology. They aspire to the good life and upward mobility. In appealing to these voters, the Liberal campaign strategy needs to be seen as identifying with and being committed to their values—such as the desire to get ahead through hard work, opportunities for upward mobility, opportunities to acquire and spend wealth, promotion of personal initiative."

Before the election, urged Goldfarb, Peterson and key ministers had to get out and sell their record, especially the balanced budget and "the unprecedented economic growth, job creation and business investment Ontario has achieved under Liberal leadership and policy direction." Such tours would help "make the premier and his key ministers appear to be more accessible to the public to help re-establish the original open, accessible image appeal of the premier's style of leadership." Goldfarb also recommended the Liberals crank up a propaganda machine by undertaking "government advertising leading up to the election campaign to remind people of these successes, achievements and accomplishments."

Although he found most voters knew little of the Liberal record, Goldfarb wanted the Liberals to project "a clearly defined agenda and vision for where they want to lead the province in the 1990s" that would "link the past record of accomplishment and successes that the government has achieved in the area of economic growth, job creation, equal pay for work of equal value, the environment and health care with a visionary, progressive direction for the future." That plan assumed the Liberals would get their record out before the election, allowing them to point to it as a touchstone and foundation for their new agenda.

Goldfarb's suggested campaign platform included a strategy for economic growth and job creation that focused on skills training, the free trade adjustment program, environmental and law and order announcements and one notable new idea: "a GST tax relief adjustment program for 1991 to ease the inflationary impact of the GST in its introductory year. The government could offer to rebate to Ontario taxpayers all additional revenue it will collect as a result of the introduction of the GST. This initiative would be designed to speak to the integrity-in-government issue. It could be held in reserve and used if the Liberal lead falters. In order to keep GST tax relief in reserve as a potential tactic, early in the campaign the Liberals should launch a major attack on the GST. Then, if the Liberals' lead falters, there will still be an opportunity to legitimately introduce such a measure later in the campaign, without being seen as cynical." This rebate of the "tax on tax"—distinctly different from a reduction in the retail sales tax—was hotly debated by the strategy committee. It was known to be opposed by the province's treasury, which saw it as an administrative nightmare that would have bureaucrats parading to the window ledge.

*　　*　　*

Robinson, Gagnier and MacNaughton received the first copies of Goldfarb's strategic paper and circulated it to other members of the strategy committee. Gagnier arranged a meeting late in May for an initial discussion of the paper with Peterson.

Robinson was adamant that the committee come forward with one voice to present its strategic recommendations, mindful that Peterson expected her to work out the strategists' differences. "Kathy was very concerned about this," said Webster, "to go as a consolidated group; they must go only on a consensus basis or else they weren't going to go."

The strategists gathered as scheduled and kept their knives sheathed in Peterson's presence as MacNaughton presented the report on behalf of the group. "They were all as happy as clams" said Webster. "They were all so supportive and happy with it you would have thought they had all written it together."

Goldfarb's role remained up in the air. Concerned he not be provided with opportunities to mainline his views to Peterson over those of the committee, Robinson invited him to attend the meetings with the premier on one condition: "He wasn't to speak," said Webster. "He was only to explain." Always eager to hear everyone, however, Peterson thwarted the committee's bid to muzzle Goldfarb. "The premier asked him, 'Waddya think?'" said Webster, "and he spoke quite freely."

Goldfarb predicted the government would lose seats in southwestern Ontario, where he identified problems in London, Chatham and Windsor, and in northern Ontario. Zeroing in on Liberal vulnerabilities, he reported a sense that "our legislation has been aimed at pacifying the public, not solving problems," and that the government lacked decisiveness and a clearly perceived agenda, and was becoming too Toronto-centered. And he warned that "the premier has lost some of his appeal as being the open, accessible guy next door."

Goldfarb laid out his best version of the Liberals' reason for calling the election, the "rationale for going: in the last three years, the Feds have substantially restructured the country through free trade, the GST and Meech Lake—we need a mandate to counter and respond to these changes to maintain Ontario's strengths." He distilled his strategy: the Liberals could win with an agenda for the 1990s delivered under Peterson's leadership; they should build on their record and conduct a "value-driven" campaign emphasizing policy and middle-class values as opposed to costly programs.

The strategists heard Goldfarb out and the meeting ended peacefully. But after displaying unanimity on the strategic paper in front of Peterson, the strategists proceeded to carve it up. Rather than swallow Goldfarb's offering whole, they picked at it like birds, taking tentative, darting nibbles from its recommendations.

Preoccupied with Meech Lake in the months before the election, Peterson did not embark on a road show to sell the government's record on the balanced budget or Ontario's economic growth. Nor did the Liberals take the plunge on propaganda: they did not want to reverse a well-publicized 1985 decision to restrict government advertising. Goldfarb urged developing a series of strategy papers on how to deal with attacks on the government's weak points during the campaign; with the demands of Meech, Peterson's office did not have time for the project. His proposal for separate regional campaign strategies targeting the NDP, although mulled over by the strategists, was similarly left by the wayside.

Goldfarb recommended the campaign focus on economic issues; while the strategists agreed to emphasize the economy, their platform would not target the self-interest of the middle class as Goldfarb suggested. Although Goldfarb's paper hinted at concerns about excessive taxes, his idea for a separate strategy paper on taxation would end up lost in the shuffle; his pitch for a huge free trade adjustment program would be deemed too costly. Guided by Peterson's reluctance to "bash Mulroney," the strategists turned down Goldfarb's proposal to start off the campaign by attacking the federal government over the GST and free trade.

The strategists did agree with Goldfarb on the need for ministers' tours independent of the premier's campaign tour, to complement Peterson's daily announcements. Goldfarb thought such tours "would also take some of the pressure off the premier, who was sitting out there all alone with a lot of warts that he wasn't aware of himself." But enthusiasm for the "kinder, gentler" objectives of the ministers' tours dwindled among the strategists as they agreed ministers stood to win media attention only if they offered negative messages. They agreed ministers' tours should be organized chiefly to provide counterpoint to a good-vibe campaign by Peterson. Mindful of the Tories' lessons of 1988 they envisioned a "slime squad": a low-road role for a couple of cabinet members. Treasurer Nixon, they thought, would be perfect to bash the NDP and make it "the party of taxation"; Health Minister Caplan had the credibility to bash the Tories effectively.

Goldfarb contended his colleagues damaged the integrity of his master plan by altering or dropping components and erasing subtle linkages. "It's a good document," he maintained. "We expend a lot of energy into that when we do those documents. But I don't honestly know how much the document was used. It didn't show up in the platform. And you can choose five of seven things, except the two you leave out are the ones that hold the other five together." As the strategists ignored or discarded his ideas, Goldfarb was incensed: "It wasn't one thing, it was a hundred things that didn't get done because they thought victory was in the bag anyway and it didn't really matter if you won with 90 seats or 80 seats."

Nothing infuriated Goldfarb more than watching Mac-Naughton and the strategy committee drop his schemes for appealing to the Liberals' "middle-class constituency." "We didn't deliver for the middle class," he charged. "Remember, it's only 10 percent of the population that float. They floated away from us. They used to be with us. That middle-class vote that's fickle, that's selfish, that worries about 'How am I going to make my mortgage payment because I'm overcommitted now?'—we didn't help that guy. That's what makes you get elected over and over again."

The strategists had other ideas, different from Goldfarb's. From May through July as they chose bits and pieces of the pollster's strategy, they would build on it with plans of their own. One central theme would be roundly endorsed and retained: Goldfarb's edict that "the premier is the campaign." It was the most vulnerable theme in his strategy—but the strategists bought it outright. The reason: even after MacNaughton's crusade for access to Goldfarb's data, the right to take part in its interpretation and the opportunity to look for inconsistencies

between the detailed findings and the pollster's recommendations, the strategists failed to critically probe and question the
data Goldfarb delivered. "Not many people read those cross-
tabs," admitted Gagnier. "They basically took it in either from
the presentation or from the executive summary." MacNaughton
shared the blame and offered the reason: "The big problem was
that there was a sort of mental laziness about the campaign.
There was no sort of big threat. Too much was being taken for
granted. There was a laziness about analyzing the data." Had
they scrutinized their hard-won data the strategists could have
ferreted out crucial problems, understood more fully the Liberals' soft spots and prepared responses to them, and obtained a
truer sense of the mood of Ontarians as they entered the summer of 1990. Instead, they eagerly awaited the results of Goldfarb's focus group research, confident it would provide them
with the deeper understanding of what voters liked about
the premier that they needed to hone the edge of a Peterson-
centered campaign.

*   *   *

Between May 22 and 24 Goldfarb vice-president Doug Hurley
conducted four focus groups, one each with men and women in
Toronto and mixed groups in Hamilton and Windsor, to gather
information to paint a portrait of Peterson's public image. Goldfarb decided the participants in the groups would be screened to
ensure they were Liberal or Liberal-leaning: half were determined to be "very likely" to vote Liberal, half were deemed
"somewhat likely." His rationale: the Liberal campaign had to
concentrate on "holding our existing constituency of voters
together," the vaunted Liberal core vote.

"What we were playing to was our strength," said Goldfarb.
"We were also playing to potential conquests, which is what the
leaners were all about." But the decision to give the focus groups
a strong Liberal slant was criticized by Goldfarb's vice-president
and fellow strategist Kirby: "Normally, frequently when you do
groups, when I've done them, I do them with undecideds."

The resulting report by Hurley made an exuberant conclusion: "Premier Peterson's image is very positive and strong across the province, even in regions where the Liberals are doing less well, such as southwestern Ontario and Hamilton-Niagara. His image appeal is consistently strong in all three regions where interviewing was conducted.

"The premier's image is so positive that some people have difficulty finding anything negative or critical to say about him," the report read. "These findings suggest that the reasons why the Liberals are doing less well in regions such as southwestern Ontario and Hamilton-Niagara have little or nothing to do with the premier's personal appeal or image performance. Rather, it is other localized factors or issues that are contributing to the weaker Liberal standing in these regions.

"The other implication," the report intoned, "is that the premier's universally strong image appeal across the province means that personal attention and campaigning by the premier in regions where the Liberals are doing less well should help strengthen the party's appeal in these regions."

The focus groups fortified the strategists' plan for a Peterson-centered campaign. Hurley's report cited "a host of positive qualities or attributes which people see in Premier Peterson which are central to his strong image appeal: his perceived warm, friendly, open, accessible, approachable image appeal; his perceived down-to-earth, average-guy-next-door image appeal," and his "sincerity, honesty and integrity," "frankness and forthrightness," "empathy and compassion for people," "strong family man image," "youthful, contemporary, fit, energetic image," "commitment and dedication to the job," "handsome, distinguished leaderlike appearance" and "charm or charismatic image appeal."

The report suggested "these are the key kinds of image strengths and appeals of the premier that need to be emphasized and reinforced in the campaign. It is these qualities which attract people to him and give them trust and confidence in his leadership . . . make people feel he understands and genuinely cares about their concerns, values and aspirations in life . . . help set

Premier Peterson apart, in a favorable way, from other politicians whom people have less respect for generally."

In its detailed findings the report revealed that people liked
Peterson because he "comes across as a 'winner' and people
want to identify with and follow winners. He has the appeal of
a winner because he has it all." One focus group participant
was cited as calling Peterson "a role model that all the rest of us
aspire to be like or emulate in life. He seems to have everything
that everyone else aspires to in life. He is successful, charming,
articulate, self-assured, well-liked, handsome, well-to-do financially, has the ideal family and a beautiful wife." Such observations yielded the conclusion that "Premier Peterson stands for
or symbolizes the good life, success and happiness, everything
that people want to identify with, and this is a big part of his
personal appeal."

These observations by Liberals and Liberal leaners were
deemed so solid and Peterson's image qualities so positive and
durable that they would be worked like mulch into the ground
on which the Liberal strategists would build their campaign.
"People love his main-streeting and picnics," said the report.
"They love to see him mingling with ordinary, everyday people."

Buried behind its first 10 pages of praise the report bore
disturbing news for the strategists. "One of the chief criticisms," the report warned, "is the perception that not much
has been accomplished or achieved since the Liberals were re-
elected. People have difficulty pointing to specific accomplishments or achievements. Some feel this reflects negatively on
Premier Peterson's leadership ability and ability to get things
done. There is a sense of inertia or that too many issues are
dragging on with no resolution. There is some feeling that the
government has been slow to take decisive action in dealing
with issues such as car insurance, the Patti Starr case, health
care problems, housing problems. The premier tends to be
blamed for this perceived lack of action and is the focal point
for criticism about the government's handling of these issues."

The danger, the report flagged, was "a public perception that
the premier and the government have become overly cautious,

evasive and wishy-washy in their approach toward issues which are potentially controversial. This is being interpreted as a weakness of leadership by some people. It contributes to a perception that the premier and the government tend to duck controversial issues. This is, in turn, contributing to a perception that Premier Peterson is becoming more of a day-to-day manager or caretaker and administrator than a visionary leader. That is, it is contributing to a perception that . . . the premier lacks a longer-term leadership vision for the province and is not spending enough time or is giving inadequate forethought to how to guide Ontario through the tougher times that some people think are coming."

Even the last sentence, a fleeting glimpse of prescience behind a sweeping curtain of platitude, was soft-pedaled: "This perceived cautious, tentative, consensus-seeking, deliberate style of governing is not, however, entirely negative in people's minds, particularly given the recent strong economic performance of the province. It does convey a sense of stability and people like this. They do not like or want too much controversy."

The report recommended that the Liberal campaign steer clear of dealing with Meech: "Most would like to see some sort of compromise over Meech Lake. They feel that this country was built on a willingness to compromise and feel the current impasse should also be solved through compromise. Many also find it hard to believe that if Meech Lake fails, Quebec will actually separate. They believe Quebec is bluffing when it talks about the consequences if Meech fails. There continues to be evidence of some feeling that the premier has been too preoccupied with Meech Lake and has been neglecting more important provincial concerns because of this. Moreover, the premier is seen to be largely reacting to events instead of playing a central role in shaping events insofar as Meech Lake is concerned."

To address perceptions the Liberals had become inactive and had no agenda for the future, the image report made two simple strategic recommendations: get the record out before the election and have Peterson "take some clear, decisive action on a couple of carefully chosen issues where he can make a concrete

commitment and take action and deliver on his commitment."
In the hectic months to come, neither recommendation would be
followed.

The Peterson-centered campaign approved by the strategists
was locked in by Hurley's report. The strategists were aware of
the perceived flaws listed in the back pages. But they believed
Peterson's positives would outstrip his negatives. "The strengths
far outweighed the weaknesses by an overwhelming margin,"
said Robinson. Kirby concurred: "I guess I wasn't all that worried about it because the voting intention data was very high.
I've never seen data on anybody where there weren't negatives.
I've seen Trudeau get a massive majority on negative data." The
negatives would not have much impact when conveyed by the
opposition leaders, the strategists believed. "I guess we figured
they couldn't make the negatives stick," said MacNaughton,
"that while the negatives were there, they weren't credible
deliverers of the message."

The Liberal strategists anticipated their opponents might
run negative campaigns. But Peterson's vulnerabilities were not
explored in detail in Goldfarb's focus groups through "projective" interviewing techniques—asking participants a series of
"what-if" questions. "The question really was: What was going
to be the impact of a negative campaign?" MacNaughton later
realized. The Liberals obtained no information on exactly what
might dislodge Liberal supporters.

"We should have had better information on what happened
to people when you started introducing consistently negative
messages and you really started probing some of the negatives,"
MacNaughton admitted. "What if you were told that there were
33 tax increases, if somebody told you that David Peterson and
Bourassa had a secret deal, that kind of stuff?" But zombified by
their top-line polling numbers and their confidence in the
strength of Peterson's positive image qualities, the strategists
failed to prepare for the worst.

*　　*　　*

With Goldfarb's work in hand, the Liberals knuckled down to a two-month grind on the homestretch of election preparation. Under Dan Gagnier and Beth Webster's direction, Peterson's policy chief Jan Whitelaw began pulling the government's record together in an 800-page policy manual for candidates. Started in April, the work was not completed until July, leaving no time to get the achievements across to voters before the election—a measure vital to enabling the government to campaign on its record. In May, Whitelaw came up with an impressive statistic: since taking office, the Liberals had kept, or implemented partly or through alternate means, 109 of the 115 election promises they made in 1985 and 1987. While some major pledges had fallen by the wayside, including the 1985 promises to sell beer and wine in corner stores and expand political rights for public servants, the finding showed the Liberals were good at keeping their word. But with Peterson busy with Meech and the government's corporate communications inadequate, that claim would not be offered up to Ontarians.

After coming together once to deal with Goldfarb's strategy paper, the strategists did not meet regularly or deal with the details of campaign readiness. Expected to serve as the committee's whip, Webster found the strategists' differences made progress all but impossible. The committee had not laid out a critical path when she came on stream in April; its meetings seldom included the same people and it had not produced a shred of paper on its plans. Since all were volunteers busy with their day jobs, the strategists had to be chased down by Webster for every meeting. "It was hard to get an ironclad commitment by everybody," she found to her frustration. "It was so painful to try to get hold of these people and get them working.

"As time evolved, the whole group of them became obsessed with the issue of the polling," said Webster, "and all of the other essential chores were neglected as a result of that."

The strategists assumed Gagnier would ride herd on the staff gathering policy materials together, but Peterson demanded his attention in the roll-up to the final Meech Lake sessions in

June. Webster was kept on the run by the nomination challenges against four caucus members.

As the summer arrived and the certainty of a fall election grew, Webster was stuck with a growing pile of critical tasks: "Suddenly it would be like, 'There's no campaign manual—Oh my God, do something!'" With time running out and confidentiality of the essence, Webster and Robinson became convinced that much of the pre-election preparation would get done only one way—if they did it themselves, drawing in as few people as possible.

* * *

In his office overlooking the Humber Valley, advertising consultant Ken Tilley stared down at the mountain of paper and photographs on his desk. It was early in June and information on the Peterson government's record was still being shipped out to him in bits and pieces by Webster. Two months after Tilley had explained his pre-election needs in a letter to Robinson, the details of the Liberals' accomplishments were finally showing up. "Of all the times I've done this, this is the least understanding of the process I've seen," he observed. "Kathy was sort of naive on this. It was Beth and her, Beth talking to her about why we couldn't deliver on a certain day for a certain meeting—the blind talking to the blind."

Tilley forged ahead, knowing from experience that Liberals across the province needed his products if they were going to be fighting an election later in the summer. "We're making the tools for the guys in the street," was how he described his job— the same job he had been called on to perform for years for Liberal campaigns across Canada. In the weeks ahead Tilley's copywriters and art directors would work to assemble the Liberals' "riding services package," an essential communications vehicle for their campaign.

The package would include the 6.5 million pieces of literature that Liberal candidates and workers would carry from door to door, poking through mail slots or thrusting into the hands of voters. Robinson wanted a brochure on the government's record, personalized for each of 130 candidates, ready to go by late June, then a tabloid-size newspaper, a second personalized brochure and a fistful of flyers on different issues, ready to ship across the province by August, when the election was expected. Along with stickers, buttons, banners, manuals and training sessions, the package would cost Liberal ridings between $3,500 and $4,100 each, payable to the central campaign.

Like most parties in an election, the Peterson Liberals would rely on three communications vehicles in 1990: news coverage, paid campaign advertising and the riding services package. Tilley's package, along with the paid ads, represented the Liberals' purest means of getting messages across to people. His task was to cook down the Liberals' best selling points and work them into the printed materials. But unlike other elections he had worked on, Tilley found the most critical part of his job had been done for him. The main theme of the campaign materials was decided and conveyed to him with no explanation by Robinson and Webster: make Peterson the center of everything in the package.

Tilley was not pleased. He felt he was being turned into what he called an "executional bum boy." In other campaigns with the Peterson Liberals and other Liberal teams across Canada, he had been invited to pore over the research materials, including strategy papers and focus group findings, to get a feel for the message. But this time, Tilley found that information was being clutched with unprecedented tightness by Robinson and Webster, and the veteran advertiser was frustrated: "Any commercial client, the more he invites you in to be part of his marketing organization, the better job you can do for him. You have to be part of the process. My model is the other places," he said, referring to other Liberal campaigns. "I sit in the meetings and I hear it all. You have a feel for the whole thing."

Tilley was uneasy with the idea of making Peterson the focus of the Liberal campaign materials. He had a feeling Peterson's public image was far from perfect and the premier might not be the Liberals' strongest selling point. But like other experienced

Liberals drawn into the campaign and given their marching orders by Robinson and Webster, he found there was no way to voice his criticism. "It seemed not to be our task to do that kind of quality control on thematics and stuff," he found. With the campaign looming he shelved his concerns and began churning out the Liberals' brochures and flyers. "I just thought it was me being more critical than I should have been, to be honest," he said, "because the polls said he was as popular as hell."

But Tilley was not alone among Liberals who were worried about Peterson's image. On July 13, 80 Liberal candidates and campaign managers gathered in the government caucus room at Queen's Park to start a two-day "campaign college." Robinson, MacNaughton and organizational chief Debbie Nash opened the intensive training session with a two-hour rundown on campaign preparations. That evening at a nearby hotel they relaxed for cocktails and dinner, and MPPs began lining up to speak privately to MacNaughton about the campaign. They had some serious concerns about Peterson and his image.

"You'd better know," whispered an Ottawa area incumbent, "that David isn't really the biggest thing since sliced bread in our area and we'd really rather that you didn't send him in." MacNaughton rolled his eyes. The same member had given him the same sage advice before the 1987 election. "Part of that you have to recognize as real, and I was concerned about it," MacNaughton thought. "On the other hand, I've never been in a campaign in my whole life where a lot of the candidates don't think they're going to win it on their own, regardless of whether they've got a 2 percent identification rating." MacNaughton began to wonder, however, when members from the predominantly Liberal Hamilton area—and even Peterson's own London area—approached him with the same warning. He left the training session uneasy, but convinced himself that "the preponderance of the advice was, 'David Peterson continues to be one of the strongest assets the party has.'"

* * *

Robinson and Webster led Liberal troops through a revealing array of gymnastic manoeuvres in an attempt to select the perfect photograph and slogan for the Liberal campaign poster. The choices were critical: in a Peterson-centered campaign, the poster meant everything. It had to capture and convey precisely the correct qualities of Peterson's image. The large, glossy photo, trimmed with bands of Liberal red, would be a trademark of the campaign. About 6,500 copies would be printed and distributed to campaign managers across the province and used to splash the Peterson theme across the walls and windows of campaign headquarters, to announce the Liberal presence at all-candidates meetings and on canvasses to adorn the sides of vans carrying candidates and workers.

The Liberal poster was created through a mind-warping comedy of errors. In early July, when a late-summer election had become a certainty, the need for carefully chosen promotional materials suddenly became a crisis. The Liberal caucus service bureau's photo files, barely recovered from the pillaging they had endured weeks earlier for the riding services package, were turned upside down to find that one perfect shot.

After several days of frantic digging, the search yielded nine versions of a campaign poster based on three hopeful photos: the poster shot from the 1987 campaign, with Peterson looking pensive and powerful; a jovial shot of Peterson laughing with an adoring woman at a Canada Day celebration in front of Queen's Park, and an intriguing picture of Peterson wearing a humble expression, standing and listening with concern to an elderly couple under a canopy. The choices were sped off to Goldfarb's offices for focus group testing on July 16 by consultant Hurley.

After an evening of evoking reactions from participants screened to be "very" or "somewhat" likely to vote Liberal, Hurley recommended a version of the third poster as the best of the options available. The look on Peterson's face in the 1987 poster conveyed "a more serious, businesslike, leadership image for the premier," he found, but Robinson and other Liberals worried that it appeared remote and detached in 1990, as if the premier were daydreaming about distant events. The lighthearted poster was found to be "relaxed and upbeat in tone," but Liberals fretted that the premier should be seen to be more serious, rather than yukking it up at some featherweight event.

Of the choices available, the focus groups agreed that the third set of posters using the "listening" photo best conveyed Peterson's positive image qualities. Hurley wrote in his analysis that "these versions appeal because they emphasize or showcase the premier's key strength—his strong rapport with people. They function to reinforce the perception that the premier is an open, approachable, concerned, caring and likable person." Hurley fired the posters back to Queen's Park with his recommendation. Still wavering, Webster invited a campaign staffer to study the choices with her that night. After tucking in her year-old son, Webster lined up the prospects on a wall in her basement.

"They're all shit, Beth," the aide pronounced. "We better set up a shoot with Peterson and get it right."

"Well, we can't," she said. "This is all we've got; there's not enough time. We can't bother him for something like this."

"So which one is it?"

"The groups liked that one," said Webster, pointing at the "listening" poster.

"Ugh," the aide responded. "Well, it's kind of a neat look on his face. And it's not our constituency, but I guess talking to old folks shows intergenerational bonding, which is supposed to be a good thing these days. There's a couple of problems with it, though."

"Such as?"

"Well, the old guy's got a drink in his hand. Maybe it's only orange juice, but do we want to see the preem walking around at some piss-up? And the old girl's wearing a big string of pearls. Maybe they're fake, but who cares: she looks too rich. And look at those age spots. Geez!" The aide glanced over at Webster, who had blanched.

"Shit," she muttered. "You're right. We can have the guys work on it."

The next day, Webster shipped the offending poster to long-time Liberal advertising expert Donald Murphy of the ad agency

Vickers and Benson for a few touch-ups. At the end of the day, it came back to Webster. Through the magic of airbrushing, the poster had been cleaned up. A note confirmed the changes: "Glass is out. Jewelry is out—necklace and earring. Liver spots, etc."

Relieved, Webster had one minor detail to look after: the elderly couple had to be tracked down to sign a release form. Bill Murray, executive director of the Liberal caucus, was assigned the mission. He knew from the photographer that the photo had been taken at the opening of a hospital in Ingersoll, near London. Murray told the story in his gravelly voice:

"First I called Charlie's office [local MPP Charlie Tatham] and they didn't know, so I called the hospital. I talked to the administrator and he thought at first it might be his mother. Then I went down there and he looks at it and says it's not her. Then he thought the old guy was someone he knew who was heading off to the golf course. So we got there and found this old guy who wasn't the right guy, but he knew who it was—another old guy who was off playing golf. We didn't think we could find him wandering around out there, so we went over to his house. His wife answers the door and she looks at the picture and says, 'Yes, that's us.' She said the only reason she went up to Peterson was she liked what he did on Meech. And then she says they're Tories and there was no way she was going to sign the release I'd brought. I didn't even tell her it was going to be on the poster—I just said it was for some promotional materials. I didn't tell her it was going to be plastered all over every goddamned arena and Liberal campaign office all over the province."

Murray rushed to phone Robinson with the disastrous news. Thoroughly frazzled and with only days to go before the election call, Robinson and Webster appealed to Donald Murphy again for help. "Send it back up here and leave it with me," said Murphy. He called down to the reception desk in the agency's lobby. "Hello," he said sweetly to the woman who answered the phone. "Could you and your husband come in and have your picture taken in a studio this weekend?"

The poster problem was solved with an artist's razor blade. The Tory couple, first sanitized with an airbrush, were cut out of the picture and replaced with stand-ins posed and photographed to complement Peterson's intently listening face. The scene meant to encapsulate the Liberal campaign never actually happened.

Similar attention was applied by Robinson and Webster to devising a campaign slogan. In the same focus group sessions on July 16, Hurley exhaustively tested campaign theme lines that began "Premier Peterson" and ended with variations on a similar theme: "Effective Leadership for a Strong Ontario," "Leadership that Works for Ontario," "Strong Leadership for a Strong Ontario," "Proven Leadership for a Strong Ontario," and "Leadership You Can Count On." Hurley recommended the first line, finding "it has an impact and an emotional kind of ring or appeal that some of the other themes lack. It conveys a feeling of competence, self-confidence and reassurance. It is appealing to people's hopes for the future and their sense of trust and confidence in the premier's leadership. It is telling people what they want to hear or believe, that is, that Ontario is going to remain strong in the face of some of the problems confronting Canada . . . People also tend to accept or buy into the notion that Premier Peterson's leadership will help keep Ontario strong. . . . that he has been an effective leader." The phrase "Leadership that Works" was found to be unimaginative and open to opposition attack; "Strong Leadership for a Strong Ontario" was called redundant and reminiscent of "dictatorial autocratic government, more along the lines of Mulroney-style government"; "Proven Leadership" focused too closely on Peterson's record rather than on his abilities; "Leadership You Can Count On" had "a ring of hackneyed sloganism and used-car-salesman hype associated with it."

Hurley also recommended the Liberals describe the premier as "Premier David Peterson" rather than "Premier Peterson," a key difference when the title had to appear on millions of pieces of campaign literature. "Premier David Peterson" was found to be "more personal and less formal." With less than two weeks to go before the election call, the Liberal campaign theme line was finally pieced together: "Premier David Peterson: Effective Leadership for a Strong Ontario."

5

The NDP and Tories
Get Ready

The NDP will listen to you.

–DAVID REVILLE, NDP STRATEGIST

*The bottom line was we didn't think we could make
much of a difference.*

–LARRY GROSSMAN, PC STRATEGIST

Gerald Caplan needed a "them"—as in "us against them." It
was May 4 and the senior NDP strategist had been asked to create a strategic overview for the aggressive attack Bob Rae's team
had in mind for the expected election campaign. Such challenges were old hat to the self-described old hack who had run
his first campaign for Ontario NDP leader Donald MacDonald
in 1959, magnificently increasing the party's holdings from three
seats to five.

In 1990 Caplan had bought into the Rae team's single, simple objective: align Peterson and the Liberals with a group of rich and powerful interests to create a "them" who were not like "us"— not like the remarkably large column of people in the NDP's "universe" of potential voters, those who had not ruled out voting New Democrat in a provincial election, including hard-core NDPers, soft NDP-leaners and soft Liberals and Tories. To many New Democrats, bringing down the Peterson government was another in an endless series of quixotic undertakings by the party of eternal pessimism. If the New Democrats ever won an Ontario or federal election, they chided one another, they would no doubt ask for a recount.

For months, feelings of frustration and drift had been turning the NDP's once-feisty little caucus sclerotic. After gruelling but successful spring and fall sessions in the legislature in 1989, the spring session of 1990 had been a disappointment, highlighted in spirit and in publicity only by Peter Kormos' 17-hour filibuster, his inventive tirade against the government's no-fault auto insurance plan. Major polls publicized the legacy of failure of the opposition's ritual of assaults on the Liberals over the no-fault issue, health care, the environment and the Starr affair: nothing was sticking to the Teflon-coated premier.

"We took a poll sometime in the middle of '89 before we were doing our pre-election work," said Rae. "We were at 23 percent. And we worked and we sweated and we took our issues across the province. We did campaigns at the door. We did everything we possibly could. And at the end of that we got it up to 24 percent."

In the fall of 1989, Rae held a view, lonely among his colleagues, that Peterson would call an election for sometime late in 1990; he was prescient of the potential for future difficulty posed by the struggle around the Meech Lake deal and envisioned several scenarios that could lead the premier to send the province to the polls early. With his like-minded chief of staff, David Agnew, he ordered the party to escalate its election-readiness activities.

The NDP organization looked good on paper. Its 50-member Election Planning Committee (EPC), a subset of its 300-member provincial council, had been staying its course by meeting four times a year. Prodded from the top, the EPC commissioned its steering committee to begin holding meetings once a week. Sub-committees were struck on fund-raising, organization, communications and other election-readiness functions, all reporting back to the provincial council—a unique, fastidiously democratic approach to campaign planning.

As their election preparation and perennial frustration were underscored by the spring polls that pointed to a Peterson coronation, the New Democrats were truly miserable. Rae feared defeat in his own York South riding, where he had barely pulled through in 1987; early in the summer he canvassed heavily in his own backyard.

Windsor-Riverside incumbent Dave Cooke did not believe his region's antipathy toward the Liberals was real enough to keep him ensconced; Winnipeg pollster David Gotthilf of Viewpoints Research had made initial projections in Windsor and southwestern Ontario that were gloomy for the NDP, while those obtained by Martin Goldfarb for the Liberals had found Rae's personal popularity exceeding Peterson's in the region. "We would have been gratified if we held on to the official opposition and we had got up over 30 seats," said NDP strategist David Reville.

Street-smart and irreverent, Reville was one of a small group of New Democrats who became the core of the EPC's steering committee. A former Toronto alderman, Reville had decided he had shot his bolt as the member for the Toronto riding of Riverdale; in the months leading to the election he turned his attention to election strategy preparation. Joining him on the steering committee were campaign chair and EPC chair Julie Davis, secretary-treasurer of the Ontario Federation of Labour; Ontario NDP president Janet Solberg; the party's provincial secretary Jill Marzetti, campaign manager; former Toronto NDP member Ross McClellan, the campaign's key link to labor groups; Chuck Rachlis, Rae's research director; and Agnew, who as campaign director had responsibility for the key areas of polling, communications and advertising. Perennial strategist

Caplan was called on when the assistance of a "gray eminence" was felt to be needed and former party leader Stephen Lewis brought occasional moral and strategic support.

Until the end of April, as it searched for a cohesive attack-based strategy, the steering group had chased its tail in ever-tightening circles. Draft after draft of a strategy paper had left the group unfulfilled; the approach to the campaign, like the caucus's disconnected flurry of assaults in the legislature, was not gelling. To break the spell, the group asked Caplan to develop a strategic overview it could refine in its election planning process.

Pollster Gotthilf distilled the results of his spring poll into a concise problem the New Democrats had to solve: there was a serious gap between voter beliefs about the NDP's ability to perform well on important issues, and voting intentions. Gotthilf reported the NDP had reached a ceiling of support of about 28 percent of decided voters. If they were to break through, they had to reach some of the 60 percent of Ontarians who fell into the NDP's universe of potential supporters. Gotthilf found when he asked those people which party and leader would be best at cleaning up the environment, protecting jobs and other top issues, the NDP came first across the board. But that did not change the way that people were planning to vote; Peterson and the Liberals remained far in front. The lines of voter beliefs and voting intentions refused to move closer together.

"Our task was to try and get in under the blanket that we felt Peterson had been able to drape over the electorate," said Reville. "Everything we had been trying to do both legislatively and outside the house did not seem to have a whole lot of effect on the general attractiveness of the Peterson government."

To complement Gotthilf's quantitative findings, Agnew ordered up focus groups from Toronto consultant Peter Donegan. A 20-year veteran of several major Toronto advertising agencies, Donegan was a market researcher specializing in psychographic techniques. He adhered to the theory that people say different things than they do and are motivated by deeply held feelings and beliefs they do not often articulate and of which they might not even be aware. Donegan's consulting firm told corporate clients how to peddle consumer products by exploiting people's subconscious thoughts. He was fascinated by the challenge of applying the principles to a political product.

To help the NDP find a hook for its campaign strategy, Donegan organized a series of three pairs of focus groups in Hamilton, Sudbury and Toronto, using a group size of eight at a time in sessions of no less than two hours each, in contrast to the twelve-member groups of one to two hours conducted by Goldfarb vice-president Doug Hurley for the Liberals. The NDP strategists and their pollster insisted the groups be composed of members of the NDP's broad universe of potential supporters, unlike the Liberal groups that were made up of Liberals and Liberal-leaners. By including soft supporters of other parties and undecideds, the NDP groups were designed to provide a broader range of voters' perspectives; the composition of the Liberal groups was based on the premise the Liberal campaign would be targeted at keeping the Liberals' existing constituency of voters together.

On May 4, Caplan, Agnew, Reville and Rachlis attended the two Toronto groups. As Caplan watched for hints to help him craft his strategic overview, Donegan revealed to him both the problem and the seeds of the solution.

"That focus group was all-important for me," said Caplan. "I sat there watching the focus group leader try to worm something out of these people and it was like pulling teeth, so neutral were they, so semi-satisfied were they with the government. It suddenly occurred to me that what I was seeing was true: in fact, they didn't give a fuck about the NDP. They were largely happy as pigs in shit. They largely thought David Peterson was okay. And if they were worried about Meech Lake or how sleazy he was, it sure wasn't there."

But Donegan's technique, something akin to mass psycho-analysis, helped him burrow under Peterson's cozy blanket. He passed out crayons and paper to his participants and asked them to make simple sketches that described their feelings about the Liberals, then about the NDP. The results yielded some heavy symbolism. One pair of sketches showed Peterson as a devil brandishing a pitchfork on top of a hill, with Rae represented as a farmer in a valley by a clear stream. Another effort showed a large hairy arm wielding a mallet over a tiny stick figure, under the heading of "Liberal"; the NDP was represented by a giant question mark. Donegan was getting underneath the sweeping Liberal support indicated by the widely known top-line polling results, support the NDP had suspected was "a mile wide and an inch deep." "Beneath their initial complacency, these people were really quite unhappy," Donegan said. "They painted a very pessimistic picture about what the next five years had in store for them and there was a great deal of anger and resentment when they opened up and talked about how they felt."

Donegan coaxed his participants along and found that, with careful prompting, they latched on willingly to the idea their feelings could be linked to a sense of frustration with big government, big corporations and big business. "People felt that even when they had taken a self-empowering step such as writing a letter, they were always ignored," said Donegan. Those discoveries were not novel; the trick for Donegan and the NDP was to take advantage of those feelings by translating them into a strategy for fighting an election in 1990.

Caplan wanted to lift the acrimony Donegan detected out of the confines of the focus groups and cultivate it among potential NDP voters. "The idea was to build a bridge between that which was theoretically credible about the NDP and that which actually was salient to voters," he said. Caplan had to choose a group that would help him build that bridge—a group that represented rich and powerful private interests that could be believed to be working against the public interest. By linking that group to Peterson in the minds of voters, he would clearly identify a "them" in the "us-against-them" equation that made people draw a mallet poised over a little person to describe their feelings. With "them" singled out, the NDP campaign could play variations on the theme through its tour and advertising. Caplan made his choice when he watched Donegan test out on his participants, at the strategists' request, the idea that developers were one group that represented private interests working against "people like us." "They accepted that immediately," Donegan found.

"It was a question of was David Peterson too much in the pockets of private interests; the private interests that I thought were the most useful to us given the record of the Peterson government were the developers," said Caplan. "Basing a campaign primarily on the role of the developers in David Peterson's Ontario hit a couple of notes. It allowed obviously for the implication of the Patti Starr affair to be raised without actually raising it. I didn't want myself to make a big issue of Starr specifically; I wanted to make a big issue of the Peterson government being too close to ritzy developers."

Caplan was taking chances. Other than the evidence Donegan exhorted from his focus group guinea pigs, Caplan had no concrete proof Ontarians would accept and respond to that line of attack. "It was frankly a recommendation of last resort," he admitted. "Neither anyone else on the EPC nor I could think of any other way to get the attention of voters."

Caplan's colleagues bought in. To Reville, who also watched Donegan's focus groups, "the strategy was really simple: Peterson doesn't listen to you, he listens to a select group of powerful people who can rent space in his ear. He doesn't listen to you and the NDP will listen to you. We were starting to pick up the sort of fat-cat complaint: you can talk to him if you're the president of this or that, but if you're just an ordinary Joe, he's going to hand you a hot dog and that's it." Rae would attempt to create an alliance with voters based on the common experience of "us against them" and demystify Peterson by portraying him as a typical politician in league with the rich and powerful.

On the all-important leader's tour, the strategists agreed, Rae could present his attacks at a series of venues laden with symbols of the "them" relationship. On the second day of the campaign, he would hold a news conference at Ontario Place and spell out Peterson's ties to developers in large letters; the theme would then be perpetuated as the backdrop changed to the front of a Tridel building, and so on. Caplan recommended a case-study approach day by day for two weeks to sow a bed of suspicion in the thin soil of latent public doubt about whose interests the Liberals represented. "It was by no means high on anybody's agenda," he realized. "Sometimes, I thought, it would have to be frustrating, but they'd have to build that case."

Caplan's attack strategy included no plan to dispense an NDP platform at any stage of the campaign. "The strategy didn't visit the platform part, really," said Reville. "Ultimately we did not decide on an issue campaign." But that posed a terrible risk: the NDP would be trying to get away without presenting its alternative positions—even on the leverage issues such as the environment, which all the parties knew were powerful enough to single-handedly drive voting behavior and on which NDP research showed voters preferred their party's position over the Liberals. But the NDP strategists were listening closely to Donegan, who in turn was listening to his focus groups.

"They were very scared of an NDP government," Donegan found. "They seriously questioned whether they were really going to be any different and whether they were experienced enough to run things properly if they ever did get in. I told them they had to stay away altogether from talking about the things they would do and about the possibility of an NDP government."

It was a massive gamble but the strategists had a feeling it would work, at least for a while, because the media, especially the Queen's Park press gallery, was fed up with Peterson and would find the attacks interesting. "We observed that the press was getting more and more impatient with the premier," said Reville. "You don't plan your strategy based on what you think the media is going to do, but my view is the way Peterson changed between '87 and '90 certainly wasn't helpful to him. His way of handling scrums and Question Period was starting to grate on the Queen's Park media; you could feel that, you could see it, you could watch the reactions. He seemed to get more dismissive and a bit smart-alecky or grumpy or just didn't deal with things. He basically stopped answering questions in the house, or if he did he answered them in a mumble that you couldn't hear. He was just referring stuff this way and that way, and then he'd sit down and smirk." The NDP strategists decided to make Peterson's deteriorating relationship with the media work for them.

The NDP's plan defied the conventional promise-a-day routine that had characterized Canadian campaigning for decades, but this approach to its platform would carry the party halfway through the 1990 campaign. Drawing on his small bankroll of media goodwill and patience, Rae would finesse his way along. "Part of the whole environment that we were campaigning in was this sense of real boredom and fatigue and rejection of traditional politics," said Agnew. "We decided not to do, and in fact criticized, the promise-a-day approach of the other parties. The decision wasn't easy to reach because again it was not traditionally the way we've done it." By keeping steadfastly clear of dealing with the issues, Rae would be able to emphasize his single, simple theme that Peterson and his rich and powerful developer cronies were not acting in the public interest but were motivated by private greed.

From their earliest meetings the NDP strategists had been convinced that Rae's tone for the campaign had to break new ground. Believing the NDP had become too gentle in the legislature, Agnew and Reville, backed up by Rae himself, wanted the campaign attacks to have a sharp new edge and an aggressiveness never seen in the NDP leader. In the opening days of the campaign, Rae would come out swinging, using tough, unapologetic language to go after Peterson. "We had a very clear sense of what we wanted to do on the first day that wasn't particularly affected by what Peterson said or did," said Agnew. "We had learned a lesson a couple of elections ago of not being fast and we were bound not to repeat that. We wanted to make sure that we had a very aggressive message for the first couple of weeks on each day, an aggressive message about the Liberal government."

"We were concerned that the summer election would be so boring and would be considered to be a foregone conclusion, that basically the Tories are in disarray, the voters are asleep, Peterson has just got to eat hot dogs again for a whole summer, and on September 6th it will be another Peterson majority and nothing will have happened," said Reville. "So our strategy was to be as much like an alarm clock as we could imagine and it was a very anxious decision for us because a good number of our people didn't think that was the way you ran an election. They thought you went out and talked about how Utopia was going to look when we got in some day and give long descriptions of how you were going to build a better world."

Caplan was queasy about focusing so aggressively on the honesty and integrity of Peterson and the Liberals; he preferred the subtlety of suggestion and symbolic linkages. "That was a diversion from the campaign," he complained. "The issue was not whether David Peterson was an honest man or not, whether he lied or not. The issue was whether or not he was on the wrong side of the interests of working people. I didn't like all that other stuff."

"The interests of working people": on the use of that type of terminology the old and new elements among the NDP's strategy group differed in 1990. The traditional-minded, like Caplan, regretted moving the party away from the populist language of Tommy Douglas, David Lewis and Ed Broadbent. But Agnew, young and willing to break some rules, and Reville, open-minded and ready to try anything, were both students of communications techniques, listening to a new language: the psychographic analysis of Donegan. In a detailed report that followed Caplan's strategic overview, Donegan advised he had found most voters, even some hard-core NDPers, rejected the deprecating lexicon of past generations that flogged the New Democrats as the party of "the little man," "the average worker," and "ordinary people." Those terms were too close to the grim truth for Donegan's research subjects; they seemed to confirm people's worst anxieties about themselves and their futures. "When the NDP continued to describe people in those terms," said Donegan, "they were implying that if they were ever in power, that was how they would treat people." For the first time, Agnew's group deemed, the NDP campaign would strike those references; Rae would stick to talking about "Ontarians" or just "people."

With their plan nailed down, the strategists, old and new, reached one firm consensus: they would not be thrown off-strategy. "We were very tough about our strategy and about our approach," said Agnew. "We were bound and determined not to get pushed off it by external events." The plan was not an easy sell when the party's candidates and campaign managers gathered at a series of four "campaign colleges" across Ontario in June and July.

"There were a lot of people, a lot of activists and ideologues who would have been quite happy to go out and explain universal sickness, accident and disability insurance the whole time," said Reville. "One of the hard jobs was to say, 'No, we've got the strategy': the strategy is Peterson listens to the fat cats, he doesn't listen to you, we will listen to you—and we've got to go after that every day in spite of how bored the media is getting, in spite of how irritated they're getting, in spite of how they're going to say more and more, Where's your policy? Where's your platform? What are you going to do?' We thought it was really important to keep driving home that simple message because it was clear to us it was going to take a long time to get in under this kind of fuzzy feeling people had about Peterson and the Liberals."

By July NDP organizers were having trouble getting their people interested in a campaign because the Liberals were running so far ahead in the polls. For the strategists that dilemma made the central messages and the leader's tour doubly critical. "Our concern was everybody was going to think the thing was a yawner and we were really worried that if it was a yawner that would be very bad news for us," said Reville. "Given our ground strength, if people were not getting our message anywhere and it was not getting in under the summer blahs, then the turnout would be low and they'd all go, 'Ho-hum—Peterson,' and we'd be dead ducks. So our major concern was to sort of punch the thing up a bit."

Caucus administrator Richard McLellan was placed in charge of the NDP leader's tour, which was tailored to use morning and early-afternoon events and careful mapping of its routes to help the province's Toronto-centered media propagate the NDP message. More than the Liberal or Conservative tours, the NDP's tour would adhere faithfully to a ritual of returning to Toronto at the end of each day.

In early July, Rae and his wife Arlene Perly Rae took their children to the family's Rideau Lakes cottage near Ottawa. "Arlene and I were at the cottage together," he said. "As we were chatting about where we had been, I said, 'Well, it's been 10 years, almost. This will be the third election . . .' Going into this election campaign, I believed that it would be my last election campaign as leader of the party." Feeling less pressure than he had in years Rae would enter the campaign relaxed, sure and feisty. He made a prediction to his wife: the party could get 30 seats and 30 percent of the vote and he would be able to retire gracefully, having taken the New Democrats back to a level that paralleled their strongest showing in Ontario, under Stephen Lewis in 1975.

But Rae, like other New Democrats in July 1990, was unaware of the timeliness of the strategy the Election Planning Committee had settled on, of the neat fit it would enjoy with the strategy of the Tories, of the chaos and bad chemistry in the Liberal camp, of the opportune events that would unfold in the campaign. He was as unsuspecting as other Ontario politicians of the changing backdrop of national and international events against which Ontario's election would play out. And he had no idea he was about to summarily dehorse a once-white knight and claim the Pink Palace as his own.

*   *   *

Mike Harris needed a miracle. The Big Blue Machine, the mighty Ontario Progressive Conservative Party led by Bill Davis, was three leaders and five years removed from the smoking hulk he inherited by winning the Tory leadership on May 10, 1990. With an expensive election looming ahead the Ontario Progressive Conservative Party now led by Mike Harris was towing around a $4-million debt, which sucked up $500,000 a year in servicing costs from any new funds raised. Strategic planning by the Tories had been nonexistent since 1987, as the party felt its way around in the twilight zone created by the interim leadership of stalwart Andy Brandt and the nonleadership of would-be party leader Tom Long, the party president.

Brandt replaced Larry Grossman as leader when Grossman resigned after losing his seat on election night in 1987. Getting ready for the next election was far removed from Brandt's mind: he chose to home in on maintaining a strong presence in the legislature and restoring the morale of a badly beaten and divided party, while helping try to get the party's finances back on track.

Long saw himself as a cheerleader who had to travel extensively to keep the party motivated but, intent on taking a run at the leadership, had spent little time readying the Tory organization to enter the fray again—let alone fight an early election in 1990. The Tories had failed to get their act together by conducting a poll-by-poll rebuilding process in the ridings where they had a good shot at winning; that process had served them well after the 1977 election, when they recovered from minority status to win a majority in 1981. No strategy for gradually paying down the debt had been conceived, agreed on and implemented. Under Long, no campaign organization, election planning group or critical path had been established.

A small committee of Tory veterans began taking up the organizational slack early in 1990. While most of the party was caught up in its laborious, diluted and dull leadership process, leading to the selection of Brandt's replacement in May 1990, a sketchy package of campaign plans was developed to be handed over to the new leader. But the makeup job was no substitute for a long-term planning effort. Harris was dead-on after his victory when he sized up the situation on May 11: "I am a bit behind the eight ball."

One saving grace for Harris was the speed with which his opponent, London MPP Dianne Cunningham, laid down arms to ensure unity; a lesson had been learned from 1985 Tory leadership loser Alan Pope, who had sulked in his office for more than a year after being beaten, much to the party's embarrassment.

Another side benefit of the leadership contest was a list of 33,000 Tories who had registered to cast ballots. While it did not provide Harris with 33,000 canvassers, the list came in handy for Tory fund-raisers. They used it to persuade five chartered banks and several trust companies to lend the party $1.2 million to finance the Tory campaign, with the promise the up-to-date membership rolls would help them pay back the loans before the campaign ended, a promise they would keep.

A large, lumbering man with an unassuming manner, Harris was the antithesis of modern political charisma. His network of established Tories helped him defeat Cunningham, who had served as an MPP for only two years. Harris's less-than-effervescent personality made him appear to be a difficult commodity to sell, although during the campaign his self-effacing style would serve him well. His image was hampered somewhat by his well-known previous career as a golf pro, a job not commonly recognized as preparing one for public office, and by his right-wing inclinations. "I personally think Frank Miller is one of the brightest, freshest things to come on the political scene," he said in 1985, shortly before Miller's throwback Conservatism was chucked on the scrap heap by Ontarians.

His meager binder of campaign plans in hand, Harris was willing to overlook the philosophical differences dividing the Tories in his search for strategic campaign advice. By early July a campaign team and strategy committee were assembled that included a handful of Harris's staff, with a core group that included top strategist John Laschinger, Davis veterans John Tory and Hugh Segal, ex-leader Grossman, communications consultant and former MPP Phil Gillies, party president Long, strategist Nancy McLean and campaign secretary Leslie Noble, with pollster Allan Gregg. The coalition was a mixture of left and right, young and not-too-old—mostly left and young, however, in contrast to the right-wing policy orientation Harris had displayed vividly during the leadership contest.

The Tories' dire circumstances were assessed in July in a pre-election poll by Gregg. Peterson's top-line supremacy was starkly evident when the strategists gathered three weeks before the election call: the Liberals enjoyed the support of slightly more than 50 percent of decided voters; their overall performance rating was topping 60 percent. The prospects for the Tories were sickening: 14 percent of Ontarians could name Harris as leader without help; their support among decided voters had withered to 17 percent, barely a few blips better than support for the Mulroney Tories. On paper, Harris and company were good for as few as four seats. "The bottom line," said Grossman, "was we didn't think we could make much of a difference."

But Gregg drew the strategists' attention to the thinness of the support for the Liberals. How satisfied were Ontarians with the way the Liberals had managed taxation and avoided tax increases? More than 60 per cent were dissatisfied. How about the Liberals' control over government spending? More than 60 percent were dissatisfied. The pattern was a haunting one for some of the Tories, who had watched Premier Frank Miller's 55 percent support level, also described at the time as a mile wide and an inch deep, fall away during the campaign in 1985.

Gregg's data confirmed what the strategists had been suspecting: a single-issue campaign based on the tax issue offered the best chance to make up ground. Taxes were a leverage issue, Gregg advised them—whipped up properly, the pocketbook nature of overtaxation had the potential to break people away from maintaining their voting intentions by pushing them to make a choice based on self-interest. Harris could benefit by harnessing perceptions that the Liberals were tax-drunk and spending people's money like sailors on shore leave.

"It was the one issue on which the Liberals were faulted, the one issue on which people were angry or could be persuaded to be angry, and the one issue on which the PCs had any credibility at all," said communications chief Gillies. "In a rather hostile environment for Tories, this was the issue where those three factors coincided." Still, even the tax issue was not driving voters out the door with a rope in their hands, hunting for politicians. Only about 10 percent of Gregg's respondents rated it a strong concern; only relative to other issues did it come into its own.

"When you look at formulating a strategy when you're 35 points behind, you have to look for that chink in the armour," said John Tory. "It was also the federal government's fault and the municipal governments' fault; there was just a general sort of attitude of being fed up with taxes and this was the first government that came along and offered itself up for re-election."

Some of the strategists adhered to the nowhere-to-go-but-up theory: "Take any issue," Grossman told the group to demonstrate his point. "Now flip a coin. Pro or con, whichever issue you pick, whichever side you pick, you're higher than 14 percent. Everything is running ahead of us." Swinging wildly at too many issues would not work for the Tories, Gregg discovered. "Whenever we got too ambitious about all those things that were wrong in the province and how it was the dirty Liberals' fault, they weren't buying," Gillies observed. "Not from us, anyway."

The Tories also decided early on not to have Harris go on the attack against Peterson over the Starr affair. While Gregg found half of his respondents were aware of the fund-raising scandal, they did not believe Peterson was personally culpable. Most believed "That's just government" or "That's just politicians"; a smaller number believed it was an Ontario Liberal Party problem; only a small fraction thought Peterson himself had erred.

To veteran strategist Laschinger, the campaign plan was taking shape: get Harris out the door fast and hard with simple, sharp jabs at the Liberals' soft, tax-related underbelly. Do not let him respond to extraneous issues; do not relent to any media pressure to start presenting a platform. Set the news agenda for the campaign and make sure every penny spent on advertising supports the single theme and reinforces what people hear on the news every night. And stay on strategy. Throughout the campaign, Grossman would drill that message into Harris: "Stay on the thing; stay there, don't move; don't be lured into anything else." To keep the story alive without going off course, Grossman suggested the Tories try a "tax of the day" message instead of making the usual announcement-a-day on a different policy.

Laschinger had a basic theory he wanted to put into play, one familiar to experienced strategists. He believed successful

early attacks had the potential to cripple the Liberals by undermining their credibility if they tried to respond on taxes or any
other issue. If people could be convinced the Liberals were
responsible for the highly sensitive problem of high taxes and
out-of-control government spending, Peterson's ability to deliver believable messages in other areas would be neutered. If he
can't handle our money, people would think, how can he handle
anything less important? The Tories were convinced a strong
negative reaction from voters on the powerful tax issue even
had the potential to overwhelm Peterson's strong, positive
image. "People would say, 'Look, they've screwed that up so
badly I think I want to get rid of them for that reason, and I
don't really care what else they plan to do or what a nice fellow
David Peterson is,'" Tory believed.

Gregg's July poll also carefully probed the question of an
early-election call and convinced the Tories their strategy would
have to include raising the idea of an unnecessary election just
before Peterson made the announcement. The strategists were
mindful of their 1977 experience with Davis, who extricated
himself from difficulties in the legislature by calling an election
after two years of minority government. Both opposition parties
used the unnecessary-election charge effectively against the
Tories in the campaign and prevented Davis from getting a
majority. "We knew that if you did it right, you could exploit it
through the campaign and cause them some grief," said Tory.

Doing it right meant doing it with all guns blazing.
Laschinger's commitment to hard-edged, early attacks was reinforced by the low level of concern and engagement with an election
the strategists observed in focus groups conducted by Decima
just before the campaign. Focus group leader Marcel Proulx had
to prod and provoke his participants to get them to react to any
issue, even overtaxation and the early election call. "People
were mad or people did or didn't like this or that, but that's all
against a background of relative ambivalence," observed Gillies.
"They were fed up with politics, it was just past the Meech collapse, they were wanting to enjoy their summer holiday and not
focus on all this stuff." That complacency, the Tories hoped,

could be turned into a negative factor for Peterson if Harris harped loudly enough on the issues they targeted, starting with the early call. From the outset of the campaign, they decided, the climate of public opinion would be theirs to shape.

Gregg used projective polling techniques to word his critical early-election call questions, setting up a "what-if" situation for his respondents. He wanted to obtain answers that would reflect the context of critical reaction by the media and opposition in which Peterson would be announcing an early election. He told his respondents the Liberals might be about to call an election less than three years after the last one, then asked them whether they thought the Liberals were calling it because it was necessary for them to get a mandate to deal with something or because they were being opportunistic. He followed up by asking whether people approved of the early call, then asked if people felt more or less likely to vote Liberal with the Liberals going early.

On all three questions Gregg found that about 60 percent of Ontarians would condemn an early election and reject the Liberals when prompted with the right critical context. No such projective analysis was provided by Goldfarb for the Liberals in his strategic paper. The Liberal strategy team did not demand that a projective analysis of the early-call issue be undertaken to enable a defense to be prepared.

Sending Harris off without a platform did not trouble his strategists. Gregg's research had revealed that on most of the top issues, such as the environment, education and social policy questions, the Liberals could be faulted, but not by Tories in 1990. Only the NDP could effectively criticize the Liberals in every area except taxes, where the Tories had modest credibility. But on all issues, including overtaxation, Gregg found people were not interested in hearing solutions from Harris. "They didn't want to hear that we were gonna do anything differently," said Gillies. "So we had to start off indicating that this is an area where the government has fallen down; you have every right to be angry about this. But that was about as far as we could take it."

In a broader sense, the Tories decided, it was Peterson's election and people would be looking to him alone to come up with substantive reasons to re-elect him. "People don't expect opposition parties to do anything," said Tory. "They look at the government and say, 'Do I like these people and what they're doing or not?' By and large, the opposition parties don't even get a look. You could be standing on your head spitting silver dollars at the corner of Bloor and Yonge and nobody cares. That's what happened to us in '87. We could have gone around the province giving away money, just literally handing out cash, and it wouldn't have mattered." Even Harris's main campaign promise, a tax freeze, would be a way of attacking the Liberals over taxes.

The Tories, like the NDP, had no interest in fighting an issue campaign. Their decisions predetermined that the election would be fought not over substance but over image and perceptions of performance; they helped create conditions that ensured the outcome of the election would represent primarily a judgment of the incumbent Liberals and not an endorsement by voters of the positions of either challenger on the issues. Both the Tories and the NDP decided the election, for them, was no place to put forward policies.

With 86 percent of Ontarians unable to identify Harris as leader in the weeks before the election, the Tory strategists saw him as a blank sheet of paper ready to be filled in. But they were worried about the opposition and the media doing that job for them. One thing was a given: Harris was going to have plenty of trouble trying to walk, let alone run, with Mulroney draped around his neck. It was in spite of Mulroney and the proposed GST that the Tories had the shred of credibility on "management issues" on which they were basing their overtaxation attack strategy.

Gregg had confirmed that most people did not differentiate strongly between federal and provincial Tories. He suggested Harris try to draw clear lines to distinguish himself from Mulroney, show he was not accountable for federal policies such as the GST and assert an Ontario election was about Ontario issues. The strategists were split over how aggressively Harris should hammer Mulroney, concerned such attacks would alienate hard-core Conservatives without deterring anti-Mulroney protest votes. But they agreed the faster they could run away from their perceived links to the least-liked politician in Canada, the greater their chances of appealing to undecided voters and switchers from the Liberals.

The Tory deep-thinkers devoted considerable time to the issue of what to do with the "real" Mike Harris—the right-wing dinosaur many center-and-left Tories, along with a sizable chunk of the province's media, were certain they had seen during the leadership process. Harris's extreme views and his astonishing vacillations on vital policy areas were widely documented in the media, and the Tories cringed at the thought of the other party leaders or reporters raising his vulnerabilities at every opportunity on the campaign trail. Harris's record on user fees for visits to the doctor was a prime embarrassment: "I don't see anything wrong with $5 every time you access the system, say, for example, to a maximum of $100 a year," he said on April 21. On May 6 he stated "This province is also introducing a whole host of social programs that no other province can afford."

Harris was also eager to tell reporters he wanted to dump rent controls, scrap private sector pay equity, eliminate property tax rebates for the elderly and combine the provincial sales tax with the GST to create a new supertax he would extend to cover GST-exempt items ranging from visits to the doctor to groceries.

Harris had a rubber-ball approach to policy that threatened to undermine his credibility when he attempted to pull off the overtaxation lines the campaign would be built on. On March 6 he was quoted as saying he wanted to reduce provincial taxes; by May 13 he was reportedly ready to freeze them. On May 9 reporters found he wanted to freeze hiring in the public service and start cutting it back by 2 percent per year. Four days later he wanted to slash it; two months after that he was willing only to stop its growth. "We spent quite a bit of time working on those because we knew those were weaknesses," said Tory. "We spent quite a bit of time talking about that."

Early in the campaign, when challenged by reporters on such highlights of his record, Harris would variously alter his position, claim he had been quoted out of context or recant entirely. "Clearly there was some attempt to sort of recast some of those initiatives," said Tory. "The best way to deal with these things is to say, 'That was then and this is now, I've made a mistake or I've changed my mind.' I think people are looking for that right now." During the campaign's debate, Harris would set matters straight for everyone by announcing: "I am the only honest politician."

In spite of her efforts to encourage her supporters to rally around the new leader, Tory leadership loser Cunningham's attacks on Harris in the heat of battle also threatened to be dredged up at any time. "Mike," she told him publicly in April, "you want a party of the narrow right, a party that justifies its existence by being different and by being on the far right of the spectrum." In May she told a reporter, "Harris is yesterday's man. Appealing to Conservatives with the old tried and truism of the past is how we got into this mess to begin with."

In the weeks before the election, Harris often seemed determined to position himself as a poor alternative for voters. "They [the Liberals] know that Mike Harris and the PC party of Ontario really does need and could use a year," he told reporters on July 15. "We could very well use another year to get our financial situation in order, and our candidates in order, and to be as completely ready as we'd like to be for an election."

Harris was as accurate as he was up-front. The Tories guaranteed themselves organizational problems for a 1990 election by ordering their ridings not to nominate candidates until the leadership contest was over. Even after the ban was lifted they were slow to get their organization cranked up. Only about 30 of the province's 130 ridings would have Tory candidates nominated by the time the election was called; about 17 were identified but not nominated at that time and in more than 50 ridings, the Tories did not have a clue who they were going to run until well into the campaign. The Tory campaign strategy would acknowledge these shortfalls by targeting only 50 to 60 seats as having the potential for victory.

From Gregg's earliest pre-election poll for Harris the Tories had a strong sense of where their overtaxation attack strategy could send voters. Gregg asked his respondents which party they thought was the most likely to hold the line on excessive tax increases. By a wide margin, people said the NDP. "It just blew our minds," said Gillies. Through Davis, Miller, Grossman and Brandt, the Tories had always been picked by Ontarians as the most reliable managers of the public purse. "They certainly did not trust the Liberal administration any more on taxes and government spending; they thought it was way out of control," said Gillies. "They didn't attribute any great virtue to us on that same issue, because of the way they perceived the federal Tories."

With an attack strategy that moved voters off the Liberals, the Tories were ready to let loose with what Grossman described as "a fairly effective hard-hitting campaign by a party that was an ineligible receiver downfield." But the Tories did not enter the campaign dreaming their attacks would do anything more damaging than chip away at Peterson's majority by dislodging Liberal voters. Only late in the campaign would they have to decide whether to back off their attacks—or maintain them, knowing they would be helping to send Rae into the premier's office.

Note: Documents filed by the three parties with the Election Finances Commission in 1991 revealed the following expenditures on polling in 1990: The Ontario Liberal Party made a payment to Goldfarb Consultants of $370,000 during the campaign period, in addition to a payment of $184,500 to Goldfarb for "campaign consulting" after the campaign, for total campaign period research and polling expenditures of about $550,000. Goldfarb was also paid $40,000 by OLP for work before the campaign. The New Democratic Party reported research and polling expenditures during the campaign of $114,000, including $112,000 paid to Viewpoints Research. Viewpoints also received a payment of $9,000 for work before the campaign. The NDP paid Donegan Consulting $24,700 for research before the campaign. The Progressive Conservative Party reported research and polling expenditures during the campaign of $105,000, including $99,000 paid to Decima Research, and $6,000 to John Mykytyshyn, the private pollster described in Chapter 10. No payments to Decima for work outside the campaign period were reported.

6

A Platform and a Reason for Going

We knew we were flimsy as hell on the substance, we knew we were flimsy on the focus, but it wasn't any sense of impending doom.

*–DAVID MACNAUGHTON,
LIBERAL STRATEGIST*

"Beth, you're going to be like Gordon; Kathy, you're going to be like Hershell," Peterson told Webster and Robinson early in June. In those few words the premier laid out his expectation of how the duties of the Liberal campaign director and campaign chair would be divided—to replicate the team of Ashworth and Ezrin that had delivered victory in 1987. Peterson seemed to be searching for a level of comfort with the management of the campaign. But he was confirming what the two already knew: Robinson had decided early on that she would command the policy and communications functions of the campaign; Webster would be in charge of organization.

At the beginning of June the strategy committee was still spinning its wheels dealing with the broad-strokes "theming" of the campaign. As Robinson continued to be occupied with the strategy committee and its problems, Webster and Dan Gagnier, when he was not busy with Meech, were left with the task of overlaying substance onto the style represented by Peterson's image. They decided they had to take up the slack and started pulling every available lever: the premier's policy staff began to work with Nixon aides from treasury and deputy cabinet secretary Bernard Shapiro to assemble a platform. The group merged Martin Goldfarb's recommended policy priorities with suggestions sought from ministers and their deputies. Peterson's policy chief Jan Whitelaw moved to the fore as coordinator of the Liberal platform.

The strategists and policy staff debated the philosophy of what their platform should look like. Although they did not meet regularly to thrash out the platform, the strategists, touching base through Robinson and Webster, settled on going ahead with a low-cost platform that would be represented by a series of inexpensive promises.

The strategists accepted Goldfarb's premise that, on the verge of tougher times, high-dollar programs were best supplanted by a "value-driven" campaign promoting policy and middle-class values. That recommendation represented a change in strategic thinking for Goldfarb who, in David MacNaughton's view, "has often said that the guy who wins campaigns is the first who promises the most."

But Goldfarb had sensed a sea change in public opinion and convinced his colleagues, as MacNaughton said, "that going into this campaign with a general concern about waste and inefficiency in government and taxes, anybody who went out and promised the moon—it was part of the problem that contributed to the defeat in the '88 federal election." The strategists had strong allies among Peterson's most influential staff. Whitelaw sensed a public concern she described as "a real correlation that people were drawing between election promises and increased taxes in the next budget." Nixon's staff were pressing for a platform that would start coming to grips with program growth.

When Robinson reported the strategists' consensus to cabinet in early June she found strong support for a low-cost platform among ministers who had spent nearly three years struggling to implement the costly promises of the 1987 campaign. "A consensus did evolve around the fact that we could not buy an election," said one minister. "But with what we were told the polling was showing, we thought we wouldn't need to. There wasn't a person in that room who didn't think we'd get returned with at least a reduced majority."

The Liberals had another reason for keeping their campaign promises low-cost. Cabinet secretary Peter Barnes and deputy secretary Shapiro were proceeding on the Tomorrow Project, an enormous reorganization of the government that promised to slash the fat in the interface between ministries, potentially eliminating thousands of public service jobs and cutting hundreds of millions in annual cash requirements from the province's treasury—all while improving the delivery of the province's services to people.

The overhaul had been pushed by Peterson's first cabinet secretary Bob Carman. Although only in its infancy, the Tomorrow Project helped clear the decks for an early election. A clean break was needed, the Liberals believed, before they could plunge into a massive and politically dangerous undertaking that would get to the very heart of the Ontario government's structural inefficiencies. The likelihood of giving the Tomorrow Project a green light after the election reinforced the need for a platform that would demonstrate a political commitment by the Liberals to cut programs and stop making costly promises. A conservatively priced, fiscally responsible platform, the Liberals thought, would earn them precious credibility as they attempted to justify the project's painful cuts and dislocations in the years ahead.

For the Liberal platform the strategists rejected costly economic initiatives proposed in the spring 1990 budget. "The budget provided for being exploded into a platform for the campaign," said Nixon's policy advisor George Cooke. The budget's plan for a massive retraining program, supporting the industrial restructuring Ontario needed to deal with free trade, would receive only token representation in the platform. A labor market adjustment plan that served as the cornerstone of the Liberals' skills training and retraining program had fallen between the cracks in the spring. Other budget programs springing from the Premier's Council on Technology and such high-cost promises as a $5-billion transportation plan could have sent Peterson on an old-fashioned campaign spending spree. The strategists and policy staff weighed those options but decided frugality should prevail as the timely campaign theme.

The pieces of the low-cost platform came together late in June and were sent for testing by Goldfarb's vice-president Doug Hurley with five focus groups composed of Liberal and Liberal-leaning voters. The participants endorsed initiatives that would soon become the Liberal offerings to voters. Among them: scaled-down skills training improvements to create a "science and technology culture"; programs for clean air, improved water quality and expanded recycling; drug and impaired driving crackdowns; in-home care for seniors and persons with disabilities; a breakfast program for children.

The focus groups rejected two initiatives that were dropped like hot coals from the Liberal campaign platform: an "Ontario Investment Fund" and a mandatory employment equity plan for private sector employers.

The Ontario Investment Fund was to have set up a government-appointed board to use Canada Pension Plan funds to invest in Ontario firms picked to improve the province's international competitiveness. The groups did not understand the concept; Hurley said it prompted concerns about "putting people's pension money at risk" and the potential for "political patronage to help 'friends' of those in power."

Hurley's groups turned thumbs down to private sector employment equity for "racial minorities, persons with disabilities, women and aboriginal people." The groups lashed out,

Hurley reported: "There is a concern that this kind of policy is pandering too much to minorities. There is a tendency to view this kind of policy as putting the needs and interests of minorities and immigrants ahead of those of 'Canadians' and there is strong negative reaction to this." Employment equity was promptly dropped from the platform. Whitelaw found Peterson fearful of a recession-prompted "racial backlash in terms of, 'I've lost my job, why should they get help?' That was dominant in his mind and I would say he made a conscious decision," she said.

In its final form the Liberal platform would cost little more than $200 million in "new money" (funds not previously accounted for in a budget), much less than their 1987 platform.

As he watched the low-cost platform come together, Mac-Naughton was uncomfortable. Along with some of Nixon's and Peterson's staff he believed the Liberals needed a sharper economic edge in their platform to address people's concerns about the deterioration of the economy, excessive government spending and tax hikes. MacNaughton wanted something that would lure voters into the Liberal tent, catching their eye and forcing them to focus on the Liberal's economic agenda. He decided to devise a plan to reallocate tax dollars that would show the Liberals could set priorities and demonstrate fiscal responsibility. The "mismanaging" federal Tories would provide a convenient foil.

MacNaughton and the sympathetic staffers drew up a program of spending cuts worth $900 million, including scuttling Toronto's ballet-opera house by withdrawing provincial support for the project; selling the province's shares in Suncor, worth about $350 million; slashing 3,000 public service jobs, and saving $100 million on the Ontario Drug Benefit Plan by having benefit recipients pay pharmacy dispensing fees while the government continued to pay for drugs. Further actions were outlined, including program reductions across dozens of ministries, that could have raised the cuts to between $1.5 and $2.5 billion.

Early in June Liberal staffers, MacNaughton, Robinson and Webster met to put the pieces together. MacNaughton stood and sketched out a massive balance sheet: potential policy announcements on one side, spending cuts to pay for them on the other.

The plan for the campaign, MacNaughton suggested, was "to start by saying we were going to cut and then the rest of the week would be, 'Here's how we're going to spend this money.' Principally to drive the NDP nuts on the first day with the cuts and they'd then come and kick the shit out of us and say, 'How are we going to spend the money?'" The goal was to force the NDP to choose either supporting the cuts, or increasing taxes or digging a deficit to pay for new promises. MacNaughton thought the strategy would identify the NDP as the party of taxation while the Harris Tories would remain tainted by their links to Mulroney, whose GST defined his stand on tax hikes.

But the cuts were not to be. "We had gone over this stuff with the premier," said MacNaughton, "not the specifics but the generalities of it, and I was of the view that it was all coming together and the next thing I would see would be the whole thing in an integrated way." Instead, after a week of consideration by Peterson, Nixon, their staff and others on the strategy committee, the plan was dumped. When the cuts were examined in detail, complications mounted up. Each cut had downsides considered too risky to deal with in a campaign, and as the list of problems grew, enthusiasm for the program fizzled. While each cut "might make one segment of the electorate happy, it would annoy another interest group and therefore there would be too much muddle and backlash to the cut," said Whitelaw. "You would lose the overall message that the government was trying to reallocate to meet its priorities."

The Liberals' decision to reject a program of cuts and enter the campaign with a simple, low-cost platform was also linked to the belief of the treasury's economic analysts that the recession, while looming closer, would not be lengthy or severe. "I don't think anybody really appreciated it would come as quickly or be as deep," said Nixon's policy advisor Cooke. "It was supposed to come more slowly and be far more shallow, and everybody was wrong on that. There was also a hesitancy to spend your way into a recession. You want to spend your way out." Cooke and treasury officials had a project of their own on the go: developing a set of recession-relief programs, including a $750-million capital works scheme to create jobs that could be brought forward to stimulate Ontario's economy when a downturn hit.

Had the proponents of the cuts held firm, their plan could have provided the Liberal platform with a sharper recession-protection edge in the climate of plummeting consumer confidence and anxiety that would take hold in Ontario late in the summer. But as the campaign drew closer MacNaughton chose not to fight. "I basically rolled over," he said, "because I just figured even if we screwed it up, we couldn't screw it up all that bad."

For months Goldfarb had been pushing his own ideas for the Liberal platform, dramatically different from MacNaughton's. He wanted Peterson to announce that, should the sale of Toronto-based Consumers Gas to British Gas be approved by the Ontario Energy Board, cabinet would reverse the board's decision on the grounds the Liberal government was not going to sell an Ontario utility to a foreign company. The strategists and Liberal staff looked warily at the proposal: complicating matters for MacNaughton was the fact his government relations firm was under contract to British Gas to assist in securing the takeover. It was also recognized that Goldfarb was advocating the veto in spite of past business ties to Consumers Gas and executive-level friendship with the firm. But the proposal was rejected for practical reasons that kept potential business considerations out of the mix: the group agreed announcing a government veto in advance of the board's decision would abrogate due process and call the board's independence into question.

Goldfarb's proposal represented a view of liberalism that was left leaning and nationalistic. As a Trudeau Liberal, Goldfarb was enamored of nationalism, individual rights over collective rights, compromise among competing interests and government intervention in the economy; he was not overwrought about actions that would increase the deficit. Like Trudeau, Goldfarb was vehemently opposed to the Meech Lake Accord. Goldfarb was convinced economic nationalism always sold in Ontario, and felt a veto of the Consumers Gas takeover would be widely supported. He also suggested Peterson speak out against the privatization of Petro-Canada by the federal Tories. "One of the pieces of advice he had was that we should go on the nationalistic kick, with absolutely no evidence in the data I saw that economic nationalism was the thing," said MacNaughton. "It was a throwback to the Trudeau years."

Again the split in the Liberal brain trust was polarized around MacNaughton and Goldfarb. This time the differences were more profound than an argument about the methodology or purposes of polling: they were rooted in strongly differing views about liberalism and what it should mean in the 1990s.

MacNaughton's view held that there are limits to government activity and spending. Control of deficits and increased productivity and competitiveness are to be pursued, and nationalist economic policies and government intervention are not the optimum methods through which Canadians can achieve prosperity.

"Governments in this country have to fundamentally redefine the role of government," believed MacNaughton. "The old notions of strong central government, weak central government, activist government are completely out of touch with reality, both from a fiscal point of view and the ability to effectively deliver what you're promising."

MacNaughton's program of spending cuts was an example of Liberal economics seen through his view of liberalism. "I tried to encourage David [Peterson] to look at the assets side of the government's balance sheet rather than simply looking at taxes and the spending side," he said, "to look at the huge assets and start using them as leverage to both raise money and accomplish your goals rather than always looking at simple spending programs and delivery by public servants." MacNaughton and like-minded Liberals called for more partnerships among the private sector, community and volunteer groups and the government as a way to provide better services. He also espoused increased cooperation and coordination between the federal, provincial and municipal levels of government, especially around fiscal planning and delivery of services, to control spending and reduce taxes while improving services. When it came to satisfying interest groups, this view of liberalism held that in the 1990s there are too many interest groups and intractable positions to be effectively brokered. MacNaughton believed politicians cannot always forge consensus but must show leadership and make hard choices.

MacNaughton backed off from fighting to have his ideas included in the Liberal platform, not only because he felt the Liberals had an insurmountable lead but also to protect what traces of cooperation could still be found among members of the embattled strategy committee. "I'd gotten into a fight about the polling and decided you can only sustain a certain number of fights, combined with the fact that I've got other things in my life to deal with," he said. "Rather than getting into a great pissing match, I would just say, 'Okay, fine. Bugger off.'"

The strategists' chemistry problem played a part in locking the Liberals into a narrow platform without a sweeping economic plan and minimized their discussion of options and alternatives. Goldfarb opposed the cuts; Ezrin vacillated, depending on the difficulty of implementing whatever component was being discussed. But underlying all the strategists' discussion was a sense their platform was not a life-and-death proposition: with the polls looking good and Peterson's image positive, they could win even if their campaign was less than perfect.

As the election approached MacNaughton did huddle with Gagnier to contemplate a backup plan—a sort of auxiliary parachute. "Gagnier and I talked," said MacNaughton, "and decided that what we would do was we would see how it was going for the first week or so, and if we started to have problems then we could get Hershell, you know, to make it up, make up some other stuff as we went along. We knew we were flimsy as hell on the substance, we knew we were flimsy on the focus, but it wasn't any sense of impending doom." But MacNaughton, Gagnier and Ezrin would not get a chance to reach for that second rip-cord.

Peterson had little to do with creating the Liberal platform. "He was like an audience; he wasn't a participant," said Whitelaw. "He certainly interjected on a couple of things, but he did not play an active role in determining what would or wouldn't be there." But Peterson supported the theory behind a low-cost platform that did not have a strong recession-protection emphasis. He believed he should not lead a charge into economic oblivion.

"If you get too negative it becomes a self-fulfilling prophecy," Peterson said. "So you've got to be very, very careful about not talking yourself into a recession. You listen to the best economists in the world and a large percentage of what causes a recession very often is the psychology: if people are negative they don't spend, if people are positive they do spend, and so you've got to be very, very careful you don't tilt the psychology adversely against the economy."

Peterson's ministers also played a part in creating a Liberal platform that was not hard-hitting and innovative, but safe and unobtrusive. They made that contribution in the same way they ensured that the activities of cabinet and the decisions of the government in the months leading up to the election were free from controversy. Cabinet informally created, in the spring of 1990, what was referred to none too jokingly as "the October List," a repository for controversial decisions that could wait until after a September election.

"Employment equity, extending pay equity, the doctors' negotiations—they all went on the October List," admitted a member of cabinet's policy and priorities board. "Every nondecision was driven by election preparedness. The polling was driving us and leading us not to make decisions." One policy option, expanding pay equity, was put off to avoid a backlash from the province's business community in the spring's teetering economic climate. Two cabinet submissions on employment equity were brought forward and rejected during the same period.

Peterson's ministers did not expect to be directly involved in the detail of the campaign strategy and platform. "The assumption was always that the strategy committee would come from the premier's office and outsiders," said a senior minister; keeping elected members out of the mix had worked fine in the two previous elections and few were prepared to argue with success.

Some ministers expecting a strategy and platform to back up an economic rationale for calling the election thought the "good stuff" in the platform would emerge magically from the premier as it did in 1987, when Ezrin churned out policy and programs overnight.

What they did expect to be consulted on was the political climate of the day. But Peterson's six ministers with regional political responsibilities, all experienced campaigners and political veterans, were not invited to meet with Robinson or the strategy committee to discuss plans for the campaign or contribute their views on the political mood in the province in the months before the election. Members of the group might have raised concerns about the strength and resilience of Peterson's image based on what they had been picking up on the hustings. Instead, without the benefit of that critique, Robinson and the strategists toiled covertly, convinced their view of the world was right: Peterson was a hot commodity with a solid core of Liberal support and a Peterson-centered campaign would pull them through. Rather than fighting to be heard, admitted one senior political minister, "We didn't bother pushing it. We just rolled over."

As Liberal staffers worked up the campaign platform, the Liberal caucus found itself stuck out in the bleacher seats, straining for a glimpse of the action. Robinson provided the caucus with progress reports that explained the strategists' process and the themes for the platform: the economy, the environment, social policy—but no detail. Determined that their local concerns be heard, the Liberal backbenchers formed their own campaign policy groups and fed suggestions to Gagnier, who passed them on at meetings of the strategy committee. The strategists found the caucus supported their central themes but the lists of local needs—a hospital here, a highway there—were rejected. Buying votes with local goodies was deemed a dated approach.

By July, as Peterson departed for a pre-election vacation, most of the Liberal strategists and staff hoped their low-cost platform responded adequately to the anxieties of Ontarians facing the possibilities of harder times. "The platform itself was designed to target what were seen to be key vulnerabilities and show that the government was managing the change that was necessary in the economy, and to try to make that change tangible to people," said Whitelaw. "If you're losing your job because of free trade or the recession or global competitiveness in your sector, here's what we are doing to help you as an individual, and it was designed to try and be more touchy-feely and relevant to the individual. But there certainly could have been more stated."

"The platform we came up with was not a platform," charged Goldfarb. "It was a bureaucratic managerial document that didn't help people. It wasn't a political document. It was a list of things that the bureaucracy were going to do." Mac-Naughton, his program of cuts gone, was deflated: "It wasn't strung together; it didn't hang together particularly well." And Vince Borg, who would spend the campaign on the road trying to help Peterson sell the promises, asked "How does your mother relate to this stuff? Is there any resonance here to this policy stuff? Like, who cares about this? None of our stuff connected." But as the campaign approached, it was all the stuff they had to go on.

* * *

Since the end of 1988 the Liberal cabinet had fretted that if Meech failed, Peterson would persist in putting forward concerns about national unity as a rationale for calling an election in Ontario. That December the Supreme Court of Canada struck down a portion of Bill 178, Quebec's sign law, ruling that French-only signs and advertisements constituted an unreasonable restriction on the Charter of Rights and Freedoms' free speech guarantee. Quebec responded by invoking the notwithstanding clause in the Charter, overriding the guarantee.

To Peterson, the events planted a seed of anti-Quebec feeling that could lead to the death of Meech. "It is my belief that the thing that killed Meech was Bill 178," he said. "The mood shifted after 178." Polls confirmed Peterson's belief. A spring 1989 Decima poll showed 76 percent of Canadians outside Quebec opposed the bill; most felt it would hurt francophones outside Quebec and provoke an anti-French backlash; 60 percent said the law would hurt Meech's chance of being passed by all the provinces.

But as many Ontarians developed hardening attitudes against Quebec's actions and Meech, Peterson continued to back the deal and maintain his support for his old friend Robert Bourassa, in spite of Bill 178. "I was totally against it," said Peterson, "But then what do I do, turn on him? The country had a vested interest in him doing well. We each had to help him keep credible in Quebec." Worries that Peterson was getting too preoccupied with national unity, and becoming too closely identified with "Boo-boo" and "Lyin' Brian" Mulroney prompted a memorable exchange early in 1989 around the Liberal cabinet table.

"We appreciate your efforts at trying to hold this country together," a cabinet veteran ventured, "but it's going to kill us politically."

"Look," said Peterson, "in this business, there are some things you die for." He would repeat the same words with no less conviction in a post-election cabinet meeting in September 1990.

Meech discussions devoured great chunks of time in Peterson's cabinet meetings in 1989 and 1990. Attorney General Scott produced five possible scenarios for how Meech might collapse and the aftermath of each; the options for Ontario in each case were exhaustively debated. But the discussion also zeroed in on the possibility that, if Meech failed, Peterson might try to work the ensuing national unity crisis into some sort of reason for calling an election. The fears escalated as the final round of Meech talks approached in 1990.

On June 3 Peterson and Ontario's delegation of a dozen lawyers and constitutional advisors arrived in Ottawa. The Liberal campaign strategy committee was represented by MacNaughton, Ezrin and Gagnier. For a frustrating, complicated week, Peterson applied himself to trying to forge a deal he believed was critical to preserving the country. There were serious setbacks. An Ontario strategy paper on how to discredit Meech's opponents leaked out, to Peterson's embarrassment and anger. The backroom nature of the process chosen by Mulroney for the talks was emerging as a concern for all the participants. The risk of failure was constantly on Peterson's mind.

One night, Peterson walked from his hotel with a handful of staffers, and found a few well-chosen words for a speechwriter.

"I want you to write three speeches for me," Peterson said. "One for a success, one for a failure."

"And the third one?" the writer asked.

"Make it a suicide note," said Peterson.

The campaign strategists were already at work on a strategy for dealing with Meech's collapse. Ezrin and MacNaughton worked up a scenario and a speech to assist Peterson if he had to leave Ottawa without being part of a deal. As the week wore on it appeared more and more likely he would have to use them.

Late on the Friday of that long week, the first ministers' best efforts bearing no fruit, Peterson appealed to his advisors for a way to break the deadlock. At 4 p.m. the closed session recessed and a disheartened Peterson sat down with his team.

"It's all over," he told the delegation. "It's lost. We're coming back at six but it's going to break up. [Newfoundland premier] Clyde Wells is not going to sign and the thing is going to collapse. Unless anybody here has any bright ideas?"

"What about giving up some Senate seats?" suggested James MacPherson, the dean of Osgoode Hall law school.

"Well now, that's interesting," said Peterson. "You guys go and discuss it." Peterson left the group to work out the details of the proposal, sent Gagnier to pitch the idea to the federal delegation and walked to his hotel room, where he phoned Shelley in grim resignation. "I could lose my job because of this decision I'm going to make," he told her.

Peterson's advisors began to have second thoughts about the idea. "As the matter was debated a little more, the tide began to turn," said one. "It was probably something the premier should not do." Lawyer Rob Prichard, president of the University of Toronto, was dispatched with a memo listing the group's reasons for rejecting the proposal. He arrived after the first ministers had resumed their closed session; Peterson was back in the meeting room. Prichard could only wait until Peterson came out.

"Our advice, premier, is that you should not give up the seats," said Prichard. "Do you want to hear why?"

"I've already done it," said Peterson. He wheeled and went back into the session. Prichard tore up the memo. The offer proved critical to making a tentative Meech deal come together.

When Peterson returned to Toronto, Ezrin called him with a message. "Well, I guess I was really wrong," he said to his old boss. "I was certain this wasn't going to work."

*   *   *

The tentative Meech deal neither helped nor hindered the Liberal strategists or the Liberals who watched the campaign train continue to roll along in June. Worsening economic prospects still made a fall election likely, and while the Meech talks were initially successful, they were creating more problems. Peterson had been involved in a closed-door process that was heavily criticized and the deal had many hoops to go through—most significantly Wells and Manitoba native MLA Elijah Harper.

For two harrowing weeks in June, Peterson watched and waited as the deal fell apart. He was first off the mark to accept Wells' invitation to speak to Newfoundland's House of Assembly in support of the deal. He watched with frustration the decisions by Wells not to allow a vote on the deal and by Harper to stand fast on a procedural challenge that delayed introduction of the Accord into Manitoba's legislature until it was too late to complete ratification. Both succeeded in scuttling Meech by delaying ratification past Ottawa's deadline. Mulroney evoked nationwide disbelief and contempt with his cynical choice of words to describe the developments: Meech was "a roll of the dice," he was widely quoted as saying.

"When I read that roll-the-dice thing, I was almost sick to my stomach," said Peterson. "It ceded the moral high ground to Clyde Wells, who was very fragile at that point. It looked so cavalier, and it wasn't a roll-the-dice situation." Suddenly Peterson was stuck in a difficult bind. He had linked himself intimately with a failed deal, a questionable process and Mulroney and Bourassa at the worst possible time.

*   *   *

Meech's death on June 22 brought Peterson face to face with the reality of a fall election. His conviction began to steel. "The reason I called the election was I did not want an election in the province of Ontario in the future that would be a referendum on what's happening in Quebec," he said, referring to the activities of the Bélanger-Campeau commission on Quebec's future relationship with the rest of Canada. "I feared the consequences. I thought the situation would become absolutely ripe for oversimplified politics with a racist overtone that would be so destructive as everything reverberated across the country. I thought the voices of moderation and conciliation would be drowned in an impossible situation that would do irreparable harm to the country. That's why I did it—and I thought we could win. I thought we could have a strong hand to deal with things in a sensitive way to try to keep the country together in some semblance where you could recognize it."

Peterson made clear to close advisors his will to put his nation-building objectives ahead of his own political fortunes. "I would rather lose the election," he told Gagnier. "This is something worth being defeated over, rather than have an election a year and a half or so later that would be extremely divisive."

Peterson heard from members of his family about the critical decision. In July, Marie Peterson told her son not to call the election. "Clarence and I would go for walks along Dundas Street in London east, in his core area," she said. "I could just feel when we'd go for walks and I'd see people with poorer clothes than they had two years ago. I just had a feeling about it: people are not going to like this." But observations about the economic downturn were only a part of her motherly advice. "In Canada, there's no idealism," she told him. "People are becoming cynical of politics. You are the most credible man in

Canada today politically. Don't disappoint people. Because people rightly or wrongly will think you are becoming an opportunist."

"The mood wasn't right, but I feel he felt the mood would get worse," said Shelley Peterson. "I was in the end convinced that he had to do it, but right until the day that he announced it, I was advising him to back out. Just because of this angry mood that I was feeling in my bones. I just had this horrible feeling that something awful would happen. In the end, the reason he made his decision was very noble. I understood David's motives completely. I was behind him 100 percent at that point."

Driving for an early election also closed the loop on Peterson's decision not to run for the federal Liberal leadership. After deciding he could make his best contribution to national unity from the position of premier of Ontario rather than federal opposition leader, it was clear to him that he had to time his election call to reinforce his position and extend his mandate, if he were to continue to serve as a nation-builder.

But while Peterson believed he had to call an early election, he was reluctant to use warnings about Quebec's future troubles as his rationale. He feared that would antagonize and alienate Quebecers—and impair his ability to act as a conciliator between Quebec and English Canada and deliver a future solution to the constitutional impasse. "We knew what his real reason was," said one minister. "We knew in his heart of hearts that was why, but he couldn't say it because of the fear of antagonizing Quebec.

Peterson turned to his constitutional advisors to back up his personal rationale. He got what he wanted on July 12 at a dinner meeting with five of his top constitutional experts. "They all felt that he was correct," said his policy advisor Patrick Monahan, "that if an election were held a year from now, it would tend to become a referendum on Quebec's place in Canada. They also felt that if there were to be an election in the summer of 1990, the Quebec issue should not become a focus for the campaign."

Peterson's ministers understood his reasoning but were certain his pro-Meech stance was unpopular. They were ready to support him in calling an early election but rather than make his concerns about national unity the focus, they wanted to put forward the rationale that the Liberals needed a renewed mandate to guide the province through worsening economic times. "Meech's failure made a decent rationale for Peterson," said a top minister, "but it wasn't what we were prepared to stand behind as the reason—that had to be tied in to the economy."

Peterson accepted that his rationale would not be a winner with Ontarians. "There was no tolerance level for those reasons," he realized. "Frankly, I don't think my view of the situation was particularly popular. I'm not sure that's the stuff of which great elections are made. What do I say, 'I'm going to have an election now so we can have a strong hand to deal with Quebec whatever they come up with as a result of this commission'? It doesn't fly. You can't turn that into a campaign. You had to campaign on other issues, the record and other things, the economy and all that kind of stuff."

For months realistic Liberals were not bucking the tide of an early election but grasping for the right reason to justify it. Now the need was urgent. In cabinet after Meech's demise, one minister voiced the thoughts of her colleagues. "We have to have a clear reason for going," she told Peterson, "and we have to be prepared to get it across clearly and stand by it." Peterson was ready with an answer: "We will," he said.

Peterson knew his national unity agenda could be served by coming up with an economic rationale for an election. "The world was changing and there was the onslaught of recession," he said. ""We all knew about that, about the deterioration of the economy. We knew the boom was over. There was lots of anxiety about that, about jobs and other issues as well." Supporting an economic focus for an election, Peterson believed, were "the problems and consequences of free trade and the interest rates, which were continuing to be much higher than Michael Wilson had forecast. All of us were victims of that and every other bloody problem."

Three weeks before the election would be called, the Liberal strategy committee convened again—a rare meeting with all of its members in attendance. Peterson came to listen—the last time he would meet with the group—and Borg, Whitelaw and other campaign staff joined in.

Robinson and Webster knew the meeting was critical to the final stages of ramping-up to the campaign: the strategists had to review the strategy, the campaign team had to understand it, everyone had to decide what the platform would finally be and the premier's tour, again directed by wagon master Doug Kirkpatrick, had to be matched to the platform announcements. But those details took a backseat at the meeting to one task: ensuring Peterson would adhere to a plan to keep national unity in the background of the campaign. The strategists were guided by their strong sense that Canadians were "Meeched-out."

"People were trying to break through to him constantly at that point," said Webster. "It was that those are not issues people are responding to. Everybody did a very good job of reiterating that. They all understood by that point the numbers clearly said people do not like his position on Meech."

The strategists could reach firm agreement on only a single point: Peterson would get only one kick at the constitutional can during the campaign—a major speech. "The strategy committee spent most of its time deciding on the timing of it so that it had the minimal negative impact," said Webster. "That seemed to be much more important than the day-to-day, bread-and-butter issues. The strategy committee was preoccupied with how we get through this with minimum damage." Peterson accepted the one-speech limit. The group agreed he should also attend a meeting of premiers in Winnipeg during the campaign.

But the rationale to be used for calling the election remained undecided. Ideas were kicked around among the strategists and staffers, all with an economic slant, but no conclusion could be reached. A solution was proposed: Peterson's staff would write half-a-dozen different rationales and Goldfarb would test them with focus groups to find the best one.

When the meeting ended it was clear to Robinson that vital campaign chores were still not getting done. The strategists were not meeting regularly or working together and the group's volatility and mutual distrust were rendering it dysfunctional. If the campaign were to come together for the Liberals, Robinson decided, she and Webster would have to take total control of it. "Once Kathy and Beth were on it full time," said Gagnier, "any concept of a well-managed, well-focused strategy committee ceased to exist."

Robinson saw a further need to divide up the campaign duties to get the job done. She had spent little time on the details of the campaign's policy and communications; Webster had been doing most of that work for weeks. Three weeks before the campaign Robinson insisted she and Webster reverse the Ashworth-Ezrin roles Peterson had envisioned for them.

"I feel my strengths lie in doing more of what Gordon did," she told Webster. That meant giving marching orders to the campaign organization and dealing with ministers and other candidates. Webster was given Ezrin's policy and communications jobs and faced the monstrous task of pulling together the details of each plank in the Liberal platform. "I just about freaked," said Webster. "It was three weeks before, and I just thought, 'Holy cow.'" After nearly two years of ramping up, the Liberals at the heart of the campaign were scrambling, as one observed, to get their "feces correlated."

*　　*　　*

"People love his main-streeting and picnics. They love to see him mingling with ordinary, everyday people." Seizing on that advice in Goldfarb's report on Peterson's image, Robinson and Webster looked for opportunities before the campaign to place Peterson in high-profile situations that would let him interact with people in front of the television cameras.

A golden opportunity surfaced in early July: a charity event in downtown Toronto, sponsored by Shopsy's and the Toronto Blue Jays. The setup seemed ideal: Peterson could mingle with office workers on their lunch hour as the cameras rolled. Peterson's press aides were sent to persuade members of the Queen's Park press gallery to attend.

When the day arrived a horde of reporters and cameramen showed up for the event at an outdoor cafe. To their dismay they were treated to an all-too-familiar sight: Peterson, wearing a red apron, was passing out hot dogs to the crowd. Reporters might have been even more perturbed had they known that many of the smiling faces belonged to Liberal staff from Queen's Park, who had been ordered to attend to ensure a large and friendly gathering.

The scene, and a few others like it after Meech's demise, incensed many reporters, who recalled Peterson's summer picnics of previous years. The Liberals, they suspected, were about to favor style over substance again, with an election coming up. Inexperienced at dealing with the media, Robinson and Webster underestimated the cynicism about Peterson that had been building among many reporters. In the weeks before the election call they placed Peterson in situations that exacerbated that feeling and helped make members of the media more wary of the Liberals. And more determined to ask the tough questions that would make Peterson earn re-election.

As Robinson and other Liberals worked toward election preparation, they repeatedly fell back on Goldfarb's May report on Peterson's image. That report had backed up their plan to make sure "the premier is the campaign." But after Meech's collapse, they did not seek a new report to update their understanding of perceptions of Peterson's image in the wake of the failure, among either Liberals or Ontarians at large. Robinson believed such updating was taken care of through other research for the Liberal campaign, when the platform, possible rationales and campaign advertisements were tested with focus groups. "You automatically test the image when you're testing the advertising and the poster and those sorts of things," she said.

But the Liberals did not specifically test whether Peterson's image, in which they were placing so much faith, had been changed by the events of Meech. They would go ahead with a Peterson-centered campaign without carefully determining whether, or to what extent, Meech had scratched Peterson's Teflon coating and settled instead for warning Peterson away from talking about national unity.

*　　*　　*

On July 19 and 20 four focus group interview sessions were held at Goldfarb's offices to discover how people would react to six possible rationales for an early election. Three sessions were conducted by Hurley. The first was conducted by Goldfarb. Eleven men and women, including Liberals, Liberal-leaners and Liberal "rejecters," were assembled for Goldfarb; each would collect $30 for about two hours of his or her time and opinions.

"We're gonna bounce some ideas off you and see what you think," Goldfarb announced as he took his place at the head of the long table. "I think you'll have a good experience tonight. There's lots to do and interesting stuff to talk about. So first of all, first name, and what you do for a living."

Around the room Goldfarb went, noting the names of each participant: Tammy, an office administrative assistant; Stephen, a Canada Post employee; Mary, retired; Sid, a real estate agent; Bert, a part-time office temp; Ken, retired; Veronica, a baby sitter; Anne, a computer trainer; Luke, a printer; Reign, an office temp; Ed, a computer operator.

"Some of you may have heard talk about an election," said Goldfarb. "I want to play with a few ideas. I'm gonna read a statement to you, and I'm gonna playact, and I want you to respond to the statement. I want to read a statement on why there would be an election called at this time, and tell me how you respond to the rationale in that statement and the way I've expressed the idea why we want to call an election or why somebody might want to call an election."

Goldfarb pulled out the first of the six rationales written by Peterson's staff. "'For several years, the federal government has been leading Canadians along a dangerous and harmful path,'" he read, citing free trade, the GST and other federal Tory policies. "'We need to send a strong and clear message now that the federal government must change its course.' How do you respond to what I have read as the reason for calling the election?"

"I feel it's a good time for an election because I feel the federal government has flip-flopped so much the time is right," said Mary. "People want an election, they want to get that commitment."

"A commitment from————?" Goldfarb prompted.

"The provincial government to put pressure on the federal government," Mary answered.

"I think it's right to have an election," said Tammy. "Perhaps change the course and clear up some issues and state that we want things to be clarified."

"But remember, this is a provincial election," Goldfarb said. "Why is this the right statement to make if the party in power in Ontario wants to have an election?"

"We're going to lose parts of Canada," said Ed with concern. "It makes me think that eventually we're going to lose it all, just might as well join the whole thing to America."

"But what about this statement?" Goldfarb interjected. "What does it mean to you?"

"At the present time we have a provincial government which has a Liberal party in position which has a very strong majority," said Sid. "I don't see an issue where there is a necessity for having a provincial election, because the major issue is at the federal level."

"What the provincial government should be doing is tightening up on the social services that are offered to people," said Anne. "Freeloaders, our taxes are keeping them all." The room hummed in agreement.

"Hold on a second," Goldfarb interrupted. "Let me see if I can keep you focused. Does this statement explain why, satisfy you why, they would want to call an election?"

"No, because that's federal," Anne concluded.

Goldfarb tried the second rationale: "'Canada is headed for some uncertain times. Economically, we may be facing a recession. Over the next few years, we'll need to fight to protect Ontario's interests and keep Canada a strong and united country. We won't be able to do that if we have to take time out for an election.'"

"No validity at all," replied Sid. "To me, it's an empty, pompous statement, full of rhetoricals, which doesn't make sense. It's not supportable. A provincial election is not gonna resolve those problems."

"I do feel that we need a federal election," offered Luke.

"We're talking about a provincial election," Goldfarb reminded him firmly.

"I know," Luke replied, "but again I believe that the provincial government can only do so much."

"The question I'm asking you is, based on the statement I read, does that justify in your mind an election?" Goldfarb said. He wanted to keep the session on target by getting reactions to the statements but his respondents were aching to tell him about other things.

"I don't like either statement," said Stephen. "I don't like it when one politician tries to blame another one as an excuse for an election. I want to hear what he's gonna do positively. If he wants a mandate, he should explain what he's gonna do, not say what the other government hasn't done."

"I think he should do a little housecleaning before he calls an election," Mary interjected in a loud, raspy voice.

"What kind of housecleaning, Mary?" Goldfarb asked.

"I just think with Patricia Starr there's a little cloud hanging over them," Mary explained, "and you can't just call an election and just sweep that under the rug."

"What I'm picking up is that they're using the reason to call an election is 'cause we have problems," said Reign. "What a lot of the people fall for is that their problems, the thing that will solve them is a change, and it has to go beyond it, not just a change."

"Maybe the next party in favor will help if they work harder," Ed suggested. "From what I've seen, every party that's in power, it starts off, they have their promises, they attack their problems, I think they do their best."

"Okay," Goldfarb interrupted. "But this government is facing a decision of why it may or may not call an election, and I've read you one rationale and I'll read it again." He repeated the second statement. "Okay, let's go back to Reign."

"Tomorrow, after the election, we'll have problems still,"

Reign said earnestly. "It's not the issue of the election that's going to solve things, as with past elections."

"Is this not a rationale then," Goldfarb cut her off, "for calling the election?"

"It's not a promise that it's going to work," Reign said. "To me, I don't see the solving as being an election."

"To me, I don't see it as a reason to call an election either," said Stephen. "It's very wishy-washy. It's not saying anything but calling an election now will save us the trouble later, 'cause we may have other things to work on later."

"I don't like that speech; it's full of platitudes," said Ken with disgust. "It's like you've heard that speech a hundred times."

"All right, I'll give you another one," Goldfarb said. "I'm the premier and you're the voters and you have to decide whether that's adequate, a decent rationale for calling an election. 'Over the next few years, Canada's facing a great deal of uncertainty. Uncertainty about the future shape of our country and uncertainty about the future state of our economy. Uncertainty can be very harmful: it drives away investment. We need to balance the uncertainty taking place outside Ontario with the certainty of a strong Ontario that has a clear and purposeful agenda for the '90s.'"

"I'd like to see him get more specific still," said Ken. "If he's been doing things good in some areas, he should keep saying how he's gonna build on it. The ones that haven't worked out he should be bringing them up. I'd like to see a speech that's a little specific, but it's better than the other one."

"I think the part about people investing in Ontario, that they're not going to do that if there's uncertainty about Canada as a nation, is right," said Anne. "That's the only thing that would help if there was an election."

"You think that's a legitimate reason for calling the election?" Goldfarb asked. "The uncertainty about future investment in the economy? The political uncertainty would mean————?" and he looked to Anne to complete the sentence.

"People won't invest," she answered.

"And that's an issue. Okay," Goldfarb concluded.

Sid had a point to make. "I think it's a great speech for Brian, rather than David," he suggested.

"It's too bad Brian wouldn't make it," added Luke.

"I think Mr. Peterson, it looks like he tries to do a good job and I think he is," said Bert. "But he's got so damn many problems that I don't think the poor guy knows which one to tackle first. And I go back to saying, I think we need a federal election, let alone a provincial one."

"I accept that opinion," Goldfarb said firmly. "But I really want to know whether this statement explains to you why he might call a provincial election."

"I think it's true in practically every word," Bert said.

Goldfarb shuffled his papers and found another statement.

"Again, I'm Mr. Peterson," he said. "It would be nice, wouldn't it?"

"I don't know," Mary muttered; the others tittered.

"'Canada's changing very quickly. Rapid economic and politicial changes are reshaping our country. An election will allow Ontarians to decide which agenda they wish to follow for building a strong economy, preserving and protecting our environment and building safe, healthy and caring communities.' I'm gonna start with Anne this time."

"This one seems to be a little bit better than the other ones," she replied, "'cause you're talking about what's going on in the province with the environment, which people are not doing much about."

"Mary?"

"I wish politicians would quit talking to people like they were dunderheads," Mary snarled.

"What happened here?" Goldfarb tried to interject.

"They give us this nice, slick statement every time they get in front of the television and nobody listens because they've heard it all before," Mary said, her voice sharp with contempt. "If they'd just get up and talk like a neighbor, or the guy who lives upstairs, and say, 'I didn't make these problems but I'm gonna do what I can.' But there's no input from the people. It doesn't matter what we want. You put somebody in and they say, 'Well, we haven't got the money for this, and we haven't got the manpower for that, but this was here before we got in.' So it's just the same old thing over and over."

"All right," said Goldfarb, "now that you've made your little speech, Mary, how do you respond to this statement?"

"Agh," Mary spat, "I'm indifferent."

"It is quite a bit more provincially focused," offered Tammy.

"What do you mean by 'provincially focused'?" Goldfarb asked.

"It doesn't make me think of federal government issues, those things like Meech Lake and free trade, things like that."

"So you feel more comfortable when it concentrates on provincial issues?"

"Yes."

Goldfarb went to the fifth possible rationale: "'We've called an election at this time because we feel we have a good chance of winning and renewing our mandate. Placing the issue of winning to one side, we believe this is the right time for the people of Ontario to decide on the best approach to strengthening our economy and setting the standard that will determine the quality of our lives for the decades ahead.'"

"It sounds somewhat smug," said Sid. "But it's self-confident at the same time and you get brownie points on that."

"I think he's calling an election because he's sure he's going to win," Mary announced.

"And you think it's legitimate to call an election because he can win?" Goldfarb asked.

"You bet," Mary fired back. "You wouldn't call one if you were in Mulroney's position."

"Do you think, Bert," asked Goldfarb, "it's legitimate for the premier to call an election on the basis of the fact that he feels he can win?"

"If it's getting near the end of his term and he knows he can win," Bert replied.

"He's in his third year now," Goldfarb said.

"So he's got, what, one year to go?" Bert reasoned. "Yeah, I'd say he has the right to call an election. Sure, it's the time to go for it, when you're on a roll. If he puts it off for six months or a year from now, who knows what could happen then, he might not have the same chance."

"So you don't hold it against him that he would use his recent, whatever success he's had, and this positive feeling that the public has for him, to call an election now?" Goldfarb asked.

"I think he's smart to do it."

"You don't think he's cynical?"

"All politicians are cynical," Bert shot back.

"Independent of that," Goldfarb pressed on, "you don't think he's cynical about calling the election now?"

"Sure, he's the same as any other politician," Bert replied.

"So you're not saying he's more cynical than anybody else?"

"No, no."

"You wouldn't hold it against him?"

"No, it's a political animal," Bert said. "You're going to go when you can win."

"I don't think it's a reason for calling an election just because he thinks he can win," said Anne. "I think they can go for five years, can't they? He's got lots of time to do more."

"Costs a lot of money for an election," said Mary.

"I think he should wait," Anne decided.

"Is there any real justification for holding a provincial election if there's no necessity for having one?" wondered Sid. "Looking at the reality of things, and not being cynical, I wonder how much respect the Liberal party will lose in this exercise."

"Well, if you listen to the room that you're in," said Goldfarb, "seven out of ten say he would call it, he should go."

"But the individuals, some of the seven that made those comments, said it on a cynical basis," Sid pointed out.

"Let me ask you a question," Goldfarb said. "You're the premier now. What would you do?"

"I think that if you stop and consider the Quebec situation," Bert suggested, "Mr. Peterson would be very smart if he calls an election now, and he knows that he's gonna be in command for the next four years no matter what. If Quebec separates, we're gonna be practically a country of our own, Ontario."

"That's another subject," Goldfarb said. "One more rationale. Again, I'm Mr. Peterson. 'It's never easy deciding when is the best time to call an election. I've decided, given the public uncertainty and difficult economic challenges that lie ahead, now is the time for the people of Ontario to decide on an agenda for the future.'"

"At least this time he's considering the people a bit more," said Mary.

"This one is for the people, the other one was for his party," said Anne.

"Now if you're the premier," Goldfarb proposed, "and you're faced with a circumstance where the numbers are pretty good—somebody's done some polling and you know that the public is feeling pretty good about you and your government. You also went through an experience where the country and Quebec are politically unstable, the federal government seems to be, doesn't seem to know what it wants to do or how to anything right now, especially as it relates to national issues, the economy is struggling. You also know you're going to go through the next two or three years of very aggressive negotiations deciding what does Ontario want, what does English Canada want, so that when you come to the table with Quebec, you have a point of view. Why would you call an election? What rationale would you put on the table?"

"If you want to call an election to renew confidence in what our opinions are and renew the strength of the province," Tammy offered, "in order to work together to make a stronger English Canada, then I would say that's a good rationale."

"That one's reason for going right now," Ken agreed, "because things could get worse. There's no doubt about it that things with Quebec and the GST and everything, it's only gonna get worse, especially with Quebec."

"What rationale would you say?" Goldfarb interrupted.

"If he's re-elected, which I think he will be, he can say he's in there for another four-year term, and he's probably gonna get a big majority," Ken reasoned. "You figure he's gonna have more clout at the table discussing these things with Quebec in federal-provincial meetings."

"I agree," said Stephen. "I would say to people there are unsettled times ahead, I need a mandate from you now for the next four years because there's a lot of things to come in the next four years with the GST and Meech Lake and everything."

"I think that Mr. Peterson would be very wise in calling an election," said Bert. "Mr. Peterson is a family man, he has a wife and kids. He's probably thinking of his kids' future too and what kind of a country they're going to live in. And if he can make it a little better for them in the future by inaugurating certain programs now, it'll help everybody in the end. So I think he's very wise to have the election and get it over with before all these other events happen."

"It would certainly support Peterson and the Liberal government in the future negotiations at the federal-provincial level," Sid pointed out.

"If you were Mr. Peterson, who would you consult about this decision?" Goldfarb asked the group. "It's a totally different pressure than most of us ever experience as ordinary citizens."

"Sit down with members of the cabinet," Sid suggested.

"I guess that's why you're talking to us," Stephen observed.

"Probably Nixon's a pretty good one to talk to," said Ed.

"I would say his wife," Anne offered.

"His wife," Goldfarb stopped the discussion. "Why his wife?"

"Because she's a force behind him," Anne explained.

"And she's not a political animal," Sid added.

"She's a nice person," said Anne.

"Would you trust her advice?" Goldfarb asked. "You're the premier, now. Or would you trust your advisors?"

"I think she'd be giving him different advice," said Ed. "She'd have deeper insight into different things than a political pro. Sometimes I wonder if she's got a sixth sense that someone's going to plunge a knife into him or something. It's like she has a people's brain, and is sort of part of the people rather than just a politician's wife."

Goldfarb wrapped up the conversation: "Are you telling him to call an election or aren't you?"

"Well, I don't want to take the blame for it," said Luke.

"I think he should go out on the street and talk to the common people and ask them whether they think is he doing the right thing," said Bert.

"He's doing that right now," Goldfarb reassured them all.

Goldfarb's approach to his focus group was different from the techniques employed by pollsters for the NDP and Tories in their pre-election work. He did not use a projective interviewing style—the type of "what-if" questioning that might have clued him in to how people would respond to charges the election was unnecessary, a waste of money or a coronation for Peterson. Unlike the other parties' pollsters, Goldfarb did not attempt to provoke strong negative reactions to Peterson, which could have provided the Liberals with information they might have used to defend against attacks. Nor did Goldfarb seem to be interested in listening to what the people in his focus group were trying to tell him. Participants tried to reveal their concerns about the need for a federal election, overtaxation, government waste, the Starr affair and contempt, indifference and cynicism toward politicians—some even hinted at agreement with Peterson's own national unity-based rationale for calling the election. Rather than probe these thoughts to discover what they might mean for Peterson and the Liberals, Goldfarb seemed to disregard the concerns people were raising and forced them to respond only to the statements.

Later that evening and the next night, Hurley would conduct his three groups in a similar style, keeping the participants focused on each statement, preventing them from getting sidetracked. Audiotapes of the sessions were sent to the premier's office, where they were passed about among top campaign staff, none of whom had time to listen to the full eight hours of recordings. Hurley and Goldfarb worked with Peterson's staff to assemble the statement the premier would read to call the election. In its final form, Peterson's statement would be a grab bag that combined lines from the six rationales with phrases picked up from the groups; it would be fine-tuned the day before the election call when Peterson held a day-long session of preparation with his strategists and campaign staff.

*   *   *

Attempts by people close to Peterson to "play the media" before the election yielded disastrous results for the Liberals. Robinson had been concerned about leaks of confidential information since June, when a secret projection by Goldfarb known only to the campaign strategists that the Liberals could win 103 seats surfaced in some media reports. On July 23 a three-page article appeared in *Maclean's* magazine that obliterated any remaining traces of cooperation and trust among the strategists. At first glance the coverage seemed to be excellent publicity for the Liberals. Peterson was shown in a half-page color photo posing with a couple of Blue Jay players at the Shopsy's charity event. But the article horrified Robinson. It contained, almost verbatim, detailed deliberations by the strategy committee, including its concerns about going to the polls after the collapse of Meech. Also revealed were the results of a confidential Liberal poll by Goldfarb that showed the party holding the support of 50 percent of decided voters, with the NDP at 28 percent and the Tories drawing 20 percent. To Robinson, the story represented a leak of the highest order: on the eve of an election, portions of the government's campaign strategy along with polling results known only to a privileged few were turning up in a national magazine. The leak was far too accurate and embarassing to ignore, too great a threat to the security of the Liberal campaign. To Robinson, the leak warranted a decisive and fail-safe response.

After surveying the strategists, Robinson concluded the source of the leak was Gagnier, who maintained he was unfairly singled out: while he spoke freely to reporters about the Liberal campaign in the weeks before the election call, other members of the strategy committee were also being quoted widely in the media, including MacNaughton, whose name appeared in sections on

Liberal strategy in the *Maclean's* article. No members of the strategy committee would accept responsibility for leaking Goldfarb's numbers. Gagnier believed he was implicated because he was not a dyed-in-the-wool Liberal partisan, but a seconded public servant who had made it clear he would be returning to the public service the day an election was called.

The question of Gagnier's role in the election came to a head in mid-June, after Peterson addressed the Newfoundland legislature in a bid to save the Meech deal. Flying back to Toronto from St. John's in an Ontario government plane with a handful of staff, Peterson turned to his principal secretary. "The premier basically confided that he was going to drop the writ," Gagnier said. "The question was, 'What do you want to do in the campaign?' I said to him, 'Well, look, I've got to go back to cabinet office. I'm not going to resign from the public service.'"

Gagnier believed Peterson felt fundamentally let down. "That set a tone, from that moment on: Dan may be a good guy and he helped us a lot and he may be politically sensitive, but he's basically out of it," said Gagnier. "That was the first point at which the dynamics of the relationship changed. The second point was when the order-in-council got passed in cabinet, converting me back to cabinet office."

By the time the election began, Gagnier would be relegated to sitting in the premier's office, running a housekeeping operation. To many Liberals, his decision to adhere to the terms of his contract and not "cross over" to partisan activity capped months of misgivings: many had questioned Peterson's decision to ask a bureaucrat to become principal secretary, even if Gagnier provided the constitutional expertise and problem-solving skills the premier needed at the time. "Clearly, one of the problems with him coming in was that there was really no great affection from within the party system for the guy," MacNaughton observed. "There was all sorts of sniping going on and people just didn't like him at all." The issue of who actually leaked the information would not be resolved, and there was no evidence that pointed to one person specifically as the source of the leak. But the events had a profound effect on the Liberal campaign.

The leak was the last straw for Robinson. Convinced the strategy committee had self-destructed, she made a decision that hobbled the Liberal campaign. To eliminate the potential for future leaks, Robinson decided to invoke the "dictatorial powers" granted to her by Peterson: she would not share with the strategists the all-important, day-to-day "rolling poll" data that would be gathered by Goldfarb during the campaign. Rolling polls, normally analyzed and their trends predicted by strategists, are used to modify campaign tactics on the fly, to respond to the way a campaign is going. Absolutely vital to running a campaign, rolling polls, when properly used, permit connections to be made between actions taken and effects noted that can make the difference between winning and losing.

"It had always been agreed that the numbers would be kept very tight," said Robinson. "The discussions that we had were that when there was any significant change it would be dealt with by the strategy committee, and that was done. But on a day-by-day basis in the early stages of the campaign, everyone agreed that it was important that there not be extensive sharing of the numbers and that's how things worked."

Gagnier was resigned to being cut out of the action. "Kathy made it clear in no uncertain terms that the relationship, once the party's money was being used in a campaign situation, was between her as the client and Goldfarb as the guy doing the service," he said. But Gagnier believed Robinson's decision to go beyond him and keep the rolling polls away from all the strategists was tied to a broader sense of distrust. "It goes all the way back to the premier's concern over MacNaughton talking to the press at one time," he said. "They tightened it up to the point where either the premier or Kathy felt comfortable that nothing was going to get out."

MacNaughton was aghast at the ruling. "When Kathy decided she didn't want to show the numbers to anybody because she thought Gagnier would leak them, I thought that was incredible," he said. "It seemed to be appropriate, seeing Gagnier as being the principal source of the problem. But I said, 'Look, I don't care if that's the way you want to handle it, but if it starts going to the shitters, you've got to let us know.'"

Peterson kept his nose out of the mess. "Hell, I'm rather sanguine about these things because there are leaks throughout the entire process," he said. "I'm not one of those up nights worrying about it. When you see things that sort of harden the chemistry of the group, that develop distrust, obviously it's not a very good thing. I never worry too much about all that stuff because there's always stuff in the paper and speculation and people making up stuff. Can't worry about it."

Robinson's resolve was cemented on the Saturday before Peterson called the election. The *Globe*'s Richard Mackie produced a story even more detailed on strategy than the *Maclean's* report. The leak, Robinson feared, was turning into a torrent. Her mind was made up: she would begin the campaign determined to keep the rolling polls out of the hands of her fellow strategists. That would prove easy to do. At the same time, she would convene no meetings of the strategy committee until far into the campaign.

The strategists would claim Robinson's decision lobotomized the Liberal brain trust: her ultra-tight grip on Goldfarb's numbers would fundamentally impair the advice they would be able to offer Peterson. "Kathy certainly said that her policy vis-à-vis data from there on was done with the full support of the premier, but strategically it was a huge mistake," said senior strategist Michael Kirby. "The result of it was devastating because more than any other single activity, it destroyed the campaign. It destroyed the way the campaign was to be run." MacNaughton agreed. "Kathy decided that nobody should see the polling results except for her," he said. "So we were flying blind." Or so they would claim.

7

The Protester Phenomenon

Can we hear your answer, sir?

*—AN ANONYMOUS TV REPORTER
TO DAVID PETERSON*

The weather, as it often does, said it all the day the election was called—close, stifling, irritating. People in Toronto woke up on Monday, July 30, to find their week starting with a day so hot it hurt to breathe.

On this first day of the election campaign, Peterson was exhausted. The Meech talks and the ordeal of watching the deal die had worn him down. Anxious over his decision to call an early election, he had been unable to truly rest on his three-week holiday at Grand Bend on Lake Huron.

The previous day's arduous rehearsal of the campaign kick-off statement and news conference with the strategy committee and campaign staff had filled his head with facts, answers and explanations, but little comfort. He appeared refreshed at the rehearsal but now faced the reality of a hard, grinding campaign. For weeks, the papers had been bristling with criticism that an early election would be unjustified and self-serving for the Liberals. Peterson had agreed with his strategists to put forward a catch-all reason they were convinced would be accepted by Ontarians: there is no good time to call an election and profound changes in the world and in Canada had put new pressures on Ontario; the Liberals needed a new mandate to meet those challenges with a full agenda they would reveal during the campaign. Flak about the early call, the strategists believed, would fade as a one-day wonder.

The morning was already stifling when the premier's dark-blue Chevrolet Caprice arrived at the red door of his Rosedale home. Anticipation hummed through the Peterson house, spurring the last-minute packing and preparation for 37 days on the road. Various combinations of the Peterson children—Ben, Chloe and Adam—would join Peterson on the Liberal bus; Shelley would come on board when her television shooting schedule permitted.

Ten minutes later, when the car pulled up to the east door of the legislature, a mob of television cameras and reporters was waiting outside in the heat, straining to scrum Peterson before he entered the building—a rare event, since the cameras normally waited inside, in the cool hall by his second-floor office.

The reason for the urgency was a weekend Toronto *Sun* story that alleged Kathy Robinson had received advance notice from a Liberal representative on the Election Finances Commission of its proposed charges against the Liberal party and two top officials related to the Starr fund-raising scandal. The story suggested that the party had pressured the commission not to lay the charges. Reporters wanted Peterson's reaction so they could meet early deadlines, lest the story be lost in the expected flood of election-call news.

Swarmed by reporters barking out questions as he opened the car door, Peterson mumbled that he knew only what he had read in the paper. The exchange turned ugly as Peterson refused to budge; he went inside leaving reporters incensed.

"You're just about to ask the voters to reaffirm your mandate; you can't just get away with 'No comment,'" thought the *Globe*'s Richard Mackie. "It was a very hostile scrum. It was like, you're going early to avoid things because there's something really dangerous in the Starr revelations and you're desperate to get the election over with."

That exchange set the tone for the day, sharpening media impatience with Peterson and fueling a belief that the early call was blatant opportunism by the poll-conscious Liberals.

At about 9:30 a.m., Peterson's ministers filed into the cabinet room to be advised officially of the election date. As they gathered around the table, sipping coffee and talking in low voices, the mood was subdued: some were resigned to five weeks of gruelling door-knocking, some were upbeat, some still doubted the wisdom of going early. All had one question: what will be the publicly stated reason for going early? As recently as July 25, cabinet had been promised a campaign strategy and a platform focused on the economy. But Peterson's ministers still had not been told exactly how the rationale for going early would be expressed and presented.

Peterson spoke succinctly as Robinson and Webster stood by. The election date, he said, was September 6. The campaign would be hard work but the polls still looked good—so, good luck. That was it. Ministers exchanged concerned glances. One veteran broke in quickly with the all-important question, inexplicably overlooked: "Well, premier, what's the reason going to be?"

"It's in the statement," replied Peterson. "It'll all be in the statement."

"The statement will be sent out to everyone later on today," added Robinson. "Just get it and read it; everything is in there."

With that, the meeting was over. The Liberal cabinet would start the campaign without debating or discussing an official, universally accepted version of the reason for the early call. They'd be given their "lines" later in the day—or so they believed.

Shortly before 11 a.m., Peterson left his office and walked

down the red-carpeted stairs to the Queen's Park media studio. Shelley and the children by his side, circled by glaring television cameras that held his pace to a crawl, Peterson made his way down the wide hall of the legislative building. Some of the cameras picked up Peterson's whisper to his wife as they walked slowly: "This is almost like a funeral procession." It was an ominous portent from a man whose slide toward political death was about to begin.

*   *   *

"Mr. Peterson!" The tape-recorded words crackled through the static:

> Mr. Peterson, this is a message from Greenpeace. We are here today to protest your government's failure to protect the environment. There are five reasons why we are doing this. First, you failed to protect us from toxic chemicals going into the water. In 1986 you promised to eliminate toxic chemicals from going into our water system and not one single regulation has been passed by your government. In 1987 you promised clean air legislation. There is no clean air legislation. Your promise is a lie. Before you were elected you promised not to build any more nuclear reactors . . . Mr. Peterson, your record is a record of failure. It is not acceptable to us or Ontarians.

Exactly 15 seconds after starting to read his statement at the campaign kickoff news conference, Peterson was fighting a losing battle. Before the premier could complete his first sentence, Greenpeace activist Gord Perks leaped from a chair where he had been sitting among reporters in the media studio. Shelley Peterson had noticed him as she walked in.

"His face came out of the crowd at me because he looked scared," she said. "I worried, and then I thought, no, the press has checked everybody, I'm sure he's legitimate, maybe it's the first thing he's ever covered."

But Perks was no reporter and no novice. An experienced activist, he made it to the platform in two strides and laid a "talking briefcase" on the table in front of the startled premier.

"When he was the one that stood up, I grabbed my children," said Shelley. "I thought he was going to shoot David. I thought he was going to kill him." Others in the room thought the same for an instant but Perks' real purpose became clear in seconds: from the sturdy metal case handcuffed to his thin wrist, the taped message spewed out, slamming the Liberals' record on environmental issues.

As the scruffy young man in shorts and the blue-suited premier faced off in an impromptu confrontation, Ontarians suddenly had some compelling television to watch—far more exciting than the staged events of a typical election campaign. Reporters leaned forward, smelling blood as Peterson, ashen-faced in spite of his deep tan, listened in stony silence to the litany of charges of broken promises.

Perks picked up the attack when the tape ended: "Mr. Peterson, we want to know why it is that you have failed on so many important environmental issues."

"Do you have anything else you'd like to say?" Peterson asked tersely.

Perks persisted. "I want to hear your answer, sir."

"Maybe you'd be good enough to sit down and we could have a discussion," Peterson responded, dropping his voice to the trademark mumble.

Perks remained standing. "I'd like to hear your answer first, sir."

"Well, there are many other people here and we'll be discussing a lot of these issues," Peterson murmured.

"Can we hear your answer, sir?" a reporter called from the back. "Can we hear your answer up louder, please?"

Peterson glanced over at Gene Allen, the *Globe* reporter moderating the news conference. "Gene, I'm in your hands. Is that the way you want to conduct things?"

Allen moved to Perks' side and put a hand on his arm, telling him awkwardly that the news conference was being conducted by the "parliamentary news gallery," and he was preventing it from proceeding. Believing Allen to be a Peterson aide, Perks ignored him.

"Get the fuck out of the way, Gene," a cameraman hissed. "Sit down, Gene," barked another. "You're blockin' the fuckin' shot." Allen looked around in confusion and stepped off to the side.

Perks held his ground. He stood facing Peterson, his back to the reporters. By now, a half dozen cameramen had yanked their cameras off their tripods and moved closer for better shots of the standoff. A soundman standing behind Peterson could be seen grinning broadly as he dipped his microphone over the duel. Perks, a skilled on-camera performer, continued to press Peterson.

"He's made his point," a reporter called out impatiently.

Emboldened, Allen moved toward Perks and tried again. "Can you please sit down and allow us to proceed? You've made your point."

Perks finally relented. But before backing off, he declared loudly, "The premier of Ontario has no answer for these issues."

As Perks walked away, a shocked and sweating Peterson wiped his mouth and looked around. "It's going to be an interesting campaign," he announced. Uneasy laughter greeted his attempt to brush off the confrontation. Outside in the hall, Peterson's staff huddled to sort out the breach of security: they realized that no one had thought to case the studio in advance.

Perks had made an impression in more ways than one. Not only had he conveyed Greenpeace's message of dissatisfaction with the Liberals on an issue important to Ontarians, he had hijacked the premier's crucial news conference—and obliterated the Liberals' opening day message.

Peterson rushed through the rest of his statement about the rationale for going early, as if he just wanted to get it over with. The carefully crafted lines, well rehearsed the day before, were lost in the chaos and overwhelmed by the gripping imagery of the standoff.

"You couldn't have asked for a better confrontation—for better television," said Global TV's Robert Fisher.

The atmosphere of confrontation persisted as the news conference moved into a question-and-answer session. Why was Peterson going to the voters only three years into his term when he had a huge majority? One reporter suggested that, with the Liberals running at 50 percent in the polls, the reason was political opportunism, pure and simple.

Perks' intrusion had diverted attention from the critical lines of the opening statement. Peterson stuck to the script and repeated his rationale, adding that he took nothing for granted and expected a rough ride. But in spite of his painstaking rehearsal, Peterson reiterated the vital message with little conviction. Still shaken by Perks' attack, he wore a look of defeat. Ticked off by their acrimonious exchange earlier in the morning, many reporters were not buying the premier's answer—or his vague rationale.

Bad turned to worse for Peterson. Following up the previous weekend's story, Toronto *Sun* reporters demanded his response to the allegations that Robinson had received advance notice of the latest Starr-related charges. Peterson said again that he first heard the story when he read it in the paper and added that the commission was an independent body. But that sounded evasive; the reporters dug in and repeated their questions more aggressively. Other reporters joined in. Peterson began to argue with them.

"You appear to be vexed about this," one reporter observed. "I'm not vexed at all!" Peterson snapped in a high voice. So much for the scrupulous rehearsal the day before.

The only issues about which Peterson displayed enthusiasm during the half-hour news conference were national unity and, belatedly, the Liberal's environmental record. When the questions turned to the environment, Peterson got rolling: he listed his government's programs and acknowledged they might not be enough to satisfy everyone, especially people with strong views. The Liberals were not perfect, he said, and more work had to be done, but important gains had been made. It was not a bad answer by most standards; it took some of the bite out of Greenpeace's rhetoric. But it came too late. On tonight's news, the pictures of confrontation would tell the story on the environment.

On national unity and the failure of Meech, Peterson's tone was firm and deliberate, his personal conviction clear. But problems surfaced to further muddy the Liberals' message. When asked for his solutions to the national unity crisis, Peterson said he would reveal his position in a speech later in the campaign. By talking about "protecting Ontario's interests" without being more explicit, Peterson gave some reporters the impression he was "fucking us around," one would complain later.

Reporters felt that Peterson wanted to save the constitutional goodies and dispense them at a strategic pace. They could sense another "burger-a-day" campaign—media lingo for pre-formed, conveniently packaged stories, served to them each day on a plate. In fact, Peterson was steering clear of detail on the constitutional question to stay "on-strategy": he had agreed with his strategists that he would not make national unity the focus of the Liberal platform. The Liberals were not about to be thrown off-track by reporters hungering for a half-cooked burger.

But getting no immediate news on the national unity front from "Captain Canada" was simply unacceptable to some of the media. The Toronto *Star* would pursue Peterson throughout the day, until it obtained enough comments from him to prepare a national unity story. The next day's *Star* would run the headline, "Ontario's role in Canada is the key issue, Premier says." But that was not the issue or message the Liberals wanted to convey.

Other major media would also give short shrift to the Liberals' intended message. CBC-TV flagship CBLT stressed its surprise at Peterson's reluctance to deal with the failure of Meech. It featured the Greenpeace incident, commenting that the campaign promised to be much tougher than 1987, labeled Peterson "vexed" and criticized him for taking a combative approach to "questions he did not like, specifically Starr, taxes and the environment." A *Globe* editorial would chastise Peterson for failing to show his cards on national unity and spell out his agenda for nation-building.

Rather than exhaust itself as a "one-day wonder," the early-call story penetrated deeply; few reporters were interested in Peterson's wordy, unclear rationale. "There was no central message other than business as usual," concluded the *Star*'s Matt Maychak. "He was asked literally dozens of times, 'Why an election now?'; he never answered it satisfactorily for us and, ultimately, for the electorate."

By not offering a substantive, well-delivered reason for the call, a front-and-center statement on national unity or an immediate, detailed agenda on the economy, the Liberals created a gaping news hole. Ready to fill it were some great headlines: Perks' dramatic protest, an unnecessary election, more Starr scandal and a "vexed" premier who did not like people raining on his parade.

"There was no reaffirmation of national unity, there was no reaffirmation of the need to rebuild the economy," said the *Globe*'s Mackie. "He's still calling this election because he thinks he can win it. He's taking us for granted. It's a $40-million waste of time."

In less than an hour the die was cast and the tone set: "Government under assault," as Peterson would label it. Their strategy under heavy fire, the Liberals had no ammunition with which to mount a defense, let alone launch a counterattack.

* * *

NDP leader Bob Rae moved into the media ring and came out swinging. He belted out the NDP's line of attack, saying the election was about choices, about "who's been running the province and who gets what in the province and who has benefited from the Liberals." He charged that the Liberals had consistently taken the side of the "polluters . . . developers . . . and tax freeloaders which fund them," and when asked if Peterson was a liar, said five times that the premier had lied to Ontarians. "Mr. Peterson lied to the people of the province about car insurance; he also lied to them about taxes; he also lied to them about free trade," said Rae. Reporters found Rae confident, upbeat and enthusiastic, and contrasted his demeanor with Peterson's defensiveness.

Hard on Rae's heels came Tory leader Mike Harris, hammering away with his own assault. The election was unnecessary, he said, before unveiling his campaign theme: taxes were the issue and Peterson had introduced 33 new ones. The Liberals were hoping to get away with a campaign that would see Peterson attend picnics and ignore the issues, Harris charged. "The premier can eat hot dogs while food banks run dry," he asserted. Without offering alternatives, both Rae and Harris unleashed their attack strategies—plans that turned out to be a perfect match for the mood of the day.

Peterson retreated to his office to cool down after the events of the morning and prepare to board the Liberal bus for his first campaign stop in Dundas, near Hamilton. He did not watch his opponents make their statements. A campaign aide found Peterson sitting alone behind his desk, staring out the window and smoking.

"Waddya think?" the premier asked. "How'd it go?"

"Well, the door's open now," the aide replied. "I think you got the lines across on the reason, but now every nutbar and his brother is going to come out of the woodwork."

"How should I handle them?" Peterson asked. "What do I do?"

"You can't just sit there and say nothing again. You have to be magnanimous. You're the premier; you can afford to be magnanimous. Talk about how great a country this is, that everybody can state their mind. Then invite the guy to make his point to the media, or talk with you afterwards. And don't get irked, or whatever they called it."

"Vexed," said Peterson. "Yeah."

Another campaign staffer came in; Robinson and Webster followed.

"What's the TV perspective on this?" asked Peterson. "Waddya think, are we gonna be okay?"

"The Greenpeace thing will get covered because it's good TV," came the second staffer's reply. "The key is always to turn it around and put yourself in control of the situation. You have to deal with these guys; then you can concentrate on getting our message out."

Peterson had been inhaling the advice along with his cigarette smoke. He pushed away from his desk and walked over to a cabinet that he opened to expose a small TV set.

"Where's the thing, the clicker?" he wondered aloud, scanning the stuffed armchairs and plump couches. He picked up the remote control and aimed it at the set. "How do I get *Newsworld* on this thing?" he asked.

"You were already on," said Webster. "It was live."

*   *   *

The "Liberal bus," in 1990, meant two buses, not one: gleaming silver Greyhounds, with two-foot-high red lettering blazing down the sides to proclaim the arrival or passage of "Premier David Peterson." The media bus would usually arrive or depart each event before the premier's bus. Press gallery members were stunned to discover that Peterson's familiar press aides were nowhere near the front lines: they were squirreled away at Liberal headquarters, dealing with the media by phone. New faces were brought in; the Liberals wanted neutral people who would not encumber their campaign messages with the baggage of previous problems and strained relationships.

But press gallery members believed that this move betrayed a long-standing problem with Peterson's office: the top brass placed no trust in the press office. The newcomers faced the daunting hurdle of trying to get to know reporters from scratch and develop relationships of trust on the fly, in the heat of a campaign.

Peterson's bus was a rolling luxury hotel suite, typical of a leader's campaign bus, with every amenity for a comfortable life on the road. Crammed aboard was enough high-tech communications equipment to command a space flight: hand-held cellular phones, portable fax machines, televisions, computers linked by electronic mail to campaign headquarters and hands-free walkie-talkies set to the frequencies used by Liberal advance crews.

Sticking to Peterson like Velcro throughout the campaign would be aide Vince Borg, a calming, soothing influence who could guide his old friend through anything; he would also work with the media. Rounding out the tour staff were other longtime aides chosen by Robinson with the premier's "comfort level" in mind: they would be the soft lining of his silver cocoon.

As the buses swung onto the highway on the campaign's first day, the Liberals' campaign headquarters started to come to life. Two weeks earlier, the former Toronto head office of National Cash Register on Eglinton Avenue near Yonge Street had been leased by the party. Robinson had claimed a large office in the executive suite, and had an enormous antique pine desk hauled in, which she surrounded with hoop-back chairs. Webster and campaign vice-chairs Debbie Nash and Bill Murray took offices nearby.

About 40 staff members began moving into Liberal headquarters as the campaign started, toting boxes filled with policy and organizational papers, slapping up the freshly minted campaign posters, and vying for desks and chairs that were in working order.

But as the Liberals settled into their summer quarters, problems began popping up like cruel practical jokes. The phones had not been connected as promised; the fax machines, lined up in banks, were neutered without phone links. Half of a vaunted internal computer network was still in boxes as technicians tried to piece it together; its electronic mail links to the campaign bus were lifeless until the phones were hooked up.

Worse still, as staffers tripped over repair crews and ran back and forth to Queen's Park to find phones, faxes and computers that worked, the air-conditioning kept breaking down. Liberals fortunate enough to find desks near windows that worked could open them for refreshing blasts of the 40°C August breeze. There were no coffee cups—or toilet paper.

In the midst of the chaotic inferno, Robinson and Webster tried to sort out priorities. The phones were number one. Robinson spent precious hours persuading Bell Canada to respond to the urgent need. Installers would not complete the massive job for several days.

As the afternoon wore on, unable to transmit Peterson's opening statement to Liberal candidates, the fax machines sat idle. But the province's media did not. Across Ontario, news of the early-election call spread, with the angle that Peterson could not come up with a good reason. As cabinet members and other Liberals arrived in their ridings, they found no messages from headquarters—nothing to help them explain why the election had been called. A few tried calling Queen's Park, searching desperately for someone who could read them a few lines from Peterson's statement. But as they headed out to begin knocking on doors and talking to local reporters, most Liberal candidates, including cabinet ministers, did not know their "lines" on the reason for the election call. The promised copies of the statement would have helped Liberal candidates and workers spread the rationale across the province when, as it turned out, Peterson could not.

*　　*　　*

The phones began to ring early that afternoon in Dundas, at the constituency office of Government House Leader Chris Ward, the Liberal candidate in the riding of Wentworth North. The inquiries were all the same, and they were strange.

"Could you give me directions to the Collins Hotel?" caller after caller asked. Peterson's first stop on his campaign tour was scheduled at the Collins for midafternoon, where he would officially open Ward's campaign office. That morning, Ward's campaign team had been furiously assembling a welcoming event in what the Liberal tour organizers believed was "the safest place on earth." A hundred local Liberals were coming to help.

Ward's workers were disturbed by the calls. The Collins had been a popular watering hole in the same location since 1841; everyone local knew where it was.

"I think there's some out-of-towners coming," a worker said to Ward when he arrived from Toronto. Indeed there were, and they were bringing yet another surprise for Peterson—a surprise that would define the Liberal campaign for the next 37 days.

There was no sign of trouble as the shining Liberal buses pulled up in front of the old hotel's huge white pillars. Peterson descended the steps of the bus, smiling and waving, and disappeared amid a throng of welcoming Liberals, through the doors and into Ward's campaign headquarters. Inside, Peterson and Ward approached the microphones.

"All of a sudden, up go the signs," Ward said. "We couldn't do anything." Several dozen protesters from Greenpeace, the antibilingualism Confederation of Regions party and the local teachers' union had followed the cheering Liberals into the room. The attacks were aimed straight at Peterson. Members of Greenpeace carrying placards lambasted the premier, accusing him of reneging on an old promise to stop building nuclear reactors. The others yelled a simpler message: "You're lying!" Scuffles broke out as two Liberals tried to block Greenpeace banners from the television cameras. When Confederation of Regions members heckled Peterson on bilingualism, Liberal workers tried to shout them down.

Peterson moved to a microphone and launched into his first campaign speech, heavy on the Liberal lines about calling the election to protect Ontario's economic and political interests. He looked toward the chanting protesters at the back of the room. "If they feel so strongly, they should run in the next election," Peterson told the cheering Liberals. "I think that would be a very important thing to do, because this is a democratic system, and everybody should be heard, everybody with views. I'm proud of what we have, and I'm proud of the fact that anybody can stand up and say anything they want anytime, including my friends over here." As the Liberals applauded, Peterson left the stage and pressed through the crowd toward the campaign bus.

Accepting Peterson's invitation, a Greenpeace protester pushed upstream through the departing Liberals. He approached the microphone and began speaking, then suddenly stopped. No one could hear him—someone had pulled the plug. Greenpeace would never find out if the microphone had been shut down to shut them up, but they learned a lesson: never again in this campaign would they let Peterson stage-manage their protest.

The sign-wielding protesters chased after Peterson, catching him just before he reached the sanctuary of the bus. For several minutes they surrounded the premier's entourage, jostling, pushing and shoving, shouting and screaming.

Mashed against each other in the heaving crush of bodies, Ward and Borg found themselves face to face.

"So, Chris," Borg grunted, "what the hell are we supposed to do when this happens?"

"I thought *you* knew," Ward called out as Borg was swept onto the bus.

The Liberals had expected to run into the odd protester on the road, but already, at Peterson's first campaign stop, even the "safest place on earth" had turned into a battle zone.

*   *   *

"Operation Alienation," the Peterson government's pattern of turning off certain sectors of the electorate, yielded a bitter harvest for the Liberals in the 1990 campaign. Special-interest groups, unhappy with their treatment by the Liberals, combined with a wide range of protesters to create a phenomenon without precedent in a Canadian election, taking advantage of Peterson's open, accessible tour to challenge the Liberals with anger and persistence. Free trade protesters who tried to attack Mulroney in the 1988 federal campaign did not come close to making such an impact. In earlier Ontario elections, third-party activism was tempered and sporadic: in 1985 Premier Frank Miller often ran into organized protesters but their numbers were small and their attacks mild; in 1987 protests against Peterson came daily, but were also smaller and less vociferous.

But in Ontario in 1990 the threads of disparate protest wove together into a mighty rope. Over 37 days, the rope formed itself into a noose, and Peterson and the Liberals would be publicly hanged nightly on the news. The repeated attacks would affect the attitude of voters toward Peterson by helping to transform his image as a popular leader into that of a politician subject to widespread attack and ridicule.

Many of the groups active in the 1990 Ontario election fully believed that the Peterson government could not be toppled. They protested only to be heard by the "returning" government. "You had interest groups who decided, much like the general population, that this government was going to get re-elected with a majority," said Borg, "and therefore, 'This is going to be our last shot, so let's make sure they hear it loud and clear.'"

*   *   *

Greenpeace was typical in its expectation: "We got a list of the ridings that were close," explained Perks, "and said, 'These are the people who will listen if we go in and start knocking on doors.' Not to knock people off, because there was no expectation that we would knock the Liberals off, none."

Greenpeace members began planning their strategy for the election campaign in April. While polls showed Ontarians placed the environment high on the public policy agenda, Greenpeace believed that all three parties were waffling. "Intervening in such a direct way in the electoral process was a first for Greenpeace," said Perks, "but we weren't prepared to let any of the parties ignore such serious problems. The environment had to be what the voters wanted it to be: the number one priority." Unless it took action, Greenpeace decided, environmental issues would be buried in a "pit of recycled promises."

Perks, a 27-year-old Torontonian, had been Greenpeace's central Canada pulp-and-paper campaigner for one and a half years when the 1990 election was called. A former student Liberal at the University of Toronto, Perks found his calling at Greenpeace along with others who shared his passion to "protect the planet." Perks spoke with messianic fervor of the feelings that gave him the nerve to confront Peterson: "I'm a person whose son was born with all these toxic chemicals in his body, higher concentrations, multiple times higher, than David Peterson's body was born with. We let people become premier and they don't care. That's what this campaign was about."

Perks jumped at the chance to be at the hub of the Greenpeace effort. He preferred the "personally empowering" tactic of face-to-face confrontation with politicians over other Greenpeace protest tactics, such as commando-style assaults on polluting factories or nuclear plants. He understood how to grab and hold media attention. "I have a couple of rules in terms of the media," he said. "I believe that if the mountain won't come to Mohammed, Mohammed must go to the mountain. Go find some live TV somewhere and, hey, you're rolling."

When Greenpeace began to plan its involvement in the election, members argued over who to target: Environment Minister Jim Bradley, Treasurer Bob Nixon, Peterson, the entire Liberal government or the other two parties. With a campaign budget of just $15,000, Greenpeace chose to invest its energies where the payoff would be highest: Peterson, on whom the media would be focusing.

One weekend early in April, Greenpeace staff headed north from Toronto for a retreat at the Taoist Tai Chi Centre in Orangeville, with election strategy as one item on the agenda. Discussions turned to how best to get the environmental message out into the political arena.

In past elections, both federal and provincial, Greenpeace had joined with others in the environmental community to send a questionnaire to every candidate in every riding, requesting responses to a number of issues for publication midway through the election. They found with dismay that identical responses came back from each party's candidates—the answers espoused the party line and were fudged, Greenpeace felt, to prevent the reader from determining if the line was yes, no or maybe. For 1990 Greenpeace decided to take "direct action" to tell the public that there was a difference between empty words and real change, and to send the Peterson government that message.

A two-part strategy was devised: get voters to ask candidates at the door their position on 12 critical environmental issues, and convince the media to recognize the distinction between rhetoric and concrete steps to "protect the planet." A Greenpeace election pamphlet, mailed to its 125,000 Ontario members, led with the headline, "The Peterson government has talked a lot about the environment. Too bad it's just talk." A photo of Peterson looking insincere and confused filled the front page. Inside was a chart containing the "Peterson Government's Environmental Report Card." A scorecard on the back asked the voter to rate the candidate's responses at the door. The same scorecard was published in several Ontario newspapers and distributed for Greenpeace by community groups.

During the campaign, about 400,000 Greenpeace pamphlets would find their way into the hands of Ontario voters. "In the long run," Perks felt, "that's going to be the most important thing we do. We taught 400,000 people what 12 issues on the environment were, and to ask the candidates these questions because it's going to matter."

Backing up the pamphlet was a carefully targeted door-to-door canvass by Greenpeace members in 20 ridings where the races were believed to be close. Many candidates from all parties found the tactic working—voters began to give them a tough time on the environment at the door. But Greenpeace inflicted deeper, more direct damage on the ruling Liberals by re-enacting their one-on-one attacks on Peterson every day on the campaign trail.

A green minibus filled with five Greenpeace activists and a sixth dressed as a seven-foot-tall green rat shadowed Peterson, confronting him at virtually every stop on his tour. The litany of alleged broken Liberal promises was repeated like a broken record. Standoffs between Peterson and Perks became a daily ritual, with Perks often clean-shaven and wearing a suit if necessary to gain access to events. The giant green rat, which symbolized the somewhat obscure proposal that even a rat could be green, became a fixture on the campaign trail. A four-foot-square blowup of the scorecard was hauled out for public viewing at every opportunity. Greenpeace protests became an integral part of the campaign's news agenda.

Many Liberals and reporters speculated about collusion between Greenpeace and the NDP but both vehemently denied any coordination. Greenpeace claims a policy of nonpartisan campaigning and refuses to endorse candidates. In Ontario in 1990 its doorstep activities were targeted at all three parties.

Rae and Harris drew some Greenpeace heat but a stronger focus was placed on Peterson, said Perks, because "we really thought that he was going to win." But as Greenpeace read polls published during the campaign that revealed NDP strength, "it was like, Jesus Christ, we'd better get a commitment out of this guy on nuclear power because he hasn't said a word yet," Perks said.

Midway through the campaign, Greenpeace and five other environmental groups would send a letter to all three party leaders, demanding straight answers on environmental issues. Only Rae would reply, answering "yes" to such questions as "Will you phase out nuclear power?" and "Will you ban garbage incinerators?" Rae's response was prepared one week before NDP polls would show that his party had a chance of winning. "We've got him now," Perks would say.

Greenpeace achieved its goal in the Ontario election: bring environmental issues into prominence and make politicians deal with them. "From here on in," said Perks, "any politician who figures he's going to go out on the hustings has to be prepared to talk about what the people they run into want to talk about and not what their policy director has scripted and they read the night before. If you want to be premier, you've got to be prepared to answer Greenpeace. Politicians do everything they can to avoid these situations. I think that's changed."

Greenpeace plans similar activities for future Canadian elections, to force both incumbents and challengers to respond to environmental issues. "There were probably a couple of million people in Ontario who wished they were in my shoes at that point, that they could stand up in front of the premier and ask their five favorite questions," said Perks. "The sense that government is getting more closed and not more open, that's what I think played really well. We created a sense that here's this guy who can't even afford a nice shirt, he's got no power in the world and there he is, he's able to ruin the day of the most powerful man in the province."

From the moment of Perks' opening-day confrontation, Peterson knew what he was up against. "It set a tone in the campaign," he said. "That's all everybody saw, and that invites other people to do the same thing. There was no question that every dissident group came out during the campaign and that was played every night, even if there were three guys with signs on sticks. It looked like government under assault all the time. It sure as hell didn't help the campaign."

*   *   *

"Silly," Peterson blurted out early in 1989—Ontario teachers' concerns about their pensions were "silly." It was the wrong word, to the wrong group, at the wrong time. "Are you silly?" became a rallying cry for teachers that rang loudly, right through the 1990 campaign, at the Liberals' expense.

Vying for a piece of Peterson's hide on the Liberal campaign trail was the union representing Ontario's 60,000 public secondary school teachers, a political force in the province for decades that flexed its muscle in the 1990 election. Teachers' unions across Canada have strong mandates to become involved in provincial politics; provincial governments control virtually every tax dollar spent on education, including federal transfer payments. Some teachers' unions have earned a reputation as a candidate's best ally during a campaign. But if teachers are ticked off at a government, party or candidate, they can be powerful enemies.

In 1990 the Ontario Secondary School Teachers' Federation (OSSTF), the province's most politically charged teachers' union, obtained its first-ever mandate to seek a specific election outcome. The aim of the group, approved by its provincial assembly in March 1990, was to work toward a minority government—of any party. In the process, some Liberals would have to go.

OSSTF believed that minority government was responsive government, more conducive to conventional lobbying and open to negotiation. No significant education legislation could be enacted by a minority government, the teachers knew, without passing through the scrutiny of all-party committees of MPPs, where opportunities to pressure members to meet teachers' concerns could be used to full advantage. When dealing directly with a minority government, the teachers found open doors and could count on frequent consultation with the premier and ministers, who were anxious to keep the teachers from aligning too closely with the opposition. To Jim Head, president of OSSTF, "Majority governments have never been kind to teachers."

When OSSTF's mandate to secure a "minority-responsive" government in Ontario was set, few teachers believed the goal was attainable—they too read the polls. But OSSTF was determined to take action to get a "government that listens." The union maintained it had been conducting a "dialogue with the deaf" at Queen's Park with Education Minister Sean Conway; similar acrimony had soured its relationships with Peterson and Nixon. Sweeping changes in curriculum and the structure of elementary and secondary education had been introduced since 1987, including a plan to reduce the pupil to teacher ratio in Grades 1 and 2 to 20:1. These changes were all part of a broad education platform unveiled by the Liberals in the last election, which the teachers complained had been devised without adequate funding or implementation time and without consulting educators.

But OSSTF considered the Peterson government's handling of the teachers' pension issue the most blatant of all the Liberal affronts to the teaching profession. More than any other irritant, this pocketbook issue, said the teachers, drove them to the hustings.

The teachers' and public servants' pension funds had built up a $4-billion unfunded liability since the mid-1970s—that huge shortfall was projected when all the funds' contributors tried to collect their pensions. The crisis was the result of flaws in the design and management of the funds by the Tories. The teachers' fund alone had a $2.3-billion deficit.

To bring the problem under control the Liberals wanted to combine the teachers' fund with its separate indexation fund and legislate a one percent increase in contributions from teachers'

LEFT: 1990 Ontario Liberal campaign chair Kathy Robinson. Peterson was impressed with her hard work as party president and gave her the top job in the 1990 election.

RIGHT: Peterson's last principal secretary, Dan Gagnier. The lifelong bureaucrat advised Peterson on constitutional matters, but fell out of favor before the 1990 campaign.

LEFT: David MacNaughton. 1987 campaign co-chair for the Peterson Liberals, he headed their 1990 campaign strategy committee. When he couldn't get the platform he wanted, he said he "rolled over."

RIGHT: Martin Goldfarb. The perennial Liberal pollster missed the Trudeau years—when he felt his advice was followed. His 1990 election strategy, "the premier is the campaign," went awry when voters turned against Peterson.

LEFT: Senator Michael Kirby. In the 1990 campaign, he supported the Liberals' $1.1-billion cut in Ontario's retail sales tax—but the voters did not buy it.

RIGHT: Beth Webster. The 1990 Ontario Liberal campaign director, she followed in the footsteps of her husband John, director of the federal Liberals' 1988 campaign.

ABOVE: The premier, the "three-legged stool" and the cushion. From 1985-88, Peterson was supported by a delicate balance of personalities. Clockwise from top left: Hershell Ezrin, the policy and communications mastermind who left without grooming a successor; Peterson; Bob Carman, the diligent head of the public service; Gordon Ashworth, "the conscience of the Liberal party" who resigned during the Starr fund-raising scandal; Vince Borg, Peterson's friend and closest aide, who shared the body blows on the 1990 campaign trail.

Liberal Caucus Service Bureau

ABOVE: A man in motion: Peterson was on the move in 1985, with a bright future ahead of him.

LEFT: Peterson with children (l-r) Adam, Ben and Chloe and his wife Shelley. The image of the successful premier and his family was well-suited to the prosperous 1980s. Peterson kept his family out of the limelight, although they often joined him on the campaign trail at election time.

Liberal Caucus Service Bureau

Courtesy David and Shelley Peterson

ABOVE: In the backroom at Meech in 1987: (l-r) premiers Don Getty, Richard Hatfield, Robert Bourassa, Bill Vander Zalm, Peterson, Howard Pawley and Grant Devine. Peterson loved clubbing with his fellow premiers, often calling Getty and Bourassa for political advice—including whether to call an early election in 1990.

BELOW: The "four horsemen": (l-r) Attorney General Ian Scott, Education Minister Sean Conway, Peterson and Treasurer Bob Nixon. In its last months, the Liberal cabinet joked about an "October List" of decisions it could put off until after the September 1990 election.

Liberal Caucus Service Bureau

Liberal Caucus Service Bureau

LEFT: In the 1987 election, people clamored to "touch the border of his Roots sweatshirt," one reporter observed. By 1990, Peterson's yuppie image was wearing thin.

RIGHT: On Canada Day 1989, Ontarians lined up for hotdogs when Peterson handed them out. But by 1990 voters were fed up with style over substance.

Julie Matus photo

Randy Rath/CHCH TV photo

LEFT: Patti Starr. In June 1991, the former Liberal fund-raiser was sentenced to six months in jail for criminal breach of trust and fraud.

Julie Matus photo

LEFT: Claiming they had been neglected by the Liberals, members of the Toronto-area Sikh community mounted nomination challenges to three Liberal incumbents before the 1990 election. Peterson visited a Sikh temple and donned a makeshift turban, but the belated gesture underscored communication and community relations problems in the premier's office.

Ontario Liberal Party poster

Julie Matus photo

ABOVE: Snip snip #1: The original photo for the Liberal campaign poster featured a couple discovered at the last minute to be Tories. A receptionist and her husband were posed and spliced in to create a theme picture that never happened.

Courtesy John Laschinger

Courtesy Phil Gillies

NDP Caucus Service Bureau

Courtesy Gerald Caplan

UPPER LEFT: John Laschinger. The 1990 Tory campaign manager used every trick in the book. The Tories set the tone and determined the issues of the 1990 campaign, and helped send NDP leader Bob Rae to the premier's office.

UPPER RIGHT: Phil Gillies. The Tory spin-doctor played the media like a violin in the 1990 campaign.

LOWER LEFT: NDP strategist David Reville. The former MPP tried to keep pace with Gillies in the battle of the spin-doctors.

LOWER RIGHT: Gerald Caplan. This veteran NDP strategist abhorred his party's attack strategy and campaign television commercials filled with what he called "lies."

John Felstead/Canapress

ABOVE: The protester phenomenon begins at the 1990 campaign kickoff: "There were probably a couple of million people who wished they were in my shoes," said Greenpeace activist Gord Perks.

Julie Matus photo

Ilan Scott campaign brochure

ON SEPTEMBER 6
RE-ELECT IAN SCOTT

"The workhorse of the Ontario Government" Ottawa Citizen

IAN SCOTT HEADQUARTERS
439 Parliament Street
975-5000

ABOVE: Snip snip #2: Attorney General Ian Scott posed with the premier for a publicity shot before the 1990 election was called. But when Peterson became a liability during the campaign, a Scott brochure used half the picture and covered Peterson with a self-adhesive note.

salaries, to be matched by taxpayers. Teachers lashed out at the demand for more of their money and were incensed with the Liberals' refusal to permit them to share in managing the fund. The two sides believed different actuarial assumptions about the fund: the Liberals argued it might continue to lose money at public expense and were reluctant to share its management; the teachers claimed it could earn money and wanted joint management of the fund with the opportunity to use profits to improve benefits.

In April 1989, shortly after Peterson's "silly" remark, Head told a rally of 17,000 teachers outside the Liberal party's annual general meeting in Hamilton that all OSSTF wanted was a "fair ride,"and that the Peterson government ignored teachers at its own peril. Seven months later, when the Liberals passed new teachers' pension legislation that rejected the teachers' position, OSSTF saw the ballot box as its court of appeal.

The Liberals had plenty of warning of the union's plan to state its case in the 1990 election. "They made their intentions known very clearly," said Dan Gagnier. "They talked to everybody who'd listen, the treasurer and people in the premier's office. They published their position and made it known they would be using the full weight of their organization and their membership to militate actively against the government, either to help defeat Liberal candidates and incumbents or to run their own people against them, whichever led to the greatest amount of difficulty for the government."

But the Liberals believed the pension fight was far too complicated to become an election issue. They felt that Ontarians would not sympathize with well-paid teachers and public servants who claimed rich pension plans with inflation protections and enjoyed good job security. OSSTF, however, wisely decided not to make the pension issue the focus of its attack on the Liberals. Teachers did not want to be painted as "pampered whiners" by Peterson, Head explained. The emphasis, OSSTF determined, had to be on broad educational concerns that would sell to the average person.

"Spending too little on public schools is child neglect" was the campaign slogan used by OSSTF; it appeared on brochures, buttons, billboards and in newspaper ads in major dailies. Backing up the theme were the teachers' charges that the Liberals had steadily reduced the province's share of the costs of education, a claim made in spite of the Liberals' unprecedented increases in school construction grants and operating grants to school boards.

OSSTF set up an election desk in May to coordinate its campaign communications and media functions and an army of "teacher-activists."A budget of $250,000 was allocated to "send the message": $100,000 went into a media campaign, with most of the remainder donated to candidates and used to support campaign activities in the union's local districts. The Ontario Teachers' Federation (OTF), a larger umbrella organization including public elementary school teachers, ran a similar program of campaign activity with a $100,000 budget. OSSTF's plan was to put teachers in ridings to work for candidates who were "friendly to education and had a reasonable chance of election." Twenty-two ridings were targeted for "direct action."

But like other players in the 1990 election, OSSTF's strategy was affected by the polls that showed strong support for Peterson and the Liberals. Priority was initially given by the teachers to winning opposition seats and improving the chances of achieving a minority government.

Reporters found these activities newsworthy. In July a CBC-TV news report featured OSSTF's election-readiness team, stressing that disenchantment with the Liberals was the reason for the activism. Nixon, Peterson and Conway were tagged as "pirates" by a union organizer. Other major media also took note of OSSTF's campaign planning. Part of the teachers' strategy was already working: grab media attention early.

During the campaign, OSSTF's demands for minority-responsive government were revealed at a well-attended news conference. At a widely reported debate in Peterborough, OSSTF and the Ontario English Catholic Teachers' Association argued with candidates from all three parties to call attention to teachers' concerns. The debate marked the first time in Ontario that the two teachers' groups collaborated in a common cause.

More than 300 teachers volunteered to work in the ridings targeted by OSSTF. A majority of the teachers worked for NDP candidates; some worked for Tories, including party leader Harris in North Bay and education critic Cam Jackson in Burlington; only a few worked for Liberals, including ministers Lyn McLeod in Thunder Bay and Gerry Phillips in Scarborough. OSSTF decided to leave Peterson, Nixon and Bradley alone because it considered their grip on their ridings too tight.

The union wanted local teachers involved in local campaigns under a master plan that tended to work against Liberal candidates. But executing that plan was made difficult by the pattern of traditional party affiliation of OSSTF's members: "About 40 percent of our membership are Liberal, about 40 percent are Tory and about 20 percent are NDP," Head estimated. "So when you run these kinds of campaigns you've got to remember that, and you've got to convince people why they are going to vote against their own party this time." Many teachers proved willing to snip their partisan ties to advance their own cause. By election day OSSTF would boast it had more than 900 people engaged in the fight. The union believed its most significant impact on the campaign was to reduce the number of teachers who were active Liberal supporters.

Like Greenpeace, OSSTF ran a traveling road show that dogged Peterson and other candidates throughout Ontario. At all-candidates meetings and leaders' appearances, teachers faithfully showed up with picket signs to shout that the election was about education and demand that Peterson account for his government's record. Head acted as a general: cellular phone in hand, he personally directed three motor homes filled with teachers to wherever the action was.

With teachers involved in all 130 local campaigns, an intricate and extensive intelligence network provided timely data that allowed the union's resources to be best allocated. Reinforcing the ground assault was the media campaign: billboards were rented in a dozen cities and ads were placed in major newspapers before and during the election.

OSSTF would claim a share of the responsibility for the election result—although the union's objective of a minority government would not be achieved. Some Liberals would credit the teachers with ending their political careers. Peterson cabinet minister Ken Black, a former teacher and principal, found himself abandoned in 1990 by many teachers who helped him in 1987. "I could understand," he said. In Brantford, secondary school teachers had helped elect former teacher Dave Neumann, who discovered that few of his former colleagues were moved to support his bid for re-election. In the Windsor-area riding of Essex-Kent, one of the longest-sitting Liberals, Jim McGuigan, complained publicly about the role teachers played in the campaign.

After the election, OSSTF would herald its success at "sending a message." That message, Head would say, was clear: Never again can teachers be taken for granted, because they have the power to "make a difference." But while teachers demonstrated their clout in Ontario in 1990, their activism was driven chiefly by the pension issue. While the teachers' unions demonstrated they can mobilize their members and influence a campaign, repeat performances will depend on how strongly their members feel motivated to get involved. "It's the same old problem," said Head. "Unless it affects individuals, they don't get interested."

*   *   *

Another special-interest group that took a supporting role in the campaign was the Ontario Medical Association (OMA), representing 18,500 doctors. After their experience with extra billing from 1985 to 1987, Ontario doctors were anxious not to be cast again in the role of "black hats" or obvious villains that Peterson and the Liberals could oppose so easily in an election.

In the aftermath of the extra-billing fight, the OMA overhauled its public and government relations operation to rebuild the image of doctors and communicate OMA concerns internally and to Ontarians. Like many special-interest groups the OMA used public opinion research to develop its communications planning—and its strategy in the 1990 election. The OMA learned that, while Ontarians were concerned about accessibility and quality of health care, they did not want to see doctors and government engaged in pitched battle.

"The polling has shown if you have two large and powerful organizations battling with each other, public opinion could shift either way," said Paul Rhodes, the OMA's manager of government relations. "But in the end, the individual is going to think that he's the person who's getting hurt by this, and a pox on both your houses."

The polling revealed the OMA had considerable credibility when it raised the quality and accessibility issues but Ontarians were turned off by doctors complaining publicly about their fees or health care funding. The findings led the OMA to rule out a campaign strategy that visibly pitted doctors against Liberals or focused on dollars and cents, and opt instead for a theme of quality and accessibility in the health care system.

But the OMA's leadership faced a dilemma. The association had been embroiled for more than a year in renegotiating the doctors' fee schedule with the Peterson government. The fees had not been increased since a 1.75 percent raise imposed by the Liberals in 1988. The OMA was seeking binding arbitration to end the dispute and get more money. Backing up their argument was Justice Emmett Hall's 1979 federal report on health care, which concluded that binding arbitration should be a condition of any health care system that did not allow extra billing.

In June 1990 the OMA dropped a long-standing legal challenge to the Canada Health Act and the province's extra-billing legislation to clear the path for binding arbitration. But the Liberals did not want the doctors to be subject, union-style, to binding arbitration, and wanted the fee schedule talks to be the framework for "a new, more cooperative relationship between the province and the medical profession."

The OMA was pessimistic, explained Rhodes. It believed the Liberals were going to be returned to power with another majority and might again unilaterally impose a fee schedule that doctors would find inadequate. Significant membership problems would arise, OMA leaders thought, if doctors believed their association was failing to seize a good opportunity to criticize the government in the election campaign.

For months, relations between the OMA and the province had spiraled downward. Health Minister Elinor Caplan and Peterson infuriated doctors by alleging that a doctor in a controversial suicide case had not used the province's crisis care system properly; Caplan erroneously claimed the OMA had endorsed a plan to reduce caesarean section births by 25 percent; the OMA felt swindled over the implementation of the Liberals' Independent Health Facilities Act, a plan to license facilities providing services traditionally available only in hospitals. "Caplan stood up in the house day after day talking about how much cooperation was going on, when in fact there was very little," said Rhodes. "And what was going on was clouded in such suspicion and antagonism as to be almost meaningless."

Before pushing forward with a full-blown strategy for the election, OMA leaders blitzed Peterson's office with warnings that they were going to turn on the heat. The response, Rhodes found, was "Go ahead. We don't care. Do what you feel you have to do." The Liberals believed the doctors would not risk another public flogging over money issues, and voters would not be sympathetic to their "plight." Gagnier was among those who received a warning call. When he relayed the warnings, he said, cabinet was indifferent: "They felt, 'Well, we put them in their place, and if they give us an issue we'll get them this time as well,'" said Gagnier.

That response sealed it for the OMA. Although resigned that the Liberals could not be turfed, the association felt obliged to go after them. "We had two purposes," said Rhodes. "One, to show the government we would because they didn't believe we would, and two, we felt the Liberals were going to get back in and there would be a continuation of the kind of attitude we faced. We could not have faced our membership without having done something of a high profile nature, particularly in light of the fact that Manitoba doctors went on strike during the election campaign and got a deal."

The OMA came up with a strategy it believed was salable to both the public and its members. Late in July, days before the election call, the association spent $100,000 to mail letters to 300,000 Ontario households, criticizing the Liberals over quality and accessibility issues. Calling for cooperation between doctors and government, the letter, signed by OMA president Dr. Basil Johnston, warned of worsening shortages of nurses, equipment, and hospital and emergency services. Attached was a questionnaire on health care. The mailing reached Ontario homes in the first days of the campaign, but Rhodes told reporters that this was a coincidence: "We're not tying it to the election campaign," he said. The letter enabled the doctors to attack the government without setting themselves up again as a foil for Peterson.

OMA ads placed in Ontario newspapers at the same time as the mailing carried the message about cooperative doctors and the intransigent Liberal government. "The OMA wants to make the health care system better for all Ontarians; we want to work together." Photos of caring doctors examining babies and talking to elderly people accompanied the message. The ads were tested with focus groups in June—and unearthed a surprise for the OMA.

"People were incredibly angry at the government," Rhodes observed. "There was a definite anger out there. We were just sitting there and then suddenly this government dump came out of nowhere. We were quite surprised because the doctors weren't being blamed. It was an antigovernment focus." The groups confirmed the OMA message would sell, but the doctors' did not realize they were on to a sentiment strong and pervasive enough to mean serious trouble for the Liberals.

*   *   *

The special-interest group working hardest against the Liberals in the 1990 election was the union representing the government's own 105,000 employees. The Ontario Public Service Employees Union (OPSEU) executed a massive and intricate plan of political activity aimed at bringing its issues—and a vehement anti-Liberal message—to the attention of voters. Groups of prison guards and clerical, provincial welfare, hospital and highway workers rallied at all-candidates meetings and invaded Liberal events to protest neglect of their concerns. OPSEU was active in the 1985 and 1987 elections but its level of organization, the sophistication of its tactics and the confidence of its members in the 1990 campaign were unprecedented.

As they did with many other special-interest groups, the Liberals gave little credence to the potential impact of OPSEU's activism. "I think they grossly underestimated us, as the Conservatives did in 1985," said Jim Clancy, president of OPSEU from 1984 until September 1990, when he became president of the National Union of Provincial Government Employees. "They grossly underestimated our style of organizing, campaigning and reaching out to members. We represent members in every two-horse town in Ontario."

Clancy and top New Democrats refuted suggestions that the giant union had a deal with the NDP in the 1990 campaign to develop and unleash a cooperative anti-Liberal strategy. But in ridings across Ontario, evidence abounded of long-standing ties between OPSEU and the NDP, the party closest to labor. "To the degree that would happen," said Clancy, "it would happen naturally because the people who were organizing locally were also active in the NDP. But formally, nothing."

But OPSEU's messages during the election were a neat overlay of the NDP attacks. OPSEU's campaign jabbed at the Liberals with the question, "Who's in charge here? Is it private greed or the public interest?" This loudly echoed what Rae called the NDP's essential question for the campaign: "Who should run the province? The people or the special interests?"

The "Who's in charge here?" theme was conceived in April, 1990 by Clancy and other union heads. OPSEU believed "Peterson's a nice guy. We all really like him but when working with special-interest groups, nothing was happening. So, 'Who's in charge here?' The answer could be the bureaucrats and, for other constituencies, maybe the developers." And "during this period," Clancy noted, "he's increasingly playing the role of

Captain Canada," raising the question of who was in charge of Ontario and looking out for Ontarians' interests.

Battles between OPSEU and the government included the Liberals' failure to deliver enhanced rights to political activity for public servants and a trend toward privatization, divestment and downloading of provincial services to community agencies and municipal governments—a trend that eliminated the jobs of some provincial public servants.

But like their counterparts in the teaching profession, Ontario public servants had a pension bone to pick with the Liberals. OPSEU was also enraged by the government's move to increase members' financial contributions without sharing the management of their pension plan. Clancy found he could motivate his members by encouraging them to think about the pension issue in terms of "somebody coming up to your front door once every week or two weeks and saying, 'I want 9 per-cent of your earnings, but I'm not going to tell you how I'm investing it and you don't have any say in how it's invested.' OPSEU members will vote in their own self-interest. Externally, I hit the government on other issues."

OPSEU's campaign strategy worked at two levels, said Clancy: clobbering the government in public on a wide range of popular issues and whipping up the union membership about their pensions and job security. In the fall of 1989 OPSEU leaders began to plot campaign strategy. OPSEU's board of directors approved a "public outreach campaign" with a budget of $1 million—nearly half the campaign budgets of each of the three main parties.

Just as the Liberals, NDP and Tories held intensive campaign training sessions, OPSEU called in its troops for pre-election orders. Top officers from the union's provincewide network of area councils gathered in Toronto on July 28 to learn how to put the union's strategy into action on the ground against Liberal candidates.

In a session called "Picnics," the OPSEU members were taught how to disrupt Liberal picnics and barbeques. Printed instructions told them to recruit "people on unemployment insurance, retirees and anyone else who has a beef against the government" to supplement their own members in assaults on Liberal events. The advice included where to stand and what to do. "Ten OPSEU members half-moon around the premier or MPP with placards and OPSEU flags," the instructions read. "The 10 members in front and members picketing throughout the crowd create domination and publicity for the TV and press." The crash course in campaign activism was rounded out with budgeting tips, media training and policy review. OPSEU members fanned out across the province in search of Liberal candidates, armed with an arsenal of facts and tactics, ready to turn the Liberal's expected easy win into trench warfare.

But these local activities were only the background for OPSEU's solidly financed central strategy, which attacked the Liberals on four fronts: a "SWAT team" trailed Peterson on his tour; OPSEU ads inundated radio and newspapers, all-candidates forums were sponsored and stacked with union members and direct mailings on election issues poured out to the members before and during the campaign, urging them "to tell the province's politicians what they should be doing."

The SWAT team had been given a trial run in summer 1989 at Peterson's Liberal membership drive picnics; it had been all but ignored by reporters. In the summer of 1990 the union's attack squad was ready to move when the election was called. The SWAT team was composed of OPSEU members who worked in correctional facilities, psychiatric hospitals and institutions for the criminally insane. Clancy wanted people who were afraid of nothing, people who had seen it all. They were "big," articulated well and were trained to stay on a question. During the campaign a dozen OPSEU members would work on the squad, three or four at a time.

Clancy delivered his directions personally. "Look for an opening where the guy can be harassed," he instructed. The SWAT team caught up with Peterson on the second day of the Liberal tour and immediately staked out its turf as an effective conveyer of its message. Armed with booming voices, daunting physiques and fearless attitudes, the SWAT team made commanding appearances at almost every stop on Peterson's tour. Its approach was straightforward: wade in, shove aside whomever was unfortunate enough to be standing in the way—including other protesters—and follow Clancy's orders to "jam on Peterson and ask him questions." To keep reporters interested and to appear not to be strictly self-serving, OPSEU's own messages were often set aside during these confrontational dances with Peterson and replaced with loud questions on the environment, the economy, housing and poverty.

By the midpoint of the campaign, OPSEU's delegates had made a deep impression on the Liberals. In Cornwall on the day Peterson was to make an important announcement, the SWAT team and the premier's entourage were booked into the same hotel. The Liberals wanted the event to go off without a hitch. Before Peterson's announcement, some of his staff knocked on the door of the OPSEU room and asked the SWAT team to refrain from interrupting the premier. The reply: OPSEU members did not intend to interrupt the event, but they would be there.

All went well for the Liberals until the event ended. Six-foot-two-inch corrections officer Mike Oliver approached Peterson, who was being scrummed by reporters, and muscled his way through. He demanded that Peterson explain whether the announcement meant the Liberals "were not going to follow through on the promise to reduce overcrowding in Ontario's jails." Peterson tried to brush off the suggestion that he would reduce funding of public services to save money. But Oliver, adhering to his training, stayed on the question.

"Well," Peterson said, "let me look into that."

"That's what you've been telling us for a long time," Oliver replied.

"When I tell you I'm going to look into it for you, I mean it," Peterson said firmly. "If you'd be so kind as to leave me your business card."

"Business card?" Oliver bellowed. "What do you think I am, a developer or something? I'm a corrections officer; we don't have business cards." Everyone within earshot, including reporters, broke into laughter while Peterson turned beet red. OPSEU spread the word on the exchange, convinced it showed Peterson was out of touch with the average Ontarian.

About $700,000 of OPSEU's million-dollar campaign fund was pumped into advertising. Four broad public concerns were targeted: the environment, housing, poverty, and health, social and other public services, all drawn together under the "Who's in charge here?" theme. Five subjects were selected for radio and newspaper ads that tied those concerns to those of OPSEU members: privatization of water and sewer operations, forests, homelessness, closure of psychiatric hospitals and mental retardation facilities and the larger issue of privatization of public services. Clancy and other OPSEU leaders arbitrarily picked the subjects for the ads based on their "read" of what voters and members were concerned about; the union had not resolved an internal debate over the use of polling. The ads were further tailored to play to local OPSEU concerns in individual communities.

OPSEU, like other special-interest groups, was able to place its ads at any point during the campaign—in the opening days, to make early impressions, or in the closing days, to hit voters who saved their decisions for the end. Special-interest groups remain unaffected by limits on spending and timing of advertising that regulate the activity of political parties during a campaign.

A master stroke in OPSEU's campaign strategy was its plan to seize control of all-candidates meetings in ridings. In the two previous Ontario elections the union taught its local officers to be the first to set up all-candidates meetings, before other local organizations or the candidates themselves could reach agreement on debates. In 1990 the system worked so efficiently that OPSEU-sponsored debates were the only all-candidates sessions in scores of ridings. Although the union encouraged the public to attend, OPSEU locals stacked the crowd with members, ensuring that the agenda adhered closely to OPSEU's antigovernment bent. Union officers heavily promoted the forums in the local media; reporters who attended were provided with a display of animosity toward the local Liberal candidate, which was often reported as spontaneous and broad-based. "The members could answer a broader range of policy issues than most of the candidates that came out," Clancy boasted. "They could go toe to toe with them."

Many of the activities of OPSEU members during the campaign appeared to be in defiance of provincial laws governing political activity by public servants—laws the Liberals promised to change in their 1985 accord with the NDP and did not, to the lingering resentment of the union.

OPSEU advised its members that "civil servants are barred by law from canvassing and may not comment publicly in a partisan manner." OPSEU publications and advertisements carefully avoided specific partisan attacks on the Liberals. But to Clancy, OPSEU's actions spoke louder than words: "I remember in 1989 saying to the management board of cabinet, 'Well, fuck political rights. You think that's number one on our list?' I mean, we've taken it. In 1990 I didn't hire one lawyer to protect my members. Our members just went out and took it."*

With members who "took it," a million-dollar war chest, a powerful provincewide organization and a comprehensive strategy, OPSEU too would claim a share in turning voters against the Peterson government.

"I said to Nixon," Clancy recalled about the pension fight, "'It's a long road that doesn't have a curve in it, and I'll catch you at the curve. I'll catch you.'"

*   *   *

"At first blush, it may seem a peculiar group of three musketeers," said Dr. Basil Johnston as he looked out across the roomful of reporters and TV cameras assembled for a news conference at

---

* On June 6, 1991, the Supreme Court of Canada ruled that the Charter of Rights and Freedoms gives most public servants the right to support political parties and publicly support candidates during an election. The 6 to 1 decision struck down as unconstitutional a section of the federal public service employment act which forbade a deputy head and any government employee from engaging in work for or against a candidate or a political party. Top bureaucrats, those regularly involved in developing government policy, must remain politically neutral, the court decided.

a Toronto hotel on August 14. "The fact we're together is an expression of our concern that this government is unwilling or unable to respond responsibly to the people."

As president of the OMA, Johnston was engaging in a rare form of coalition building. Two weeks into the Ontario election, he was flanked by Beverly Polowy, president of OTF, and OPSEU president Clancy to denounce the Peterson Liberals.

Joint election campaign action by some of Ontario's most politically charged special-interest groups emerged for the first time in 1990. Believing that voters would notice several groups carrying a common message, the province's doctors, teachers and unionized public servants teamed up to take a collective slap at the Liberals. The three issued a joint statement that attacked Peterson for failing to live up to promises of open, consultative government, improved health care, better social services, more money for education and lower car insurance rates. They called for "a new government that is more responsive to the needs of Ontarians and to the concerns of the frontline providers of health, education and public service."

Nine months before the election OMA executives began to feel out groups, including OTF and OPSEU, for their assessments of relations with the Liberals. That first step was difficult but the doctors believed their organization had to become less isolated from other interest groups. "There was a lot of mistrust and prejudice that had to be overcome," said the OMA's Rhodes. A face-to-face meeting was arranged, with immediate results. "We were stunned, because the way we believed we had been treated by the government, in an arbitrary and unilateral way, was exactly the same complaint from the others," said Rhodes. "Suddenly you could see the lights going on around the room: 'Well, maybe we should all be involved in a joint project.'" The coalition anticipated that the Liberal campaign would steer clear of substance, and agreed to make sure the vacuum was filled by its issues, which Peterson would be forced to discuss, rather than "how the local hot dogs are the best he's tasted," said Clancy.

As Johnston, Polowy and Clancy each read antigovernment statements, there was no doubt about the message. "Here are three representative organizations within the community who believe that the way the current government is dealing with them is poor," said Rhodes. "We have a government in place that is more interested in confrontation and who acted as political machismos without solving any problems."

The never-before-seen coalition grabbed the spotlight. Its news conference received wide coverage and made the lead story on most Ontario newscasts that evening. Few reporters suggested the groups were motivated by self-interest. Most were impressed by the image of three major organizations uniting, each believing another Liberal majority was almost a certainty but still angry enough to raise the issues and voice their problems, regardless of the consequences when the Liberals were re-elected. News of the collaboration fed the growing climate of rejection of the Liberals.

*   *   *

Although caught flat-footed by Peterson's early-election call, Ontario's fringe parties emerged as a critical political force in the summer of 1990—they would increase their share of the popular vote from about 2 percent to 7 percent. In more than two dozen ridings, the vote for fringe party candidates would exceed the margin of victory—usually at the expense of the Liberals.

Like the special-interest groups active in the Ontario election, the fringe parties represented collective voices of protest. Their growing attractiveness to voters pointed to weakening allegiances to traditional parties, primarily among people whose political activity and voting behavior is driven by interest in a single issue. Supporters of the fringe parties tended to be people who felt their narrow interests were not being served by the brokerage politics practiced by the mainstream parties—political decision making based on the principles of compromise and "making as many people as satisfied as possible" by convincing divergent interests to accept limits and trade-offs in their demands.

By the midpoint of the campaign, fringe candidates were popping up in ridings across Ontario. Most were put forward by the antiabortion Family Coalition Party (FCP); by the Confederation of Regions Party (CoR), linked to the anti-French and antibilingual Alliance for the Preservation of English in Canada (APEC); and the Green Party, with its strong environmental bent.

Strongest and best organized of the fringe parties was the Family Coalition Party, affiliated with the national Campaign Life Coalition. In the 1987 Ontario election the FCP recruited 36 candidates; only one received more than 3,000 votes. But by 1990, its organization and membership were bolstered by the fight against Bill C–43, the federal abortion law, and by its involvement in the national Liberal leadership campaign of pro-lifer Tom Wappel. The FCP's ground-level activism was hardened by years of militating against abortion clinics in Toronto and women's health centers, a creation of the Liberal government that broadened access to services, including abortion, in other Ontario communities. Its skills and resolve tougher than ever, the abortion-fighting FCP put forward a slate of 68 candidates in 1990; five would top the 3,000-vote mark as their party increased its total vote by 130 percent. FCP organizers claimed up to 90 percent of their votes in some ridings came from the Liberals. The organization estimated in 1990 that 70 percent of its members were Catholics, traditionally a strong constituency of the Liberal party.

The FCP entered the campaign determined to make abortion "a real live issue," said its organizers. Accepting that it could not come close to winning a seat, the FCP had a more modest objective: "Give our supporters a chance not to have to spoil their ballots." It sought to lay the groundwork for the next provincial election, when it planned to run a full slate of pro-life candidates. Like the other special-interest groups active in the campaign, the FCP believed that defeating the Liberals was impossible. Nor were the pro-life candidates interested in helping the Tories.

"The Tories? No, different-colored slime," said Frank Kennedy, a FCP organizer. The NDP? "We felt they were like dogs chasing a car. However, not our enemies. They did not create killing centers. They were like us—on the outside looking in. We decided to aim all of our blows against the Liberals and the Tories."

FCP's three regional directors, part of the Toronto-based party's executive of fourteen, slowly pulled their organizations together in local ridings. Candidates were recruited from the pro-life movement; some were disenchanted members of mainstream parties. "I've been a Liberal for 25 years," said Gordon Maloney, FCP candidate in Perth. "I couldn't live with my conscience any more. I wasn't even going to vote, but it was like a gift from God when the FCP came to my door. It was a real pleasure to find a party that represented all the family values I believe in."

The pro-lifers' election arsenal was not extensive or sophisticated, consisting of two pieces of literature and a cartoon book. The pamphlets condemned the three major parties for betraying the Ontario people by discarding "the essential values on which the province was built." They contained promises to increase funding for schools, reduce taxes and toughen penalties for polluters—interspersed with commitments to ban abortion clinics, condom machines in high schools and Sunday shopping.

"Our election literature read like a Sunday School paper," admitted Kennedy, "but we tried to present alternatives and solutions to problems." The party's 1990 Ontario Election Cartoon Book, filled with editorial cartoons from *The Interim*, a pro-life newspaper, invited Ontarians to read the jokes, "if you're concerned about the $45-million coronation that David Peterson has planned for himself on September 6."

"In this election, vote for families, honesty, morality," read the FCP tracts. That message was also conveyed in a television advertisement, which received limited exposure on the FCP's tiny budget of $30,000.

Unlike other special-interest groups on the hustings, the FCP received scant attention from reporters. "The media listed us under 'fringe' and treated us with mild disdain," said Kennedy.

But the FCP made a tangible difference in several ridings where Liberals would suffer. In Willowdale, in north Toronto, incumbent Gino Matrundola was considered "safe" by the Liberal campaign but the Tory candidate would displace him by 790 votes; Matrundola would attribute his defeat to the 1,078 votes that would go to the FCP. The most dramatic evidence of the cumulative clout of the fringe parties would be felt in Peterborough by Liberal incumbent Peter Adams. FCP, CoR and Green candidates would combine to account for 5,500 votes, or 13 percent of the total vote. NDP candidate Jenny Carter would prevail by only 138 votes over second-place Adams.

Fringe parties in the election snatched votes away from the mainstream parties over single issues strong enough to change people's voting behavior—abortion, French-language rights, the environment. By the end of the campaign, it would become evident that the fringe parties' ability to increase their share of the popular vote was tied closely to their success in fielding an increasing number of candidates linked to these issues. A small increase in the fringe parties' share of the popular vote would emerge, suggesting that protest votes were lodged by people who did not believe the Liberal government could be defeated and wanted to make a protest they believed would be "cost-free"—that would not affect the result of the election—or who refused to accept either the Tories or NDP as an alternative.

The FCP would show signs of reaching a growth ceiling. The average vote for its candidates would rise only from 4 percent to 5.2 percent; just four FCP candidates would achieve more than 10 percent of the vote. In seven ridings won by the NDP by small margins the FCP would claim responsibility for the difference. Combined with other fringe groups who fielded candidates the FCP would prove statistically to have a significant role in helping the NDP overtake the Liberals. Recognizing that the NDP's position on abortion is nearly identical to the Liberals', FCP organizer Kennedy would be encouraged by the outcome. "We were not able to reward our friends," he said, "but we were able to punish our enemies."

*   *   *

For 37 steamy summer days David Peterson was chased across Ontario by protesters who pursued him like an angry mob of bill collectors. By the end of the first week of the campaign, all the protest acts, road shows, shadow tours and SWAT teams were up and running hard. As they jockeyed for openings to deliver slap after slap, they created a clutter of confusion and chaos from which one primary message emerged: people are mad as hell at Peterson.

For reporters, the ever-strengthening protester story represented an important angle to the campaign that had to be covered. It helped provide what many of them thought was missing—a sense of balance to a government that was going largely unchallenged as it continued to ride high in the polls. "The media started out sort of feeling that they had to be skeptical because that was the only way there would be some balance in the eventual victory," explained the *Globe*'s Mackie. "The Liberal government had been so arrogant before, that if they won another sweeping victory, you knew they'd get absolutely nothing done."

The protester story also helped fill the giant news hole the Liberals seemed to reporters to be intent on creating. Their first announcement, a $65-million skills training plan unveiled on the second day of the campaign, came off badly. Following the recommendations of a report released just one week earlier by the Premier's Council on Technology, Peterson's first campaign goody promised money to businesses to help them train employees and hire apprentices. In the tough, "show-me" climate on Peterson's media bus, the *Globe*'s Mackie scanned the skills training news release with a critical eye.

"I've got a problem with these numbers," he told Liberal media officers Martha Durdin and Moira McIntyre. "The figures are phony," he said, pointing out that the figures in the announcement could be added up to $220 million.

As Mackie argued loudly with Peterson's staff, other print and television reporters picked up on the dispute. Peterson agreed the calculation could be interpreted either way. Instead of transmitting a clear-cut, positive message, the Liberals' first announcement was muddied by a dispute over cost—and the relationship between reporters and Peterson's tour staff was off to a bad start.

Day after day, the Liberal offerings failed to impress the news-hungry reporters. Even their expectations of a burger a day were not being met. "This isn't a Gainsburger," one scoffed, reading a Liberal release that first week, "it's a piece of Kibbles and Bits."

"The stuff he was saying just wasn't playing," said Mackie. "On the first three days of the campaign he hadn't mentioned Rae, Harris or Mulroney. He hadn't talked about anything serious; it was just the vague generalities about Canada's a great country. You knew how vacuous the campaign was. It was a total vacuum."

For reporters tiring of the Liberals' bland little burgers, the protester story was a spicy new dish. "I think it filled the gap," said Mackie. "It was something to focus on when there wasn't anything else to focus on. If someone stood up and confronted Peterson, that was a story." This sudden symbiosis between protesters and media would prove disastrous for the Liberals as their summer sleepwalk became a nightmare.

Nightly news reports on Peterson's tour began to reflect the growing importance of the protesters as the only campaign story with real substance. Story after story led off with or included the cacophony of the day's attack. This focus became even sharper as "ordinary" Ontarians, out to vent their spleen, began to join the organized protesters.

On the second day of the campaign, as the Liberal buses rolled out of downtown Toronto, Peterson's bus ground to a halt at an intersection. Vince Borg glanced out through the tinted glass window. On the sidewalk, "a 45-year-old elegantly dressed woman" was grappling with her designer shopping bags in an effort to raise her hand. Borg began to smile, expecting the woman to wave. But his eyes bulged as the woman jabbed a vigorous one-finger salute. It was the first of many times that gesture would be glimpsed through the windows of the Liberal buses.

The "couple of million people" Greenpeace's Perks thought wanted to be in his shoes at Peterson's kickoff news conference seemed to start showing up in person on the Liberal tour, signs in hand. In the first eight days of the campaign, Peterson faced six different local protests from what his tour staff called "garbage folks"—residents of communities with sites being considered as repositories for Toronto's garbage. Local environmentalists joined them, clad in skeleton suits and silver antiradiation gear to protest everything from dump sites to water quality at the local beach to nuclear power. For several weeks, Peterson was chased around by a person dressed as a tree.

As the protest story took hold, it legitimized for ordinary people the act of confronting a powerful politician. In the second week of the campaign, a group of sign-wielding elderly women showed up to challenge Peterson over a dangerous intersection in their town.

As the protest story outgrew its special-interest group genesis, its importance in the eyes of the media solidified. "We made a conscious decision to include those people in our stories," said the Toronto *Star*'s Matt Maychak. He consulted with *Star* editors, who had come to regret their decision not to cover the protesters who pestered Miller in the 1985 election, believing they did not represent dissatisfaction with the Tories. In 1990 when ordinary people began coming out to take a swing at Peterson, reporters felt they had to pay attention.

"It's hard to walk up to a premier and say, 'I think what you're doing stinks,'" said Maychak. "For every person who finds the guts or has the personality that allows someone to do that, I believe there's probably a thousand or several thousand who feel the same way. That approach by the media may have been abused at times, but in general I would defend that. But I think you'd find Liberals who felt our coverage of those people created thousands like them. We made the judgment they already represented thousands like them."

*   *   *

The outpouring of acrimony by the protesters, both organized and ad hoc, was unexpected by the Liberals only in its degree. As early as May, Goldfarb's focus group research on Peterson's image revealed the anti-Liberal trend, with much of it directed against Peterson himself. The findings had noted beliefs that "the premier and the government tend to duck controversial issues" and "the government does not act until it is forced to act by public or media pressure." But the Liberals, overconfident about the positive side of Peterson's image, did not give full weight to the danger those negatives represented or how people might respond to them if they were widely exposed.

The louder the chorus of voices rose against Peterson, the more the negative aspects of his image emerged—especially to the unblinking eye of the television camera. The problem the Liberal strategists had glossed over was being realized, as Peterson began to look and act like the "evasive," "wishy-washy" politician that Goldfarb's focus groups found so offensive. Peterson usually lacked concrete answers to the problems he was presented with—and in most cases there were no quick and easy answers to the issues being shoved in his face. But without being able to deliver definitive replies, Peterson was not able to come out on top in the confrontations and take ownership of each exchange.

The Liberals' answer was to have Peterson attempt to include in each exchange a simple "value statement"—that he would not want a garbage dump placed in a town without due process having been followed, for example. But those replies were rendered ineffective by his inability to deliver a bottom-line answer that met the expectations of the protesters challenging him. Nor was Peterson able to consistently get across a visceral sense of honest passion strong enough to compensate for what appeared to be his failure to deliver the goods. He appeared not to have good answers and he did not sound sincere.

Ontarians who viewed these episodes on the news night after night began to believe they were watching a politician who did not have a set of values that shaped his political beliefs, who lacked principles and trustworthiness and who spoke without honest passion. This confirmed Goldfarb's groups' earlier suspicions. Nightly "evidence" of Peterson's hollowness tapped into long-held feelings of doubt about the honesty and integrity of the Liberal government. The Liberal strategists knew that concerns about these qualities meant a great deal to voters—Goldfarb had identified "each party's stance on honesty and integrity in government" as the number one leverage issue for voters. But the strategists believed the Liberals were not vulnerable in this area. Goldfarb had assured them "the overall honesty and integrity of the Liberal provincial government is not a sensitivity for most people," a conclusion he reached based on the wording of a question in his polling questionnaire.

The tendency of the protester phenomenon to convince people that Peterson lacked values fueled the resentment that he called an early election for what many felt were self-serving purposes, rather than for a compelling reason that spoke directly to people's concerns and served the public interest. And people would look elsewhere for the values they found missing in Peterson.

*   *   *

Nine days into the campaign Peterson was finally able to provide Ontarians with a searing glimpse of honest passion—but the message he conveyed was a damaging one. At his London Centre nomination meeting on August 8, demonstrators from the local Union of Unemployed Workers forced Peterson and his wife to run the gauntlet to enter the building. Inside, what began as a routine Peterson thank-you speech to 400 cheering supporters turned into bedlam. When Peterson tried to speak, a well-known anti-poverty protester leaped to his feet to berate him. An angry exchange raged.

"You're the poverty premier!" the man seethed, shaking a clenched fist as the television cameras lit up around him.

"Some day you're going to grow up and find a responsible job," Peterson replied. "The issue tonight is your rudeness. Nobody takes you seriously because you've worn out your welcome in this city."

"You don't care about justice for those living in poverty; you're the poverty premier!" the protester screeched.

"If you went out and got a job you could make a decent contribution to this country," Peterson shot back. "I think it's time you left." The exchange came to an abrupt conclusion when two large Liberal supporters seized the man and dragged him out the back door.

"Get a job!" In context, Peterson's message was perfectly appropriate. In London the protester was well-known as a professional troublemaker and antagonistic toward Peterson; he had exhausted his credibility with the local media. A long-time union activist, he had disrupted scores of events in southwestern Ontario by verbally attacking politicians. He had even turned off Queen's Park reporters by making "cold calls" to them to voice his unwanted opinions and by interfering with their interviews in the halls of the legislature. "Get a job!" could have been lifted from the thoughts of most Liberals and reporters that night.

"At the time that [Peterson] said it to him," said the Globe's Mackie, "I thought, yeah, well, I'd like to say that to him, too. The number of times we've been in a scrum and he has been yelling in the background. He was a professional shit-disturber."

"He really overdid it and people were quite sympathetic to Peterson," said Global TV's Fisher. But contempt for the protester did not prevent Fisher and other television reporters from seizing on the exchange as one of the highlights of the campaign. Edited down to a few tight seconds, the image of Peterson sneering at an "unemployed" person to "Get a job!" was riveting, revealing television. The clip became one of the most widely repeated of the campaign, showing up on the news in summaries, weekly reports and campaign features until election day. "That got heavy, heavy play because you have the tape, so you play it," said Fisher.

Television was not the only medium that took Peterson's lines out of context. The Toronto Star gave Peterson an editorial "dart" for "arrogant insensitivity" for his comments, without explaining the circumstances.

Outside the narrow context of that event, Peterson's line was disastrous: it seemed to encapsulate the worst suspicions about him, especially when Ontarians were feeling growing unease and anxiety about the economic outlook. Although he delivered a perfect TV clip, tight, visceral and emotive, that message and its timing were wrong. Filtered through the prism of television in the summer of 1990, Peterson, once the messenger of prosperity and good times, began to appear in a different light: insensitivity and arrogance seemed to be replacing vision, compassion and any sense of ordinary people's concerns.

Peterson's once-masterly use of television to transmit his likable image was short-circuited by the protester phenomenon. Many people who followed Peterson closely during the campaign believe he was partly to blame for the different image he began to project—because he was behaving differently. Peterson maintained he did not change his approach or his style. But as the protesters refused to let up, Peterson became increasingly impatient and unwilling to talk to them. At the same time, he shut down his communicativeness with reporters—his critical link to the electorate.

"I expected to see the David Peterson I met in 1986: patient with the reporters, affable, friendly, joking," said the *Star*'s Maychak. "But he quickly became irritated with us. I'm not trying to say that he did not have a right to be irritated with us— I'm trying to be fair. But he wasn't just talking to us anymore, or the audience we reach on a daily basis. He was talking to the electorate at a time when their antennae are up and they are interested in him." But Peterson, in 1990, did not appear to be interested in them.

* * *

As the clashes between Peterson and an assortment of protesters filled Ontario television screens night after night, Liberal strategists were banging their heads against the wall. At Liberal campaign headquarters the atmosphere grew increasingly uncommunicative. Robinson and Webster were barely talking to tour director Doug Kirkpatrick. As events on the premier's tour worsened, the hostilities grew. Robinson could not get the campaign staff to work together to solve the problem. Peterson and the staffers on the Liberal bus were left to handle the protesters on their own, day by day, with mixed results.

Peterson's ways of handling the protesters were all over the map as the Liberal campaign lurched and bumped along. He tried out the early advice: be magnanimous when confronted and praise the democratic process, invite the protesters to share their views, then move on.

In Trenton, east of Toronto, on August 11, "garbage folks" from nearby Marmora turned out to confront Peterson over fears that a local iron mine pit would be used as a dump for Toronto's garbage. The protesters were fuming. "A dump here will make Oka look like a Sunday school picnic," one local had warned reporters during a visit a week earlier by Tory Leader Harris.

Peterson waved off his handlers and waded into the middle of the seething mass. "He talked to people and ended up convincing everybody that he had their best interests in mind," said the *Globe's* Mackie. "Afterwards, they were all satisfied." Quinte MPP Hugh O'Neil, whose nomination meeting Peterson was there to attend, was impressed by the premier's unique way of defusing the crowd: "He invited their leader into the meeting and the guy sat at a table with us up near the front. It worked."

But Peterson's diplomacy did not cut it for long. The protesters found that as long as they kept shrieking, the cameras kept rolling. Peterson's reaction went from being nice, to being patronizing, to making fun of the demonstrators, to hostility: Perks said that Peterson whispered to him near the end of the campaign, "Don't breathe on me."

The battling Liberal strategists did not prepare a plan for dealing with the relentless bombardment. The Liberal tour was designed around the premise that "the premier is the campaign." A wide-open, Peterson-centered tour, the strategists believed, would showcase the premier's strengths of openness and rapport with the average person. But the strategy backfired: "the premier is the campaign" became "the premier is the punching bag."

Borg, who as Peterson's closest campaign aide shared many of the body blows, had found the strategists uninterested in planning for protesters. "I would mention it to folks and I know others did, but somehow it didn't get through the system and work its way through with recommendations made and accepted and dealt with," said Borg. "People would say that this is going to be a rough campaign, media are going to be tough; there was that mind-set, but there was also this incredible arrogance about the numbers: it's going to be a tough campaign and everything else, but there's no alternative, and we'd do okay in the end. We've got lots of miles to go before we lose a bunch of seats."

Ad hoc advice trickled out to Peterson. Strategists David MacNaughton and Hershell Ezrin connected with him or with Borg, who threw in his own ideas. Early on, they counseled him to be nice—but also to look for a few protesters who could be used as a foil, permitting him to say, "The reason these people are angry is they want to push their self-serving agenda against what is good for the rest of Ontario; I will not be pushed around and I'm going to stand up for the interest of the many over those of a few." There was nothing novel about the approach. Decades earlier, Republican presidential campaign organizers allowed antiwar demonstrators into events to let Richard Nixon play off against them.

But Peterson never tried the tactic. There was no agreement about which group to focus on. With so many protesters appearing with individual beefs on local issues, a blanket approach was ruled out because of fears that it would backfire. "It wasn't easy to pick over," MacNaughton said. "You didn't want to pick on the little old lady from Elmira protesting the dump; you had to pick the right group."

As the protester phenomenon flourished, other approaches were canvassed by the Liberals. Although the strategy committee was not meeting in the early weeks of the campaign, Robinson consulted with one or two strategists at a time and talked to Borg and Webster. She wrestled with the dilemma of trying to keep Peterson looking open and accessible in the face of the reality of the premier stepping off the bus at every campaign stop to boos, shouts and a poor television message. She rejected the idea of shifting to a "bubble campaign" that, in the style of Mulroney's

1988 campaign, placed the leader in the middle of a ring of police officers, with protesters and media kept at a safe distance. Robinson concluded the bubble tactic would be so far off-strategy that it would destroy the Liberal campaign. Tighter controls on Liberal events were also ruled out after a handful of failed attempts; protesters found Peterson on his way in or out and reporters covered the attacks rather than the events.

"There was no answer to it that would have been a complete answer," said Robinson. "As soon as you started doing more controlled events, where you don't have the same degree of access, the watchers of the event became what got covered rather than the event itself. This made sure that your message was completely obscured."

The frustrated Liberals decided to try another approach: fight fire with fire. They mounted attacks on two fronts: against the protesters themselves and against another leader.

At the end of the second week of the campaign, organizers at Liberal events received new marching orders from headquarters to counteract anti-Peterson protesters with pro-Peterson forces. Dozens of Ontario Young Liberals were rounded up and sent to shadow Peterson, with instructions to outshout anyone who came near him. The plan was to create the impression the premier was surrounded with wildly cheering crowds trying to get close to him. Instead, the effect was mass confusion and chaos. Peterson was besieged by protesters screaming so loudly to outgun one another that he could not be heard speaking into reporters' microphones. People on both sides were shoved so violently organizers were worried someone would be seriously injured. Embarrassed, the Liberals quickly scrubbed that scheme.

At the same time, in darkest secrecy, Liberal headquarters decided to organize protesters of its own to go after Tory Leader Harris. Six Ontario Young Liberals were recruited to stage an anti-GST protest at a Tory event at Toronto's St. Lawrence Market. Eager to help out the cause, the band of earnest youths, carrying hand-painted signs, marched through the doors and smack into the middle of several hundred Tories. Minutes later, bruised, scratched and their clothes hanging in tatters, they were tossed out onto the street. Back to the drawing board for the Liberal campaign.

The worst fear for the Liberals as the protesters took hold was that overzealous Peterson supporters would take matters into their own hands. The last thing the Liberals wanted was people duking it out in front of the TV cameras. The danger became clear when Peterson walked off his bus in a small town and into a heated confrontation between local protesters and local Liberals. "Vince jumped on one of our guys because the guy was going after some protester," said Peterson. "The guy was going to go and take him out and beat the hell out of him. Our guys were really the peacemakers, the guys on the bus." But the lid could be kept on the volatile mix of excited, protective Liberals and increasingly angry protesters for only so long. The lid blew off in Sarnia.

Word of the protester problem had reached organizers for Sarnia Liberal candidate Mike Bradley long before Peterson arrived. Rather than let their event with Peterson be another stage for confrontation, the Liberals packed their hall with supporters and prepared for the worst. Minutes before the Liberal buses arrived, the protesters began to materialize: OPSEU's SWAT team, the teachers, Greenpeace and a slew of locals riled about their own issues.

As Peterson worked his way through the human logjam, the overcrowded event turned into a donnybrook. The protesters moved in to get at Peterson and the Liberal faithful massed around him to offer protection. Shoving matches broke out and dozens of people on all sides were jostled and pushed. Some fell on the floor; others fell on top of them and were walked on. Reporters excitedly recorded the wild melee. Their coverage, said Robinson, was "all out of proportion to the nature of the event." But the tactic of trying to outnumber the protesters and squeeze them out the door was quickly discarded. "That was not something that was an ongoing realistic option," Robinson solemnly explained.

On August 15 the Liberals appeared to reporters to be trying a new approach: avoidance. The morning after flying into Windsor from the premiers' conference in Winnipeg, Peterson and his tour staff were informed that about 30 angry autoworkers were circling on the sidewalk between the door of the hotel and Peterson's bus. They seemed unusually aggressive, as suggested by their unique chant: "Liberals lie, Liberals die!" Rather than "meet and greet" this particular crowd, Peterson opted to slip out another door of the hotel and into a waiting car, which sped him to meet the bus at another location.

The official explanation for Peterson's manoeuvre was that his OPP bodyguards determined that the crowd posed a security risk. But the decision was more closely tied to Peterson's mood that morning. After the long flight the previous night, Peterson had been visibly tired. As a result of a miscommunication with his staff, the key to his hotel room was misplaced and he was accidentally locked out in the hall. The premier had to persuade hotel staff to give him another key. The following morning, Peterson declined to take his usual sunrise jog. His temperament was not well suited to dealing with a potentially explosive crowd.

"One of the things you're always worried about is that one of these times you'll get hit, you'll get pounded on the head," Peterson said about the incident. "It would be wonderful for me to take a swing; it was very tempting some days, you know, the old pugilist coming out in me. I just can't do that stuff."

Some reporters appreciated the context of the Liberals' decision to keep Peterson away from that particular group of protesters. "A lot of them had been in jail overnight," said Mackie. "Most of them were semidrunk." But the reporters' sympathy did not restrain them from extensive, critical coverage of what Mackie described to *Globe* readers as "the first confrontation he has backed away from since the campaign started." Mackie's report on the day's events devoted 20 paragraphs to the protester phenomenon and one paragraph to the Liberal announcement of the day, a $19-million program to encourage the development of innovative agricultural products.

Word of the avoidance spread across the province. "Peterson takes back route to avoid angry workers," reported the Toronto *Sun*.

The security-risk explanation was not holding water. "Everybody thought that was bullshit," said Global TV's Fisher. "The OPP was being used as Peterson's personal army here to protect him. No one believed there was a security risk. He can walk into the angriest group of people you can possibly imagine and say, 'Hi, how are ya, come in and have coffee, sit down, tell me I'm a jerk and we'll work on it.'"

The story about Peterson "ducking" helped kill the Liberals in Windsor: "Those people were suffering down there," said Goldfarb. "We weren't prepared to face the crowd. The day after that, our numbers plummeted. The optics of not facing the crowd hurt us in that part of the country."

Reporters and Peterson's staffers agreed on one result of the Windsor incident: the mood on the Liberal bus was never the same afterward and Peterson's approach to protesters changed perceptibly. Reporters began to sense anger and hostility toward them from the Liberal bus. Answers, they claimed, were getting shorter and sharper. The Liberals were getting frustrated: they tried quietly to persuade some reporters to pay less attention to the protesters. Some reporters simply ignored the requests; others included them in their reports, citing the pleas as further evidence of sagging Liberal fortunes. The Liberals complained to no avail that reporters failed to point out that many of the same protesters were showing up again and again, to investigate any organizational links between protest groups and the opposition parties or to look critically at what the protesters were trying to accomplish. Peterson, felt Robinson, "had made a point of dealing with the protesters, talking to them, but talking and responding only works if dialogue is possible and if someone is prepared to listen. The protesters wanted to harangue, to overwhelm our message."

Escaping unscathed from the protesters were Rae and Harris. On August 7, reporters accompanied Rae to a staged event in front of a Tridel apartment building, where the NDP leader made his first call in the campaign for a minimum corporate tax. The reporters were taken aback when a tenant marched out and interrupted the NDP leader with a tirade of abuse, attacking him for unfairly picking on Tridel and making claims that were "horse manure." The novelty of the assault earned it a place in most newspaper reports; and it showed up widely on television. Liberals watching the news at their campaign headquarters that night guffawed as Rae stammered and sputtered, clearly caught off guard. But the incident did nothing to help the Liberal campaign. The tenant, shirtless, tanned, and wearing a gold chain as thick as a garden hose, was hardly an effective conveyer of a protest message. And no pattern of anti-Rae protests sprang up: the protesters representing special-interest groups had decided to go after only Peterson.

Rae and Harris became the happy beneficiaries of the protester phenomenon. Not only was Peterson's image turned upside down and the Liberal message lost in the noise, but the NDP and Tories were handed an opportunity to get their messages out with minimal challenge and critique. "In a campaign, there's seldom time to get the other side of the story," said the Star's Maychak. "You just get the one side. What the protesters provided was an instant flip side of whatever Peterson was saying. So for every punch that was delivered by the governing party, there was a counterpunch. For every punch that was delivered by the NDP, there was no counterpunch." That was the price Peterson paid for being the incumbent in 1990 and entering the campaign far ahead in the polls: his record, promises, perceived values, style and every word were stuck under a microscope that had only his name on it.

The emergence of the protester phenomenon as a media focal point would prove of seminal importance in the campaign. A major post-election poll would reveal that two-thirds of voters said media coverage of the campaign was important in helping them decide which party or candidate to support. "The protesters hurt us badly," said Goldfarb. "But worse than them hurting us, we had no tactic on how to deal with them. When you're running a campaign, these kinds of things are going to happen, whether it's protesters or negative media stories, and you've got to have a response. We had no response. We did nothing, we just let them beat the hell out of us and we looked wimpy."

*   *   *

In their attitude before the election, their creation of a strategy and their inability to respond to the protesters during the campaign, the Liberals running the show ignored a simple political rule: never go into a campaign thinking you are going to win; run every campaign assuming you are going to lose. They would pay dearly for their mistake. Special-interest groups, pleased with their role in the Ontario campaign, plan to re-enact their success in future campaigns; strategists will fail to factor them in at their own peril.

Without a plan for protesters or a message strong enough to overcome them, Peterson was lost. The phenomenon the Liberals helped cultivate and did not deal with was a critical ingredient in the mix of factors that turned Ontarians off Peterson. It got them thinking about the other products on the campaign shelf and how they might be different.

8

Sultans of Spin

Send the Liberals a letter they can't ignore.
                    —NDP TELEVISION COMMERCIAL

If you're thinking of voting Liberal, think again.
                    —PC TELEVISION COMMERCIAL

The steaks at George Bigliardi's restaurant on Church Street, just north of Maple Leaf Gardens in Toronto, draw politicians of every stripe. Ontario cabinet ministers have dined at "Big's" for many decades, filling its dark rooms with smoke late into the night, hoisting cognacs, arguing, laughing and partying, often exiting discreetly through a back door to the rear lane.

Peterson and his top constitutional advisors met at Bigliardi's on July 12 to ponder the implications of the death of Meech over

George's finest steaks. Sequestered in a private room, the group confirmed Peterson's view that he had to go for an early election. Late in the evening, the group walked to the front door, where Peterson found himself face to face with Tory Leader Mike Harris and what was clearly an election preparation team headed by campaign manager John Laschinger. They had been having their own private dinner meeting in the upstairs dining room and were on the way out.

Both groups broke into belly laughs but some nervous glances were exchanged. As Peterson walked away an aide slipped up to him. "Do you know who that was with them?" he hissed.

"That one guy I didn't recognize, no," said Peterson.

"It was Mike Murphy from Washington," whispered the fretting assistant.

"Oh yeah, of course," said Peterson. "Well, who the hell's that?"

"He's a consultant who specializes in negative advertising. A real nasty guy."

Murphy was an acquaintance of Laschinger, invited up for a few days to give informal—and reputedly unpaid—advice on the Tory campaign. A Republican campaign consultant, Murphy had made his name in 1984 as a key player in the North Carolina Senate race. He helped the incumbent senior senator, Jesse Helms, turn away challenger Governor Jim Hunt. The race was a watershed in negative advertising in the United States—more than 7,000 negative television commercial "spots" were aired in a five-week period in a multimillion dollar campaign for a single seat. The campaign featured ads so vicious and character-assassinating they made headlines in a nation where negative advertising has been part of the campaign game for nearly four decades.

Murphy specialized in helping candidates control the agenda in a campaign by developing negative themes early, building recognition among voters of an opponent's vulnerability, then moving on quickly to another line of attack.

News of Murphy's sighting, nearly a month before the election call, flashed through Liberal circles. It was even mentioned by reporters on some Toronto newscasts. Negative ads were coming, in some way, shape or form, as part of a Tory attack strategy, and the Liberals knew it well in advance. But the Liberal strategists paid little heed. They pondered the implications of getting hammered by Harris and Bob Rae, and even asked Hershell Ezrin to draw up scenarios for Tory and NDP campaign attacks. But they made no strategic preparations to accommodate negative campaigns by their opponents. They were convinced Harris and Rae were not "credible deliverers" of anti-Liberal messages and certain that with their big lead and Peterson's strong, positive image, they could withstand whatever the other guys were getting ready to throw at them.

* * *

Phil Gillies had a problem, to put it mildly. As communications director for the Tory campaign, he had a leader nobody knew, a party nobody liked and a severe shortage of money. But he had an understanding of the campaign tactics of Michael Murphy and an idea. A former junior minister under premiers Bill Davis and Frank Miller, Gillies had entered the public relations business after losing his seat in 1987. Gillies decided to take the Tories way out on a limb.

Gillies and Laschinger agreed they had to make a bold move before Peterson called the election: as the third-place party they could count on receiving the least attention from reporters when the campaign got going, and would have to sit through the legally required 16-day blackout before they could put campaign advertising on the air. All they needed was the right negative theme. Focus group testing at Decima had shown Ontarians were touchiest about two broad areas: taxes and an unnecessary early election.

"Let's run a pre-writ ad blitz based on the premise that they're gonna call an unnecessary election," proposed Gillies, "and we'll tell people how much that unnecessary election is gonna cost." The cost of an Ontario election was estimated at $40 million, including all spending by the parties, individual candidates and Elections Ontario as a Toronto *Sun* story had revealed early in July. The theme of an unnecessary $40-million election was dangled in front of focus groups at Decima, with a distinct response: "They were mad," Gillies observed. "Real mad."

The Tories' campaign communications committee was built around ad agency Bowen & Binstock, which had handled Larry Grossman's leadership campaigns in 1985. With strategists Nancy McLean, Mitch Patton and Perry Miele, Gillies directed a relatively tiny team that included writer Linda Laiken, B&B account executive Kevin Viner and producer-director Andy Rice. Strapped for time, the small squad drew up a concept for a print ad that looked simple but would prove to be dynamite: a theme line saying "Don't let Peterson fish you in," with a picture of a fish. The ad and a supporting radio spot were quickly approved by the Tory campaign committee.

To make the critical pre-campaign attack work, Gillies needed to make a splash. But he had to make his impact with a paltry budget of $35,000, all that the cash-strapped Tories could afford. Gillies didn't mind: he had a scheme up his sleeve.

Gillies placed the ads judiciously. He bought two-thirds of a page in just one newspaper, the *Globe*, and airtime on Toronto radio station CFRB, staying below budget. Then he spent the rest of his pre-campaign money running off scores of copies of both ads. On July 26, the Thursday before Peterson would call the election, he raced out to the Tories' major pre-writ campaign planning session at a Toronto hotel with the copies stuffed in boxes. Some 60 Tories were assembled, candidates, campaign managers and party staff—and Gillies made certain the Queen's Park press gallery had been invited along.

As reporters watched, Gillies unveiled giant copies of the print ad and blared out the radio message over the public address system to the cheers of the Tories. "They loved it, they went bananas," said Gillies—and so did the reporters. "It was the first assault in a campaign that was expected to be called any day," said Gillies. He had read bang-on the press gallery's view that Peterson's plan for an early election was cynical. Reporters left with copies of the tape and the ad.

But Gillies was not through. He announced that copies of both were available to every riding and asked the Tories from across the province to put them into play as fast as they could, using riding association funds before the campaign that would not have to be declared as campaign expenses.

"They snapped up every copy; in fact, we ran out," said Gillies. "They took all the radio tapes. They were all running to the pay phones in the lobby, phoning their local radio stations and their local newspapers and booking space for the next day. The thing was seen and heard right across the province, and the bulk of the cost of the advertising was actually borne by our riding associations." Tory ridings happily coughed up $150,000 to get the ads out over the next three days.

The news media impact was stunning. "They were fairly nasty, hard-hitting ads," said Gillies. "They were on every major newscast the day we unveiled them; most of the dailies ran an article noting that we were doing this." Gillies later tallied up the value of the news coverage, or "earned media," and added on the cost of his advertising purchases and those of the ridings. The result was astonishing: "As best I can tell, we ran about a $300,000 advertising campaign," gloated Gillies, "and it cost us $35,000 bucks. I think the press gallery caught on to what we were up to, but it worked once."

Gillies' scheme worked beyond the Tories' wildest expectations. It achieved the Murphyesque objective of making a profound impact early with a negative theme, permitting Harris to move on to another attack. With reporters already questioning an early election call, the Tories' attack line was not bracketed by critical media analysis, beginning a pattern that would characterize much reporting of the NDP and Tory negative attacks during the campaign.

The Liberals' assumption that the early-call story would die as a "one-day wonder" was blown out of the water. The idea of a "$40-million coronation for Peterson" that was a waste of taxpayers' money penetrated deeply and remained one of the most decisive themes of the campaign. It played on people's doubts about Peterson's honesty and integrity, suggesting he wanted power for power's sake and would blow $40 million of "your money" to get it. Gillies' scheme was a stunning success—but like many subsequent Tory tactics, its chief beneficiary would prove to be Rae, not Harris.

*   *   *

Roughly half of each dollar spent by the three major parties in the 1990 Ontario election would be devoted to advertising: $1.4 million of $2.9 million for the Liberals, $850,000 of $1.6 million for the NDP, and $980,000 of $2.4 million for the Tories, supplemented by $400,000 provided by individual Tory ridings for advertising.

In Ontario and other provincial jurisdictions, political advertising by parties during election campaigns is tightly regulated. The parties' ads can be sent to air or published starting on the twenty-first day before voting day, as permitted by Ontario election laws, and must be removed at midnight, 48 hours before voting day. Each party was intent on making advertising an integral part of its strategy that would co-mingle with other events, be used for tactical purposes and play a critical role in shaping the perceptions of voters.

Political advertising for the federal and Ontario Liberals has involved many of the same people since the 1970s. Volunteer representatives of ad agencies were brought together in an organization called Red Leaf Communications in 1972 for the federal party; in 1975, a similar group called Red Trillium Productions was created for the Ontario party. In 1985 and 1987 strategic direction for the group came from Ezrin. In 1990 Red Trillium's first outside chair was appointed.

In 1988 strategist Senator Michael Kirby, a member of the board of directors of Peterborough's Quaker Oats company, invited the company's vice-president of marketing, David Morton to act as chair of Red Leaf for Turner. Kirby wanted an independent in charge of the constantly jockeying volunteer advertisers; Morton had a sound reputation and filled the bill. After seeing the highly rated 1988 Liberal ads against free trade, including the famous "map ad" in which a U.S. negotiator erased the border between Canada and the United States, Peterson decided he wanted Morton to run Red Trillium in 1990 and called him to offer the invitation.

"I thought it would be fun to win one for a change," said Morton. "Plus it should have been easier: we had a better product to sell." He jumped at the chance but on a single condition: "I had one caveat—I wanted to be on the strategy committee. In '88 I felt like a bit of a lackey—I'd get a call from somebody in Ottawa saying do this, or you should be doing that. I wanted to understand a little more the thought process that went on before that phone call went out." Morton's federal experience had convinced him he couldn't run advertising in another campaign without having direct access to strategic information. Peterson agreed.

Morton attended his first meeting of the strategy committee in April. Soft-spoken and diplomatic, he became the strategists' main conduit to Red Trillium. Morton inherited a 1990 version of the organization that included veterans Terry O'Malley, Donald Murphy and Ron Bremner of Vickers and Benson, Tony Miller and Hugh Dow of MacLaren-Lintas, creative staff from both agencies and consultants including Peterson's image-shaper Gabor Apor and Ken Tilley, who had left MacLaren to join Marbury Advertising, where he maintained a steady political business.

First set loose on pre-campaign activities in March many of the ad execs had months to think about how they would like to market Peterson and the Liberals. In 1985 Red Trillium had conceived a gently humorous campaign that sniped at closed-door Tory politics and referred to smoke-filled back rooms. In 1987 the group had scalped the theme line from Ronald Reagan's 1984 presidential campaign, "Leadership that's Working," and counted on Peterson's yuppie image to convey a timely message of success, prosperity and reform-minded leadership.

The advertisers arrived on May 16 at their first formal Red Trillium meeting with Morton in charge. Placed on the table was a creative strategy drawn from Martin Goldfarb's strategic recommendations. Worked up by Morton with Goldfarb's counsel, the directions were unequivocal: the campaign's advertising theme would match the umbrella theme for the Liberal strategy, "the premier is the campaign." Tilley would adhere to that line in the printed riding services materials; Apor would follow it in the creation of the Liberals' "free-time" television production.

"Based on the research we were getting, there were a few little niggles but fundamentally he was the guy," said Morton. The ad execs, all Peterson fans, were happy to apply their talents to developing a theme around his leadership. Some were not personally comfortable with the idea of an early election but quickly discovered the Liberal strategists were not interested in hearing their opinions.

"We were the executors," said Tilley; or, as O'Malley said wryly, "I'm not a strategist, I'm an executioner." Morton realized "most of the people involved outside the strategy group really didn't think we ought to be going [early]. I was never able to explain it."

At the end of the first Red Trillium meeting, the question was put: Should Peterson make the early call? One by one the advertisers said no, until O'Malley's turn came. He held up a notepad on which he had written, "Remember Mike Tyson." "All that flashed through my mind was here was this unbeatable, invincible guy that no one can beat, and the next thing here's Buster Douglas standing over him from nowhere," he said. "I just didn't feel right because I couldn't get my hands around a why, which is fundamental. It's like anything in our business: if there's a product or service, there has to be a reason. What's the benefit to the public: You're going to get this guy again for the next five years, isn't that a great deal? That's a tough equation for people to make."

O'Malley heard another message coming back loud and clear from the strategists: "There's lots of room to lose some, that's a reality. It can't be as good as the last time, so relax."

Casting personal reservations aside, the advertisers turned to peddling their theme. Morton laid out a critical path to have creative executions tested and ready for production by the end of June and Red Trillium's volunteers went to work, eager to pitch Peterson instead of beer or laundry detergent.

Morton's communications strategy was to sell the message "David Peterson's Liberals will provide the province with superior leadership in the uncertain times that are ahead. The benefits of Peterson's leadership for the electorate are stability, a sense of direction and a rudder in uncertain economic and political times." Goldfarb's views could be heard in Morton's plan to talk about "a more optimistic, secure future for the middle class," "a genuine concern for the values and dreams of the middle class" and "integrity—we did what we said we would, the middle class can trust us, we will not let them down." Morton accepted the premise that Liberal votes could be retained by plugging Peterson.

"If you read this, this is like Superman," said Morton, holding Goldfarb's focus group research on Peterson's image. Like others on the strategy committee he was not put off by the negative findings on Peterson's image in the back of the report: "The general assessment was they weren't that dangerous," he said. "We thought he was resilient enough to go through it, even those of us who didn't think it was a good time for an election. My interpretation of the research was that the Liberal Party in Ontario was David Peterson and that he was so powerful, relative to what else was out there, Rae and Harris, that he was the guy we had to play."

With their mandate defined in mid-May, Red Trillium's members toiled toward a June 28 deadline. While they worked away, Peterson's image was subjected to the events surrounding Meech and its collapse—the closed-door process, the alignment with Bourassa and Mulroney. But the Liberal strategists did not update the report on Peterson's image to find out whether it had been changed by those events. Red Trillium continued to use the May report as its resource material.

The Liberal ads' creative concepts were tested July 11. Again, to appeal to what was believed to be a solid Liberal core vote, only people who said they were Liberals or Liberal-leaning were assembled for focus groups.

Goldfarb's vice-president Doug Hurley recommended as his top choice a series of ad concepts built around a "Buses" theme. These spots showed Peterson traveling around the province on his campaign bus, mingling with people and talking directly to the camera with his tie loosened and sleeves rolled up. Hurley found this approach was the best way to convey Peterson's positive attributes. The imagery, found Hurley, "has a down-to-earth, modest, ordinary-guy kind of appeal"; "it suggests the premier is out meeting and mixing with ordinary people from all parts of the province"; and "it provides an opportunity for intimate and candid, one-on-one dialogue between the viewer and the premier."

Another spot recommended by Hurley was "Office," a "vision" ad that showed Peterson talking from behind his desk, giving a sweeping "value statement" about his personal beliefs. "The government's job is to determine the straightest course for a strong, prosperous future," Peterson was to say earnestly to the camera, "and then provide the right encouragement, popular or not, to get us on that course and keep us on it." The camera was to pan across the objects on his desk, showing official papers and family pictures, then cut back to Peterson in profile, gazing out his window, saying, "I love Ontario. In my mind, it's the greatest place in the world to live." The groups found the concept "credible, sincere and believable" and thought it proved Peterson was "a very dedicated, hard-working man."

But the groups rejected one concept strongly: an ad that showed Peterson at the Meech talks in June surrounded by the other premiers, who were standing and applauding him. "It does succeed in conveying a positive and strong leadership image for the premier," said Hurley. "The problem is it revisits and resurrects a very emotional, contentious issue that people would like to forget about. It also associates the premier with the failure of Meech Lake, and people feel it is negative to associate him with failure even though he, personally, was not responsible for the failure." Through the one-way glass of the observation room next to the focus groups, Morton sat and watched the reactions. "They were protective of their premier," he thought. "They were sick of him doing the national stuff, they wanted him to care for Ontario." Morton believed the groups were rejecting Meech and its failure, not Peterson.

Through further testing the selection of Liberal ads was narrowed down by the last week in July to the "Buses" series alone. The "Office" spot had to be scrubbed: its concept had been accepted when the focus groups saw printed storyboards illustrating the ad. But when the groups were shown the actual spot, they were repulsed. While Liberals and the advertisers loved the spot, Donald Murphy was astonished at how it was misinterpreted and angrily rejected when tested in its final form: "Him saying that to the camera, people hated that—'Who does he think he is? Just because I wasn't born in Ontario I'm not as good?' You could never think of all the ways that people get angry." The advertisers blamed their script and dumped the spot. They would rely on the "Buses" ads to convey Peterson's "visionary leadership."

"Buses" became a series of four ads, keying on the themes of visionary leadership, education, the environment and economic management. In the featured ad in the series, "Vision," the Liberals worked in the value statements they believed Peterson had to convey to appeal to and hold the Liberal core vote. "Ontario is the engine that drives Canada; we have to stay strong," Peterson intoned as the Liberal bus rolled down a tree-lined highway. Looking sincerely into the camera Peterson continued: "Ontario has created over 700,000 jobs in the last five years. In the same time, we've made major investments in social assistance. We have quality health care but I want to make it even better. Our streets must be safe, our air, land and water clean. That's my vision for Ontario. Let's work on it together." The ad ended with a rousing jolt of up-tempo music as an announcer read the campaign's theme line, "Premier David Peterson: Effective Leadership . . ." and a chorus sang, ". . . for a Strong Ontario."

Morton's plan brought the Liberals' Peterson-centered campaign to television through "positive" political advertising. The spots pointed to the Liberals' record and asked for a mandate to implement a visionary agenda, which was described in the sketchiest of detail. That was the theme Peterson tried to bring forward on writ day—but when the ads were released 16 days later, their message had not matured beyond that basic theme and viewers expecting more information from them were destined to be disappointed. "At some of the meetings of the advertising committee, we said, 'We need more meat to start backing up what we're saying,'" said Morton. "We didn't have the meat, so we went back to the record a lot."

The Liberals believed that associating the government's record of performance with Peterson's positive image could elevate viewers' perceptions of what the Liberals had done and what they would do if re-elected. They tried to make their issue and image messages merge and reinforce one another by wrapping the issues in Peterson's personality and using Peterson to make voters feel secure. The "Buses" ads used the messenger as their key message. They attempted to convey information by piggybacking it on Peterson's persona. Hurley pronounced the "Buses" series successful when his focus group testing confirmed Peterson's positive image qualities were being picked up from the spots; they registered the impressions the Liberals wanted.

But the Liberal ads went against the established grain of positive political advertising. Designed to enhance the government's performance on the issues by marrying it to Peterson, the ads defied the concept of "referential" political advertising, the practice of transferring meaning from pleasing objects or experiences onto the politician. A referential ad might have shown Peterson with his family, in a classroom or visiting a busy workplace.

Nor did the Liberal ads measure up to the basic standard for commercial product advertising: they did not engage viewers, provoke them to react and convince them to do something, in this case, vote for Peterson. Testing only for the conveyance of Peterson's positive image as directed by the Liberal campaign, Hurley did not gauge the ads, as a commercial client would expect, for clarity, empathy and persuasiveness. Although the ads tried to convey that Peterson shared values important to people, they failed to prove to viewers he could relate to their personal lives and concerns. As he rolled along in his cocoonlike bus, talking about his accomplishments and making vague promises, he did nothing to demonstrate he was like ordinary people and cared about their interests; he did not provide solid evidence he could fulfill the needs of viewers and was therefore qualified to be re-elected by them. Rather than take advantage of television by using visual or aural symbols to convey its messages, the ads channeled verbal information through Peterson, assuming he would imbue it with the "right" appeals simply by saying the words. If Peterson said it, the Liberals assumed, it would sell.

The "Buses" ads ultimately relied on Peterson's own on-camera performing ability to close the loop between himself and the viewer. To make the commercials work, Peterson was called on to achieve consistency between his verbal and nonverbal communications: he had to look and sound convincing. Although he had years of experience performing in front of the camera and appearing in scrums on the news, Peterson had never been called on to perform as a pure actor, and it showed. With his deep tan enhanced by his white shirt, he looked more like a movie star than an empathetic leader. Presented with five scripts one day before the commercials were shot, he had little time to rehearse and get comfortable with his material. To viewers, Peterson was clearly "reading" his script, with several flaws in his narration the Liberals did not have time to correct.

But the final testing of the ads was not aimed at rooting out any hidden messages in Peterson's on-camera performance. Satisfied the ads registered Peterson's positive qualities as the Liberal campaign wanted, Hurley did not check on what the premier was saying to viewers with his body language, inflection and pacing. The Liberals' positive ads, intended to help Peterson build a bond of trust between himself and viewers, might in fact have done the opposite. And by the time they were sent to air the events of the campaign would make them irrelevant and even harmful.

*　　*　　*

Campaign director Beth Webster was worried that the Liberal ads were too positive. On June 14, she had flown to Washington with campaign chair Kathy Robinson and organizational co-chair Bill Murray to attend a conference sponsored by Campaigns and Elections, a U.S. political publication and research company. While Murray and Robinson went to seminars on organization, Webster sat through as many sessions as she could on advertising. She found a common theme: the Americans were uniformly committed to using negative advertising, both to unseat incumbents and to defend them against attacks. She came home worried that Peterson's opponents would use negative tactics against him and the Liberals would have no reply.

Webster anxiously attended the next scheduled Red Trillium meeting with Morton and the advertisers. The initial concept stage of their Peterson-centered positive ads was nearing completion. When Webster suggested Red Trillium also work up some negative ad concepts, the advertisers turned thumbs down.

"I felt we should have done and bagged negative commercials," said Webster. "They didn't want to engage in it; they thought it was bad advertising." Backing up the advertisers was Robinson, who was under pressure from the party to keep campaign spending under control. That meant starting with one set of ads, and with the positive ads nearing production, changing directions was ruled out. The idea of negative Liberal advertising had one more key opponent: Peterson. "The premier never wanted to do negative advertising," said Donald Murphy.

Although they opposed using negative ads against their opponents, the members of Red Trillium agreed to write examples of attack ads the NDP and Tories might launch at Peterson and test them to come up with responses. O'Malley came up with four vicious 30-second television spots. One pseudo-Tory ad used a "Scales" theme, with Peterson's honesty and integrity on one side and anti-Liberal issues stacked up on the other—the Starr scandal, auto insurance, taxes.

Hurley tested the concepts with focus groups as Morton and Murphy looked on. "We asked people if they would believe those ads if they saw them running," said Murphy. "People said they didn't like negative ads of any kind and they wouldn't affect how they would vote. They said right away they didn't like them. But they still listened to them and they made a difference." Later, while shooting one of the Liberal ads, Murphy showed the negative ad scripts to the premier. "I'm glad you guys aren't working for the Tories," Peterson gulped.

But Morton and the strategists believed Tory and NDP negative ads would not be a major problem for the Liberals. "We had tested enough negative stuff that I thought, certainly, given the premier's image at the time we tested the thing, that wouldn't play well," said Morton. "It wouldn't hurt us that much."

With the Liberal ads in the final stages of tweaking late in July, Morton found a few minutes to chat with a friend from Peterborough who was working on the campaign of local Liberal incumbent Peter Adams.

"What are you guys doing strategically?" his friend asked.

"Well, it's pretty straightforward," said Morton. "The general thrust is leadership with the premier, and the premier's going to be the central focus."

"Oh, we're not going to do that," his friend replied.

"Why not?" demanded Morton.

"People here don't like the premier as much as they did," the local Liberal said matter-of-factly.

"What are you talking about?" asked Morton. "You guys are smokin' dope!" Later Morton would realize he had accepted the strategists' conviction that Peterson's image was strong, positive and resilient. When he heard something different, he simply did not believe it, because the research showed otherwise.

Peterson took one day away from his vacation to shoot the ads. On July 26 a production team gathered early in the morning in Toronto's Don Valley around a nondescript Greyhound bus. Peterson was in uniform: red tie, white shirt with the sleeves rolled up and a tan so deep that the inside of the bus had to be specially lighted to make his facial features visible on camera. To provide a generic backdrop outside the window, the bus rolled slowly up and down the tree-lined Bayview Avenue extension, which was almost free of traffic on the scorching afternoon. "It was very hot," said Donald Murphy. "You couldn't have the air-conditioning on because the sound drowned out the premier's voice. And you had to chug along because if you started changing gears on the bus that drowned out the premier, too." To ensure that the "optics" of the scene were demographically correct, members of Peterson's staff were carefully placed in the shots, including a pregnant woman and an East Indian man.

After three hours of shooting, Morton called for a lunch break. The bus pulled off near a patch of grass where sandwiches and soft drinks had been laid out on a picnic table. A support van rolled up and Morton and Murphy hopped into the air-conditioned sanctuary, waving at Peterson to follow them.

"No, that's okay," said Peterson. "I'll eat out here with these guys." He walked over to sit in the sun with the camera crew, technicians and staff. Morton and Murphy followed. As the group ate, a huge truck from a nearby brickworks roared past. Its occupants craned their necks at the scene and the truck ground to a halt nearby. Morton approached it cautiously.

"Hey!" barked out one of the truckers. "Is that the premier over there?"

"Uh, yeah," Morton replied warily.

"What are you doing?" the trucker demanded.

"Oh, we're just shooting some commercials," Morton replied.

"Do you think we could go over and meet him?" asked the trucker.

"Uh, sure," said Morton, and the truckers jumped out and walked up to Peterson, who stood, smiled and shook their hands.

"Why don't you guys join us for lunch?" the premier offered. The truckers sat and talked with Peterson and the crew; when the lunch break ended, they shook hands with Peterson again and walked back to their truck.

"My wife's not gonna believe this," one said to Morton. "I had lunch with the premier!"

Later Morton would recall the scene wistfully. "I wish," he sighed, "that we'd had a commercial like that."

*   *   *

Canadian elections have avoided negative advertising. One campaign in British Columbia offered an exception to the rule. An anti-NDP ad by the Social Credit Party showed a chameleon changing colors to demonstrate the policy vacillations of the NDP, until the lizard died. The ads were vilified by some viewers, especially animal rights activists, but the Socreds still won the election. Morton's 1988 "map ad" was negative in nature but its tone was gentle compared to the mildest of U.S. attack ads.

Americans eat up negative political advertising. Their pollsters have found that some Americans like it better than positive advertising. "They welcome ads that give negative information about an opponent's voting record or conduct in office," said Democratic pollster Paul Maislin in 1986. "There used to be a saying in our business that you could never find anyone who would tell you they liked a negative ad. This year, for the first time, we're finding people who are saying, 'Hey, that's interesting.' It's the positive stuff they're more cynical about."

U.S. pollsters believe negative ads that tap into existing beliefs are especially persuasive and capable of prompting stronger recall among viewers. "We know from years of research psychology that people process negative information more deeply than positive information," said Democratic pollster Paul Melman. "When we ask people about negative ads they'll say they don't like them . . . the point is that they absorb the information." U.S. research has revealed that negative television ads work best when they go after the character of an opponent and plug away at a single issue, to break through the blur of a medium based on entertaining people.

Laschinger, Gillies and the Tories set out in the early weeks of the campaign to find the best themes with which to sustain their strategy of negative attacks. Michael Murphy's advice had helped open the door for the Tories but Gillies declined Laschinger's offer of further help from the U.S. consultant. "I think we can run an advertising campaign that will do just what we want," said Gillies, "and I think it can be made right here in Canada."

The focus group sessions at Decima were disheartening for the Tories; few participants knew Harris. The Tories concluded their ads should not identify their leader or offer up anything related to the Conservative party as an alternative. "The atmosphere in which we were operating was not only antigovernment, it was anti-Tory," said Gillies. "We were treading a very fine line on what people would accept from us. In the first 15 minutes of discussion on a provincial election, you'd see venom just about spitted across the room about Brian Mulroney. Against that kind of background, for the Ontario PC party to go in and say, 'We're having an election, David Peterson is the devil and the Liberals are wrong on this, this and this, they've screwed up your taxes, they've screwed up health care, so vote for us'—people would just glaze over. There would be comments like 'Come on, do you guys think you'd do any better?'"

Overtaxation emerged as the Tories' line of attack for their ads, as participants responded angrily to information about Liberal tax hikes. "When you put the numbers to them, that under the Peterson administration there have been 33 different tax increases and taxes have gone up 132 percent, they said, 'Are those the numbers?'—and there was absolute, complete acceptance," said Gillies. But when Decima asked if people believed that Harris and the Tories would change things, the response, observed Gillies, was skeptical: "'Nope, we don't believe it from any party. We don't believe any politicians anymore, they're all a pack of vagabonds, bunch of scoundrels.' They didn't want to hear any solutions from us."

Gillies reported back to the Tory campaign committee: "All I can really recommend is we attack, that it be a fairly hard-hitting negative attack on the advertising front. At least in the early stages of the campaign there is not a market for us proposing any great solutions. People don't care." That was fine with the Tory strategists. Coming up with answers, they believed, was the government's job in most Ontarians' eyes.

The Tory creative group began churning out initial ad concepts built on the tax theme. On his tour Harris would adopt overtaxation as his central attack on Peterson and the tenor of his early attacks would have the same objective as the criticism of the early, unnecessary $40-million election—to create doubt about the Liberals. The ads would reinforce Harris's message.

On the first Wednesday night of the campaign, focus groups at Decima were treated to the Tories' ideas. Each ad concept was demonstrated through "animatics," a series of slides, with scripts and some voice tracks provided. One of the Tory ads was truly "venomous": it showed a spider web with a dark, sinister spider in the middle, representing Peterson. "David Peterson's been tying you up in a web of taxes," the script read, raising the charge of 33 tax hikes. "Oh, what a tangled web he weaves."

The heavy-handed, personalized attack was shot down by the groups. "People were horrified," said Gillies. "People said, 'Ugh, I hate that ad, I'm scared of spiders.'" Many were offended by the personal slap at Peterson: "The man has spent a lot of money but that is a bit much, isn't it?," said one participant. Direct, character-based attacks on Peterson would not work, the Tories agreed.

The focus groups also vetoed a series of Tory ad scripts that clobbered the Liberals over the Starr affair. "They didn't see it as a scandal that was exclusively owned by David Peterson as an individual or by the Liberal government," said Gillies. "You got, 'All politicians are dishonest, all governments screw up.'" The ads were dropped before production.

The same groups provided the Tories with the closing line for all their ads. Several dull "kickers" had been rejected, such as "It's Time for a Change" and "A New March Forward for Ontario." Toward the end of one group session, late at night, Decima's moderator asked a middle-aged man what he took from the concepts he had been shown.

"It doesn't really offer anything particularly as an alternative," the man replied. "But it sure tells you that if you're thinking of voting Liberal you should think about it again." Behind the one-way glass Gillies bolted to his feet: "That's it!" he shouted, startling Decima's Allan Gregg and strategist Nancy McLean. Both were unimpressed: "What kind of an election slogan is that?" they demanded.

"Maybe that's all the room we have to manoeuvre," said Gillies. "If the idea of the first wave of the campaign is to create doubt, maybe that's all we can tell people."

As the focus group session drew to a close, McLean sat quietly thinking. Five minutes later she was on her feet excitedly. "That *is* it!" she exclaimed. "That *is* the message!" Approved that week by the Tory campaign committee the line would be used as the kicker on every Tory commercial: "If you're thinking of voting Liberal, think again."

Four ad concepts emerged from the focus group research: "Light Bulb," which showed a flickering bulb as the voice-over recited Liberal tax hikes and asked, "Still think Peterson's a bright idea?"; "Faucet," with a red-handled tap dripping to the same tax-hike tune; "Heart Monitor," with a computer-generated electrocardiogram beeping wildly to represent Liberal over-taxation, then flat-lining; and "Piggy Bank," featuring a hapless ceramic piggy bank getting squashed in a vise as the announcer said, "Don't let Peterson put the squeeze on you again." All four television spots went into production as "split-30s," fast-paced 15-second ads run in pairs.

Shot on a tight budget on video in a harshly lit studio, the ads had a cheap, gritty quality that turned out to be perfectly matched to their message. Gillies was delighted. "We wouldn't have wanted our ads to look too flashy," he said. "It was a distinctly unflashy message, which was 'Your money is being squandered.'"

The Piggy Bank spot was by far the most expensive to make. Locked in a vise, the pink porker had to explode on cue as it was squeezed, spraying its contents into the air. Producer-director Andy Rice had a small explosive charge loaded into the bank, and the camera rolled. Ka-boom! The piggy bank was blown to smithereens, firing coins around the studio like bullets as the crew dived for cover. The tape was replayed in slow motion to see if the effect could be captured. No such luck: in one frame the piggy bank was there; in the next, it was pink powder. Rice tried another bank and a smaller explosive charge, then another and another. But the coins presented a problem: when the bank blew up just right, the money tinkled unimpressively onto the ground. Rice came up with the solution: he turned the piggy bank over and shot the explosion with the camera upside down. The coins appeared to fly dramatically into the air. By the end of the day, the Tories had their ad but 37 piggy banks were sacrificed to the cause, at a cost of $28 each.

In their final form the Tory ads were exceptionally effective commercial television spots. Gillies found they all scored high with focus groups on the essential qualities for political ads of believability and likability. But the ads were also simply good television. All four focused on the single emotional issue of overtaxation and presented their theme with simple, memorable symbols. The storytelling devices of the light bulb, faucet, heart monitor and piggy bank were graphic and easily grasped by even an inattentive viewer. The Tory message had a serious and personal pocketbook connotation, but the motifs of each ad were cartoonish and undemanding—in the case of the piggy bank, the imagery was also funny and cute. That presentation style, using humor and simple imagery, helped the Tory's negative ads escape a negative backlash from the media and television viewers.

*　　*　　*

NDP strategist David Reville caught on quickly as he watched psychographic researcher Peter Donegan conduct focus groups for his party. "They think all politicians are liars," he said. "But they kind of think the New Democrats are lying less." Honesty and integrity in government was among the deepest concerns of voters. That issue held the key to the NDP's campaign strategy, the strategists decided—and to its advertising.

Following strategist Gerald Caplan's outline, the NDP communications team, driven by David Agnew, wove together a communications plan that would hammer home a series of simple anti-Liberal messages linking Peterson to "rich and powerful interests" while presenting Rae as a reasonable, trustworthy alternative more representative of average Ontarians. On the

NDP leader's tour, in the party's free-time political broadcasts and at all his public appearances during the campaign, Rae would present a firm, authoritative image, wearing a dark, leaderlike three-button suit.

Only a set of disruptive, negative messages remained to be crafted for the NDP advertising campaign. A competition was held to choose an agency and the tiny Toronto firm of Ryan Mac-Donald Edwards (RME) Advertising, which had no previous connection with the NDP, was selected. "Like most everybody else, we thought of the NDP as being sandals, gum boots, long floppy dresses or beards and pipes," said RME writer Bruce MacDonald. "But we went in there and we found that these people had their act together." Reville, Agnew and party communications director Dianna Rienstra explained the ad strategy to MacDonald and RME art director Michael Edwards and gave them plenty of creative leeway.

Within weeks, RME's team devised a set of television ad concepts that were devastating—negative attack ads that made a lot of U.S. negative ads look wholesome and gentle.

The two spots settled on were nearly identical. Both were shot over the shoulder of a television viewer with his arm lazily holding out a remote control. Clicking his way from channel to channel the viewer was treated to a jarring, machine-gun-style series of snippets of simulated news reports, each one presenting a fabricated Liberal scandal or negative story from Queen's Park.

Recognizing the value of having external third parties validate its points of view, the NDP used phony versions of the most trusted third party it could think of—unbiased television reporters—to make its attacks. As the events of the campaign unfolded the NDP would be treated to an unexpected surprise: the actors in their ads were imitating the reality of what the news looked like, as real television reporters conveyed the primary message of the news agenda of the campaign: government under assault.

"Drinking water has sent hundreds to hospital but the Liberal government says it cannot pass legislation," said an anchor in the NDP ads. "He accepted a Caribbean vacation and a food processor; the Liberal minister reacted angrily," said a reporter on the next station. "Peterson was shaking hands on yet another new tax," said a female anchor as a photo of Peterson and Mulroney shaking hands was displayed behind her. In the NDP version of Peterson's Ontario, hospitals were being closed, Ontario Place was being bought and paved over by developers and unemployment had jumped to 17 percent. "You can change channels," said a voice dripping with sarcasm, "but you won't change a thing." The spots ended with the incitement, "Send the Liberals a letter they can't ignore" as a large black X was slashed across the screen, followed by a brief glimpse of the NDP logo.

The NDP Election Planning Committee was aghast. Many of its members, though fully supportive of the attack strategy, thought the spots were offensive, extreme and riddled with outright lies. "I thought, oh this is so fantastic," said Reville. "But the committee didn't think they were so fantastic. They were very anxious about this stuff." Many of the New Democrats abhorred the idea of blatant misstatements going on the air on behalf of their party. "It was all lies," said Caplan. "I am embarrassed to have been part of it and I think it was very embarrassing for the party and I hope we never do it again. Morally they were destructive and therefore unacceptable. I thought it was not at all helpful to the theme. It seemed to emphasize quite different themes and it emphasized much more the integrity issue than made me comfortable."

But Agnew and Reville were ready with rationalizations. "The only reason that you'll find the debate about the negative is because of the American connotation," said Agnew. "We didn't get personal; we didn't talk about people's drug habits or sex lives. It was an aggressive, issue-based campaign." Reville offered his own explanation: "There was a mixture of hyperbole but it was true in a sort of thematic sense. Obviously, the facts were not correct. In the end the words or looks weren't that important, it was the ideas." Agnew defended the ads in the Toronto *Star*: "They weren't in themselves reality, but they reflected reality. They were designed to trigger a recognition with the voter that this is the kind of thing that has been going on or will continue to go on if the Liberals were re-elected."

The rat-a-tat-tat format of the ads, disruptive, confusing and hard to understand, made them even more unsatisfactory to some of the NDP strategists. "I can't hear that, what did he say?" one of Rae's advisors complained as the ads were screened. "You're not supposed to hear it; you watch the TV, you don't listen," explained Reville. "They didn't get the concept very well," he said of his fellow strategists. "This kind of smorgasbord, clipped thing was very post-modern, but it was a very jarring exercise for the committee to get a grip on and some of us had to sling a lot of lead to get those ads approved."

Traditional-minded members of the committee demanded the spots be dropped and replaced by a cut-down version of Rae's free-time production, which featured the NDP leader wearing a conservative suit, sitting in a chair being interviewed. The battle heated up even more when Rae started off the campaign by saying Peterson had lied. An internal struggle raged for the first weeks of the campaign, with pollster David Gotthilf lining up against the controversial spots. But Agnew's communications group prevailed.

Strangely, the edited ads were not tested with focus groups, which almost certainly would have rejected their negativity; Agnew claimed the communications budget did not allow it. The twin TV ads were a go and they would be complemented by a radio campaign that featured the Peterson Liberals "striking out" six times in a baseball game. One radio spot was rejected unanimously by the NDP strategists as too outrageous. Called "Bedsprings," it featured the sounds of a vigorously squeaking bed as a voice asked, "Who are the Liberals in bed with now?"

The NDP's alarm-clock-style campaign rang out with Rae's follow-up to Peterson's election-call news conference. His "Peterson lied" comments received strong news coverage and Rae would cling to his attack theme, with enough variations to keep the media interested.

Sixteen days into the campaign, the NDP's advertising would be ready to come on-stream. The ads would assist the

NDP strategy by building the impression of Peterson as a dema-gogue rather than a representative of ordinary people, as "just another politician" rather than an honest leader who cared about everyday Ontarians and their concerns.

Like the Tories' negative ads, the NDP offerings were clever examples of how to use the unique medium of television to get a point across—and how to incorporate advertising into a cam-paign strategy with maximum impact. By hooking together their news and advertising agendas the New Democrats adhered to the principle of single-message marketing. Rigid control of their messages was a trademark of the NDP strategy: the ads stuck to it on the air and Rae stuck to it on the ground, as he resisted dealing with issues and making news other than with his attacks.

The qualities that turned many of the NDP strategists off the ads were precisely what made them good television. The spots were turbulent and disruptive, employing an intricate inter-weaving of information with visual and aural messages to seize and hold the attention of viewers and provoke a reaction. They were unique enough to crack through the din of other ads, news and entertainment programming. Their abrasive editing, similar in style to many music videos, was provocative in itself: the ads "wiggled," and made people notice them. They made a series of exaggerated points linked to the single theme of honesty and integrity and provided a one-line resolution at the end of each spot, all without addressing superfluous issues. Consistent with the NDP strategy the spots were designed to register suspicion and uncertainty and to tap into feelings of distrust of Peterson and the Liberals by suggesting they were linked to powerful special interests and different from "us."

Even the use of the remote control in the spots carried a hid-den message. The "clicker" was a visual and aural cue that view-ers could connect to a common personal experience—one that conveyed symbolically that changing channels to the NDP was a simple, self-empowering act that could make a difference. The channel-changing television viewer was clearly "bored with the program," much like many Ontarians in the summer of 1990.

*   *   *

Three days before the parties' ads could legally go to air Tory communications director Gillies struck again. It was a Sunday, with little news coming from either the Liberal or NDP camp, and Gillies decided to try to steal the show on campaign advertising. He tipped off reporters from major Toronto media that Harris was going to unveil his campaign ads early at a strategy session for party workers. Reporters again showed up to cover the "story," unaware they were supplementing Gillies' anemic media budget. Introduced by Harris the ads were screened to the hoots and cheers of the Tory throng. The week's media coverage was launched the following day with headlines Gillies would gladly have written himself: "Tory ads target Liberal 'tax grab'" and "Ad blitz assails Grit tax record." The NDP and Liberals scurried to get copies of their ads together to release to reporters but the tactical chess game had again gone to the Tories.

Media response to the ads tended to reflect the tone of the coverage elsewhere in the campaign. The first reports on the Tory ads called them "aggressive" and "tough," playing down any mention of negative advertising. When all the ads were finally released at mid-week, the Tory and NDP negativity was picked up, while the Liberals were praised for taking a high-road approach.

But with a focus on style, the substance of all the ads, including the Liberals' positive ads, was subjected to minimal scrutiny. Even the "lies" and "hyperbole" that NDP strategists would later admit formed their ads were not rooted out and bracketed with critical analysis by reporters or looked at in the light of Rae's prominent statement that Peterson had lied to Ontarians. Reporters did not point out the ads were bereft of Tory or NDP alternatives.

One report claimed to discover the "reason" why Rae and Harris were missing from their parties' ads: "Party officials say that's because the leaders are already being seen in daily election reports." Reville and Gillies were earning their keep by spinning such lines. Both opposition parties, in fact, had determined viewers were not interested in what their leaders had to say. Analytical reports prompted by the ads began to surface about two weeks after the spots were released but tended to ponder whether the negative trends of the Ontario campaign represented a permanent shift in political advertising in Canada.

As they began to infiltrate the province's airwaves the video offerings of the three parties enjoyed dramatically different strategic positioning. While the NDP and Tory ads were consistent with those parties' news messages—and with the overwhelming direction of the campaign—the Liberal spots were out of sync with the news agenda. Rae's daily attacks had sustained the theme of questioning the Liberals' honesty and integrity. Harris had shaken off the stigma of being an unknown and christened his campaign buses "Taxfighter I" and "Taxfighter II," just in time for the launch of the Tories' overtaxation commercials. But the Liberals were in trouble and their ads didn't help: by the time they made it to air, Peterson was no longer the sincere and smiling traveler portrayed in the 30-second Liberal spots. In the "real" world seen every night on the news he was being pelted with abuse each time he ventured out of the safe sanctuary of his bus.

While the NDP and Tories achieved the highly prized strategic objective of consistency between their advertising and the news the Liberals now had a whole new problem to contend with. Rather than reinforce the news agenda, their ads provided a contrast by being dated and inappropriate. The spots were a throwback to the way the Liberals would have liked to have seen Peterson perceived throughout the campaign. The ads' positivity, ironically, had a backlash effect, as they became a subject of scorn and ridicule in the days after their release. An Ottawa reviewer wrote "Peterson, fixing his soft brown eyes on the camera, is a cross between a basset hound waiting for another bone and a latter-day Don Juan assuring a young maiden that she can trust him to behave—this time. If Ontario is the engine driving Canada and Peterson the engineer, the voters are meant to be in the sleeping car."

The members of Red Trillium were beginning to worry before their ads went to air. They watched the news and wondered how badly the buffeting of Peterson's image was damaging the Liberal fortunes and undermining their ads. If people began moving away from the Liberals, they realized, the ads might not be sending out the right message to stop that movement and bring people back. But with Robinson holding Goldfarb's rolling poll numbers tightly to herself in the early stages of the campaign, David Morton received no information that led him to think seriously about reconsidering the ad strategy. Red Trillium received no signals about whether the Liberal strategy was working, or about any plans to alter it, until well after their positive Peterson-centered ads had started to air. "I didn't know we were softening up," said Morton, "so there was no reason for us to think the ads we were putting on weren't going to play well."

The ads went to air on August 15 and Morton was dying for information. He called Goldfarb and pleaded with him to part with a shred of data that would tell him about the climate of public opinion in which the ads were being seen. "If it hadn't been for my good friend Marty I wouldn't have had any data at that point," said Morton. Goldfarb ignored Robinson's orders and told Morton that support for the Liberals had fallen badly. Getting word from Goldfarb that the Liberal campaign was in trouble only made matters worse for Morton. He felt he could not disclose to Robinson that Goldfarb had shared the numbers with him and he could not arbitrarily start rejigging the ads without authorization from the strategy committee. Red Trillium's positive ads were going ahead as planned but Morton was plagued with doubt: "We sure as hell are smart enough not to run nice David Peterson-on-a-bus things when his image has fallen flat in the can. We basically were wasting money running that kind of campaign. Had we known earlier, I suspect the bus campaign wouldn't have gone that way." Had Morton been provided with early confirmation that the opposition attacks on honesty and integrity and taxes were registering, the Liberals could have used their first wave of ads to try to inoculate Peterson against further attacks on those issues.

Robinson, determined not to be forced off-strategy by the events of the campaign, told Morton to hang tough and said the Liberal numbers were holding. They agreed to see if the ads could help the Liberal campaign balance the attacks of the protesters and the tough media coverage. But their assumption was bucking a fundamental rule of election campaigns: the news is by far the most important thing that goes on the air. The likelihood the Liberal ads could have overwhelmed the news agenda was never strong.

But Morton agreed to wait and see, hoping the ads would help: "If the numbers are holding, that's the premise we're working under, if everything is going fine, our advertising was going to help alleviate that negative stuff we're seeing," said Morton. "As long as there's an impression that there's this negative stuff here, but it's not having much of an impact on the voters, and let's offset that with this, then it made sense at the time to continue to do that."

But five days after the ads started to air, Morton and the strategists agreed the attack messages in the NDP and Tory ads were buttressing their negative themes and registering with Ontarians as if they were Peterson's campaign slogans. The word went out quickly from Morton to Red Trillium: we need a new approach that goes after Rae and Harris in the same way.

"We were about a week into the ads before we got any data that said we were in trouble," said Morton. "What do you do? We never had a chance to think about it because it was too late to be anything other than reactive. We lost a valuable number of days by deluding ourselves. A well-thought-out strategy ought to be good enough to drive a campaign for three weeks but you also have to adjust. You've got to adjust quickly but you can only adjust if you get the information. We clearly didn't get enough information early on."

By now Red Trillium had been all but dissolved. Believing their jobs had been done, most of its members had taken off for holidays or were away on business. Morton and Murphy were left holding down the fort with a few of their staff. If they were going to launch an attack against Rae and Harris they needed good ammunition fast. To their relief it was ready and waiting.

*   *   *

On the first day of the campaign Dan Gagnier began to hold twice-a-week meetings with three Liberal communications advisors, all former reporters in the Queen's Park press gallery.

"I want to get some alternate points of view on how the campaign is going," Gagnier announced at the group's first meeting. "I want to get a critical perspective and a media perspective."

"Oh, I get it," said one of the ex-reporters. "You want us to be pricks."

"You might say that," Gagnier smiled.

At the end of the first week of the campaign the four assembled for their second meeting. All had come to the same conclusion: the negative campaigns of Rae and Harris were hitting home; reporters were conveying the attack messages and Peterson was being slapped around without offering a defense. Gagnier asked for the group's advice.

"I think we should look at the vulnerabilities of both Rae and Harris and think about some way of getting the facts out on them," said one of the group. Gagnier agreed to assign a researcher to gather newspaper clippings and party policy documents for the advisor, who would put together a package of little-known facts about the background, record and commitments of the opposition leaders and their parties.

The group agreed that an opportunity to spread the information might come up during the second week of the campaign, when the Liberal ministers' tours were scheduled to start. Within days, two documents were prepared, filled with embarrassing and unsavory facts. The research showed that the resolutions from an Ontario NDP policy convention in 1988 would technically require an NDP government to drastically alter the decision-making process of cabinet and caucus to defer to resolutions of the party. The NDP was still on record as demanding the nationalization of Inco, Falconbridge, Denison Mines and Rio Algom; it would replace the provincial sales tax with a progressive income tax system, institute a payroll tax to fund provincial pensions and willingly run the province's deficit up into the billions. Noteworthy quotes from Rae were unearthed, such as "Taxes are a way of sharing. It's a way of getting into a relationship with society" and "I don't know any government in Canada which operates on the basis that all expenditures have to be paid for out of immediate revenue."

Harris's statements during the Tory leadership campaign had produced a bounty of right-wing positions, including extension of the GST to cover food, $5 user fees for doctor visits and an end to rent controls and affordable housing construction. The research found that Harris was a sitting duck for personal, character-based attacks, quoting him as saying he agreed to run for MPP after he was told "that the legislature sat only six months a year and that I could fly down on Tuesday morning and back to North Bay on Thursday night and have lots of fun." One reporter was found to have written about Harris, "One popular topic was the MPP's widely publicized criticism of the dimensions of the steaks served at the provincial legislature."

Days later, with the help of the Liberals in Harris's riding, another interesting fact was added to the list: Harris, who was calling himself the "Taxfighter" on the campaign trail as he pounded the Liberals' tax hikes, had a less-than-enviable record on taxation. From 1977 to 1981 he had served as chair of the Nipissing Public School Board. During that time, the mill rate was increased by 51.17 percent, rising from 63 in 1977 to 95.24 in 1981.*

When Gagnier and his group finished hooting over the discoveries the papers were forwarded to Liberal campaign headquarters staff attempting to organize the ministers' tours. The strategists had agreed with Goldfarb's proposal to assign several

---

* Documents filed with the Election Finances Commission in May 1991 also reveal that the Nipissing Progressive Conservative Association spent $7,241 in riding association funds to buy suits for the "Taxfighter" in 1990. The expense was listed as "MPP wardrobe."

ministers to both echo Peterson's campaigning efforts and provide negative counterpoint to the NDP and Tories. Copies of the
findings on Rae and Harris were forwarded to Liberal ministers
Ian Scott, Sean Conway, Bob Nixon and Lyn McLeod. Each was
persuaded by Robinson to pry loose from local campaigning and
get on the road for a day to deliver the negative attack messages
that the papers supplied.

The plan backfired dismally. Conway took a tour of centers in
Northern Ontario, where he was promptly attacked by media,
teachers and other candidates over Liberal education policies.
Nixon marched off to Kitchener, where the Kitchener-Waterloo
Record reported he told its editorial board he had opposed the
early election call all along. Others failed to draw the regional
media coverage the Liberals anticipated. In each case the ministers
were reluctant to use the negative information.

Robinson phoned each one repeatedly but was unable to
convince them to go along. Only Nixon came through with a
strong attack. He told the crowd at Peterson's nomination meeting in London on August 7 that he had little time for "El Pinko
Bobby Rae." But Nixon's words, flashed across the province by
the media and often rerun as one of the highlights of the campaign, appeared several decades out of touch with many Ontarians' view of the NDP leader. Midway through the campaign,
Nixon finally agreed to deliver some of the attacks on Rae and
Harris as they had been scripted. In a west Toronto riding he
railed about the threat Rae and the NDP posed on taxes and the
deficit, in front of three television cameras and three print
reporters. Only one of them used the story.

*   *   *

The papers on Rae and Harris sat at Liberal headquarters until
they were spirited off by Morton to Donald Murphy. Their plan
was simple: with Liberal support dropping they would produce
a series of negative "response" ads as a counterpunch to the successful campaigns of the Tories and NDP. Morton and Murphy
would produce two anti-Tory television commercials and three

radio spots, one attacking each opposition party and one attacking the GST. On the creative side the door was wide open.

Murphy scanned the information from Gagnier's group and went to work with his writers. The first script was called "Clothesline": "Open on a short, fat candle that says 'Mike Harris,'" read the video copy. "Over the candle is a piece of clothesline, leading to the camera. We hear the creak of a clothesline as a card is pulled up with a clothespeg holding it. It reads 'health care.' It catches fire and disappears." The audio copy was blunt: "Let's shed some realistic light on Mike Harris and the Tories," the announcer was to say. "They want to burn you with renewed extra billing by doctors and by turning our health system over to private business. They want to torch pay equity for women and put a match to plans for more child care centers in schools. Rent controls will go up in flames . . ." and so on. "Clothesline" was ruled too heavy-handed when members of the Liberal strategy committee saw the concept; it was relegated to the back "burner." The strategists wanted to start their attacks by hitting the Tories where they were weakest. They wanted something that could transfer voters' well-known anti-Mulroney sentiments onto Harris.

Murphy and his writers tried again. "Open on a balloon on a stick. On one side is a caricature of Mulroney. On the other side is a caricature of Harris. Their names are under their caricatures. The faces flip back and forth." Male and female announcers shared the reading: "It's easy to confuse one Tory with another Tory. This Tory [Mulroney was shown] got us into the free trade mess. This Tory [Harris] stands for free trade too. This Tory brought us the GST; this Tory likes it so much he'd extend it to cover food and doctor bills . . . A Tory is a Tory is a Tory [Balloon spins and pops]. Don't let them hurt Ontario."

That did the job, agreed Robinson, Webster and Goldfarb. Morton went along reluctantly. He was not happy to be associated with a negative ad, thought the concept was hokey and had difficulty accepting the Tories as the main target. But the campaign brass prevailed and "Balloon" was rushed into production along with the three radio spots.

A different tack was tried with the radio scripts. Rather than simply attack the GST, the Tories and the NDP, each spot was written to offer a line of criticism followed by a line describing the Liberals' alternative position. All four spots arrived at Goldfarb's offices for focus group testing by Hurley. "Balloon" was roundly criticized for its negative style but the message was clearly registering—Harris was in cahoots with Mulroney, whom nobody liked. But the radio spots produced an unexpected result. Hurley walked into the observation room when the groups were completed. "I can't believe it," he said. "These are negative ads but they're testing as positive. Those people think they're fair and reasonable."

Morton reworked his weighting of the Liberal ads to have "Balloon" occupy 60 percent of the television spots booked. Some of the positive ads were retained. As "Balloon" began to run, "Clothesline"'s candle motif was revived and worked into another negative spot called "Candle," which showed a series of candles, representing different issues, being snuffed by the Tories, and then relighted by the Liberals. It replaced the last two positive spots, and in the last days of the campaign Liberal television advertising would contain nothing but negative attacks aimed at the Tories.

Reporters, prompted by the dramatic change in ad strategy, immediately jumped on the Liberals for going for the jugular. "The gloves are off and Premier David Peterson is fighting for his job," reported the Toronto *Star*. Again, Tory spin-doctor Gillies convinced reporters to pass along his interpretation of what was happening in the election. Straight faced, he led a Toronto *Star* reporter to write, "The new Liberal campaign 'is the most negative' in campaign history, Gillies said. He's astounded by the strong-armed Liberal tactics."

By reading the inclinations of reporters and feeding them carefully crafted lines, Gillies was able to enhance the effectiveness of many components of the Tory strategy. His efforts helped build consistency between the Tories' advertising and the news agenda, and ensured that key events were often bracketed with his anti-Liberal analysis by reporters. Reville, the

NDP's main spin-doctor, ran a distant second but with his friendly, self-deprecating manner was similarly effective at the art of media manipulation. Robinson, who insisted on handling such duties for the Liberals in spite of a lack of experience in dealing with the media, was simply skated off the rink.

*   *   *

Within a few days of entering Ontarians' living rooms, the attack ads of the Tories and NDP began to register on viewers. Echoing and complementing the news agenda of the campaign the spots aired by both parties continued the erosion of Liberal support. But as the Tory strategists had suspected would happen, the attacks worked to the benefit of the NDP. At Decima, focus groups began to reveal the trend to Gillies: "I sensed that our campaign was taking hold, that our ads were having an effect, but that we were not the beneficiaries of the bulk of the drop-off in the Liberal vote. For every three votes that dropped away from the Liberals the NDP were picking up two to our one. When they were sitting in a room watching Tory ads, by a ratio of about two to one, those disaffected would then say they were going to vote NDP. That tracked with our quantitative polling."

The NDP strategists were delighted as they observed the same trend. "It was almost like having an advertising budget you didn't have to put down on your election finances form," said Reville. "You weren't paying for it, those other guys were." The New Democrats locked even more firmly onto their attack theme but wondered how long it would be before the bottom fell out of the trend that was bringing them votes.

The Tories, however, had a tough choice to make: Should they keep running ads that helped shovel Liberal votes over to Rae? The Tory campaign committee made its first critical decision of the election, one that caused nightmares for the right-wing Tories on the team: the ads would stay. Self-preservation was the determining factor. "We had to keep chipping away at the Liberal vote even if the NDP picked up a disproportionate number of those votes, because it was the only way we could save our skins," said Gillies. "We knew if we got up into the 20 percent range we would be okay, we would at least win as many seats as we had in the previous election and maybe a few more."

The attack ads served a secondary purpose for the Tories and NDP: they helped demoralize the Liberals. Many Liberals were shaken as the attacks on the integrity of their leader and their party filled the airwaves. While the Liberal strategists had anticipated negative attacks they had failed to prepare for them and had not passed along a warning to the troops. Instead, a few days after the ads were released, Robinson passed along encouragement in a bid to shore up morale: "The opposition's failure to score a significant hit constitutes the failure of their 'last, best hope' at knocking us off our positive agenda," she said in an August 22 memo to Liberal candidates and campaign managers. "Their negative campaigns and negative advertising have had little discernable impact."

9

Summer of Discontent

People are cranky.

—*DAVID PETERSON*

For the first few days of the campaign, Government House Leader Chris Ward was confident about being elected for a third time in the sprawling riding of Wentworth North—confident enough that he was willing to spread his strength around by campaigning for neighboring candidates. On the first evening of the campaign he offered to help Burlington South Liberal Marvin Townsend. With a handful of canvassers, Ward drove from Dundas through Waterdown and crossed the border into Burlington South. They picked up Townsend materials and found the new residential development they were assigned to canvass.

Brimming with energy and enthusiasm Ward bounded out of the car and jogged down the street. He sprinted up the steps of the first house like an outfielder chasing a fly ball and rapped on the front door. A middle-aged woman opened it.

"Hello, ma'am, I'm Chris Ward," he said with a smile. "I'm here to ask for your support for Marv Townsend in the election on September 6." He thrust out a Townsend brochure done up in Liberal red and white.

The woman looked Ward in the eye and took the leaflet. Without breaking her gaze or saying a word she tore it in half and handed it back to him.

"Thank you, ma'am," said Ward. He turned and walked limply off the porch.

Ward was not alone. Other Peterson Liberals going door to door in the search for votes in the summer of 1990 became accustomed to similarly chilly greetings. Liberal canvassers across Ontario found people at the door silent and stoic or painfully polite: worrisome signs they recognized as signals for "No, but I'm too nice to tell you" or "I haven't decided but don't get your hopes up." "Either way," said one Liberal candidate, "you know you're in big trouble."

Some candidates were asked important questions; their opinions counted to some people. In the first week of the campaign, Attorney General Ian Scott went door-knocking in the upscale Toronto neighborhood of Moore Park. At the door of an old stone home he was greeted warmly by a woman in her eighties.

"Hello, Mr. Scott, how are you?" she said. "You look so well—you've lost a little weight since the campaign started."

"Yes, I think I have," Scott replied. "You look well also."

"Do you have any competition this time?" she asked.

"Well, yes, I do," said Scott. "Keith Norton, the former Davis cabinet minister, is running for the Tories and a young woman by the name of Carolanne Wright is the NDP candidate."

"That's nice. Well, don't work too hard, you're not as young as you used to be," said the woman. "And tell me one thing, Mr. Scott. Which one of those two should I vote for?"

That incident encapsulated the campaign for Scott. "She wasn't being sarcastic, she was too old, and she wasn't putting me down," he sighed. "She was just saying, 'I like you well enough but I'm not voting for your party this time. By the way, I respect your judgment and which one of them is the best?' Within two weeks, for me, it was the story of the campaign."

*　　*　　*

Seven days into the campaign the pollsters for the three parties were reporting in with dramatic first-week findings. As expected all around, support for the Liberals dropped off from the 50 percent-plus ratings in July. But the fluctuations were wilder in the day-to-day rolling polls than any of the pollsters had ever seen. Some days, the Liberals were coming in as low as 42 percent, an unheard-of drop of eight or more points within days of the election call; in other samplings, the Liberals were slipping by three or four points, a more characteristic early-campaign drop-off by an incumbent party. "Volatility of the electorate" quickly took over as the buzzword in all three camps. But ten days into the campaign, the trend was clear: in the hot summer of 1990, support for Peterson was peeling off like a bad sunburn.

At Tory headquarters the puzzled strategists looked to Decima's Wednesday night focus groups for correlations that could help them understand Allan Gregg's early findings. Putting the "pattern" of volatility together with the groups' responses, the Tories began to realize that the potential effect of their overtaxation attack strategy was now unfolding before their eyes: voters were being driven away from Peterson and were latching onto Rae. The protester phenomenon seemed to be mixing with the NDP and Tory attacks in an alchemy that produced something potent enough to penetrate the Liberals' skin.

At first the apparent willingness of voters to abandon Peterson seemed to the opposition camps to be a cruel flirtation, giving them exciting little thrills every other day, then drawing back, then teasing them again. As the axis of the swings began to shift away from the Liberals, both the Tory and NDP brain trusts started to look at their overnight and weekly summaries without doubting the trend was genuine. They still did not believe in their guts that the Liberals were beatable but they could tell their strategies were working and they were bound and determined to stick to them.

*   *   *

Liberals, New Democrats and Tories alike had problems at Ontario's doors in the summer of 1990. All wore the stigma of being politicians at a time when contempt for politicians was rampant. NDP and Tory candidates and workers found the same range of reactions as Liberals: from bitterness to complacency to fury about an election people did not think they wanted or needed. But only the Liberals were burdened with Peterson's image.

In the campaign's first week the protesters clamoring to take shots at Peterson made it impossible to mistake who was becoming the target for people's frustrations: it was the premier everyone wanted to get at. That created a terrible dilemma for many Liberal candidates who had accepted the wisdom of the strategists' Peterson-centered campaign. For the first weeks of the campaign they also accepted what they assumed was a well-considered plan by Liberal headquarters to ignore the ground swell of anti-Peterson feelings and stay on course. They did not know about the strategists' feuding.

Most Liberals across the province were left with only their wits or instincts to guide them. Most, but not all—11 had acquired the services of their own pollster, Michael Marzolini.

In 1985 Marzolini tried to latch on with the Ontario Liberal campaign and convinced Hershell Ezrin to let him do overnight tracking for the Liberals. Each day during the 1985 campaign Marzolini had sent a three-page summary to Liberal headquarters where Ezrin, Gordon Ashworth and campaign chair Ross McGregor would arm wrestle for it; the tracking was extremely accurate and had high strategic value. But two years later Martin Goldfarb moved in as Peterson's full-time campaign pollster; kicked down to second-string status, Marzolini hooked up with 27 Liberal challengers and incumbent Elinor Caplan, offering his services during the election for about $5,000 per riding. He helped 23 of those candidates win.

By 1990 Marzolini's Insight Canada Research had grown to become the fifth-largest polling operation in Canada, with a lineup of prime commercial clients. Goldfarb seemed destined to have the Ontario Liberal Party account as long as the Peterson government stayed in power. But Marzolini believed he could still provide a useful service to individual Liberal candidates.

One of Marzolini's clients was Remo Mancini, a young Liberal minister from Essex South in the Windsor area. Mancini had only to look at the anti-Liberal demonstrations at the party's April convention to know that few people in his region would be prepared to vote for his party. Early in July Mancini came to Marzolini to get a sense of which public attitudes in his riding he could tap to overcome that disadvantage.

"We did a complete study at the beginning of the campaign," said Marzolini. "We worked out all the variances, what options would change the vote by one point, two points, whatever. We have a much different approach to electoral polling than Goldfarb does. We like to throw options, strategic scenarios, at the public." Marzolini's interviewers phoned residents of Essex South and built a profile of their top issues. "The number one issue in that riding wasn't what it was everywhere else: the environment, the rate of inflation, or whatever," found Marzolini. "It was job loss due to free trade. That was big in the whole Windsor area."

Mancini knew that if he was going to survive he had to speak directly to the concerns of people in his riding. "I had him attack Mulroney all the way through and build on his own record in the community," said Marzolini. "He was nervous about that. He said, 'The NDP are gaining. I can feel them breathing down my neck.' We talked every single day. He was getting bad advice from the central campaign." After the election Mancini would publicly credit Marzolini with saving his skin in an NDP sweep of Windsor ridings.

Thunder Bay Liberal Lyn McLeod hooked up with Marzolini for similar advice two months before the campaign. He took the temperature in her riding of Fort William and found that worries about the economic slowdown were beginning to hit harder there than in most other parts of Ontario. "The shipyards and the grain elevators were lying idle," he found. "These people were not in the mood to receive beer and hot dogs." McLeod's campaign began in June, combining her record of service to the riding with anti-Mulroney sentiment and promoting the Liberals as the best party to see the area through a recession. She would be re-elected in spite of an NDP surge in northern Ontario.

As the central Liberal campaign unfolded Marzolini told his candidate clients to ignore it outright. It was based, he said, on "shifting sands, a house of cards." He had no confidence in the vague, issueless rationale Peterson had offered up. "You need a reason, whether it's your own personality or whatever," he told his select group of Liberal candidates. "You've got to be able to get people angry at somebody and say, 'You gotta elect me because if you don't, all sorts of horrible things are gonna happen out there, and it's Mulroney who's at fault. We're gonna direct the provincial resources in the riding necessary to counteract the federal threat: we're gonna protect you.'" Marzolini told most of his clients to go after Mulroney on the GST; he could not understand why Peterson did not do the same right from the kickoff of the campaign: "That's what he was able to do in '87. It was a proper campaign in '87, run against free trade. He could have done that against the GST this time and looked honest doing it."

Marzolini supplied weekly tracking for his Liberal candidates. In the early weeks of the campaign Marzolini's findings reflected what was obvious to candidates at the door and to people who watched the protesters on the news at night: Ontario was putting the boots to Peterson. Paul Pellegrini, executive assistant to Elinor Caplan, who worked as the central campaign's Metro Toronto area coordinator, kept in touch with Marzolini on the progress of the campaign. Concerned about one Toronto riding, he asked Marzolini to sample voter intentions and the result showed the Liberal incumbent far behind, contrary to what the central campaign was saying.

Pellegrini was stunned at the dichotomy. Marzolini was telling him the Liberals were in serious trouble in Toronto but the central campaign was not batting an eye. Concerned about the information Robinson and Beth Webster were receiving, Pellegrini showed them the result of his small poll. He was even more confounded when they thanked him and did not flinch at the numbers. Unknown to Pellegrini, Marzolini's data simply confirmed the Goldfarb findings that the Liberal campaign was not moving on.

Eight of the eleven Liberals who purchased Marzolini's services would be re-elected. "The three who didn't listen to our advice or followed that of the central campaign were the three who lost," he said.

Marzolini pulled no punches for one Toronto Liberal who hired him.

"So, how am I doing, Mike?" asked the candidate.

"Well, my advice to you is to get out right away and start knocking on doors," Marzolini said.

"What do you mean? Seniors, ethnics, renters? Whose doors?"

"Employment agents," counseled the pollster.

* * *

From the campaign's first day, Liberal headquarters was inundated with feedback from the troops on the ground about how their local battles were going. Early on, Robinson invited that input. "I'll be looking forward to hearing from you as the campaign develops," she said in a memo to every candidate and campaign manager on July 31. "I can never get too much information from the places where it counts—the committee rooms of Liberal campaigns across Ontario." Within days Robinson was swamped with complaints: voters did not like Liberal candidates and hated Peterson. But the calls did nothing to shake the campaign manager from her commitment to stay "on-strategy."

Many campaign managers and candidates began to understand that Peterson was a serious liability, an impediment to their re-election. That meant decision time, when the reams of central campaign literature featuring a smiling Peterson began to arrive in the first week of the campaign. Some local Liberals did not think twice: they heaved the brochures and tabloids unceremoniously onto the trash heap or carted them away quietly to the recycling depot and replaced them with hastily prepared handouts focusing on their candidate alone. At the same time Ken Tilley's crew continued to crank out more Peterson-centered propaganda; Robinson and Webster gave them no new directions.

Officials of Liberal ridings that coughed up $3,500 to $4,100 each for the riding services package were ready for a rubber room when they realized they had wasted their money. To give their candidates a fighting chance they had to shell out extra cash for their own last-minute brochures. It was either spend the money or risk losing by being associated with Peterson.

"You put all that money in and you think, well, we're going to have to go with the main pamphlet," said Peterborough Liberal candidate Peter Adams. "It was the biggest mistake. All the others we tossed and we used ones that we designed. My garage is full of them." In Wentworth North, Ward's campaign staff found an ingenious way to solve the problem. They called the local Boy Scout paper drive.

In Ian Scott's campaign office, workers preparing their own "piece" to be dropped at doors found to their dismay they did not have a good photograph of Scott by himself. The only available picture showed Scott and Peterson posing together. The problem was quickly solved by the strategic use of a yellow self-adhesive note, which was stuck over Peterson. The resulting portrait of Scott was inserted into the layout.

*　　*　　*

The Liberals were inclined to perform backflips over their campaign literature because of its essential role in contemporary campaigning. Local campaigns depend on a supply of suitable literature to be spread by workers as a coating of propaganda. A post-election Environics poll would rate candidates' literature as the third-most important factor in helping Ontarians decide who to vote for, following news coverage and the televised leaders' debate. Whether read in-depth or scanned and then pitched as junk mail, candidates' literature is the calling card of the critical ground campaign.

Campaigns of all political affiliations believe that two factors determine whether an election is won or lost: the central campaign, with its themes, messages and leader's tour, and the ability of each candidate to "pull the vote" on election day in each riding.

Of the systems for conducting a campaign in a large urban or suburban riding, the most popular is best described as a "poll captain system." Ontario Liberals in Toronto began to develop their own version of this system in 1985, perfected it in 1987 and by 1990 were spreading it across the province. Insiders dubbed it the "Concorde" model of campaign management.

Under the Liberals' Concorde model, each riding is divided into "areas" containing a number of polls. A riding includes 100 to 200 polls and each poll about 50 to 150 homes, in addition to apartment buildings and denser housing in urban areas. Five to ten areas make up a riding. When the Concorde flies at peak performance a poll captain is assigned to each poll with responsibility for canvassing every voter. Poll captains report to area chairs, who report to the canvass chair. The canvass chair, together with people in charge of the candidate's fund-raising, the local telephone canvass, campaign signs and volunteers, report to the campaign manager.

A fully staffed Concorde would wing through an election with the help of still more workers assigned the responsibilities of election day activities, managing policy and research, running the campaign headquarters, conducting media relations, handling advertising and literature, special events, youth organization and the candidate's canvass and scheduling. The team would be rounded out with a chief financial officer, a legal advisor, an auditor and a candidate's advisory group. The Concorde requires several hundred volunteer bodies to operate as designed.

Of all these bodies the most crucial are the poll captains, the frontline troops of the campaign. They deliver the candidate's literature to each voter, helping to spread the campaign's messages. Most importantly, they lay the groundwork for election day vote-pulling by identifying the voting intentions of every voter. In provincial elections, ridings are often won or lost by a handful of votes per poll, with only a few hundred votes separating the victor from the vanquished. Those narrow margins make identifying voting intentions critical. They help a candidate build on existing support and focus on winning over undecided voters and weak supporters of the opponents. A successful door-to-door canvass will yield the five or six votes needed to win polls and, if all goes according to plan, the riding.

First-time canvassers usually think they are in for a lot of fun: going door to door, meeting people, spreading the candidate's good news. Experienced canvassers look on the job as a necessary evil. Regardless of heat, cold, rain or snow, poll captains must trudge with enthusiasm from house to house, imagining what waits behind the next door: "Jaws" the pit bull, a lecturing member of the Communist party, a tongue-lashing from an opponent's supporter, a request for answers to all of the world's problems or a large biker who growls menacingly that, "All politicians should be shot." A remarkable encounter in the 1990 Liberal campaign was reported by a downtown Toronto canvasser who knocked bravely on the door of a basement apartment from which a foul odor was emerging. The occupant, a fat, shirtless, middle-aged man, answered the door accompanied by his pet, a full-grown pig.

The Concorde recommends that the poll captain call on each voter three times, handing out a different piece of campaign literature at each visit. The poll captain marks voting intentions on the voters' lists prepared by the district returning officer. After the third visit every voter's intentions in every poll should be known. Telephone canvassing and the candidate's canvass are used to supplement the door-to-door visits. On election day, supporters are pulled by telephone or in person.

The candidate conducts his or her own door-to-door canvass, walking from house to house or running up and down apartment stairwells for six to ten hours a day for five straight weeks. Candidates often report a weight loss after a campaign and usually wear out at least one pair of shoes.

In 1987 the Concorde served scores of Liberal candidates well; in 1990 it was towed out of the hangar again and promoted at the party's "campaign college," where it was condensed into a 13-part manual that formed part of the Liberals' riding services package.

But early in the 1990 campaign the Concorde ran into trouble. "It became obvious the Concorde was never going to fly in 1990," said Chuck Birchall, campaign manager for Ian Scott and a developer of the Concorde. "We had to take the model two weeks into the campaign and refashion it." The revamped Concorde became, in ridings across Ontario, a stripped-down "Sopwith Camel." Liberal volunteers, alienated, complacent or just not interested, were not materializing in the numbers expected. Liberal campaign organizers scrambled to assign multiple duties to the bodies that did show up. Committed volunteers found themselves working day and night in Liberal ridings.

The timing of the 1990 election created problems for every party. With two long weekends, the August 6 Civic Holiday and Labour Day, the canvass period was shortened and many people were away on vacation. A smaller number of volunteers had less time to canvass. Many local Liberal campaigns found they could not cover all of their polls the optimum three times; some were not canvassed even once and voting intentions were difficult to pin down. To counteract these problems some Liberal campaign managers bolstered their telephone canvass, especially on election day when many campaign groups did not have enough bodies to pull identified supporters. Managing a Liberal campaign in 1990 meant accepting "you weren't going to get around three times in every poll, and recognizing that given some of the discontent, it might not be appreciated in terms of getting around three times," said Birchall.

The provincewide shortage of Liberal volunteers created some dramatic contrasts with the 1987 campaign. Scott's campaign boasted 700 volunteers on day one in 1987 and retained most throughout the campaign. In 1990 fewer than 100 showed up the first day, with 300 on election day. Other Liberals were in the same boat and advised Liberal headquarters of their resource problems early in the campaign. On August 7, in a memo faxed to candidates and campaign managers, Robinson blamed the shortage of willing help on the summer campaign, a suggestion that ignored the abundance of volunteers in the 1987 summer election, and on "complacency by a front-running team." Sensing widespread organizational problems, Robinson urged Liberal campaign managers to "focus on the fundamentals—identifying Liberal support and getting it to the polls. I understand the challenge of attracting and motivating volunteers but this has to be our key effort." She urged Liberals to "take every opportunity to remind voters that your candidate is part of David Peterson's team" and told them that after the first week of the campaign "the feeling on the streets is that Ontarians are prepared to re-elect a Liberal government." Already, candidates and campaign managers were discounting Robinson's advice. They were finding the opposite to be true and wondered whether the central campaign had a clue about what was really happening out there.

*　　*　　*

Robinson had plenty of clues: reports from local campaigns, the attacks on Peterson dominating the nightly news and the rolling polls reported to her each morning by Goldfarb. But in the early weeks of the campaign, she did not make the jump from observing the problem of flagging Liberal support to believing it demanded action. Determined to stay on-strategy and not be dislodged by events, Robinson laid back, hoping to see stability emerge in the tracking. To some it seemed that Robinson was developing a siege mentality that accompanied her conviction she had to make the campaign's key decisions single-handedly. Others saw that she felt her actions were a necessary response to the climate created by the leaks.

On the second evening of the campaign Robinson and Peterson aide Vince Borg met for dinner at an Italian restaurant next

door to campaign headquarters in Toronto. "She was quite concerned about the leaks and what was happening," said Borg. "It
was a pivotal moment in her deciding what to do and what not
to do. She threw out the question about who she could trust, if
anybody, about the data."

Robinson confided her problem in a few other Liberal
friends who offered their support and confidence as she decided
to hold fast and keep Goldfarb's rolling polls tight, divulging
them only to Webster. "Kathy is fairly democratic and consultative," said Borg. "But as a result of the leaks she just freaked out.
She was another person. She became a different kind of decision
maker."

Those decisions began mounting up quickly. "Kathy, in
addition to the Gordon Ashworth role, had taken on the direction of the tour," said Webster. Like other top Liberals, tour
director Doug Kirkpatrick was kept in the dark on the results of
Goldfarb's tracking; his working relationship with Robinson
deteriorated rapidly as he found his decisions being second-
guessed without explanation. At the same time Robinson "was
the one and only conduit to the bus on a regular basis," said
Webster. Robinson ordered Peterson's executive assistant Gordon McCauley to police the phone calls accepted on the premier's bus, restricting contact between Peterson and other
sources of advice.

Goldfarb, who made recommendations to Robinson when
he supplied her with his tracking results each morning, found
himself frustrated trying to get across his observations about
Peterson. In the second week of the campaign, he phoned Dan
Gagnier. The premier had no edge, no focus, the pollster complained: he was too mellow, and his language was not cutting
through the background noise of the protesters. Gagnier had
few chances to pass along such snippets of advice—only on the
rare occasions when Peterson chose to call him. The bottom line
of the arrangement: broad-based, cohesive advice to the premier was replaced by a single source. For most of the campaign
Peterson operated without the informed input of the Liberal
brain trust.

"Everybody was cut off at the knees," said Borg. "The premier didn't feel his bearings because he was getting information primarily from one source and as a result his decision-making capacity probably suffered."

As co-chair of the 1987 campaign David MacNaughton understood the decision-making challenge Robinson took upon herself and sat back while she tried to go it alone. "The strategy unraveled for a whole series of reasons, but the fact Kathy was by herself was one reason," he said. "She became the lightning rod for everything. She had been witness to the premier's decision-making style, which was to gather eight people around in a room and have them shout out at the same time and then figure out what you're going to do. We were generally of the view that was a dumb way to do things and there was a desire to focus the advice more clearly. But what ended up happening was that the focus was not just a focus but a single channel."

MacNaughton believed that without the co-chair arrangement he had had with Debbie Nash, Robinson had no place to go for assistance, not even to Webster, who was positioned as an implementer rather than a decision maker. "Both personality-wise and structurally there wasn't any co-equal person for her to bounce ideas off of or have alternative advice to go to," said MacNaughton. "She was in a difficult—and dangerous—position."

*   *   *

As the Liberal strategists navel-gazed and Liberal candidates tried to peddle their wares on the streets, the world around Ontarians and all Canadians was rocked with rapid change and upheaval in the summer of 1990. The hopes of Meech Lake had dried up, leaving behind a bitter residue of distrust and resentment toward its participants, especially Mulroney, Bourassa and other political leaders by association. Meech's covert, closed-door deal-making among "backroom boys" and acrimonious, finger-pointing conclusion disgusted and angered Canadians.

Peterson was frowned on by some Ontarians for offering up Senate seats to break the Meech impasse. But as the summer progressed, new developments that seemed to confirm the failures of Bourassa and Mulroney made Peterson's links to those two leaders seem increasingly reprehensible to Ontarians. The events at Oka, Quebec, hardened Canadians' contempt and cynicism: they provided a vivid and violent example of the failure of traditional establishment politicians to resolve long-standing, deeply corrosive issues such as constitutional reform and native rights.

In the spring, members of a Mohawk Indian band at Kanesatake, near Oka, west of Montreal, erected a small barricade across a strip of land slated for a municipal golf course expansion, that the Mohawks claimed as their own. In June the town asked officers from the Quebec provincial police force, the Sûreté du Québec (SQ), to take it down. On July 11 the SQ conducted a dawn raid and shooting erupted between officers and the Mohawks, many of them heavily armed members of the Warrior society, leaving one SQ officer dead. The SQ retreated and the Mohawks built a bigger barricade using police cars left behind. Two days later Mohawks from a nearby reserve erected a sympathy barricade across the busy Mercier Bridge linking suburban Châteauguay with Montreal, forcing thousands of commuters to take alternate routes.

Bourassa and the Quebec government placed hundreds of SQ officers along the barricades across from the Mohawks. Mulroney was urged by opposition critics and native leaders to take action because the federal government is responsible for native affairs. But Mulroney claimed the trouble involved policing and provincial security and was therefore a provincial matter. Talks among the federal and provincial governments and native leaders were limited by Ottawa's position that it would not negotiate while the barricades were up.

As the Liberal strategists feuded and Peterson went ahead with the election call, the confrontations continued. The SQ, admitting it could no longer maintain order, was replaced at Bourassa's request by Canadian Armed Forces troops. Some 700 soldiers were deployed at Oka with machine guns, helicopters and tanks; 700 more went into Châteauguay. Natives across Canada began to stage protests.

Ontarians looking to Peterson for a position found no answers; his responses were noncommittal. Scott, as minister responsible for native affairs, began to feel a backlash from natives and other voters. "The situation at Oka was worsening day by day," he said. "And what was Oka? Oka was Mulroney and Bourassa up to their stupid tricks." In his riding, Scott started to hear an angry message: "Why hasn't your premier denounced what Mulroney and Bourassa are doing in Oka? He's just saying, well, Oka isn't in Ontario and it's not his problem," Scott said he was told. "That just reminded people once again that Peterson was on the Mulroney-Bourassa team." Peterson took the advice of his staff that there was no margin in being drawn into a fight outside his jurisdiction.

As Canadian soldiers rolled out lines of razor wire, rumbled closer to the native barricades in tanks and circled the Mohawk encampment nightly with helicopters, Canadians wondered whether their country was starting to resemble South Africa. Military action against natives on Canadian soil was, for most Canadians, unthinkable. But it was happening before their eyes on television night after night. Canadians' faith in their nation as a peaceful, stable place to live was shaken as it had not been since the FLQ crisis 20 years earlier.

In the summer of 1990 it was not only Canada that seemed to be falling apart. On the morning of August 2 Iraqi troops under President Saddam Hussein invaded Kuwait. Now Peterson had the threat of war in the Middle East as the larger backdrop of his bid for re-election.

As the Liberals tried to convey their positive messages the broader news agenda of the summer made their feel-good themes and programs seem irrelevant, even offensive. The low-cost Liberal platform had to compete on the nightly news and the front pages of the province's newspapers with such stories as the United Nations Security Council's furious denouncement of the invasion of Kuwait and imposition of economic sanctions on Iraq. While Peterson announced $5- and $10-million election tidbits, U.S. and British warships steamed to the Persian Gulf to enforce the embargo; Mulroney announced Canada would send two destroyers and a supply ship to the area. As the Liberal television commercials began to air, showing a smiling, tanned Peterson safely touring Ontario cocooned in his campaign bus, a U.S.-led coalition of countries began a massive military buildup of hundreds of thousands of soldiers and arms along the frontier between Kuwait and Saudi Arabia under the code name "Operation Desert Shield." As Peterson splashed through a Mississauga stream, acting out pro-environment messages for the television cameras, Ontarians watched live coverage of their fellow Canadians lining the rails at Halifax Harbour to wave a tearful farewell to warships packed with Canadian sailors.

As August turned into September and Iraq declared it was using foreigners, including some Canadians, as human shields against "the aggressors," the first war involving Canada in nearly 50 years seemed inevitable. Ontarians were uneasy enough about their future when Peterson called the election; as the summer progressed the scenes of national and international disruption stacked ever-deepening layers of anxiety on the province's troubled psyche.

More personally worrisome to Ontarians than the events at Oka and the looming war in the Persian Gulf was something much closer to home—a recession. Throughout August federal Finance Minister Michael Wilson, Ontario Treasurer Nixon and Peterson played down the potential severity of an impending economic slowdown. But many Ontarians were already pessimistic and depressed about the gloomy economic outlook and unhappy with the optimistic platitudes being dished out, especially by Peterson. With their caretaker, economic stewardship messages left in the dust at the campaign kickoff, the Liberals were widely reported and perceived to be running an election on the eve of a recession when many Ontarians, from autoworkers to stockbrokers, felt vulnerable and foresaw personal financial hardship.

When Ontarians wanted to hear that Peterson knew they were worried about the future and had a plan to help them, the

Liberals were reluctant to acknowledge their concerns and did not have bold, timely answers. Ontarians wanted to hear Peterson say, "Yes, the recession is going to be bad but you will survive it with this government's help." When he did not deliver he seemed to be proving he was out of touch; the promises in the Liberal platform did not meet the needs Ontarians felt were critical.

Part of the backdrop of a changing Canada against which the Ontario election played out was a severe drop in consumer confidence in the summer of 1990, centered in Ontario. Bucking a trend of slightly increasing confidence in the state of the economy that peaked in June, the drop was unanticipated by the Liberals and most economists. A post-election Decima poll asking "How would you describe Canada's economy today?" would show the percentage of Ontarians who thought the economy was good or excellent started at 26 percent in March, nudged up to 29 percent in June and dived through July and August to reach 16 percent in September. Canadians overall would be slightly less pessimistic about the state of the economy; nationwide, 29 percent offered the good-to-excellent rating in June while 17 percent would make that assessment in September.

Disenchantment was well advanced in the summer in areas such as Windsor and southwestern Ontario, already hard-hit by plant closures and job losses induced by free trade. Ontario's unemployment rate would reach 6.5 percent in August, up from an average of 5.1 percent in 1989, and was widely expected to keep growing.

The Liberal strategists recognized the faltering economy as the major issue for Ontarians in May but the low-cost platform they settled on just did not cut it as the recession took hold in Ontario. The Liberals' reluctance to talk about hard times and what they meant for people in a realistic, hard-hitting way proved costly. "The impact of the lack of an economic platform was underestimated," said Kirby. "You had a guy running a campaign in an upbeat, everything-is-fine style at a time when everybody knew it wasn't fine and, therefore, they didn't relate to him. The failure to link into the major issue of concern was the ultimate downfall. We didn't do that, so the only issue became the premier."

Ontarians were left with a sense that Peterson was untouched by the "tough times" and had no understanding of the hardships facing people in 1990. That sense was crystallized for Ontario voters and the media with the Liberals' response to a re-emerging need for increased funding for food banks.

The problems underlying the need for food banks had been addressed by the Liberals through reforms announced in 1989— the beginning of implementation of the report of the Social Assistance Review Committee (SARC). In February 1990 Toronto's Daily Bread Food Bank, the nation's largest, announced that the SARC reforms were having an effect and demand for its service was dropping. But by July Daily Bread was finding people needed its service again in increasing numbers. The recession was starting to take hold, hurting people with low incomes first.

Just before the election call, welfare activists charged that social assistance changes by the Liberals would reduce funding to food banks by $600,000 in 1990, at a time when more people were starting to need them again. Daily Bread called on the Liberals for emergency food bank funding and made certain the crisis became an election issue by persuading the three parties to allow campaign offices to be used as drop-off points for food bank donations.

But the Liberals, committed to SARC's principles, would not free up special funding, even in the name of political expediency at election time. The decision was a gold mine for the NDP, who pledged increases in food bank funding if elected. Rae was handed an issue tailor-made for his "us-against-them" attack strategy. He could claim, with strong third-party endorsement from welfare activists, that he had a sense of caring and humanity, while the Liberals would not help people who were going hungry.

*   *   *

Peterson was looking forward to Friday, August 10; the Liberal strategists were dreading the day. The premier was scheduled to speak to the Ontario Chamber of Commerce on national unity.

Peterson's desire to play nation-builder during the campaign had been trimmed back to a single speech and an appearance at a premiers' meeting in Winnipeg. The Liberal strategists had turned their minds toward damage control. Since July they had fretted over how to minimize fallout from Peterson discussing what they believed to be one of Ontarians' biggest turnoffs. Peterson had been cautioned to avoid speaking about national unity or being drawn into debates about it by reporters. Any mention of national unity elsewhere in the campaign was deemed off-strategy.

Shelley Peterson believed those restrictions accounted for her husband's attitude on the campaign trail: the lack of edge and focus that Goldfarb had complained about and other strategists would identify as Peterson's "low level of engagement" with the campaign. "It's hard to be engaged when you can't get out and talk about the issue that's most important to you," she said. "The moment you say to someone you can't say this or that because of one poll or another, you decrease his ability to perform."

Peterson wanted to deal with the issue that was his passion. He felt obliged to discuss the national unity concerns behind his own rationale for calling the election early. Much of his time over the previous year had been consumed by the issue and he felt uncomfortable about becoming silent on it once the election was called. From the first day of the campaign reporters had criticized him for not revealing his ideas, especially those that would define Ontario's interests in a post-Meech Canada.

After the decision was taken to provide Peterson with a narrow window, his constitutional advisor Patrick Monahan was asked by Gagnier to put together the principles that would form the basis of the speech. Monahan, like Peterson, recognized that Quebec would be bringing forward new proposals on federal-provincial relations and he wanted, through the speech, to lay the groundwork for Ontario's involvement in the national unity debate over the next few years. Three speechwriters were assigned to the task and Peterson would spend hours fine-tuning the text himself.

The speech tried to create a dual role for Peterson as not only a nation-builder but as a premier acting to protect Ontario's interests. Peterson decided to announce a provincewide commission to hold public hearings on what constitutional steps Ontario should take in the wake of Meech's failure. Peterson would pledge to act aggressively to ensure that Ontario's economic and political interests would be protected in future constitutional talks: "We cannot stand and wait for everyone else to fill out their wish list. We must not just respond to everyone else's demands. We have to make sure Ontario's proposals and ideas are heard loud and clear." Warning of the growth of the Bloc Québécois separatist party in Quebec and the Reform Party in western Canada, Peterson would state, "I am sending a clear message: Ontario will not let its destiny be decided by the actions of others or by the unchallenged drift of events." He would tell Bourassa not to try to negotiate sovereignty with Ottawa without involving the other provinces.

Peterson would put forward five constitutional principles to govern Ontario's participation in any future national unity debate: protection of Ottawa's powers to deal with environmental, social and regional programs; enhancement of economic ties between the regions; protection of minority and aboriginal rights; equality of all regions with no province receiving special bilateral deals; and open consultations with the people to prevent backroom deals. The five-principle approach was reminiscent of Peterson's six conditions for approving a free trade deal in 1987.

But on the morning of Peterson's speech the strategists' careful planning and scripting of the role of national unity in the campaign went out the window. When Robinson looked at her Toronto *Star* she discovered to her horror that key portions of the speech had been leaked. A front-page story detailed Peterson's call for a public commission. The article was fleshed out with direct quotes from the speech. Robinson and Webster were enraged. They immediately blamed Gagnier, whom they had suspected of leaking strategy and polling results to *Maclean's* magazine three weeks earlier.

According to Webster, Robinson told Peterson the source was Gagnier. "He [Peterson] was so upset about it," said Gagnier. "He didn't know where it came from. He even looked at me and said, 'Did you leak this?' I said, 'What the hell would I leak that for? If it had been a journalist that I knew, you could accuse me of leaking it.'" No evidence of who was responsible for the leak would ever emerge. But the incident served to further isolate Gagnier, weaken the relationship between Gagnier and Peterson and drive the strategists farther apart. It kept Robinson and the top advisors fixated on their internal strife, rather than on the bigger battles shaping up.

A leak in itself was bad enough but to Robinson, the leak put the wrong spin on the story by helping feed the impression that national unity was a pillar of the Liberal campaign. Worse still to the Liberals, Peterson the nation-builder was being emphasized over Peterson the protector of Ontario's interests. The message had not been properly massaged by the leaker, and to Robinson, the focus on national unity was now entirely out of control.

Peterson delivered the speech on schedule to the Chamber of Commerce; his tour staff were infuriated to find that some Queen's Park reporters had copies of the speech in hand when they arrived. Media reaction was almost wholly negative and the unmanaged spin fed into perceptions, sparked by the early-election call, that Peterson was opportunistic.

"Premier Peterson has made a point of being a friend to Quebec. Now he says he is disagreeing with Quebec looking for special powers and unilateral agreements," declared CBC-TV flagship CBLT. "David Peterson uses election to deliver message to Quebec," announced Global TV. The CBC's *The National* said Peterson "has been seen as a friend of Quebec but now he is sounding like a foe. He is at the point of distancing himself from Quebec." A Toronto *Star* editorial predicted the public commission and its assignment would win support but judged the announcement to be "an agenda without answers" and called on Peterson to reveal his own views because "that's what elections are for."

Most reporters believed Peterson was turning against Quebec and saying what he thought people in Ontario wanted to hear, solely to get elected. "The speech was the ultimate cynicism," said the *Globe*'s Richard Mackie. "He sold out every argument he made for keeping Canada together and became two-gun David: 'I'll take on Bourassa.' A month ago he was giving up Senate seats to keep Canada together and now he's saying he won't be held hostage to Quebec's plans. You're either one or the other: Don't you believe in anything now?"

But Peterson had not intended to reverse the stand he had taken in June. "What Peterson said at Meech wasn't changed or altered by what he said in the speech," Monahan maintained. "It was Bourassa's position that had changed. Peterson always believed individual rights were important, and the Charter, and consultation with all the other provinces. It was Bourassa that changed and now wanted bilateral negotiations and Peterson said no."

Reporters, said Peterson's constitutional experts, were not understanding the nuances of that sequence of events, or accepting that once Quebec brought forward radical proposals, Peterson felt it was appropriate to take a different approach, although one that would be consistent with his values. But to keep to the strategists' plan to play down the speech, Robinson did not ask those experts to get out and talk to reporters about it, where they might have made certain it was interpreted as intended. Whether Peterson was responding to Ontarians' desire that he start sticking up for the province's interests over those of Canada or, as he maintained, adhering to a consistent position while events around him changed, the perceptions made the difference when his actions were placed in the context of the election: he appeared again to be motivated by expediency. "If there's one speech he made in which political expediency was farthest from his mind, it was that one," said Gagnier adamantly.

The following Monday, August 13, Peterson headed to Winnipeg for a premiers' meeting where national unity and other interprovincial issues were to be discussed. Although they had reservations about further linkages between Peterson and Meech, Mulroney and Bourassa, the strategists had agreed before the campaign that Peterson should go. The downsides were counterbalanced, said Kirby: "The big upside was you got a fair bit of coverage of the man as premier. You got essentially free television time because you'll be covered in the news as well and you got a statesmanlike image." The strategists realized such events gave an incumbent premier an aura of statesmanship in a hot political climate outside the narrow strictures of partisan politics. The other party leaders, in contrast, would be seen and covered purely as partisan politicians throughout the campaign.

Peterson took center stage and declared the provinces should not "disembowel" the federal government in the wake of the collapse of Meech. "We must not conduct ourselves as tribal warlords trying to divide up a dying kingdom and ensure its death in the meantime," Peterson told the other premiers, capturing the media spotlight. He stepped up his efforts to have the premiers focus on areas the provinces had in common and to strengthen economic links holding Canada together. But this campaign for national unity, many Ontarians could believe, was more important to Peterson than the one going on in his own province. It appeared to be the campaign he was truly interested in fighting and not the one dealing with the issues that mattered to Ontarians.

Liberal candidates discovered reaction to Peterson's speech and trip to Winnipeg was not good in Ontario. It resembled the reactions found in Liberal focus groups just before the election to a television advertisement that showed Peterson being applauded by the other premiers at the Meech talks. The ad got an overwhelming thumbs down from the groups because it linked Peterson to a failed process. Although a direct connection was difficult to establish, Goldfarb reported to Robinson a finding that suggested Ontarians were making the same judgment en masse: the day after he arrived in Winnipeg, Liberal support across the province began to plummet.

* * *

From the first week of the campaign Webster was convinced that members of the strategy committee had a general knowledge of Goldfarb's rolling poll numbers: not the full range of data or its specifics, but a clear sense of what the tracking showed. Someone, somewhere, was quietly slipping the top-line numbers to some of the strategists, she believed, giving them a good understanding of the Liberals' plight.

Webster accepted Robinson's decision to be fiercely protective of the numbers, but as support for the Liberals fell, Webster faced a dilemma. She realized the numbers were critical, but only if they were used to react to public opinion as the campaign unfolded. Robinson was sitting on the numbers to prevent leaks, but not reacting as they showed Liberal support eroding. To Webster that meant the Liberals might as well not be polling. She decided to share the information on her own.

When Goldfarb's tracking revealed a serious Liberal slide after Winnipeg, Webster secretly shared the top-line numbers with MacNaughton. "I showed David two weeks in, the first or second day of a major problem," said Webster. "I showed him three numbers which were our overall standings which showed some serious erosion. He kind of looked at them and said, 'Holy shit,' and just registered it and went away. He didn't ask me to see anything more." Webster wanted to bring MacNaughton on stream to help deal with the "major problem"—but no advice followed. Webster then covertly called other strategists to let them know she was prepared to share the data.

"I tried to entice them to ask me for the numbers so that I could give them to them but it never happened," Webster explained. "They just never asked me. I would have been happy to share them. I suspected they were getting them elsewhere and that's why I did not go out of my way. I would have been so happy to talk to one of them and to have the burden of the whole thing shared." Webster had a sense the strategists knew about the problem, but did not react immediately because they were angry with Robinson for not letting them see the data and because, Webster believed, "they never thought they were going to lose."

To MacNaughton's recollection, he did not see Goldfarb's numbers until several days after Webster said she showed them to him. He believed the problem with Robinson's approach to sharing the findings was that "it affected the collegiality and sense of teamwork. The fundamental breakdown was in the sense of people working as a team."

MacNaughton sensed that some of the Liberal strategists felt Robinson's actions merited a response in kind: "It got to the point where there were a number of people who, certainly in the early stages, given the way in which things were going, were almost hoping things did not go all that well. But they didn't hope that it was going to go that badly—nobody hoped Peterson would lose. But certainly, a result that had him lose 20 seats and have it look like it wasn't a particularly glorious campaign would have caused some quiet contentment among a number of people in the back of their minds. And then, by the time where it got to the point where it looked as if it was going to be worse than it was, there wasn't any sort of cohesion to bring it back."

Whether or not they were provided formally with the detailed rolling poll data or knew Goldfarb's numbers through other means, the strategists, through their months of infighting, created a climate in which Robinson decided they could not be trusted with that information and that there was no point in bringing them together as a group to work on the campaign. When she finally relented, the tactics employed would not be enough to rescue the Liberals.

*   *   *

A few days passed; the numbers gathered by all the parties' pollsters continued to show Liberal support dropping, amid odd fluctuations that did not fit any recognizable pattern. On August 16 the Tories unleashed a tried-and-true campaign tactic: they leaked a poll to several newspapers that showed Liberal fortunes slipping. The Decima poll conducted August 11 to 13 gave the Liberals 40 percent of the decided vote, the NDP 30 percent and the Tories 28 percent; 8 percent were undecided and 2 percent said they would vote for fringe parties. Tory campaign manager John Laschinger was careful to note to reporters that the poll found substantial dissatisfaction with the Liberals' decision to call an early election, ensuring that the early-call issue maintained its high profile.

At Liberal headquarters Webster was frantic: Decima's numbers were close to Goldfarb's and now the story was public. "We had three or four bad days and by that time I was just frothing in Kathy's office," she said. "I kept saying to Kathy, 'We have serious problems.' I almost yelled at her to say, 'This is a problem. We've got to come forward and do something that gets out in front of these issues. We've got to get Marty or you've got to get to Hershell or David [MacNaughton]. You've got to get them to come up with things. We've got to get the strategy group together. They're the only group we've got,'" Webster said.

Webster believed the strategists had to meet and come to grips with the erratic shifts in the rolling polls. "We were totally blown away by the numbers. You'd get great readings one night and shitty readings the next," she said. "It was terribly volatile, more so than anyone had ever seen. I went to the extent of getting Kathy to get Marty to pull off the variables in the '87 campaign, not just the overall but the detailed ones so that she could see the differences in the regional patterns. There was nothing like that, nothing like the wild swings. It made no sense to have the decided vote moving like that."

Almost a full week would pass before the strategy committee would be called together to deal with the declining Liberal support and weird volatilities. During that critical period Goldfarb's findings sat in limbo—and so did the Liberal campaign. The strategy committee would finally be called together by Robinson on August 20, after the leaders' debate. "It was only at that point she finally agreed to give them the numbers," said Webster. But to Robinson, that timing was appropriate. "As soon as we ran into problems, all of the numbers were released," she said, "about two and a half weeks in." There were only 17 days left before voting day.

*   *   *

For the first two weeks of the campaign the NDP strategy held firm—attack and do not present options. But in the third week NDP pollster David Gotthilf found the party's support was "flat-lining" at about 32 percent of decided voters. "We had a couple of days of real deodorant-failure stuff," said strategist David Reville. Four days before the debate, succumbing to pressures from reporters and from within their party, the NDP strategists decided they could no longer get away with adhering strictly to their attack strategy. Rae would have to reveal a platform or risk being clobbered in the debate for failing to take a constructive stand on any issues. The objective had been to keep blaring out the simple message that the Liberals did not listen to Ontarians and the NDP did. But the strategists were feeling the heat to "come out with the comforting message about the new world," said Reville. The challenge became how to get a $4.2-billion platform out, far larger than the Liberals' $200-million promises, without taking away from the main message.

"The strategy was to do it all at once in a friendly crowd on a Sunday," said Reville. That would prevent careful scrutiny of the platform by either the Liberals or the media before the debate. Rae could refer to the platform without being questioned on it in detail. "There was no story there, because how are you going to cover anything that big?" Reville explained. "But it allowed us to say, 'Hey, you want to know what the platform is, here it is.'"

Furiously assembled over four days and nights from the NDP's encyclopedic policy files and rushed into print late on the morning of Rae's announcement, the 20-point *Agenda for People* promised to protect the "powerless" from a Liberal government concerned only with private interests. Rae used it to showcase his vow to make Ontario corporations pay an 8 percent minimum corporate tax on their profits and promised to exempt Ontarians living below the poverty line from paying provincial income tax. Lest the middle class be forgotten he pledged to freeze personal income taxes and the retail sales tax.

Other measures included a succession tax on estates valued at more than $1 million, an increase in the minimum wage to two-thirds of the average industrial wage of $13 per hour and passage of an environmental bill of rights. Commitments in some major areas, notably health care, were left out entirely because they were not considered by the NDP strategists to be issues on which Rae could score direct hits. Rae told reporters he planned "to take the agenda points into the debate and discuss them with the other leaders."

The NDP plan succeeded so well that the policies in the *Agenda for People* would not be thoroughly analyzed by the media for most of the campaign. "Where everything the Liberals announced could be compared to their record and their past promises, the NDP promises weren't subjected to the same scrutiny," said the Toronto *Star*'s Matt Maychak. "Bob Rae's promises were multi-billion-dollar promises. He put a $4.2-billion price tag on those. There wasn't much time spent saying, 'Can you really do this for $4 billion?' There wasn't a lot of number-crunching or scrutiny of his platform. He did that on purpose. He announced his whole platform on one day." Global TV's Robert Fisher observed, "Because Bob Rae's not winning, he can put out the Bible and who's going to read it?"

Only in the closing days of the campaign, when the NDP's strength began to be recognized, would reporters start looking more closely at the document. The *Agenda for People* was conceived, made final and presented to the media when the NDP's polls showed the party, stalled at 32 percent of decided voters, could not expect to form a government. "We, of course, had no notion that we might ever have to implement it," said Reville.

The Liberals missed out on a valuable opportunity to undercut the credibility of the NDP's platform before the debate. Liberal tour staff heard that Rae was making a major platform announcement that morning. Robinson and Webster contacted Treasurer Nixon and put him on alert to be ready to come into Toronto to hold a major news conference attacking the platform, to ensure hard-hitting criticism would be included in the critical first "news cycle" of reports on Rae's announcement. One of Peterson's press aides was ordered to the NDP event to gather intelligence on the announcement.

The Liberal mole slipped into the back of the hall and listened to Rae's speech. There was no mention of the platform. Before the applause died down the infiltrator departed, believing Rae had no plans to announce anything big. But that was part of the NDP's plan—the *Agenda for People* was meant to be kept low-key and copies were quietly handed out to reporters after Rae finished speaking.

The mole returned to Liberal headquarters to advise that no announcement had been made. Nixon was called and told he could head out into rural Brant County to knock on farmhouse doors for the rest of the day. Later that afternoon Robinson and Webster went into a screaming frenzy when they heard radio newscasts reporting the NDP's $4.2-billion agenda straight up, with no critique. Nixon could not be located and brought into Toronto in time to blast away with credible attacks. Late that night and the next morning Nixon tried offering his analysis to reporters, but the stories had been written and the opportunity to deflate Rae before the debate was lost.

*   *   *

The televised leaders' debate played out with typical fanfare on August 20. Reporters love to cover a leaders' debate for the same reason they love to cover the "horse race" aspect of a campaign marked by the release of a poll: it distills the complex process of an election into elements that can be explained in black-and-white terms, with clearly defined winners and losers.

The leaders and handlers entering the debate seemed to recognize those ground rules. But that acceptance, evidenced in their debate preparations and post-debate spin-doctoring, betrayed the reality of televised leaders' debates: rather than serving as a forum for the substantive treatment of issues, they are far more about style than substance.

On the day of the election call Peterson's opening statement contained a demand for a televised debate. Remembering Tory premier Frank Miller's extended turn on the media rotisserie in 1985 for refusing to debate, the Liberals wanted to own the issue outright. They succeeded only in neutralizing it for Rae and Harris, who were not able to make the call for a debate first, as each had hoped.

Representatives from a coalition of the CBC, CTV and Global television networks approached the parties with a proposal for a debate the week of the election call and negotiations started immediately. A 90-minute, uninterrupted program with a moderator and three-member media panel was settled on in short order, but the format of the debate was fought out furiously among the parties and with the networks. The final deal gave each leader three-minute opening and closing statements and permitted the panelists to direct questions to all three leaders at once, in an order to be determined at random before the debate. The responses would be followed by three-minute free-for-alls among the leaders.

The Liberals objected vehemently that this format stacked the deck against Peterson by permitting Rae and Harris to gang up on him in the free-for-alls, but the opposition negotiators and networks prevailed—they wanted good TV and that meant lots of uninhibited three-way action. The panelists were selected at the end of the process: Global's Fisher, CBC's Lyn Whitham and CTV's Tom Clark.

Entering the debate Peterson had the advantage best defined by Tory pollster Allan Gregg: "The only way for an incumbent to lose a debate is to eat a live rat on stage." But aside from avoiding what would be more traditionally described as "The Big Gaffe," Peterson had to be armed to the teeth to fight off a continuation of the stereo assault from Rae and Harris that had characterized the first half of the campaign. Rae's strategy was simple: keep up the negative attacks on the honesty and integrity issues that were known to be hitting home with voters. Harris's game plan was slightly more demanding: hit hard on taxes and do not insert foot in mouth too obviously.

Based on the parties' common understanding of Ontarians' viewing habits, the first five minutes of the debate were recognized as the most important, followed by the last five minutes and finally the eternal eighty-minute core, regarded all around as being unwatchable by a mass-market television audience.

The Liberals were delighted when Harris won the draw to determine who would give the first opening statement; his ponderous reading style, they believed, would ensure maximum tune-out by viewers and reduce the potential for damage should Peterson later be smitten by paralysis, spontaneously burst into flames or, worst of all, make a major mistake that would become The Big Gaffe.

Rounding out this approach by the parties was their unspoken understanding that the news coverage of the debate would be more important than the event itself. Typically this would lead to a frenzied battle of spin-doctors in the post-debate analysis, all clamoring to claim victory for their leaders.

The handlers for each leader approached the debate through the back door: they sought to ensure a victory on style by displaying a mastery of substance, a circuitous process creating the surreal impression that the debate itself really mattered. It meant exhaustive preparation to fill each candidate's brain with carefully crafted facts and arguments, massage his temperament to gird him with confidence and comfort and clothe and make him up to present a suitably premierial image to viewers.

Peterson and Harris cleared their agendas on Sunday, the day before the debate, to do nothing but rehearse; both squeezed in half-day rehearsals on Saturday. Rae, by contrast, had a full agenda on Sunday—the *Agenda for People*, released to reporters that afternoon. Rae would spend the least time in debate preparation of the three leaders.

The Liberal debate preparation was orchestrated by Ezrin, his main contribution to the campaign. Ezrin's debate committee drew in fellow strategist Senator Michael Kirby, image-shaper Gabor Apor, media consultant Patrick Gossage, long-time Peterson speechwriter Allan Golombek and a handful of top Liberal staffers. Ezrin organized the issues into eclectic categories under which attacks on Peterson could be expected: Friend to the Rich and Famous, Do-Nothing Government, Election Timing, Scandals, Taxation, Environment and Minority vs. Majority Government. Each committee member took an issue or

two, preparing a response under the categories of Desired Outcome, Premier's Positioning, and Premier's Lines. Golombek,
the Liberal's best writer, took on the opening and closing statements. Ezrin assembled the information and prepared to exhort
the best possible performance from Peterson.

In the days before the debate Goldfarb found Liberal support slipping frequently below 40 percent of decided voters in
his tracking, well into what had historically represented certain
minority government status. The NDP hovered in the low 30
percent range and the Tories continued to gain ground, even
nudging over 30 percent on some days. The Liberal campaign
decided to keep Peterson in the dark on the decline, to avoid
psyching him out and destroying his "comfort level" going into
the debate. "He was not told of that slide," said Borg. "That was
a judgment they had made, and they figured it was worthwhile
going into the debate without him knowing that." Robinson,
however, was adamant that, "The Premier had access to all of
the numbers all the way through, every day."

A pared-down group of Liberal advisors, their number cur-
tailed by Ezrin to help Peterson focus, gathered in a rented studio
in North York on Sunday to help him rehearse. Borg arrived to
help and found Robinson and Webster pacing the studio "like nervous Nellies." He sensed serious trouble and pulled Webster aside
as Peterson was being wired and positioned for the cameras.

"I know how bad things are," he told Webster, trying to flush
out what was really happening. "I've known for two weeks."

"How did you know?" Webster asked, wide-eyed.

"I know," said Borg.

"You've got to get him through this till tomorrow, then we'll
figure this out," said Webster. Relieved to have an ally, she
added, "I've been trying to get this stuff talked about."

It was sparring time, the usual procedure for debate
rehearsal. Borg walked behind one of the three podiums to
assume the role of Rae. Gossage stepped up to Harris's spot.
Peterson was ready and breezed through his opening statement.

Borg decided to get right to the point. He opened up immediately with both barrels. "Your father-in-law is a developer," he

snarled at Peterson. "You're hooked right in there with Patti Starr up to your neck. You and the rich and famous people would rather have this province run by private interests."

Borg looked up. Peterson was staring at him, speechless.

"Stop!" screamed Ezrin. "Stop the fight!" The tape was stopped and rewound. Ezrin approached Peterson on the run.

"You looked at him!" he admonished the premier. "He had you! Never look at him! You look down; do not look at him!"

Borg was aghast at the reaction he had drawn from Peterson. "You'd have thought it was four and a half minutes of a beating, but it was only 12 seconds," he said. "His face was like four kids that he'd never had, died."

Shell-shocked from three weeks of protesters, Peterson needed to take his time. It was going to be a long day. Borg eased off, and over the afternoon, Ezrin gradually conducted the type of mind-meld with Peterson he had often accomplished when working full-time for the Liberals; he slowed Peterson down, forcing him to listen to each question and think about his response. Peterson worked through the thick stack of "Premier's Lines," repeating them over and over as the questions changed, until his content, tone and pacing were satisfactory to all. By the end of the day even his spontaneity was down flat.

Miles away, in a studio in Oshawa, the Tories assembled for the second straight day of trying to turn Harris into a lean, mean debating machine. The day before, the Tory team had scrutinized tapes of the 1987 debate of Peterson, Rae and Larry Grossman, looking for clues on how to break Peterson's concentration. Grossman had first-hand advice for the new Tory leader, who was a rookie at televised leaders' debates.

"You have to interrupt David because he's okay when he's got the pre-taped message in his mind, and he delivers it well," he counseled Harris. "Under the pressure of the debate he doesn't do very well. The impromptu kills him all the time. In debates David is quite a contrast to what he is when he's running Question Period and scrums. When you've got that big old camera right in your face, boy, it's like a deer in the headlights."

The Tories threw John Tory into the ring representing Peterson and stuck Grossman behind the podium with Rae's name on it. Grossman opened up on Harris's most obvious weakness.

"Well, come on, Mr. Harris," he sneered. "The Mulroney party talking about taxes? Puh-leez, Mr. Harris!" The assembled Tories were in stitches. Grossman, they agreed, made a better Rae than he had a Tory leader.

Strategist Hugh Segal took a turn at the Peterson podium to deliver his own collection of one-liners, as his colleagues howled and Harris became increasingly at ease. The Tory strategists wanted to get Harris comfortable with the unfamiliar setting of a studio, teach him how to play to the cameras and nail down the correct interactions with the other leaders. In a televised debate, Grossman pointed out, "people never hear what you say, they just watch and they get a sense of who you are." Each set of handlers seemed to recognize that, on television, the importance of a candidate's verbal communications was dwarfed by the impact of the messages of confidence, authority and passion that gestures, body language and tone could convey.

Rather than subject Rae to the routine of sparring with a couple of stand-ins, the NDP strategists ordered a team of party workers to scour the utterances of the other leaders in the first three weeks of the campaign, searching for mistakes Rae could jump on and incorporate into his attacks. After his noon-hour speech on Sunday, Rae read the material by himself. "The thing about Bob is that he's a good debater," spun David Agnew to a reporter writing a pre-debate story. "He's not the kind of person who needs or wants little notes written all over his shirt cuffs." Rae needed few new lines to maintain the simple attack strategy he had been using since the campaign's opening day.

*　　*　　*

At eight o'clock on Monday evening, *The Wonder Years*, *Mac-Gyver* and *Murphy Brown* stepped graciously aside to help Ontarians make their political choices. At CBC's Jarvis Street studios in Toronto, protesters, surrounded by Liberal and Tory supporters, stepped begrudgingly aside to permit the entourages of the three leaders access to the waiting studio. The leaders and panelists were wired up and the most hyped event of the campaign was ready to start.

Moderator Peter Desbarats, a former television commentator serving as dean of the graduate school of journalism at the University of Western Ontario, ran through the rules and called on Harris to start. The opening statements whipped by, with Harris surprisingly sharp and lively and Peterson and Rae in top form. Desbarats turned to Global TV's Fisher for the first question.

"Premier Peterson," Fisher said solemnly. "In the three short years since the last election, your government has at times been paralyzed by a fund-raising scandal involving Patricia Starr . . . What does the Starr scandal say about the government, about your party and about you yourself as leader of both?"

Peterson stared at Fisher. "He looked at me like 'You son of a bitch,'" said Fisher. "You could see 'S.O.B.' in his eyeballs; 'The first question—how could you do this to me?' It was the obvious first question, I thought. So did the panel: 'You're going to get an easy ride? Well, we'll see about that.' It wasn't that I was out to get Peterson, I just felt the question had to be asked, and it had to be right off the top of the show because it had been so much a part of the government."

Peterson's off-camera stare could not be seen in the living rooms of Ontario. He worked through his response in calm, firm tones, pointing out he had set up an independent judicial inquiry to investigate the scandal, that the inquiry had been struck down by the Supreme Court of Canada and that Starr and others were facing criminal and election-finances charges. "Justice is being pursued in an independent way," he concluded. The question was answered but the tone of the debate was set: again, Peterson was under attack.

The debate forged ahead through the tax issue, national unity, the environment, garbage and education. Peterson was the first to break from his safe, scripted lines, with a comment that made his handlers wince: "People are cranky," he observed. It was a word he sometimes used with his children. In the anteroom holding the handlers, the Tories burst into guffaws. "Are you cranky?" howled one, slapping his nearest colleague on the back. "I think I'm feeling cranky!" Each leader delivered his prepared lines of attack and defense effectively enough to have them plucked out and repeated in the television news coverage of the debate that night and in the next day's papers.

"Mr. Rae is promising the moon, he is promising taxes, deficits, he is promising to drive business and jobs out of this province," charged Peterson. "Mr. Harris, your stated policy is to tax food, to tax people who go to the hospital. If that's your tax agenda, I reject it." He turned to Rae again, pointing at Harris. "You'll lose jobs for this province faster than he's running away from Brian Mulroney."

"You're nothing but an apologist for the Chamber of Commerce," Rae snapped at Peterson. "Powerful private interests have too much control and influence over the Liberal government. Only the most wealthy and powerful have benefited from the tax policies of David Peterson."

Harris called Peterson "an apologist for the highest taxes in Canada" and Rae "a captive of old-fashioned socialist ideas." But he made his mark by uttering a line that will stand as one of the funniest in the annals of Canadian leaders' debates: "I am the only honest politician," he exclaimed. Peterson and Rae both blinked in disbelief. In the anteroom, all of the handlers were too stunned to laugh.

Peterson at one point decided to invent policy on the fly. He suggested he was prepared to extend pay equity to all workers not covered by the law, including groups such as day care workers. Rae, surprised at the major announcement, demanded to know why the Liberals were mounting a legal challenge preventing the extension of the law. Peterson was left momentarily speechless, then managed to sputter out a convoluted reply that only confused his "announcement" further. Although it represented the hardest news of the night the dialogue went almost unnoticed by reporters.

There was no knockout blow in the debate, as analysts were quick to point out; reporters settled instead for writing excitedly about "several flurries" of "heated exchange." Coverage of the event reflected its content and style accurately. That supported the established news agenda of the campaign, with its focus on attacks from a number of sources directed at the Liberals. No clear winner emerged in the collective assessment by reporters: Peterson was deemed to have fared well by not sweating or losing his cool, Rae was judged to have failed to win big when expected and Harris was determined to have achieved victory by survival. An Environics poll published on August 29 would show 27 percent of Ontarians gave the debate to Peterson, 24 percent to Rae and 21 percent to Harris; 24 percent would say no one won.

But Harris scored the point that made the deepest impression. He insisted Peterson had deliberately fixed the election date for September 6, the day before Starr was scheduled to appear in court. In fact Starr's appearance was set for September 5; Peterson ignored the timing question and assured Harris and the viewers that the matter was being handled independently by the courts. A post-debate Decima poll would show the single snippet of information retained by most viewers was the "fact" Starr was in court the day after the election.

Popular wisdom holds leaders' debates are always of great importance in election campaigns and usually critical to the outcome. Debate moderator Desbarats shared that view: "What makes televised debates significant is that they are the only spontaneous, unrehearsed, unmediated contact between party leaders and voters," he asserted. "All other television images are manipulated by the party leaders, their handlers or the journalists. Only in the televised debate do voters have an opportunity to see their leaders unedited and make judgments based on their own assessments of a leader's personality, intelligence, debating ability and so forth."

But the 1990 Ontario campaign defied that argument, with its news agenda dominated by the spontaneous interactions on the premier's tour and the leaders' debate carefully managed. Leaders' debates in Canadian elections will likely continue to be manipulated by participants and their handlers as readily as campaign advertisements. Contemporary campaign management has made leaders' debates no more or less revealing than any other aspect of the campaign that people can watch on television.

A post-election Environics poll would suggest most Ontarians paid little attention to the leaders' debate. Environics' top-line findings labeled the debate the second-most important factor leading voters to their decision in the election, close behind media coverage: the type of simple statistic that fuels the hype surrounding such events and perpetuates the mythology of their importance. But that top-line finding was misleading. Environics' detailed findings would suggest most voters neither cared about the debate, nor used it to help make up their minds: 63 percent of Ontarians would admit they did not watch the debate, 20 percent would say they watched some of it and a scant 9 percent would own up to sitting through the full 90 minutes. And only about 6.5 percent of voters would tell Environics they made up their minds just after the debate on who they would pick.

Lacking a Big Gaffe or a knockout blow the debate provided no single event on which people could base a decision; nor did it play a subsequent strategic role in the campaign for any party. Voters searching for understanding of what the leaders really stood for found little satisfaction in the slick, carefully scripted debate. The real action, spontaneous, unpredictable and revealing, was happening in the day-to-day encounters with protesters and other people, as reported on the nightly news.

*   *   *

In the last three weeks of the campaign many Ontarians sent their own messages to the Peterson Liberals. In response to a request for funds, hundreds of people, many of them angry Liberals, made their views known loud and clear.

Liberal fund-raisers mailed form letters with Robinson's signature on August 15 to 211,000 Ontarians, most of them identified Liberals. "Does it really matter who leads Ontario's government over the next five years?" Robinson asked her fund-raising targets. "Frankly, it matters a great deal," she wrote, "because leadership is a key issue in this election." The letter included all the Liberals' campaign code words— "vision," "effective leadership," "reform agenda." "It's up to people like you and me to get involved and support the leader who has done so much to generate the prosperity we enjoy today," Robinson urged. And she used as fund-raising bait the Liberals' proud indicator of good fiscal management: "David Peterson believes that a strong, dynamic economy is the key to Ontario's future . . . that's why he's balanced this year's budget with no general tax increases." By the time many people would receive the letter the balanced budget would be discarded by the Liberals.

A sample of 200 of the 400-odd rejection letters, about half from Liberals, provided a peek at some of the reasons why Ontarians were giving that one-fingered salute to Peterson and the Liberals during the campaign. Although not a scientific sample, the letters revealed some of the feelings of people who were mad enough to write and tell the Liberals what they thought.

Topping the list of beefs: overtaxation, with 34 of 200 naming it as their reason for refusing the request for funds. Second came an early or unnecessary election, singled out by 28 writers. Most writers simply refused the request for funds with a nasty comment. A handful complained about Patti Starr or the government's relationship with developers; about issues in which they identified a vested interest, including the employee health tax, teachers' pensions and doctors' fees; about other government policies and about Peterson's leadership. Four letters were anti-French and a mere 2 out of 200 linked their rejection of the Liberals to Peterson's role in Meech Lake.

"Peterson is a tax-happy idiot who doesn't give a damn about the real people of this province, only the rich companies," wrote a Toronto man, synthesizing the campaign attacks of the Tories and NDP. "So Ontario is doing great," wrote an Etobicoke man. "Well, you certainly forgot the senior citizens. My taxes have increased substantially since 1986 because of absolute

326 / NOT WITHOUT CAUSE

waste spending. I voted for the Liberal party for the last two elections, but not this time." A Toronto insurance agent wrote bitterly, "You have managed to pump this well dry." A Cornwall man: "Tax thieves don't deserve money." And a Midhurst woman: "Don't you think you've taken enough money, you bastards?"

"I am very upset by the cynicism displayed by the decision to hold this unnecessary election," a Barrie man told the Liberals. "You had your mandate, which I helped you to obtain. I will not be supporting you in the future." A woman from Toronto asked, "You're putting us through this unnecessary election and you want money too? What are you smoking?" A Toronto man wrote, "As a Liberal supporter I am outraged by this cynical, expensive and unnecessary election. I shall not vote." And a professor from Windsor explained, "I am a lifelong Liberal, federal and provincial, but this unnecessary, expensive election is the last straw. Not only will Bill Wrye not get my vote, but the NDP will."

A willingness to turn to the NDP as an alternative emerged in many letters. A longtime party supporter from Toronto said, "I am refusing to work for any Liberal candidate. I will also hold my nose and vote NDP so that David will never call another such election." A Toronto doctor wondered, "Perhaps he will act more responsibly after a minority election win?" Many former Liberals made it clear they would be sending their support to Rae: "Sorry, I am totally annoyed at Peterson calling an early election," a woman wrote from Windsor. "For the first time, I am not voting Liberal and will vote for the NDP. My family feels the same way." A London man sent back his form plastered with an NDP sticker: "You can count on me," he scribbled beside it.

Writers who complained about the Starr affair and Liberal links to developers did not connect those issues with Peterson. But those who attacked him personally found plenty of faults: "The arrogance, conceit, promises (all lies), which your leader displays make me wonder how many people in Ontario are so naive as to fall for it all," wrote an Etobicoke woman. "Peterson is an arrogant dick and will be twisting in the wind come

September," declared a doctor from Don Mills. "David Peterson is not at all like me, your letter to the contrary," a Toronto man wrote. "Please pass this on to someone who cares about the common man," instructed a man from Ancaster.

From across Ontario sheer disgust was heaped on the Liberals: "I wouldn't support you if it were a one-party system," wrote a Willowdale man. "I would seriously consider any lunatic fringe party before yours, given the record of scandal, increased taxes and image over substance," wrote a Londoner, and a Wingham man added, "Patti Starr affair? Sucking up to developers? Temagami logging? I wish you every lack of success."

The malaise of 1990's summer of discontent seeped through in the views of many Ontarians: "I do not trust today's politicians. We need new honest people to run the country," wrote a man from Ottawa. "This current election is a power grab," charged a Toronto man. "The real problem in Canada is that the integrity of the political parties is too low. I am not suggesting the other parties have much to offer."

A woman from Willowdale summed up the feelings of frustration: "Did we ever really have a time when politicians meant what they said and were not just looking after vested interests? Was it just wishful thinking that some people went into public service with the idea that they wanted to contribute something to their community, province, country? I used to believe everyone should get involved. I remember that I couldn't wait to be able to vote. I guess you can tell that I am awash in cynicism."

One writer offered a detailed attack on Peterson's Meech dealings: "I was very disappointed with Mr. Peterson's cozying up to Quebec and Bourassa," the Thornhill man wrote. "I am worried about our future, and do not feel it is safe in his hands."

Some responses were a shock to the party. "I would like my name taken off your list of contributors," wrote the chief financial officer for a top Peterson cabinet minister's riding association. "I have been assisting the Liberal party since 1949. When the Liberal party wins this election, it will be imperative that taxes should be reduced, with fewer handouts."

The 1990 campaign fund-raising drive proved to be the most humiliating in OLP's history, with a dismal $100,000 raised from individual Ontarians. Corporate donations during the election would outstrip that total by a ratio of nine to one. The result obliterated the hard work of party fund-raisers and membership organizers. And it confirmed the virtual abandonment of the party by its grass roots as convincingly as the election-long dearth of volunteers.

Some of the names on the Liberals' mailing list were clearly not Liberals. "David Peterson ruined my summer. I intend to ruin his fall," replied David Warner, the soon-to-be-victorious NDP candidate in Scarborough-Ellesmere. And another misguided appeal produced this strikingly polite response: "Sorry, I cannot in all conscience support your cause. Signed, John Laschinger, Toronto." Oops.

10

Politics of Fear

Victory is within our grasp.

–KATHY ROBINSON

Strategists MacNaughton, Kirby, Ezrin, Morton and Goldfarb arrived on the fifth floor of Liberal campaign headquarters after the leaders' debate. There had been no clear winner or loser; the Liberals' next steps would not be affected by the debate. Finally, Kathy Robinson had decided, she would part with Goldfarb's rolling poll numbers and ask the group's advice on a solution.

Robinson grimly showed the group the top-line numbers. Like the Tories and NDP, Goldfarb was finding support for the Liberals continuing to dip below 40 percent of decided voters, with the NDP steady at about 32 percent and the Tories reaching as high as 31 percent. The Liberals were not in a free-fall, Robinson advised; the numbers still showed volatility, but clearly there was a major problem.

The strategists heard a qualitative appraisal of what the numbers meant but detailed overnight and weekly summaries were not given out. Many of the strategists would later complain they were still not provided with enough data to get a firm grip on how the numbers were trending and gain a true understanding of what was going on.

"Everyone was sobered," said Beth Webster. "They knew they had to come down to some hard decisions. They very quickly pulled together in a way that was admirable and they dropped their tangible differences. There were, under the surface though, serious problems." Kirby was the first to react and the most prophetic. He pointed out that when Metro Toronto started to go, it would be very difficult to regain momentum. Although the Liberals' Metro numbers appeared to be coming back up, Kirby's prediction would be fulfilled within 10 days.

MacNaughton expressed concern about "the premier's level of engagement" and made the point that Peterson was not handling the protesters well. With the group's support he urged Robinson to change the tour dramatically to minimize the impact of the protesters. But Robinson had been giving orders to tour director Doug Kirkpatrick to try different tactics and none of the changes were working. The group demanded to know why the ministers' tours had failed to get off the ground to attack the NDP and Tories; she explained the ministers' reluctance to take part but promised to keep trying to convince them. The strategists agreed that David Morton had to rework the campaign advertising, changing its tone from positive to negative to launch counterattacks on the Tories and NDP.

After protracted griping the strategists began to grapple with the central issue of the Liberal campaign: What rabbits could they pull out of their hats to halt and reverse the slide? At last they seemed to accept that it was time to stop the infighting and get their act together. But even at this critical stage their discussions and debate of the options reflected the fundamental rifts between MacNaughton and Goldfarb.

Goldfarb resurrected an idea he had been floating for months, an announcement by Peterson that cabinet would veto approval by the Ontario Energy Board of the sale of Consumers' Gas to British Gas. Again the scheme was rejected by the strategists, who agreed that the Liberal government could not interfere in the board's independent process by announcing a cabinet position before the board's decision.

Goldfarb was ready with other options. "The substance of Marty's advice in terms of specific things he suggested were all designed to cut through the clutter, the protesters," said MacNaughton. The strategists recognized Goldfarb was trying to come up with a dramatic breakthrough announcement, something he had a reputation for trying to do in other campaigns. "From every campaign that I've been in with Marty, one thing I know is that he loves the long bomb; it doesn't matter whether you're 15 points ahead or 15 points behind," said MacNaughton. But before the strategists could make their long-bomb decision they had to determine where Liberal support was going, so they could try to get it back.

Goldfarb explained that electoral history in Ontario had shown the NDP had never been able to increase its support above 32 percent. His tracking indicated the NDP had reached that ceiling in the days before the debate and was hovering there. Goldfarb believed the NDP had virtually flattened out at that level; he suggested that once voters had gone to the NDP, they were not going to leave them at that stage in the campaign: the NDP were not going to move up or down. He contended only the Tories could knock the Liberals down to a minority, as "Liberal-Tory" switchers abandoned Peterson, refused to go to the NDP and ended up supporting the Tories because they had nowhere else to go.

The Tories were shaping up as the preferred target for the Liberals but none of the strategists believed at any point that Harris would finish higher than third on election day. Instead of treating the Tories as a threat to win, the strategists accepted that their vote was the "softest," based on Goldfarb's belief that their newfound strength was coming from disaffected Liberals who could be recaptured and returned to the fold. The NDP had picked up more points than the Tories but the NDP vote was considered "harder," or less likely to change its mind and even less likely to vote Liberal.

Still thinking of restoring their majority and with a few weeks left to do it, the Liberals agreed to go after the vote they believed was the easiest to get back. "Under those circumstances the only way in which we could get back to the majority level was to drive the Tories down," said Kirby. "Therefore, the decision was made to go after the Tory vote as opposed to the NDP vote. That was a very clear rationale for us and the belief was if you could drive the Tories down to around 20 percent, that would be sufficient."

The strategists were also told by Goldfarb that the Tory attack on Liberal tax increases was the issue hurting the Liberals the most. A tax relief measure, the strategists concurred, might be the answer. Two tax relief options had been proposed in Goldfarb's strategic paper in May: a rebate of the "tax-on-tax" in which the Ontario government would pay back to taxpayers the additional revenue it would collect as a result of the GST, and a cut in the provincial retail sales tax from 8 percent to 7 percent.

A reduction in the sales tax of not one but two percentage points was proposed as the best way to "cut through the clutter." It would provide Peterson with an opportunity to campaign against the GST, convey an anti-Tory message that could link Mulroney and Harris and respond to the Tory tax attacks that seemed to be drawing support away from the Liberals. It was also the only long bomb the strategists could agree on. But the plan would have to go through some hoops first.

"Marty's view that night was 'We've got to announce it tomorrow morning,'" said MacNaughton. "But we said, 'Let's not panic. First of all, the premier's got to talk to Nixon. We've got to see whether or not we can organize the third party endorsements which will be critical to making it look like something other than a totally cynical ploy.' It was held back for deliberate consideration for 48 hours."

Goldfarb's strategic paper had asserted a tax relief measure could be "an extremely potent vote-getting tactic" that could be held in reserve and used without appearing cynical, if the Liberals launched a major attack on the GST early in the campaign. But in their haste to perform major surgery on their very ill patient, the strategists did not fully debate the possibility that announcing a tax cut halfway through the campaign without that buildup would be seen as blatant vote-buying.

"We were all groping a bit," said Kirby. "We realized we were in trouble, at least we were told we were in trouble. I guess, in retrospect what one should have anticipated was that the effect would be a negative reaction rather than a positive reaction, or at least not a neutral reaction. But we didn't anticipate quite how people would react to it."

MacNaughton sensed the risk, "but I did not feel strongly enough that it was going to be a negative to try and persuade them otherwise," he said. The group did not believe it had time to subject the proposal to focus group testing to find out how people would react to a tax cut at that point in the campaign.

The long bomb was the play, the strategists agreed, downplaying the risk the ball could be dropped in the mud. "You've got to remember that this is the same group that dismissed out of hand the cynicism about an early election," said one Liberal about the strategists. "There's a school of political thought in terms of buying votes that says Canadians vote with their pocketbooks or their hearts, and they weren't winning them on their hearts so let's go for their pocketbooks."

*   *   *

The next morning MacNaughton and Robinson drove to St. Catharines, southeast of Toronto, to see Treasurer Bob Nixon, who was campaigning in the riding of Liberal incumbent Mike Dietsch. The three met in a tiny cubbyhole in Dietsch's campaign office. MacNaughton dragged in a chair and sat down. Robinson opened her bag, pulled out Goldfarb's latest rolling poll results and showed Nixon the numbers.

"The view of the strategy committee is that either we do something or we're gonzo," said MacNaughton. "The recommendation is that we do some sort of a tax cut: maybe a rebate of the tax-on-tax or preferably a 2 percent cut in the retail sales tax."

"You've got to be out of your fucking minds," snarled Nixon. "If the premier wants to do it, I'll go along," he said, assuming Peterson had approved, "but I am not personally going to support this." MacNaughton and Robinson were not satisfied; they needed Nixon onside.

"If you can't be convincingly supportive, the ideas won't work," said MacNaughton. "You have to be seen as endorsing this and providing the logic and defending the balanced budget in the context of this flexibility to cut the tax. Given where the economy is headed, it's sound public policy. I have no doubts about the wisdom of the action but I do have some concerns about the perception of the politics."

Nixon was not buying. Earlier that morning he had been tipped off by a faithful staffer from campaign headquarters that the delegation was on its way. The strategists agreed with the treasurer that a 2 percent cut would look "irresponsible and bizarre," MacNaughton said. It would cost the treasury $2.2 billion a year in lost revenue and Nixon's balanced budget would be out the window. A compromise followed: "I didn't have any brighter ideas," said MacNaughton, "so my advice to him was that we go with a one percent cut and that he should try and defend it." A one percent cut would cost $1.1 billion a year; the balanced budget would still be upset but the increase in the deficit could be sold as responsible fiscal management that used the province's hard-won flexibility in a reasonable way for a just cause—the battle against the GST.

Nixon relented. He phoned Peterson on the bus to convey his support. MacNaughton stood by and followed the conversation: "He said, 'The numbers don't look great. My own view is that you did well in the debate and that may turn it around. But I'm concerned and I think that I can defend this. I'm concerned about the cynicism, but Kathy and David have convinced me that we need to do something. I don't have any problem with a one percent cut.'" By the end of the conversation, MacNaughton found Nixon "was quite supportive." Nixon handed the phone to MacNaughton, who put it to his ear. "What did you do to him?" asked Peterson. "Did you get some dirty pictures on him or something?"

Staff on the premier's bus realized Peterson had not made up his mind about doing the cut and appeared "uncomfortable" with the plan until he heard from Nixon. The treasurer's phone call tipped the balance for the premier.

Back at Liberal headquarters Webster waited for the word. That morning she told policy chief Jan Whitelaw to be ready to work up a possible tax cut announcement. Nixon's staff began trying to gather the statistics and analysis to explain and justify the cut. At mid-afternoon work began on the biggest story of the Liberal campaign, scheduled for release at noon the next day.

*   *   *

That evening Vince Borg, on the Liberal media bus on the way to Ottawa, got wind of the tax cut plan over the phone from head-quarters. He was horrified. To Borg the move was the "height of cynicism." The Liberal government had set itself up as a good economic manager by balancing the budget; Borg believed announcing a costly tax cut would mean abandoning that pow-erful indicator of the Liberals' commitment to fiscal responsibili-ty.

At the next stop Borg switched buses and approached Peter-son. "What's happening?" he asked.

"Well, we're thinking of doing this cut in the sales tax," Peterson replied. "Waddya think?"

"What's the reason for it?" Borg asked.

"Well, we've got a bit of a problem," Peterson mumbled. "We don't understand what it is. We haven't defined our prob-lem. We don't know how to quantify it. We don't know if it's stylistic. We don't know if it's substantive policy stuff. We don't know if it's the opposition." But Peterson appeared confident in the strategists' recommendation that the move was necessary and timely; he had received Nixon's support for it.

Borg was not convinced. That evening Robinson flew to Ottawa to join Peterson on the Liberal bus. Late that night Borg and some staffers from the bus met with Robinson in an Ottawa hotel.

"For the record, I'm opposed to this," Borg told Robinson. "Maybe we're clued out and completely isolated, but this is not going to go over well," he warned. "Why are we doing this? First of all, it's not sound. Second, if we're going to do it tomorrow, we have no time to set it up. How am I supposed to go and set it up with the press guys? It should be set up the night before. We've been saying to the press that the poll stuff is fine, things are just hunky-dory. It's just not gonna fly."

Robinson laid down the law: the announcement was going ahead. That night and the next day anyone else who might have expressed reservations was not given a chance to get near Peterson. It seemed to MacNaughton that, "There was a deliberate attempt to keep the premier from talking to anybody who might have a negative view on that."

The next morning at 7:30 Robinson and the staffers from the bus met with Peterson to discuss the details of the announcement. As Borg entered the meeting room, the group was debating the venue. MacNaughton had suggested the cut be announced in front of the Bank of Canada in Ottawa or in Toronto, to make it clear the move was an anti-GST tactic. But the need to get the announcement out as quickly as possible prevented major reworking of Peterson's tour schedule. The cut would be announced, Robinson decided, at a luncheon meeting of the Cornwall Multicultural Association, already on Peterson's itinerary. The deadline was tight. But as Peterson, Robinson and the bus staff hastily prepared to leave for the next stop on the tour, Borg felt he had to try again to stop the announcement.

"What are you saying, Vince?" Peterson asked.

"Well, I'm saying that my personal feelings are, instinctively, this is wrong," Borg explained feverishly. "However, I believe the scientific data. If what you've been presented with is an accurate interpretation and the whole of the strategy committee is clued in and agrees with the consensus, then you must consider that. But I think it's wrong. You have to decide, because I've got to set this up properly, if we're doing it at noon."

Robinson broke in. "What's your bottom line?"

"My bottom line is my personal view," said Borg. "But I don't know about these numbers. I'm not too sure I understand the trend." Borg, who was familiar with polling from his work at Decima, began to ask Robinson questions about the trends in the data. Her short, incomplete answers made him even more uncomfortable. "Look," he told Peterson, "if Hershell is clued into all the research and he knows exactly what the scoop is, I'd have to trust that judgment. I can't look at this stuff in 20 minutes and ask questions and give my opinion. My bottom line is no."

"Look, Vince," Robinson fumed, "you know there was a strategy committee meeting on Monday night after the debate. Why are you raising these questions at the last minute? We went over this on Monday night. You had your opportunity; you were invited to that meeting."

"I didn't go to the meeting because I didn't know about it," replied Borg. "No one told me there was a meeting happening."

Peterson's executive assistant Gordon McCauley interrupted the exchange to ask Borg to take an urgent phone call in the next room. Borg cursed profusely and stormed out.

"Hello?" he barked into the phone. "Oh, hi Hershell."

"Why are you holding this up?" demanded Ezrin.

"Hershell, before you go on, this is just too cute," Borg snapped. He realized he was being set up to have his opposition quelled. "What about this morning's numbers? He won the debate. We've stabilized. This is not the time to do this."

"I'm going to think about this," said Ezrin. "I'll call back. You're right, this is critical." Borg walked back into the meeting room.

Peterson and staffers were now going over the speech he would give in Cornwall. The premier stopped reading and looked up. "Geez, I've got to get going," he said, and turned to Borg. "So, waddya think?"

"Excuse me, Vince," interrupted McCauley. "There's another phone call for you." Borg ran into the next room and picked up the phone.

"Oh, hi David," said Borg. It was MacNaughton.

"What's the problem?" MacNaughton demanded.

"Before you go on, let me tell you what just happened," said Borg. "I mention Hershell's name and three minutes later, he's on the phone trying to get me to go along with this thing. I mean, it's too cute and now you're calling. What do you mean, what is my problem? My problem is that I don't think that this is right and I'm stating my point of view."

"Why are you holding this up?" MacNaughton asked.

"Because I think it's wrong," Borg said. He was starting to feel serious heat; the bus had to leave, the decision was becoming unstoppable and he saw a concerted effort to keep his negative influence away from Peterson. "I could be convinced," he told MacNaughton. "But the timing is not to be today. I haven't had any coherent analysis about our problems at this point."

"Oh, come on, Vince," MacNaughton said impatiently.

"I'm not talking to you guys anymore," snapped Borg. "You had better get a fucking handle on the data. Do you have this morning's stuff?"

"No, not yet," replied MacNaughton. Robinson was not there to provide it.

"This is a stabilized picture compared to yesterday. There's a lag time in the quantitative stuff that's coming through," said Borg. He was sure Peterson's reasonable performance in the debate was starting to have a leveling effect on support for the Liberals. "I think we should watch what happens tonight," he said.

Borg realized his time was running out. The meeting room had emptied and the buses would be leaving the hotel at any moment. He hung up the phone and sprinted out to take his seat on the media bus, still adamantly opposed to the announcement. The buses headed out onto the highway.

Surrounded by reporters Borg had to sit and stew in silence with bus staffer Moira McIntyre. Half an hour outside of Cornwall he was frantic: no one had called from Peterson's bus to tell him whether the plan was going ahead. Trying to maintain an air of nonchalance in front of the unsuspecting reporters, he called Peterson's bus and was told by McCauley the group was still working on the speech.

"How am I supposed to get the press ready for this when I don't even know what we're announcing?" Borg hissed through clenched teeth. "This is a fucking disaster; I want to talk to him."

"Well, he's on the phone, he'll call you back," said McCauley and hung up.

The buses were speeding up now, trying to get to Cornwall on time. The announcement was 15 minutes away. McIntyre sat next to Borg, clutching a stack of news releases on the tax cut. "Vince," she whispered. "Have they returned your call yet?"

Just outside Cornwall, Borg got the call from Peterson's bus: he could start putting out the word to reporters. He took the releases from McIntyre and strolled down the aisle, handing them out.

"Burger of the day?" a reporter asked.

"Yeah, a burger," muttered Borg. "It might get stuck in your throat it's so big." Borg began spinning as best he could, telling reporters, with a straight face, that the cut was an integral and carefully considered part of the Liberals' economic plan.

In front of 160 people in Cornwall who were expecting nothing more than a small local campaign announcement, Peterson lofted the Liberals' long bomb. He pledged to lower the sales tax from 8 percent to 7 the day that the GST came into effect.

In a hard-hitting speech he berated Mulroney and the federal government for planning to bring in the GST, charging it would wipe out 15,000 Ontario jobs per year and increase the inflation rate to 5.5 percent from 4 percent. He called the federal tax the culmination of a series of damaging Tory economic policies, including the free trade deal, high interest rates and a high dollar. Lowering the sales tax would cushion the blow of the GST in Ontario, he said. Some $1.1 billion would remain in the hands of Ontario taxpayers, with tax savings for each Ontario family of $300 to $400 per year. Over five years, 75,000 jobs would be saved and Ontario's economic growth would be boosted by an estimated 0.2 percent.

Peterson tried to refute reporters' suggestions that the cut was responding to the tax attacks of the Tories and NDP in the campaign and was not an effective way of countering the GST. "I get lots of criticisms from them on that and every other issue," he replied. "There's no shortage of criticism in politics. The question is who's got the ideas to do things."

Reporters quickly realized the move would unbalance the vaunted balanced budget. Peterson countered that the Liberal government "can produce a balanced budget when the economy is strong, but we also understand the value of a short-term deficit when the economy needs a boost."

"You mean, 'When my campaign needs a boost,'" was what reporters thought and what Rae and Harris trumpeted.

*　　*　　*

The NDP had been having its worst week of the campaign. Pollster David Gotthilf's tracking showed that Rae had reached a ceiling and could not seem to punch through it. Without scoring a decisive victory in the debate Rae had not been able to jumpstart his stalling campaign and it was losing momentum.

The morning of the tax cut Rae made a minor announcement about the impact of the GST on the purchase of supplies for schools. It fell flat and the NDP bus began to feel like a slowly sinking ship as it chugged sadly along the highway for another minor event in Cornwall, where Peterson had been scheduled to make a noon speech. When it arrived the NDP crew discovered the Liberals had thrown them a life preserver.

"I think David Peterson has made the biggest political miscalculation of his career," Rae declared, barely able to contain his excitement in a hastily called scrum. "The voters of Ontario are not for sale." Indignant, he called the tax cut a blatant attempt to buy votes by a politician who has given "the clearest possible evidence that he can neither be believed nor trusted." Rae predicted the move would backfire.

At NDP headquarters in Toronto Rae's worried team could not believe their ears. "We thought it was like a gift from heaven," said strategist David Reville. "The timing was so attackable. Hardly any man on the street thought this was a sincere effort to help. It played right into the cynicism factor, which is, 'These guys will say anything to get your vote and then once they've got it, they suddenly go deaf on you.'" What Rae could not do in the debate the Liberals had done for him: given the NDP campaign a badly needed shot in the arm. The tax cut was "good for morale because it looked like desperation time," said Reville. "It came at a good time too, because we were just flat-lined. When we heard about it we were wondering whether some of our people were actually running the Peterson campaign. We looked around to see if we were missing some people."

From that moment on the NDP had their momentum back. The Liberals' long bomb had been thrown directly into Rae's hands, allowing him to keep on running with a revived attack on the Liberals' honesty and integrity.

The Tories were astounded. They believed they had managed to knock the Liberals completely off-strategy. "It acknowledged taxation as the issue for the campaign," said Tory strategist John Tory. "But worse than that, it showed Peterson, who had always prided himself on being not just another politician who will do anything to get elected and buy your votes with your own money, in there with the best of them. That he was prepared to do something so blatant and wildly opportunistic made even those asleep voters say, 'Oh, please, stop it, this is what we're fed up with.'" Harris promptly called the tax cut "the most shameless attempt to buy an election in the history of Ontario politics." He told reporters there was no question the Liberals were panicking and "policy in a panic situation is not good policy for any government and certainly not for the province of Ontario."

Although many early news reports were receptive, media reaction to the tax measure turned overwhelmingly negative. The Toronto *Star* noted the Liberal government had raised the sales tax in May 1988 from 7 percent to 8, saying it needed the money for better health care, education, social assistance and affordable housing. The Liberals did use the extra funds to respond to legitimate needs and established an enviable record on which the campaign should have been run, the paper editorialized; while spending rose, Nixon had been able to balance the budget. "But the Liberals traded in that record for a cynical election ploy," the *Star* commented. Some benefits would be achieved by the tax cut but the deficit would increase, which meant improvements in health care, welfare reform and job training might have to wait. "This move tarnishes the Liberals' responsible fiscal record and ultimately undermines their very credibility," the newspaper concluded.

The *Globe* credited the Tories with inducing the cut, calling Harris "the billion-dollar man." It questioned whether the windfall would really end up in the pockets of taxpayers but thanked Harris for "shaking a popular premier from his complacency." The Ottawa *Citizen* criticized Peterson's pledge, telling readers "It's difficult not to come to the conclusion that the campaign promise was prompted by panic over voter hostility detected in the polls and on the hustings rather than careful policy analysis."

It was not only the opposition parties and media who were taken aback by the surprise announcement: Liberal candidates did not have a clue about the move until after it was made. The shift in policy was dramatic: on July 31 Robinson had sent a memo to Liberal candidates and campaign managers urging them to hammer home the balanced budget theme: "It's vital that both our strong record on the economy (high annual growth, balanced budgets for the last two years and a reduction of our debt for the first time in over 40 years) and our clear plan for the future be known and understood by voters," she wrote.

In a fax sent on August 22, the day of the announcement, Robinson pushed the merits of the "Peterson tax cut" and pointed out it was made possible by the Liberals' careful management of provincial finances. "David Peterson has promised to use the flexibility created by balanced budgets in order to put money in taxpayers' pockets at a time when federal policies will be generating economic challenges," she wrote. Mulroney and the GST were one target of the cut, Robinson explained, but Harris was also being hit by the Liberal measure: "Mike Harris never counts the GST when he talks about high taxes; let's make sure that voters know that a tax is a tax is a tax and a Tory is a Tory is a Tory."

The move appalled Liberal candidates across Ontario. For weeks they had been standing on porches preaching the message of Liberal fiscal responsibility. Suddenly their strongest selling point had been scuttled by a single announcement that would slice revenues and require either extensive program-cutting or deficit financing. They had been instructed by the central campaign to keep driving home the first part of the balanced budget equation, that it showed the Liberals were good economic managers, but not the second part, that the balance provided flexibility to respond to economic pressures.

Liberal candidates scrambled to revise their pitches but the damage had been done: after delivering the message of Liberal fiscal responsibility personally to voters, they were now positioned to be tarred with the brush of what appeared to be Peterson's cynical opportunism and hypocrisy. Many losing Liberals would cite the tax cut as the turning point in the campaign, when their chances of winning were shot.

Cynicism about the motivation for the cut was fueled later in the week when Nixon admitted in an interview there was no guarantee the cut would still be around in a year.

"There are varying degrees of opinion as to whether the tax cut was the right thing to do," said MacNaughton; his understatement would incense most Liberals, who shared an angry consensus that the move was absolutely the wrong thing to do: it was an invitation to attack their credibility on every score. Their economic management skills, commitment to fiscal responsibility, honesty, integrity and political savvy all became suspect. If Ontarians had doubts about these Liberal qualities, the tax cut put them to rest.

The cut might have worked had it been set up properly, had it been announced at the start of the campaign and sold on two fronts. Peterson and Liberal candidates might have told Ontarians that the province was going into rough economic times and the Liberals could afford to cut taxes because of the way they had managed the province's financial affairs. That statement could have been coupled with an unequivocal acknowledgment that a balanced budget was not an end in itself but a means to create financial flexibility to be able to respond to Ontarians' concerns in difficult times. That success could have been contrasted with the Mulroney Tories' fiscal failures, vividly demonstrated by the GST, a new tax planned in a worsening economic climate.

But the initiative was not set up with propaganda about economic benefits to Ontarians that could have blunted the attacks about political opportunism. If the Liberals had gone forward with an economic plan to deal with the recession several weeks before the election or early in the campaign, the tax cut might have held up as part of a plan. Instead, their decision to campaign with a low-cost platform and not fear-monger about a looming recession helped ensure that any break in form would stand out. Staffers on the Liberal bus and at campaign headquarters fed reams of detailed background material to reporters, trying to provide them with an economic rationale for the tax cut. But all the spin in the world could not compensate for bad timing.

Not only did the tax cut play into the prevailing atmosphere of cynicism toward the Liberals, it had an effect opposite to that anticipated by the Liberal strategists: it drove more voters to the NDP. The Liberals went after the Tories, believing their vote was the softest and that core Liberal support switching to the Tories would be prompted to come back to the Liberals by a Tory-bashing measure.

As the effect of the highly criticized announcement played out, MacNaughton realized going after the Tories to retrieve Liberal deserters had been a mistake: "Marty talked about Liberal-Tory switchers," said MacNaughton. "The trouble with all that stuff is that it doesn't matter in an election like this because there's no core Liberal vote anymore. In the 1970s you were dealing with a 28 percent solid Liberal core." The strategists mistakenly assumed Liberal voters would go only to the Tories, and then only back to the Liberals. Since voters had already decided they disliked the Liberals, it was folly to think only the Liberals would benefit from attacking the Tories.

Ironically, Goldfarb was well aware of the trouble the Liberals could find themselves in if the Tory vote fell. In his strategic document in May he noted, "the collapse of the Tory vote will function more to the advantage of the NDP than the Liberals by making the election a two-party election."

By going after the Tories with the tax cut the Liberals collapsed the Tory vote to the benefit of the NDP. In their haste to throw the long bomb the Liberal strategists failed to heed some of Goldfarb's own early advice by focusing on the Tories over the NDP. "The Liberal campaign strategy should virtually ignore the Tories," his strategic paper told the Liberals in May.

"The first decision people made was that they were going to look around because of all the negative stuff about the Liberals," said MacNaughton. "It became the successive elimination of unpalatable alternatives. Having decided to look at something else, they started to focus on the Tories. The Tories started coming up and then we kicked the shit out of them and they said, 'Well, we've clearly said we want something other than the Liberals, we've looked at the Tories and what do we end up with? The NDP.' To ask them to go through the process and come back to the Liberals required two things: something positive to get them back to the Liberals and something negative to have them not look at the NDP. That was missing." Intended as "something positive," the tax cut blew up in Peterson's face. Only in the final week of the campaign would he try his luck with "something negative."

*   *   *

The sultans of spin stayed hard at work throughout the campaign. After massaging the messages on the early-election call and the campaign's negative advertising, the Tories decided to make a move that would both undercut Peterson's personal credibility and take some steam out of the Liberals, all in one blow. They decided to leak the news that the premier was trailing badly in his own riding of London Centre—not to the Tory candidate but to New Democrat Marion Boyd. It was an astonishing finding, produced by an almost-unknown Tory pollster.

At the first Tory leadership convention in 1985, Larry Grossman's campaign manager, strategist John Laschinger, provided delegate tracking data accurate enough to permit Grossman to predict to reporters going into the convention that he would make the final ballot. No one believed him. Three days later Grossman leapfrogged over contenders Roy McMurtry and Dennis Timbrell to square off against Frank Miller in the final vote that made Miller premier. Grossman had called it. Reporters were flabbergasted.

Laschinger's information on the voting intentions of delegates came from John Mykytyshyn, a little-known private pollster often offering his services under the name of the firm Canadian Voter Contact. Laschinger had maintained his links with Mykytyshyn and brought him out to provide the Tories' 1990 Ontario campaign with data on voters in 20 ridings. Most were swing ridings but others were included where the trends might be tactically significant—such as the home turf of both Peterson and Harris. In the days after the debate Mykytyshyn surveyed 250 voters in London Centre, and by midweek had a great scoop to report to Laschinger: Peterson was going down. Boyd was ahead by 14 points with the support of 46 percent of London Centre, Peterson was in terrible shape with 32 percent and the Tory candidate was at the back of the field with 22 percent of decided voters.

Laschinger was prepared to sit on the numbers and leak them late in the campaign to demoralize the Liberals just as they were trying to rally the troops for final canvassing and election-day vote-pulling. But he made a mistake that caused his carefully timed tactic to be leaked prematurely. He let the numbers slip into Harris's hands.

Laschinger filled in Phil Gillies on the London Centre poll results on the morning of August 24. Gillies could barely contain himself. He joined Harris aboard the Tory bus for the drive to

Global TV's Don Mills studios to tape Robert Fisher's "Focus Ontario" interview program, to be aired the following day. On the way Gillies gleefully spilled the beans to Harris, who was too busy sweating bullets over the taping to celebrate.

In the studio the program went smoothly until a reporter on Fisher's panel asked Harris about ridings listed as priorities by the Tories, where they were "doing well or could win." The reporters had heard Liberals claim they had a secret poll showing their candidate in Harris's Nipissing riding, North Bay Mayor Stan Lawlor, was winning. Harris was not worried. He knew Mykytyshyn's data had already confirmed his seat was safe. But he remembered what Gillies had told him on the drive up.

"I'll tell you something interesting," he said. "London Centre is now on that list and that's David Peterson's riding."

"Going to knock him off?" Fisher asked.

"That is a priority riding now for us," said Harris. "The indication that we have is that he's not in first place in his own riding."

When Harris walked out of the studio, reporters covering his tour, who had been watching the taping in another room, raced up to him for the details. Harris was caught off-balance. He had let a major story out without warning anyone. He promised the reporters he would have more information before the show went on the air the next day.

Back on the bus Gillies had to figure out in a hurry how to turn the slip into a tactical victory. He ordered up more details of the poll from Mykytyshyn to feed to reporters, then looked at Peterson's itinerary for the day. It showed the premier was arriving at Toronto radio station CFRB for Andy Barrie's phone-in program. Gillies smiled. The Tories now had two chances to ruin Peterson's day. Back at Tory headquarters the phones were busy. Half a dozen workers were sitting down with Gillies' prepared lines in front of them. One of them got through right away.

"I really think you should get rid of the red ties," read the Tory plant. "They're so hokey, they're getting a bit embarrassing now." Next he recited an attack on the early-election call: "I believe you had no excuse to call it so soon before the end of your mandate and waste $40 million of taxpayers' money. You had every reason to wait." The Tories had struck once.

The Tory bus pulled up in front of Queen's Park and reporters took off to file their stories. Gillies darted up to the press gallery and tracked down CFRB reporter Hal Vincent, who had not attended the taping. It was spin time.

"Geez, Hal, could you believe that poll this morning?" Gillies exclaimed. "I was sure surprised when Mike just let that out."

"Hey!" demanded Vincent. "What have you got?"

"Wow, Hal, we've got a poll that shows Peterson losing London Centre by 14 percent." Gillies gave him the details.

In minutes Vincent wrote, recorded and filed the story to his newsroom. The news came on at noon, as Peterson and his entourage were leaving Barrie's studio through the hallways of CFRB, where the station's programming was being piped through. The lead story was Iraqi military activity in Kuwait. The second story, the one that stopped the Liberals dead in their tracks, was Vincent's. The Tories had struck again.

The poll was covered prominently on television newscasts that night and appeared in most papers the following day, landing more coverage than the announcements and other activities of the leaders. That afternoon, in Port Stanley, on Lake Erie near London, Peterson did the only thing the Liberals could think of under the circumstances: he attacked the Tories' credibility. "They've been making up a lot of polls, those guys," he said. "The Tories always make up polls. It's not the first one." Robinson recommended the response to Peterson but she had nothing that could help confirm or deny Laschinger's ploy or offer genuine comfort to the premier. No Liberal polling was being conducted in Peterson's riding. With a 9,000-vote plurality in 1987 there had been no concern about Peterson's ability to hold his seat.

*   *   *

Begrudging anything that took them away from campaigning in their own ridings, Peterson's ministers gathered, many as gray and angry as storm clouds, for a cabinet meeting at Queen's Park on the morning of August 27. Regular business was brushed aside; this was a political meeting and the Liberal chieftains, smarting from their personal confrontations with political reality on the doorsteps of Ontario, wanted to know the big picture.

Peterson asked the six regional political ministers for an assessment of the prospects in each section of the province. From the southwest, Windsor's Bill Wrye was still optimistic in spite of growing public antipathy; from the east, Quinte's Hugh O'Neil was encountering problems but support still seemed to be holding; from the north, central, south-central and Metro Toronto regions, each minister delivered the same message: we are running into angry, hostile or at best, apathetic voters on the doorstep, but we have no reason to believe we are in serious trouble. Or do we? What did Liberal polling say would happen to the party's majority? Was it safe or, as the leaked Decima poll 11 days earlier had suggested, was there really a chance of slipping into a minority? Around the table the heads turned to Peterson for answers. He gave the floor to Robinson.

"Our numbers don't show that," she said. "The numbers are holding; the strategy is on-track. Everything is working." But the key to keeping the majority intact, Robinson said, was making an unprecedented push at the door in the final days, to break through to voters who were still waffling. The strategy over the last week, she explained, had been to define the choices for voters. The debate had helped make the differences among the parties clearer; the tax cut had made the strongest possible anti-Mulroney statement. "We now stand very clearly as the party that will best promote Ontario's security and opportunity in the times ahead," she asserted.

As he started to do in the debate, Robinson explained, the premier would continue to expose the Tories' hidden agenda to tax the sick and abolish rent controls and pay equity. "We should have no qualms about pointing out the Tory agenda at the door," she urged. And the NDP were sitting ducks, she claimed, after dropping their costly *Agenda for People*, a spending spree that would drive businesses and jobs out of the province:

"We have to drive this message home to potential NDP support-ers wherever we find them."

Around the table Peterson's ministers were apprehensive about coming on too strong with criticism. Goldfarb's rolling polls were out of their reach and without knowing the numbers they had only their own experiences to go on. It was no time, they felt, to start arguing blindly about strategy. Some took com-fort in Robinson's reassurances; others discounted her claims and decided they would go back to their ridings and keep doing their own thing. Some talked respectfully about the negative personal reaction to Peterson they had been getting at the door. Others, tactfully trying to offer support, talked about the need to be confident and strong, but carefully suggested that Peterson not cross the line between confidence and arrogance. Only one suggestion stood out.

"I think it's time you stopped wearing those damn white shirts," said Ian Scott. "Why don't you do me a favor next week?"

"What's that?" asked Peterson.

"Wear a blue shirt all week."

"What, are you crazy?" Peterson scowled. But around the table some knowing smiles appeared. Scott was not criticizing Peterson's wardrobe: he was talking about Peterson's image and how it just was not turning out to be right for the summer of 1990.

"He had a perfect image for '85 and '87, perfect for the '80s, sort of a yuppie, upwardly mobile, handsome, well-tanned, well-dressed young Ontarian with his future before him," said Scott. "Nicely spoken, well-mannered, friendly, caring, with a nice wife, pretty with a nice sort of trendy career, three beautiful kids, a house and a farm, the tie just rakish, the shirt unbuttoned at the neck, dazzling white shirts." But in a long, hot summer of discontent, with unrest in the Middle East and at Oka and a recession threatening everyone, Scott believed people were see-ing in Peterson a leader who was not catching on.

"It wasn't that he said anything that was wrong, it was that he looked wrong, that people didn't have the sense that any of this was touching him. I felt that in my riding, with rich and poor, the people didn't feel that Peterson understood what they were going through. And their thinking was, 'Well, why should he? You know, he's an '80s figure.' Or they might say, 'He's rich himself' or 'He's the premier, he doesn't have any problems.' It wasn't that he didn't feel these things or understand these things, it was that he didn't look as if he did, and perception is everything."

It was a perception that Environics pollster Michael Adams would later echo: "The guy driving the BMW, with the red tie, saying, 'I'm having a good time, and I'd like to have a good time for a lot longer'—people just wanna scratch that car. When the pie is shrinking they start to look at things like equity and egalitarianism: 'I want people like me in there whom I can trust, not people flaunting it in front of me.'"

Peterson, Robinson and the Liberal ministers listened patiently as Scott unpacked his theory. He finished and looked around. The cabinet room was quiet. "Anything else?" asked Peterson.

"I think," said Scott, "he thought I was nuts."

*   *   *

On the day after the debate, Environics had begun four days of interviews with 1,008 Ontarians for its major poll of the campaign, sponsored by the Toronto *Star* and CFTO-TV. Its findings were devastating news for the Liberals, confirming what their own polls were showing. The findings were released over a three-day stretch as the Liberals twisted in agony in the winds of public opinion. First revealed by CFTO on the night of August 27 the top-line numbers showed that Peterson's minority was "hanging by a thread," with 40 percent of decided voters still backing the Liberals, the NDP at a record 34 percent and the Tories supported by 23 percent of Ontarians. Thirteen percent were still undecided and fringe parties were picking up 3 percent of voters.

"It's definitely not a cakewalk," Environics vice-president Donna Dasko told reporters. "Forty percent, historically, is the

level where minority governments happen." The poll showed
the Liberals still well ahead regionally in Metro Toronto and
northern Ontario, marginally in front in eastern Ontario, but taking an awful beating in southwestern Ontario, from the Metro
border to Windsor. Rae's personal strength began to emerge—34
percent of respondents told Environics' interviewers that Peterson would make the best premier but Rae was closing in fast
with 28 percent as Harris stayed out of sight at 14 percent.

For the first time there was public confirmation that the Tory
attack strategy was working. While the environment was the top
choice as the most important issue of the campaign—with the
NDP picked as the party best able to deal with environmental
issues—overtaxation had rocketed into second spot, tripling the
number of people for whom it was the top priority, compared
with findings in July. "There's no other reason for that except the
campaign," Dasko pointed out.

But the writing was already on the wall: voters shaken loose
from the Liberals by the Tory tax attacks were fastening onto the
NDP. The poll found 26 percent of voters believed the NDP
could keep taxes down, compared with 21 percent for the Liberals and 19 percent for the Tories. "Taxfighter" Harris had not
made a strong enough impression to match Rae's pledge to create a fairer tax system and introduce a minimum corporate tax.

Dasko explained that the NDP "have a very clear, very basic
story to tell on the taxation issue, that the rich have not been
paying their fair share [and] the corporations have been getting
off. That's the kind of line people have been responding to."

To most Liberals across the province there was no longer any
denying of a problem: the campaign was reeling from the combined body blows of the NDP, Tories and more protesters than
anyone had ever imagined. Most Liberals—but not all of them.
On the night of the CFTO broadcast Robinson faxed a memo to
Liberal candidates and campaign managers that blew them
away. "The poll shows that while we are headed for a solid win
on the sixth, we still have a great deal of work to do in order to
achieve the kind of victory we want for the premier and the
party," she claimed. "The poll results are in line with our original

understanding of how this campaign would develop. The only people who ever said that we would have a 'cakewalk' through this campaign were the media, and only those members of the media interested in developing a story line are showing surprise in the results."

Robinson assured the troops that the undecided segment of voters was far larger than Environics' 13 percent and urged them to keep the heat on at the door. She explained the new series of Liberal response ads would attack both opposition parties, while Peterson would start "speaking out on the flawed visions of the opposition parties" to make it clear there were fundamental differences between Liberals, New Democrats and Tories. She warned that the poll confirmed many local races would be tight, with margins of fewer than 1,000 votes. But she ended with a rah-rah line that seemed as out of touch with the Environics poll as it did with most candidates' experiences at the doorstep: "As we come down to the wire, things are looking good. Our strategy is on-track; the premier is in excellent form; the polls show that the support is there for us. Victory is within our grasp."

In Liberal campaign offices across the province, the central campaign's credibility went into the trash can as quickly as Robinson's memo. Furious campaign managers tore the fax into shreds. For candidates and Liberal veterans, Robinson's lines were the final insult. After being ignored for months in the planning and running of the election they were now being taken for idiots. They had been slapped in the face with the real story for weeks, every time they and their workers had ventured up on another porch. The contempt for the Liberals' central campaign, unleashed the previous week by the tax cut announcement, was finding a focal point in Robinson.

Peterson put on a calm face when reporters demanded his reaction to Environics' numbers. "We knew it was going to be a tough campaign," he said in Orangeville, "but I'm also very optimistic." Rae, anticipating the Liberals would start coming after him at any moment, began trying to defuse the attacks his strategists believed Peterson would launch. "The Liberals are obviously desperate," he warned reporters. "We expect them to be saying all kinds of strange things in the last few days of the campaign."

Its members now scattered around the province and country by personal and business duties, the Liberal strategy committee had begun to meet almost exclusively by conference call when the Environics poll came out. Ezrin was out of the mix entirely, in Australia on business. Kirby was on a tour of the western provinces with the Senate's finance committee, studying the GST.

On August 28, with headlines blazing the first results of the poll, most of the strategists linked up twice by phone. The prime threat, they agreed, was the potential for a bandwagon effect that would help Rae: NDP supporters would be encouraged by the results while Liberals would see no cause for alarm. But the new Liberal television and radio ads were going to air that day, attacking the Tories hardest, and Peterson was already becoming more aggressive on the tour. The best move, they agreed, was to watch and wait for both tactics to have an effect.

It was also time to reach into the campaign's $100,000 tactical advertising fund, held in reserve since the beginning of the campaign. A full-page newspaper ad laying out the Liberal record was ordered from the campaign's policy unit and David Morton was assigned to book pages in the province's four largest dailies on the weekend—a final, belated blitz of information to tell Ontarians about the Liberals' record. The ad would rhyme off dozens of Liberal promises, explain how they had been kept and lay out the full platform of the 1990 campaign.

The hardest punch from Environics' poll came the next day, when the components dealing with Peterson's handling of the Starr affair were released. The poll's questions in this area enraged the Liberals, who believed they were designed to provoke responses that would generate strong headlines. "Do you approve of the way David Peterson handled the Patti Starr affair?" the interviewers asked: 51 percent disapproved, 20 percent approved and 29 percent said they did not know. "Do you think the Patti Starr affair is an isolated incident or do you think that illegal donations and other forms of corruption are more widespread in the Ontario Liberal government?" the interviewers continued. To this question, 61 percent of respondents replied that corruption was widespread, 18 percent thought the incident was isolated and 21 percent did not know.

Environics' questions were attuned to the need of the poll's media sponsors to get responses that would allow a clear, simple story to be told by the results. Media-sponsored polls that yield complex, hard-to-explain results provide a poor return on investment; shaping the poll's questions was simply good business sense to its media backers.

In particular, the question on the depth of corruption probed perceptions and then offered up a conclusion that turned those perceptions into a fact. The "fact" became a story in itself, to which each leader was asked to react. Peterson stuck to his standard Starr response: "We moved expeditiously to deal with the situation. We dealt with it through an independent group." Rae, presented with the quintessential window through which to deliver his honesty-and-integrity attack, said, "It illustrates terrible mistakes in practices and in judgment." Harris, revealing that his advisors understood the provocative wording of the question, told reporters, "I think the perception is the reality, that he tried to cover up as much as he could."

Another question in the poll provided a truer picture of Ontarians' views on honesty and integrity in government—but it was not the stuff of which headlines are made. When asked which of the three parties was best able to provide honest government, 19 percent of respondents picked the Liberals, 27 percent the NDP, 9 percent the Tories and 26 percent said none of the above, they are all the same. Nineteen percent had no opinion.

But that story, with its nuances and shadings, was buried in a single paragraph near the bottom of the *Star*'s first story on the poll. Findings that the Liberals were seen as the best party to deal with national unity, management of the economy, health care, education and French language issues were buried or saved for the last story in the series.

*   *   *

Allan Gregg had no interest in the week-old data in the Environics poll. He walked into the regularly scheduled meeting of the Tory strategy team at Toronto's Albany Club on August 28, as the rest of the province was reading that the Liberals might be reduced to a minority. He had a finding to convey about the summary of his latest tracking data, which he placed in a binder on the table.

"It's going to be," he announced, "an NDP majority."

"Yee-hah! Hoo-hoo! All right!" the Tories yelled, and broke into applause and laughter, congratulating one another. The Tories were not on another planet: they had just, in their own way, become part of the NDP's universe.

Gregg's numbers confirmed that the Tory attack strategy, when blended with the NDP attacks and the protester phenomenon, had driven voters away from Peterson. It was as if the polarity in Peterson's personal magnetism had suddenly been reversed. And as the Tories had recognized before the campaign, confirmed in its first days and supported by sticking to their attack strategy and advertising, most of those Liberal votes were heading to Rae and the NDP by a ratio of about two to one over the Tories.

"Seriously, Allan, what odds would you give today against a Peterson majority?" Grossman asked Gregg.

"Ten to one," replied the pollster.

"Against a Peterson minority?"

"Five to one."

But the strategists were still doubtful. They expected the Liberals to launch an attack on Rae at any minute. How could Gregg be so certain the NDP numbers would hold? The reason, he explained, was that the NDP support was both firm and broad-based. It was not only urban or rural and not only traditional NDP strength. Support for Rae from all voting constituencies was multiplying, tripling in some areas, and was not below 30 percent in any region of the province. It was a quiet and uniform movement, not tenants in Toronto having a disproportionate effect or rural farmers suddenly rediscovering the United Farmers of Ontario; no single issue carrying a single group was tilting the readings. "It's everyone, everywhere, making the same move, in the same week, for the same party," Gregg said.

When they had decided the week before to hold course with their attacks, the Tories had been thinking self-preservation. The Liberal votes coming their way had promised to help them build their share of decided voters into the low 20-percent range and had meant they could expect to win a respectable 20 seats. But now the implications of maintaining their strategy were much larger: they were helping to bring about the most dramatic change in government in Ontario's history. They ran through the factors: Peterson could win back support if he started attacking Rae. If Harris laid off Peterson, he could drop out of the picture again and Rae would not be affected. In both scenarios, the Tories would lose out.

The other unsavory possibility, they realized, was that serious slippage by the NDP would give Rae a minority and place Harris in the king-maker's role, forced to decide whether to support a Liberal or NDP government. The Tory strategists made their decision, knowing exactly what it meant: the attacks against Peterson would continue, even if the Tories were doing their part to help Rae get elected with a majority by driving Liberals to the NDP.

"There was not a great deal of will on the part of our campaign committee to try to stop what seemed to be happening," said Gillies. "The mainstream opinion of our campaign committee was the NDP's gonna win this thing and it's probably just as well if they do, for a couple of reasons. One, an undoubted bitterness and antipathy toward the Liberals. Two, we knew right from the start there was no way we were gonna win this election. So looking ahead to the next election, there was a feeling among some of us that we would have a better chance against the NDP than we would against a re-entrenched Liberal government."

Helping the Tories reach their decision was an understanding with the NDP that the Liberals were the common enemy. Throughout the campaign the two camps had communicated frequently, planning their announcements to avoid conflicting with each other. "We certainly liked the way Bob and the NDP had conducted themselves during the campaign," said Gillies. "We had developed some relationships there that had never existed before, friendly relationships."

Even the Tory right-wingers, appalled at the thought of a socialist regime, begrudgingly accepted that "the reality of an NDP government in Ontario might serve to galvanize the business community in terms of making appropriate campaign contributions to the PC party so that we are a strong and viable alternative in the next election," said Gillies. Only in the last days of the campaign, to try to strengthen his position as an alternative and appease hard-core Tories, would Harris take some solid shots against Rae, while his campaign gave token airplay to an anti-NDP television ad.

One day later, pollster Gotthilf brought word to the NDP strategists of their looming majority victory. But the numbers were greeted with apprehension, not jubilation. Rae's team refused to accept that the big win was a sure thing. Gotthilf's findings were too good to be true. Nudging above 42 percent of the popular vote, the NDP was looking at as many as 78 seats. As the strategists met on August 30 in the Queen's Park office of campaign director David Agnew, it was nail-biting time. Peterson would surely have to turn the big guns on Rae before long and memories were returning of the 1975 campaign, when Bill Davis resorted to images of the "socialist hordes pounding at the door" to successfully rebuff the threat of an upset by NDP leader Stephen Lewis. Worse still, a major poll by Winnipeg's Angus Reid was coming out in two days. Its findings, the NDP strategists glumly believed, would confirm Gotthilf's data, snap voters out of their trance and send them scurrying back to Peterson.

*   *   *

One week before the election Angus Reid's interviewers worked diligently on August 29 and 30 to conduct a poll sponsored by Southam News. They made contact with 900 Ontarians; Reid's computers ate up the information as it was collected, digested it and spat out the results early Friday. By Saturday morning, the first day of the long Labour Day weekend, the findings were blazing in thick black headlines on the front pages of papers across the province: the New Democrats were out in front and a dull election had turned into a great horse race.

Reid pegged support for the NDP at 38 percent of decided voters, the highest level in the province's history. The Liberals had spiralled to 34 percent, off 16 points since the election call; the Tories were back down to 24 percent, beaten back 7 points by the Liberal attacks.

Reid's interviews were conducted after the release of Environics' finding that the Liberal majority was in danger. At the same time, follow-up stories from Environics' poll were announcing wide perceptions of corruption in the Liberal government. The Liberals were convinced the poll results were feeding one another by contributing to a bandwagon effect against Peterson; pollsters disputed the allegation, saying voters were responding to the events of the campaign.

Reid's findings helped induce a subtle change in approach among many reporters covering the campaign. Although they tended to question the accuracy of the poll and whether its findings would hold up, those trailing Rae began to ask him about the possibility of becoming premier; those covering Peterson began looking for signs that he knew he was going down.

The new atmosphere put Rae in the driver's seat. Now he could appear excited and positive while maintaining his attacks. "This election has been the most exciting experiment in democracy this province has seen in a long time," he said in Sudbury on the Friday night the poll was released. "People are waking up. What you hear out there is the voice of the people. One of the things that has moved people to come to us and to leave the Liberals is a sense that they want a government that is close to them, they want a party that is fighting for them."

The Liberals had been expecting the worst from Reid's poll. They believed his results would have to be viewed with caution because he had been fired by John Turner during the 1988 federal campaign. When the numbers came into Liberal headquarters late Friday night, they were met not with panic but with skepticism.

Backed into a corner that night in North Bay, Peterson found himself not only on the defensive but, for the first time in his experience as an incumbent, losing badly as well. Determined not to admit the Liberals were facing defeat, he struck out at the accuracy of the Reid poll: "It doesn't conform with our understanding of the situation. It's quite different from that," he told reporters. "I don't concede anything. The campaign's not over. We'll continue to fight. There's lots of volatility. There's lots of uncertainty, lots of undecideds. I'm very optimistic that at the end of the day, it will work out very well." So was Rae. In fact, he could easily have spoken Peterson's next lines himself: "People will make judgments about where they are the most comfortable, about where this province is going to go and about who can best do it."

Harris, realizing the momentum was working against him, chose to keep firing off darts: "We're going to continue to focus on the issue that has shaken the electorate up—big spending, wasteful government, high taxation." And he passed on a phrase Gregg had used with the Tory strategists: the Liberals, he told reporters in Barrie, "are clearly in a free-fall."

Reid's findings were only half of Peterson's problems that night in North Bay. From a London *Free Press* reporter came word of a new poll in Peterson's own city—a poll showing the Liberal vote had collapsed and the NDP were surging. Nordex Research of London had conducted a survey for the *Free Press* that showed Liberal support among decided voters had sunk 6 points in two weeks, to 38 percent. "Polling results and current conditions indicate the incumbent in London Centre is threatened," said Nordex pollster Kim Ainslie. "In London Centre the NDP is more popular than elsewhere in the city."

That night Robinson reached Peterson on the Liberal bus and began priming him to counter the polls' potential effect on what Peterson would describe the next day as "the psychology of the campaign"—the bandwagon effect the Liberals feared. It was time to turn his attention to Rae, Robinson told the premier, to convince voters they should stop thinking about lodging protest votes. The reason: Goldfarb was finding that 7 out of 10 voters still believed the NDP could not form the government. Robinson encouraged Borg to begin spinning the line that Reid had underestimated the number of undecided voters, that it was actually as high as 20 or 30 percent, not the 13 percent suggested by Reid. The line was designed to convince reporters and voters that Reid's findings were suspect and the NDP lead was not a given.

The next morning in Ottawa Peterson dismissed Reid's findings again. But he told reporters the poll had given him a signal, loud and clear, and now he wanted to ask voters to send a government, instead of a signal, to Queen's Park. And he began to turn subtly on the NDP: "Now people have a choice to make about who can best run the government," he said. "The government is not just a picket line. This is not a by-election. This is a general election."

In Kapuskasing Rae was ready and waiting for the slightest hint of an attack. The first anti-NDP words were barely out of Peterson's mouth when Rae countered by quoting Franklin Roosevelt: "We have nothing to fear but fear itself," he said about the possibility of an NDP government. He whipped up an excited crowd of campaign workers, urging them to get out and pull the vote: "We're on a roll, my friends, we've got the momentum, the key now is to keep it going."

Harris, several hundred miles southeast in Barrie, was continuing to distance himself from Mulroney, spurred on by the Liberals' anti-Tory "balloon" ad released late that week. He told reporters he disagreed violently with Mulroney, Peterson and Rae. "All three of them want to spend more, they all want to waste more and they are all big taxers."

At Liberal headquarters Robinson and Goldfarb suspected Reid's poll was accurate but wanted to know for themselves, firsthand. Goldfarb's rolling polls were now consistently showing the NDP well in front—and doing even better than Reid had detected. But the Liberals did not have a large body of quantitative data to confirm their overnight and weekly tracking. Robinson and Goldfarb agreed they needed their own full-blown, provincewide poll—fast. The following day, September 2,

Goldfarb's interviewers would conduct a massive instant poll that would give the Liberals a solid finding they could trust, good, bad or otherwise.

All day long Peterson spread his first seeds of doubt and apprehension about the NDP as the Liberal bus burned up the highways through eastern Ontario, in Kemptville, Kingston, Port Hope and Lindsay. Exhausted, the tour limped into Toronto that night, where Robinson met with Peterson face to face. The NDP was now poised to win, she told him, not just erode Liberal support—but there was still time to start beating Rae down. The next day, they agreed, Peterson's attacks would have to be much sharper and his language much tougher to get the message across.

At high noon on Sunday the Liberal buses chugged away from Queen's Park for Niagara Falls. Ninety minutes later, they shut down in front of the Club Italia where the Niagara region's five Liberal candidates were lined up, smiling their welcome. Party workers from across the peninsula were gathered, 300 strong. It was the area's biggest event of the campaign and the only event of the day that would make it onto the news that night. Peterson had one shot.

"My friends," he told the crowd, "it's a war! It's a war we're going to win!" Reporters exchanged surprised glances. "The NDP is proposing a round of taxation that would tax the middle class, that would tax small businesses and drive them out of our province to other places," he continued heatedly. "They will kill businesses, they will kill jobs and they will kill our economy! My friends, we cannot have everything we fought for destroyed by the socialist philosophy! The NDP will lay waste to this economy. The Tories would turn back every bit of social progress that we have made. The alternatives will get rid of the progress we've made, economically or socially, in this province!"

Peterson tried offering up statistics to back his claims. He predicted that the proposal in the NDP's *Agenda for People* to raise the minimum wage by about two dollars an hour would be a disaster for business. "The NDP has wage policies, I say to you, that would kill 100,000 jobs in this province!" he shouted.

Reporters were intrigued by the equation and asked Peterson to provide proof. But the staffers on the Liberal bus were empty-handed. Treasury staff had made the prediction after crunching the promises in the NDP platform but the breakdown could not be found until the next day. By that time reporters had sent off stories that Peterson's wild, unsubstantiated claims were starting to make him look desperate.

At two o'clock Sunday afternoon the phone bank at Gold-farb's offices was fully staffed. Over a period of eight and a half hours the pollster's callers would get through to 450 Ontarians. As the day ground on, Robinson and Webster put out the call to Peterson's speechwriters to start working on more anti-NDP lines that could be fed to the Liberal bus that night. The remaining strategists were tracked down, one by one, and ordered to be ready for a critical conference call that night.

At nine o'clock, the call came together, the members of the Liberal brain trust linking up from around the province at their homes and cottages: MacNaughton, Kirby, Morton, Webster, Robinson and even Dan Gagnier, who had been brought back into the mix to help with the desperate attempts to salvage the wreckage of the campaign. Robinson set the stage; there was no point in pulling any punches.

"We are now looking," she stated, "at an NDP majority."

From across southern Ontario, silence echoed from a dozen distant phones.

"Marty is doing a large run right now," she continued, "that will have confirmation for us, when————?"

"After midnight," Goldfarb said. "I'll see the numbers in the morning."

"It's the by-election mentality," said MacNaughton.

"They think it's a cost-free protest vote," said Kirby.

"Shit, shit, shit," said three or four voices at once.

"Umm, now we have agreement that the premier is going to go after Rae, any discussion on what else we can do along that line?" Robinson asked.

Rattled and shaken, the strategists had little to offer. It was the middle of the long weekend and any messages to Ontarians were going to have a tough time getting through. If people were paying attention to anything right then, it was what their kids would be wearing back to school the following week. There was not a worse time of year to get any type of information across to people.

As they came around slowly the strategists began to throw out a mishmash of disjointed tactics; the conference call took on a chaotic, stream-of-consciousness quality, with ideas raised and shot down in rapid succession. An ad blitz might work, someone thought—that was it, a big ad like those anti-free trade ads that were done to help the Tories in the last days of the '88 federal campaign. There might be time to get an anti-NDP print ad written and distributed to a few major newspapers to be published on Tuesday. The message: This trend is real and the possibility of an NDP government is not a joke; Rae is on the verge of getting elected, and if you're thinking of voting NDP as a protest, don't do it.

"But who could deliver the message with the most credibility, to have the maximum impact on voters? Only third parties could do it effectively, the strategists agreed—yes, yes, third parties in the business community, company presidents, lots of them. Okay, let's start a list—who can think of names? An ad would be written up immediately, the strategists decided. Robinson, Webster and Gagnier would take the list and divide it up; they would each call 30 high-powered business contacts, advise them of the dangerous NDP trend, look for takers on the ad, virtually beg for help. These presidents, the strategists thought frantically, could tell their employees about the dangers of a socialist government.

But wait—was there really time for an ad to work? They would get on it right away, Robinson decreed; Morton would look for a way to get it published in time. But the only certain way to make an impression, the strategists decided, was through the news.

The conversation became more painful as the bleakness of the situation began to register and the suggestions ventured even further into la-la land. If the message could not be conveyed as an ad, perhaps those business types could be convinced to come forward and hold a news conference. There was only one absolutely certain way to get the message out in the news, they finally agreed: through Peterson. An even more savage attack on Rae, Goldfarb predicted, might cut NDP support by 3 or 4 percent a day, if it was as high as his rolling polls had been suggesting.

Okay, that's fine, what else can we do? Let's phone up the CBC and get them to put him on Peter Gzowski's radio show in the morning, that'll do it! No, that won't work. What the hell makes you think Gzowski's going to put Peterson on just because we call? The conference call wore on for more than an hour until, one by one, exhausted and baffled, the strategists checked out. All last-ditch tactics aside, the Liberal hopes now hung on Peterson.

Early the next morning Goldfarb called Robinson. He had the results of his sweeping provincewide poll, the numbers that could confirm or dismiss Reid's contention the NDP were at 38 percent. Goldfarb's finding was apocalyptic: NDP support had bloated over the weekend to an unbelievable 43 percent of decided voters. Rae was on course for a stunning majority upset. The Liberals had buckled to 34 percent and the Tories had been driven back down to 23 percent. The Liberal campaign had been in free-fall for the past week.

Robinson broke the news to Peterson that morning before the tour departed for its final swing through eleven cities in three days. The numbers, she told him, were as bad as Reid's and even worse. It would take an all-out attack against Rae to wake people up and shake them from the protest-vote, by-election mentality. He had to tell people to take the threat of an NDP government seriously. Some suggested lines were on the way. Peterson knew the job of saving the government was now entirely on his shoulders.

"Most people just thought we were going to win," he said. "That's the mood—they wanted to register protest one way or the other. They were unhappy with the Tories because of the federal stuff and we were there, all part of the wash; whoever was out there was at a definite disadvantage. At that point, we had to make people understand the consequences of that." The Liberal buses headed north of Toronto to Uxbridge.

Behind the ploy of an assault on Rae was the strategists' conviction that of all the public emotions remaining at their disposal, only fear was strong enough to motivate people as quickly as needed to alter their planned voting behavior; fear, the team convinced itself, of a great unknown: Rae and a socialist government. They believed many voters had an innate fear of the NDP that could be played on. The theory was not tested by Goldfarb in focus groups; there was not enough time.

Committed to this "red scare" tactic the strategists agreed to hunker down and ride out the closing days of the campaign. Abandoned with that decision were alternative tactics, including triage, a damage-control exercise that would have accepted an NDP minority and refocused the election-day vote-pulling effort to save ridings where the margins were narrow. That tactic would have required extensive targeting information which was not supplied to the campaign in its last few hectic weeks.

Campaign vice-chairs Bill Murray and Debbie Nash were asked by Robinson to assign Liberal headquarters staff to ridings where extra workers might make a difference on election day. The pair were then given incomplete targeting data based on the 1987 election results and told to use it to make their decisions. Assuming the Liberals would retain their majority because they were not told otherwise, they sent their extra bodies into ridings that would be won by huge margins by opposition candidates on election day; neighboring ridings would be lost, in some cases by dozens of votes.

Later that morning the anti-NDP advertisement was finished by the campaign policy unit. But now Robinson realized there was no time to place an ad: advertising by the parties had to stop at midnight, 48 hours before voting day. With a few adjustments the ad was converted into an open letter that could be released by business leaders, if any could be convinced to sign it:

An open letter to Ontario voters:

The outcome of Thursday's election means a great deal to Ontario's future. Economists and other experts tell us that tougher times are coming. We need to be confident in our leadership. People in business in Ontario—from small business owners to large employers—want Ontario to stay competitive in the future and remain a good place to do business. They are concerned that voters may consider the NDP a reasonable alternative to the Liberal government. These are sensitive and difficult times in the life of our province. But we believe Ontario can weather the coming storm and maintain the good standard of living we've all worked hard for. That's why this is not the time to elect an NDP government. NDP policies pose a real threat to the ability of many businesses to stay in our province. We want to add our voices to the growing body of Ontarians sounding the loudest possible warning against an NDP government. And supporting a government in which we can place our trust and confidence for the future—the Liberal government led by Premier David Peterson.

Finding willing signers was the next step—and on Labour Day Monday they were hard to track down. Robinson and Webster called only a dozen people between them before giving up in embarrassment. The most common responses: incredulity and skepticism that the threat was real and suspicion the Liberals were simply seeking to protect their majority. There were no takers on the letter, no offers of tangible aid. Gagnier would strike out, too: he called deputy ministers and senior public servants, telling them exactly what the numbers were and asking them to get the word out to friends in the business community that the story was no hoax.

There were a few hopeful signs for the Liberals as the final week of campaigning began. On the weekend both the Toronto *Star* and Toronto *Sun* had published editorial endorsements for the Liberals.

Thousands of copies of the positive comments in both papers were churned out at Liberal headquarters, sent to ridings across Toronto and faxed to every Liberal campaign office to be delivered to voters. Across Ontario nearly every major daily newspaper offered editorial support for Peterson—most with the caveat that the alternatives were weak. After weeks of critical coverage the media turnaround was baffling to the Liberals.

The NDP campaign was also running off paper to stuff into mail slots. Gotthilf's tracking told Rae's strategists they could win seats in ridings where NDP candidates were not even campaigning—where candidates had to be conscripted from outside the riding to get a name on the ballot. A handful of local campaign managers were quickly ordered to print up the name of their candidate and the NDP logo on sheets of paper and jam them into as many mailboxes as they could before election day.

*   *   *

Uxbridge was the first stop on a breakneck sprint down the homestretch for the Liberal campaign. Peterson was fired up to preach the anti-NDP message and take it on through Mississauga and Alliston. Exchanging the Liberal bus for a plane he would finish the day campaigning in Fort Frances and Kenora.

An NDP government would drive Ontario into a depression, Peterson warned in Uxbridge. He said the election "is not a by-election" but the real thing and conceded—for the first time—that an NDP victory was possible.

In Alliston Peterson fervently told a lunchtime crowd of supporters, "there is a choice in this campaign between the socialist approach and a Liberal job-creating approach. The province will not survive economically with an NDP philosophy of high taxation and high spending." He railed against the Tories in the Tory-held riding, claiming Harris would "rip apart all of the social programs." Anger flared when Peterson was confronted by a man waving a placard that read, "Who's in bed with Patti Starr?" Local Liberals tried to tear it from his hands; Borg had to intervene "by sitting on the Liberal guy," as Peterson noted, to avoid a fight.

On to the north in the afternoon: "We can't afford to let the socialists get at the economic strength we have built up over the last 5 years," Peterson told Liberal supporters in Kenora. "If we turn this province over to 4 years of socialism, it would take 40 years to pick up again." Peterson began reaching for the lines the Liberal speechwriters had sent him: "If by chance an NDP government is elected, you might as well hang up a great big billboard on this province saying, 'Going out of business.'" And he claimed the NDP was "totally out of step with the modern world. We didn't adopt their crazy tax policies in 1985."

In southwestern Ontario Rae was busy spreading his anti-Liberal message to receptive crowds and replying to Peterson's attacks. It was Labour Day and at parades and rallies across the province NDP supporters were marching and celebrating; union members proudly carried NDP campaign signs along with their own. In Windsor Rae accused Peterson of using out-of-date rhetoric—"about 50 years out of date." At a rally he let fly a few counterpunches: "Last week David Peterson described himself as the 'Ultimate Warrior.' This week, he's the 'Ultimate Worrier.'"

Responding to Peterson's allegation that NDP policies would result in a loss of 100,000 Ontario jobs, Rae said, "Under Mr. Peterson, Ontario lost 50,000 jobs in one month [July]. To lose 100,000 jobs for David Peterson, that's two months' work. He's doing it all on his own." And the crowds cheered wildly as Rae delivered his knockout punch: "NDP means No David Peterson."

Rae turned on the heat. Peterson, he told reporters, was a desperate man saying "strange and ridiculous things" about the NDP. He might think the NDP would destroy Ontario's economy but the premier did just fine when he implemented NDP policy between 1985 and 1987. In Chatham that night Rae softened his tone, becoming somber and philosophical as he tried to reassure voters. The NDP, he said, believes in "a politics based on trust, not a politics based on fear."

Harris kept delivering attacks on both Rae and Peterson. An NDP government, he said, would mean higher taxes and more government waste. In Toronto he told a Tory crowd that Peterson could stop the GST if he wanted to by calling his "friends in the Senate"—a thinly veiled reference to Liberal strategist Kirby. He added a slap at the Liberal platform: "If they did a Broadway musical based on these election promises, it would be called Little Shop of Horrors," he stated, evidently hitting the bottom of his barrel of one-liners.

The unions militating against the Liberals throughout the campaign were prominent in the Labour Day activities. Even OPSEU got into the last-ditch mudslinging. At a parade in Hamilton, OPSEU vice-president Ron Martin told a huge crowd, "There's a message on the streets today and that message is David Peterson's got a problem."

Late Monday night the Liberal tour arrived in Thunder Bay. Peterson checked in with Robinson at Liberal headquarters. News reports were coming in with heavy coverage, she told him: the message was getting out but he had to keep it up and hit even harder. People had to be wakened up.

Tuesday morning in Sudbury Peterson urged Ontarians to think carefully about the difference between the Liberals and the NDP, because the NDP "would drive spending through the roof, they would punish the middle class." In response to a reporter's suggestion he was using scare tactics to get votes, Peterson fired back, "That's not fear-mongering, that's absolutely elementary economics."

His own supply of lines dwindling fast, Peterson began reaching. As he spoke to the Sudbury crowd, his script abandoned, he struggled to come up with words that could convey what he believed would be the danger of an economic downturn. An NDP government combined with Ottawa's fiscal policies, he claimed, would drive Ontario into a depression. The NDP on its own would tilt the province into a deep and painful recession. "You know what recessions are?" he asked. "It's when you don't have a job. It's when your kids don't have enough to eat. You think about that."

The words jumped out at reporters. Peterson's tour staff cringed. The NDP would make children starve? The sentence immediately became known as Peterson's "starving children" line. Ontarians were not buying it: how could such an incredible exaggeration come from the lips of their premier? In the final days of the campaign, the line would be played and replayed. It was, like Peterson's earlier "Get a job!" line, a tight, perfect clip; it became media short-form for the desperate Liberal campaign. In ridings provincewide, Liberal candidates would shudder when they heard the line, dismayed that Peterson was making statements that made him appear to be completely out of control.

Across Ontario the tour flew, to Ottawa where Peterson told Liberal workers that NDP economic policies were "a recipe for economic depression in this province." He said his job was "to make sure we build for Ontario, that we keep our strength here." He noted many people, including Liberals, assumed the Liberals would win, but "I never did." At the airport in Mount Hope, near Hamilton, Peterson told a Liberal rally, "We cannot allow the socialist philosophy to wreck what we have created in the last five years. I do not believe the people of this province want to wreck it." He warned that, "An NDP government would create jobs in Michigan, Mexico, Korea and Taiwan, but not in Ontario."

Rae made a careful, subdued reply to Peterson's charge that the NDP would let children go hungry. "There's a difference between aggressive and wacko," he said. "He just crossed the line." Surrounded by reporters in Kitchener, Rae shook his head in disbelief at Peterson's attacks. "What can I say? It's going to be 36 hours of just absolute desperation from here on in. People hear the tone of a very desperate person trying to cling on to power and who they think has badly broken faith with them and badly disappointed them." The idea that Peterson was worried about children going hungry seemed ironic, said Rae: "This is a premier who cut $600,000 from the budgets of food banks."

The *Globe*'s Richard Mackie, now covering the NDP campaign, approached Rae's campaign director Agnew in mock confusion. "I have a serious problem on procedure here," he said. "Can you do that by order-in-council or do you have to pass laws that kids will die in the streets?" In both camps, the "starving children" line was turning into a joke among reporters. "When Peterson became a subject of ridicule," said Mackie, "it was all over."

In London, Harris was beating up on Peterson in his own backyard. "As a typical politician, David Peterson dismisses the people as cranky," he said. "They're not cranky, they're fed up." On a radio phone-in show he said his party would not form a coalition with any minority government: "If they want to align themselves with me, I'm willing to talk."

*   *   *

Back at Liberal headquarters Robinson and Webster were grasping, desperately willing to try anything that might provide an answer. There was another tactic to be fleshed out, they decided: Peterson could take a mea culpa approach and come forward to voters with a written apology, telling them he had gotten the message and learned his lesson. Morton and Donald Murphy put their heads together and came up with a text:

An open letter to the people of Ontario:

I'm hearing you and I want you to know what I've learned during this election campaign. I need your support for the Liberal Party so that we can take your message to heart to expand our role to build a truly strong Ontario. I've learned that many of you are anxious about the future, worried about your jobs, about health care, about your children's education and about the environment. Many of you are impatient about the swelling burden of taxes, and angry about the threat of the Conservative GST. I hear you loud and clear and I'm giving you my personal pledge that to re-elect a Liberal government will mean giving us a mandate and duty to translate your messages into action. I'm asking you not to take out your anger by voting for NDP or Conservative policies that you don't really want. NDP high tax policies would unmistakably lead us on the road to economic ruin at this critical time, and drive more and more industry and jobs out of your province, and Conservative policies would seriously threaten the social programs that we need and value. Don't support these damaging extremes. I ask you to vote Liberal to get a government which I pledge will do better. I pledge again that a new Liberal government will do better for you and Ontario. I'm hearing you, and I'm asking you to let me and the Liberal Party work on your behalf to build a stronger Ontario.

Sincerely, David Peterson

That afternoon Robinson faxed the letter to Peterson. He discussed it with his wife Shelley, who insisted he not humiliate himself. With a quick call to Robinson the idea was killed.

The last day of campaigning brought a flurry of quick and dirty exchanges. In response to Rae's charge he was using heavy-handed language, Peterson said, "I don't think he can accuse me of using excessive language. He's been using it since day one." Peterson conducted last-minute damage control in several Toronto ridings to fend off the "socialist hordes." "This is not the time to gamble on some cockamamie socialist view of how to run this province," he warned. Rae shot back: "If any campaign has been 'cockamamie,' it's the Liberal one."

Peterson told Liberal workers in Toronto he was not conceding anything and the election was unique because of the volatility of the electorate. "There's a very high degree of undecideds," he claimed, "people who have not made up their minds about the future." Liberal polls still showed the number of undecided voters running between 20 and 30 percent, he said. And he stressed that the election "has come down to a two-way horse race. It's between the Liberals and the NDP."

Rae cautioned NDP workers against thinking victory was in the bag. "Our message is getting across. Every race is going to be close and well fought in all 130 ridings," he said. "This is a great election. We as politicians have to earn the support of the public and keep on earning it every day." And campaign director Agnew warned, "We just won't know what effect the premier's scare strategy has had until the votes are counted." Rae agreed with reporters that a minority government was a possibility but dismissed suggestions that voters might abandon his party because they feared a socialist government: "The only person who's scared by the NDP is David Peterson."

Harris wrapped up with a proud boast that the Tories "set the agenda for this entire campaign." He described Peterson's election call as "arrogant and, as it turns out, stupid." A vote for the NDP "is nothing more than a vote for even more of the same," he warned. When a reporter suggested the Tories could win fewer than 12 seats and lose official party status, Harris replied, "I would say the chances of that are about as good as of David Peterson becoming premier—none."

After the Environics poll on August 28 Rae had said he expected "all kinds of crazy things to come out of David Peterson's mouth." But he was ready with responses—and knew the "red scare" would not work.

"The red scare: we already knew that was a loser for them," said NDP strategist Reville. "We had tested it. We tried to think of the arguments that the bad guys would use against us and we tried to remind people and they said, 'Come on, we don't believe that stuff.'" Scare-mongering lines about the NDP had been fed to its focus groups as early as May. "We found that they thought we couldn't do any worse than those guys," said Reville. "They weren't all that nervous that the socialists were going to somehow wreck the thing, because they thought that the capitalists had already wrecked it. It was clear that it was a very poor message for them to try to use."

The NDP found that even if some Ontarians were nervous about socialism, they certainly were not frightened by Rae. "It's possible that the voter information level was not high enough to put many scary things into the word 'socialist,'" Reville said. "And although 'socialist' is for some people a scary word, they didn't think that Bob Rae was scary." The NDP strategists were confident the Liberal-NDP accord in 1985 helped demystify Rae and the NDP in the minds of Ontarians. In 1990, they believed, voters were finally giving the NDP the credit for the positive reforms of that period—especially after watching the Liberals go it alone, with a majority, after 1987.

On the last weekend of the campaign Goldfarb had believed that an all-out attack on Rae had the potential to drive down NDP support by 3 or 4 percent of decided voters per day. In the closing days of the campaign Goldfarb found the "red scare" did work, although not as well as he had anticipated. Peterson's attacks would have the effect of cutting Rae's support by only about 6 percent in four days.

"I think if we'd focused on the NDP a week earlier we could have made a difference," said MacNaughton. "Particularly since if we'd focused on them earlier, we would not have had to have been as extreme in the attacks. The problem with doing it with five days left was that in order to get the attention, you had to get pictures of Bob Rae with rams or sheep. By that point in time, if you didn't say something pretty outrageous, it wasn't going to get reported at all."

11

Judgment Day

I'm toast.

–DAVID PETERSON,
SEPTEMBER 6, 1990

It was election day and the people of Ontario would speak. The 37-day campaign had offered up a seesaw of potential outcomes. The published polls had contributed to the confusion—first a Liberal minority was likely, then an NDP minority. Volatility seemed to be the only voter constant. Across Ontario, Liberal candidates and workers gave little credence to the polls and felt sure they would get back in. Most believed the Liberal line that the number of undecided voters was between 20 and 30 percent, not knowing that line was intended to cast doubt on the credibility of the Angus Reid prediction and persuade soft Liberal supporters that their votes were essential to keep the party in power. Peterson's last-minute rantings had done little more than convince many Liberals that the lights had been turned out before the performance was over.

As the polls opened at nine that morning, a light rain began to drift across southern Ontario. Most of the province was gloomy all day and a chill in the air served notice that the fall was coming. The drizzle, punctuated by rumbles of thunder and downpour from dark clouds, penetrated everywhere, washing out the bright colors of summer. Rain soaked the backs and shoes of canvassers pulling the vote, who ran from car to porch, porch to car, grim and single-minded.

At three in the afternoon, Government House Leader Chris Ward darted into his campaign headquarters in Dundas to change poll kits, work some voters on the phone and head out to keep trying. He shook the rain from his nylon jacket. For six hours he had sprinted and splashed from house to house, urging the people of Wentworth North to give him support again. Now the rain was picking up, threatening to curtail the final wave of voters who might respond to his pleas. He glanced up and caught the inquiring eyes of a longtime staffer.

"We're fucked," he said matter-of-factly, with half the day to go.

"C'mon, no way!" came the reaction, half-laughing.

"Yep," said Ward, ashen-faced. "I'm pulling Liberals and they're voting NDP."

In Streetsville, an old town enveloped by the burgeoning city of Mississauga, Solicitor General Steve Offer woke on election day. He had a packed schedule: handshaking at a local GO train station as he had most mornings during the campaign, casting his own ballot, then pulling the vote. Election day was the culmination of a long struggle for political survival for Offer that began with a challenge to his nomination five months earlier. He had been campaigning since April and he and his workers were exhausted. Although his campaign team had identified 10,000 Liberals in the riding and his seat was considered safe, Offer was uneasy and tense. But the hard work, concluding with a strong vote-pulling effort, would pay off for him.

Most Liberal campaigns tried to target their vote-pulling by using their own judgment, based on intelligence gathered during more than a month of canvassing. Many had ignored the advice from Liberal headquarters for weeks, choosing to play their own game of survival by wits and savvy. But some had adhered faithfully to the tactical advice from the central campaign and were paying a terrible price as voters cast their ballots.

"Kathy Robinson said the Angus Reid numbers were wrong and that in Peterborough we weren't in any trouble," said Peterborough Liberal Peter Adams, on his way to defeat by the NDP. "We thought there was something funny going on, but because we hadn't heard, we thought, 'Well, fine, it's going to be tough, it's going to be a close win.' We were working very hard, but we weren't panicked. If we had been panicked, we'd have done better."

Robinson had decided that "panicking" Liberal candidates by telling them the facts would be destructive, causing them and their workers to give up and pack their bags. In the last week, Adams followed Robinson's advice and Peterson's lead and began a vicious anti-NDP assault. Had Adams been provided with accurate information, "I would have gone and targeted the Tory vote, particularly in the rural areas," he said. "We could have shifted to that and not raised the socialist horde stuff."

On voting day nearly two dozen Liberal staff from the central campaign were ordered to Peterson's riding of London Centre in a last-minute emergency infusion of help. Three top Peterson staffers went out as a vote-pulling team, taking a set of polls in which 708 Liberals had been identified. "We busted our asses and pulled out literally 75 percent of those 708 people," said one of the workers, an expert canvasser. "We lost every single poll by more than 50 percent. The Liberals in the premier's riding were voting NDP."

The drill of vote-pulling was the common experience of local campaigns of every political stripe. New Democrats worked tirelessly through the day, under directions from the NDP central campaign to get to every possible voter. The prospects for a breakthrough were unprecedented, NDP candidates and workers were told, but no sweeping expectation of victory had been encouraged; hard work on the ground would make all the difference. The Tories, their expectations low from the outset, aimed to extract every possible vote from the poll-by-poll effort they had been struggling to organize since their leadership campaign.

*   *   *

Liberal campaign headquarters was almost deserted. One of Peterson's press aides had been assigned to answer the phones for the day; they were not ringing. Early on, central campaign workers had stopped in to pick up their last boxes of files before running off to work in the Toronto ridings where they had been assigned. One loaded his cartons on a small handcart and lugged it through the office.

"Hey, don't lose that handcart," a voice called out. "Where we're going, we're gonna need it."

"Don't be ridiculous," the worker replied indignantly.

In the last week of the campaign, unaware of the frantic flailing of the strategists, the Liberal campaign's vice-chair of organization Bill Murray realized he had neglected to organize a pool on the outcome of the election. Murray had assumed that duty in 1985 and 1987. He put out the word he would take wagers from Liberal staff until voting day: five bucks to get in, winner take all. The calls poured in; 32 entries raised the pool to $160. The average prediction was Liberals 71, NDP 42, Tories 17. Murray himself had Liberals 81, NDP 37, Tories 12. Farther down the list, John Webster, husband of campaign director Beth Webster, believed the Liberals could get 71 seats, the NDP 45 and the Tories 14. Peterson's principal secretary Dan Gagnier put his money on Liberals 67, NDP 50, Tories 13—a slim Liberal majority. Five staffers predicted a Liberal minority and only one believed the polls: speechwriter John Duffy, who bet on NDP 62, Liberals 58, Tories 10.

The members of the Liberal strategy committee were long gone from headquarters. Robinson, Webster and David MacNaughton went to London to spend the evening with Peterson. Senator Michael Kirby stayed in Toronto to appear on television as an election-night analyst. Gagnier spent a few hours at his Queen's Park office, then went home to watch the returns with his wife. Martin Goldfarb monitored the results on television in Toronto; the night before, he had given an interview to the Windsor *Star* in which he put himself on the record with a prediction of an NDP majority. David Morton convinced Red Trillium's Donald Murphy to go to London with him; they thought the strategy committee would be assembling there to be with Peterson.

In the dying hours of the campaign Webster had fulfilled what she saw as her duty, telling top, longtime Peterson workers what she expected to happen that night. "I spent most of my time telling these people the real truths, specifically Doug Kirkpatrick and Bill Murray," she said. Like even the most pessimistic of Liberals, Webster did not believe any minority situation, Liberal or NDP, would result in the Liberals losing power. "People did not know," she said. "The worst-case scenario that people were willing to go in there with was a minority government. No one wanted to believe it."

"There was always an assumption in Ontario that short of 40 percent, you couldn't get a majority," said Kirby. "That's why, even on election night, knowing all the numbers, I thought that the outcome would be more seats for the NDP. I thought that it would be the reverse of 1985: the NDP would get more seats than we did but be short of a majority and the ball would be in Harris's court to decide who would be premier. I was quite relaxed." So were Kirby's fellow strategists, who could not envision Harris using his king-maker role to crown Rae.

"My view was every red Tory candidate would have been defeated; the only ones left would have been the real small 'c' core of the Conservative party," Kirby explained. "There was no way this group of people led by Harris would conceivably put into office the first NDP government of Ontario. It clearly wasn't going to happen. So they get 59 seats and we get 51 and we're still the government." MacNaughton, like Kirby, believed, "It was going to be between 50 and 60 seats for the Liberals and for the NDP."

In newspaper, radio and television newsrooms across Ontario the machinery of election coverage was rolled out. Satellite uplinks and mobile television trucks flanked the election-night halls of each leader; cameras were rigged and cables snaked across the floors. Radio reporters checked their audio lines. Newspaper reporters tested computer links to their newsrooms. Most reporters who had covered the campaign spent election day piecing together the picture on the voter turnout and covering the final activities of the leaders. Some, to save time in the mad flood of information after the polls closed, had prepackaged their stories, covering all the options they could imagine. "Matt Maychak for the Toronto *Star*, Mike Trickey for the *Sun* and I, had written the 'hold-for-the-leads,'" said the *Globe*'s Richard Mackie. "We'd all written 'Liberal majority,' 'Liberal minority' and 'NDP minority' leads. We thought, 'Okay fine, we're covered.'"

Reporters covering the campaign were expecting no other result because, "We were all still fighting the '85 and '87 elections," Mackie said. "If you knew something about Ontario history you knew the NDP couldn't form a government in Ontario. You knew that Bob Rae could not fight a winning campaign. These were all the givens. We believed that people at heart were too conservative. We didn't realize that the people of Canada had changed a lot, not just Ontario but Canada changed a lot."

Many reporters, hardened by election experience, refused to buy the lines fed to them in the campaign's final week of informational anarchy. "You know the old line about the first casualty of war is truth?" the *Star*'s Maychak said. "Well, an election is the closest thing to war you get in politics. The first casualty is definitely truth. So you go into the election knowing that all three parties are lying to you. They know they're lying and you know they're lying. By the end of the campaign all three parties were telling us the NDP was poised to win. I was having a hard time believing all of them for different reasons. There was a suspicion in the press that the Liberals were trying to convince us that the NDP were doing better than they were, so that everyone would be scared of the socialist hordes and return to the Liberal fold and that would make the difference between a minority and a majority government. There was an equal suspicion that the NDP were lying about how well they were doing because they were trying to convince people that they were for real. And the Tories were lying because they felt that people who really disliked the Liberals and wanted to vote against them, but did not want a socialist government, would then turn to Harris."

*   *   *

Peterson and his wife Shelley left their farm on a rural road outside London before the polls opened in the morning. Accompanied by his executive assistant Gordon McCauley, Peterson voted, knocked on a few doors in polls in London Centre, where he received polite responses, and went back to the farm. The night before he had explained to his children what might happen: he was probably going to lose and they should be prepared. "They had to be ready for it and that's politics and that's life and it's not something to weep about," he said.

Back at the farm there were chores to be done, including a summer's-end ritual that was long overdue. "I made chili sauce," said Peterson. "My tomatoes were late and I didn't have a chance to make chili sauce. I had to get my tomatoes and my peppers in. It's good chili sauce." Splitting firewood in the winter and tending his garden in the summer were therapeutic for Peterson; each of his children had a garden plot. In August, the 40 plants in the premier's tomato patch had gone unattended; the rigors of the campaign had kept the gardener busy. Now it was catch-up time.

As the jars of chili sauce cooled in the Peterson farmhouse kitchen early in the evening, the winds came up and blew down some power lines, knocking the lights out. The family dressed by candlelight and left for the Radisson Hotel in downtown London, where they would watch the election results on television with family and friends.

Gathered in Suite 2206 were Peterson's two brothers and their wives, and his parents, who had been working the phones at the London Centre campaign headquarters until shortly before the polls closed. Shelley's brother and her parents Joyce and Don Matthews had arrived; so had her sister Debbie Nash with her children, and Peterson's old friend Ted McGrath and his family. Three large television sets were on. In an adjoining room, Gabor Apor and speechwriters Allan Golombek and Seymour Kanowitch were working on an array of scenarios for Peterson's speech. Robinson, Beth and John Webster, Vince Borg, McCauley, Kirkpatrick and Peterson's OPP bodyguards were filling the room; Morton and Murphy were the last to arrive.

Just before the coverage began at eight o'clock, Shelley combed her daughter Chloe's hair in final preparation for the evening. Outside in the hall, photographers and cameramen were bunched up, waiting to be permitted in to take pictures of the assembled family. Peterson walked out of the bedroom, his red tie showing beneath his collar at the back; Shelley fixed it. He sat in a hard wooden chair, the children piled onto a couch and other family members gathered and stood around. The cameras were let in for two blinding, flashing minutes, then quickly herded out.

In the next room, through the closed French doors, a hot and cold buffet was laid out, waiting for the celebration to begin. Peterson's driver and bodyguards leaned against a bar stocked with soft drinks and mineral water.

No one was talking. Robinson was quiet and looked exhausted. Beth Webster paced; John Webster, normally ebullient and outgoing, was grave and subdued.

The coverage flashed from the television screens as the polls closed at eight. For a few minutes the events of the long campaign seemed an eternity away, as the first results put the Liberals well in front. "Liberals 12, NDP 5, Tories 2," the networks were announcing after 10 minutes.

"That's it," declared Peterson, his eyes not leaving the screen in front of him. "Let it end right there; we've won."

But within minutes, on all three televisions, the numbers began to change, first in staccato bursts, then in a cataract of upsets, thundering in. Within 25 minutes every network had declared an NDP majority. Peterson sat quietly, smoking cigarettes, still staring at the screen. He appeared completely calm and absorbed. Others clamored nervously around the room, sitting, standing, kneeling on the floor, walking in and out of the room, smoking like fiends.

Chloe slipped in beside her father, hugging him and crying softly for only a few minutes. An NDP analyst came on with a few positive words about Peterson. "Isn't that nice of him," said Shelley. The camera switched to the Tory panelist, Larry Grossman, who offered some cutting remarks about the Liberals. Shelley's face fell. "Can't he even be a little bit gracious?" she said, with a hurt look.

From the back of the room Debbie Nash moved apprehensively toward Peterson. She had just hung up the phone from the campaign headquarters for London Centre, the riding Peterson had held for 15 years. She sat down next to her brother-in-law; he turned to look at her.

"I talked to the campaign," she said gently. "We're toast."

He looked up with a weak smile. "Toast, eh?"

Shelley took her children aside. "You know this means we've lost," she told them. What will happen to Ontario now, they asked her.

Peterson finally rose and stretched his legs. Morton and Murphy, feeling like outsiders, had retreated to a corner of the room. Peterson approached them. "Well," he grimaced, "I'm toast."

"No, you're not," they choked.

Peterson moved over to his driver and bodyguards. "Remember, guys," he cracked. "Don't ever pull your guns on the new premier, even in fun." They looked at him with tears welling in their eyes. One walked out of the suite into the corridor, leaned against the wall and pounded it with his fist, rattling the doors far down the hallway.

There was no hysteria, no sobbing inside Suite 2206. Morton found himself talking to Marie Peterson.

"David told me that you said he shouldn't go," said Morton.

"You know, dear," she replied, "I saw the looks on the people's faces in London. They were pained looks, and I knew he shouldn't call an election."

"Well," he said, "Moms are always right." She gave him a sad smile. Morton and Murphy slipped out of the suite to head over to Centennial Hall. Apor and the speechwriters gave copies of their texts to Peterson and joined Morton and Murphy in the corridor.

"Here's what he's going to say," Apor told Morton, leafing through his copy.

"Is he going to resign?" Morton asked pointedly.

"Oh, no, he's not going to resign," Apor replied with certainty.

Borg approached Peterson and tapped his shoulder from behind.

"Maybe we should go in to the other room and talk about some things," he suggested. Peterson followed him; Shelley, his father and a handful of advisors came along. When should he resign the leadership? they asked one another. Should he do it that night or hold off? In the last few days of the campaign, sensing the inevitability of the loss, Peterson had wrestled with the question himself. Robinson had spoken to Nixon: Would he be prepared to accept the interim leadership of the party if called upon? Of course, said the treasurer, but let's just wait and see what happens.

Peterson stepped aside for a private word with Shelley. Her advice: deal with it all at once. "Now's the time," his father counseled. Peterson returned to the group.

"I've made my decision," he said. "I'm resigning tonight."

Kirkpatrick produced a list of phone numbers and made contact with Rae's staff. Peterson spoke to the premier-elect for a few moments, offering congratulations. They would talk later, Peterson said, and he would provide every assistance with transition. A quick call to Harris followed. Nixon called; Peterson spoke to him quietly, then sat down with Shelley to work on his speech.

*   *   *

Centennial Hall had never looked larger. It was barely half-filled with local Liberals and the red-and-white balloons and bunting were sparse. "There was nobody there," said a Peterson aide, "which really pissed me off because in '85 you couldn't move in that place and in '87 it was even better. Just because we lost, nobody showed up." MacNaughton had arrived shortly before eight; he was holding the fort, conducting one media interview after another in front of the stage. No one had assigned him the job but there was no one else around to do it. As reporters lined up to put him on the live television broadcasts, he offered his own mea culpa, sharing the blame for the defeat and the early-election call.

"It's easy in hindsight to decide that you made a mistake," he told one reporter. "I take part of the responsibility for urging the premier to call an election. I was one of those who suggested he have an early-election call. So, I've got to take the rap." Mac-Naughton moved on to the next interview. "I think people thought that it was cynical and opportunistic and they didn't like it," he said. "I think we had a view that we were running to seek a mandate for legitimate reasons but others had different ideas." Another reporter asked MacNaughton how he felt: "I can't believe this," he said. "This is hard to believe." Within the first two weeks of the campaign he knew the Liberals were in trouble, MacNaughton told another reporter: "We understood we had a problem; we misjudged the depth of it."

At Liberal headquarters in Toronto, workers from across Metro Toronto had been gathering to watch the results pour in on three mural-sized television sets. Lined up four and five deep their dazed, bewildered faces could not leave the screens. Every few minutes a groan would sweep around the room: another cabinet minister had fallen; seven in all would lose their seats although most, including Bob Nixon, Ian Scott and Elinor Caplan, would hold on.

*   *   *

Peterson finished reworking his speech. The children were left in the hotel suite where they ate chips, drank pop and turned on MuchMusic. Peterson and Shelley were driven the few short blocks to Centennial Hall and entered through a side door.

McCauley and Kirkpatrick led the way in and began cutting a path through the crowd that formed around them, guiding Peterson and his wife along, surrounded by a moving, jostling phalanx of reporters and television cameras. Peterson said nothing into the microphones thrust in front of him; the cameras caught his grim, determined face as he nudged forward to the stage.

Up ahead, Borg found MacNaughton; Peterson's arrival had stopped the deluge of interviews.

"He's gonna be resigning," Borg hissed in MacNaughton's ear above the din. "He feels he has no choice."

Borg leaned back and looked at MacNaughton, who had blanched, his eyes widening with shock. He had been caught up in his interviews, and the magnitude of the loss was finally registering. He was speechless.

Peterson reached the stage and approached the microphone, Shelley at his side. The applause in the room died down and he began to speak in a hoarse and subdued voice.

"When I called the election some 36 days ago, I said it would be an interesting campaign," he said. "I had no idea it was going to be this interesting.

"The people across this province have spoken. And I accept that judgment with equanimity. Politics is filled with highs and lows and lots of heartache and I've had mine before and I'll have it again.

"I believe strongly that politics is a noble life. I believe that the highest court in the land, the people, have the ultimate wisdom on by whom and how public policy should be carried out.

"I've also determined, my friends, that . . . I will be tendering my resignation as leader of the party. The responsibility is mine and I accept that responsibility."

A collective gasp spread through Centennial Hall, through Liberal headquarters in Toronto, through campaign offices across the province. "No! No!" workers began to shout. Shelley blinked back tears.

"I felt tears coming to my eyes because I was so proud of him," she said. "But then I looked at all the media around us, nudging and smiling at one another, and I thought, I'm not going to cry and let them think I'm crying because we've lost. I felt so totally proud of David I wanted to cry. I was proud of him because he was a noble man." Peterson continued:

"I have enormous faith in the Liberal cause. I am very proud of the things we have achieved in the last five years. We have cut new paths in social policy, in environmental policy, and we have done that, I believe, in a financially responsible way and have built a strong and respected province.

"I think all Liberals can take pride in that, and I say to you that there's no disgrace in getting knocked down. There is only disgrace in not getting up.

"As long as I have breath and energy, and I can tell you that I've still got a lot left, I will continue to fight for this country and for opportunity across this magnificent land." Cheers and applause swelled up from the crowd.

"Any shortcomings were mine and I accept that responsibility. But, my friends, that does not mean that we have to give up. It does not mean that we do not have ideals that we believe in or ideals that we will continue to fight for. I believe that the Liberal view, the view of generosity and kindness, the view that takes into account all of the citizens of Ontario and Canada, is the view that will prevail and the view that must prevail as we heal this great country."

Peterson and his wife embraced and waved as the crowd cheered. Tears streaked the faces of men and women; in Liberal headquarters, workers sobbed quietly and held one another.

As they stepped off the stage Peterson gave orders to the aide leading the way: "I don't want to go see the media." McCauley and Kirkpatrick pushed through the bodies until the couple reached a side exit, which two aides blocked behind them. Outside, disoriented, the group tried to circle the building to find their cars and ran into the crowd of reporters trying to catch up with them. A swirling melee ensued as the Liberals dragged and pushed Shelley, her sister and Peterson in the right direction, bringing them to their cars. They piled in and Peterson's driver began to pull away, when McCauley ordered him to stop. In a corner of the parking lot, a longtime aide was standing alone, crying. Peterson got out of the car and walked over.

"I'm really, really sorry," he told the aide, hugging him tightly. He went back to the car and the driver sped away, toward the farm.

Back in the hall Webster urged Robinson to help Mac-Naughton deal with the reporters. "Kathy would not go onto the floor," said Webster. "She said, 'You have to go down and do it.'" Finally, reporters caught up with Robinson, demanding to know why Peterson had chosen to resign. "It was a very personal and lonely decision," she told them. "He felt it was the honorable thing to do."

In newsrooms across the province, reporters were scrambling to respond to the unexpected turnabout. "Between a quarter to nine and nine-thirty, my deadline, I wrote about six different leads," said the *Globe*'s Mackie. "From NDP looking good, to NDP getting a minority, to NDP got a strong minority, to NDP got a majority. I was running out to the desk every five minutes and saying, excuse me, I just want to make one little change."

"Reporters were in large measure the last ones to see it coming," admitted the *Star*'s Maychak. "Even on election night I was having a hard time believing what I was seeing, because we're so close to it. You don't see what's happening. We all lived in the same bubble."

In a jam-packed banquet hall in northwest Toronto, Bob Rae and his wife moved to the stage through an ecstatic, whooping crowd of supporters. As the returns had been fed through television sets into the hall the New Democrats had screamed and cheered in delight as Liberal cabinet ministers were knocked off one by one. A huge, triumphant roar raised the roof when the networks declared Marion Boyd the landslide winner in London Centre, trampling Peterson.

"I didn't expect this result," Rae admitted with a smile as the jubilant crowd thundered in applause. "The lesson from this election is that the public trust must be earned. I am well aware that in the election victory we have been given tonight, we are only just beginning to earn that trust. And we must continue to work every day to earn it, each and every working day.

"We must think more of what we owe each other, rather than what we can make off each other," he told the crowd. And he carefully directed a message at his television audience, aimed at easing the concerns of the business community. "I am prepared to work with everyone," he promised.

The Rolling Stones blasted out from the speakers in the bowling alley in North Bay where the Harris campaign was holding its election night celebration. Three hundred Tory supporters were crammed in; their party's performance was proving better than expected and they applauded Mike Harris proudly as he took credit for the massive defeat of the Liberals.

"It was the tax issue that drove the Liberals out of office," he boasted. The vote for the NDP was not an endorsement of NDP policies, he warned, but a protest against "a high-taxing and wasteful government."

Tory campaign manager John Laschinger told reporters his party had "overachieved," pointing out that polls at the start of the campaign showed the Tories would get only four seats. The results were giving Harris five times that many. But the "taxfighter" was not to be the king-maker: he still found himself at the helm of a tiny third party, drowning in debt.

Within two hours the extent of the historic win was clear: defying the popular wisdom that a socialist government could never rule Ontario, Rae and the NDP won a solid majority of 74 seats of the 130 in the legislature, an increase of 55 seats. The Liberals were routed across Ontario, dropping an incredible 57 seats to plummet from 93 to 36 members. Harris and the Tories increased their holdings from 16 ridings to 20. Support for the NDP was uniform in all regions of the province: Rae won his majority with an unprecedented 37.6 percent of the popular vote, laying waste to the rule that a government needed more than 40 percent of the popular vote to obtain a majority. Rae would form a majority government with only three out of eight Ontarians supporting the NDP. The Liberals slid to 32.4 percent, a drop of about 20 points since the beginning of the campaign.

The Tories captured 23.5 percent of voters, while fringe parties picked up nearly 7 percent, far more than their 2.3 percent in 1987. The voter turnout of 61.5 percent was typical for an Ontario election.

Reporters and analysts were baffled by the results—and especially by the vote splits in ridings that worked with remarkable consistency in the NDP's favor. "There was a tendency to hit yourself on the head and say, 'I had everybody telling me the same thing. Why didn't I put my money in the office pool on the NDP?'" said the Star's Maychak. "In our own defense in terms of predicting the outcome, if you had shown me the popular vote figures I wouldn't have predicted an NDP majority."

Back at the Radisson Hotel, Suite 2206 was quiet. A few campaign workers returned, opened the French doors to the adjoining room and picked at the buffet. The hot food was cold and the cold food was hot. "Even the food looked sad," observed Murphy. He and Morton ordered drinks from room service as more workers arrived. The dynamics were awkward; with virtually every Liberal in the province kept in the dark throughout the campaign, the result was impossible to understand. Beth Webster walked in, and was set upon by some Liberal staffers. "You knew it was going to happen," one worker charged angrily. "No one told us—we were fooled."

Liberals were lashing out that night, as they would for months, blaming Robinson, Webster, Goldfarb, the strategists and Peterson for their demise. The personal and professional disruptions would prove enormous: 600 staff were suddenly and unexpectedly out of work. Peterson would shoulder the burden himself: "When you're leader of the party, as long as you're assuming you've got the support of the party, I had the power to pick my advisors and pick the advice I chose from them. So if I picked stupid advisors and I picked stupid advice, that was my fault, not their fault. I don't think any of them were willingly trying to subvert me. They were strong people with a difference of opinion. Hell, I had different advice on every single issue. But ultimately, you listen as best you can, do the best you can. So I don't blame anybody for this."

Just after midnight the phone rang in the hotel suite and Morton picked it up. It was Peterson, calling from the farmhouse.

"What are you people doing?" he asked.

"We're getting drunk," Morton replied.

"Well, come on over to my place," said Peterson.

Morton and Murphy found a limo and headed out of the city. When they arrived at the farmhouse Peterson and his wife were in the kitchen surrounded by Robinson, Beth and John Webster, Borg and MacNaughton.

"Shelley," Peterson turned to his wife. "Remember all the times I gave you pocket money? Well, I hope you'll give me some now that I'm unemployed." Laughter rippled around the kitchen. A handful of the Peterson clan remained; most had gone home, exhausted. The group sat around and talked: about who had won and who had lost, about the stories that stuck out from the election, about the protesters, about the tough life of politics.

"This election was like 'Whack-a-Mole,'" said Shelley. "That game they have at fairs, where the little mechanical moles stick their heads up through the holes and you hit them with a hammer. You were the first mole to stick your head up after Meech."

"Well, I guess people get the government they deserve," said Peterson. The early call, he maintained, had been the right decision; it still would have been worse had he waited a year. People nodded their heads and the room grew quiet.

"So, waddya think?" said Peterson, looking around. "What happened?"

There were no answers. Some heads hung, others shook, others looked off in the distance, thinking hard of what to say.

Peterson became reflective. "I have no regrets about being in politics," he said. "I'm not cynical about the process, I'm not mad about the process. I have absolutely no regrets about my involvement. I do believe in the nobility of the struggle of life, because you've got to try and you've got to stick your neck out and keep moving and don't look back. That's the advice from me.

"You know, you have to try, whatever your own way is, hopefully, to make the world a little better place. And that's my way of trying, and I have no regrets. It's a tough world if you do anything. This country has no heroes. This country beats up everybody, and whatever you do, the more you do, the more critics you're going to have. The more successful you are, the more critics you're going to have. That goes without saying, because there are so many people whose currency is criticism. Look, this country needs playwrights, it doesn't need critics. It needs builders, not destroyers. And for some reason, we are a country that is terribly, terribly tough on itself. I don't know of a country that is more tough on itself or on anybody that does anything than this country. We have this national preoccupation with tearing down rather than building.

"Sometimes it breaks for you, sometimes it doesn't. Sometimes you win, sometimes you lose, but you've got to try in life. Life's about trying, life's about reaching, life's about doing things you believe in. And so you fail: there's no disgrace in that. The only way not to fail is not to do anything."

It was getting late. The postmortems, clinical and messy, could wait for the next day, and the next. The last family members left and the remaining Liberal friends got up to leave. Mac-Naughton walked outside with Beth and John Webster, his ride home, and sat quietly in the backseat.

"I never thought that this would happen, never," Mac-Naughton said as they drove away. "If I had known, I would have acted differently. I was so wrapped up in my own life. The poor guy." And he began to cry.

Epilogue

On May 23, 1991, 800 Liberals gathered at the Metro Toronto Convention Centre for a tribute to David Peterson. Tickets to the event were $135 each. Nine months after leading the party to defeat, Peterson was still being used as its most powerful fund-raising attraction.

Don Smith was the master of ceremonies. A video tribute to Peterson was shown on an immense screen—a montage of the Liberal government's accomplishments. Most of the tape was devoted to the minority government years. When the announcer praised Peterson's dedication to national unity, people looked at one another uncomfortably; when a clip from the Meech talks showed Brian Mulroney praising Peterson, there were some jeers.

Peterson, named a partner in the Toronto law firm Cassels Brock & Blackwell a few weeks earlier after a stint as a lecturer-at-large at York University's Glendon College, received a standing ovation as he stood to speak on the challenges facing Canada and its leaders.

"I see an awful lot of talk today of people who have no faith in their political institutions so they want to invent parallel political institutions or some new assembly," he said. "Or they can't make decisions, so have a referendum or do a lot of things that are denials of traditional political responsibility. I say to you that the legislature of Ontario, the Parliament of Canada, the legislatures across this country, are the greatest constituent assemblies in this country, and we need a leadership that will stand up to its responsibilities."

Interim leader Bob Nixon made a few remarks; it was Peterson, he reminded the Liberals, who had given them all the privilege of governing for five years. He received cheers when he read from a news release issued by pollster Michael Marzolini: Bob Rae and the NDP government, after introducing a budget with a $9.7-billion deficit, had tumbled in support to 28 percent of decided voters in Toronto. The Liberals stood at 36 percent, the Tories at 23; support for other parties, chiefly the Reform Party, stood at 12 percent. Outside Toronto, support for the NDP remained higher, but the honeymoon was clearly over.

That weekend, Liberals at their annual general meeting decided on a process for choosing a new leader and wrestled with when to hold a leadership convention. At Queen's Park the NDP government wrestled with the tough issues of the day: a deep recession, auto insurance, Sunday shopping, rent controls and scandals involving cabinet ministers, complete with resignations. News reports showed protesters ranging from businesspeople to truckers to overtaxed homeowners, lining up to march on the legislature. The New Democrats learned quickly that being in government means making choices and that making choices means creating heat. And there is still plenty of heat.

*   *   *

Liberals at the Peterson tribute were still wondering why an early election was called and why it was lost. Some blamed the timing. Most still could not understand how their government went from the height of popularity and widespread support to the depths of rejection and humiliation.

The strategists and campaign executives were not providing any clues, although most showed up at the event: Kathy Robinson, Hershell Ezrin, Senator Michael Kirby; all, along with

David MacNaughton and Martin Goldfarb, had continued in their old jobs after the election.

Vince Borg, who helped organize the event, had joined Goldfarb's firm. Beth Webster had become a government relations consultant. Dan Gagnier did not make an appearance. His skills were being tested in a new job: director of communications in the Privy Council office for Mulroney.

For most Liberals the shock of the loss had worn off. Most believed that the Peterson Liberals had provided, on balance, good government and introduced much-needed reforms. Many saw, in retrospect, that a process of decay had been at work in their government for some time—perhaps, some would think, normal organizational decay; perhaps, some would understand, more than that.

A few in the crowd might have acknowledged that perhaps the Liberals failed to win re-election because they did not fight for or against anyone or anything; they did not give Ontarians a reason to vote for Peterson and their party; they did not close the deal.

Perception, the Liberals would agree, was reality in the election: Peterson was defeated because of how he was seen by voters. People across Canada want a leader to have vision, values and goals. Peterson had those qualities but in the form of a nationalistic imperative that did not resonate with Ontarians in the summer of 1990. At the end he would remain firm in his commitment to national unity and in his decisions.

"My single greatest regret in politics is the failure of Meech," he would say, "not the loss of the election." The validity of Peterson's personal reasons for calling the election would appear to be supported by subsequent events: an election a year later in Ontario would in all likelihood have been a referendum on Quebec, although the passage of time would have helped Peterson distance himself from Meech's demise.

In 1990, Peterson's Teflon coating, only slightly scratched by scandal, was eroded by Meech, aggravated by the early election call, then stripped away by attack strategies that identified the Liberals as something bad and promised something different.

The election result represented a triumph of style over substance. Ontarians wanted a government they felt would be more honest and open, a new and different government—though not too different. They voted for the reform-minded, problem-solving government they thought they had elected in 1987. After trying the other products on the shelf they reached for the only one they had not tested: Bob Rae and the NDP.

Ontarians did not wholeheartedly endorse the NDP or its policies. Only three in eight voted New Democrat but the vote splits produced a majority. The implications are profound for pollsters and strategists in future elections: the fractionalization of the electorate, the demise of traditional party allegiances, the rise of fourth and fifth parties and the disappearance of core votes are factors to understand and deal with. The old rules no longer apply.

In their search for the truth within politicians—the vision, values, motivations and honest passions that comprise the real person behind the public image—voters should be aware of the methods and intentions of all of the players in the game: political parties, special-interest groups, pollsters and the media, who all vie to influence voters' perceptions. Voters may separate truth from propaganda, fact from spin, reality from perception, if they undertake to inform themselves and understand what the players are up to—and not only at election time. Voters with realistic expectations will not deify politicians and look to them for panaceas; politicians ought not to cater to that attitude by promising the moon and purporting to be able to fix every problem. The cycle of heightened expectations and unrealistic promises only ensures failure, disappointment and disenchantment. Voters can use their knowledge to advance their search for sincere, committed and effective leaders, and to demand that politicians prove they are qualified to represent the people, to serve and to be trusted. Ultimately, each voter is the pivotal player in the political exercise, with the power—and the responsibility—to shape politicians, public policy, the political system and the future of the country.

Acknowledgments

This project owes much to Nancy and Stanley Colbert of Harper-Collins, who in September 1990 responded with enthusiasm to our proposal that the rise and fall of the Peterson Liberal government was an important and interesting story, with implications both national and enduring. The Colberts' approach was reflected in the assistance of our editor Iris Skeoch, under whose expert guidance we worked to make our story sharper and more readable. Our copy editor June Trusty provided flow and consistency with her excellent eye.

An exceptional service was provided by Cassandra Dennis, her sister Erica and friend Maureen Jaques, who together transcribed some 5,000 pages, representing the more than 100 interviews undertaken as background to the book.

Of those we interviewed, we particularly thank David and Shelley Peterson and Clarence and Marie Peterson, who gave freely of their time and openly of their thoughts and feelings. We are also grateful for the interest and valuable assistance of Vince Borg, Ian Scott, Bob Nixon, Elinor Caplan, David MacNaughton and Dan Gagnier.

David Agnew, David Reville and Gerald Caplan shed light on the NDP campaign, while John Tory, Phil Gillies and Larry Grossman provided astute insight into the Tory campaign.

Jim Clancy, Jim Head, Gord Perks and Paul Rhodes offered understanding of their special-interest groups.

While many members of the Queen's Park press gallery supplied information and assistance, the recollections and views of senior reporters Robert Fisher, Richard Mackie and Matt Maychak were instrumental in explaining the workings of the media during the 1990 election campaign.

The Liberal Caucus Service Bureau and Ontario Liberal Party both provided access to records and documents that assisted in our research.

We would like to thank the following individuals who submitted themselves to detailed and often lengthy interviews: principals involved in the 1990 Liberal campaign including Kathy Robinson, Beth Webster, David Morton, Michael Kirby, Hershell Ezrin, Doug Kirkpatrick, Gordon McCauley, Debbie Nash, Bill Murray and Jan Whitelaw, and pollsters Martin Goldfarb, Michael Marzolini and Michael Adams.

Others whose input was invaluable include Gabor Apor, Chuck Birchall, Sue Callum, Bob Carman, George Cooke, Peter Donegan, Gordon Floyd, Allan Golombek, Patrick Gossage, Steve Goudge, Jan Innes, Patrick Johnson, Marc Kealey, Ted McGrath, Ross McGregor, Patrick Monahan, Donald Murphy, Terry O'Malley, Paul Pellegrini, Heather Peterson, Pat Sorbara, Ken Tilley, John Webster, and former and current Liberal caucus members Peter Adams, Ken Black, Jim Bradley, Murray Elston, Chaviva Hosek, Lyn McLeod, Steve Offer, Hugh O'Neil and Chris Ward.

Friends and family also provided much needed support as the project unfolded. Georgette Gagnon is especially grateful to Cheryl and Ranji Persad and Jenifer Lass for their enthusiasm and patience. Most of all, she acknowledges and thanks Denis and Yolande Gagnon and the Gagnon siblings for their unlimited love, support and understanding. Dan Rath is grateful to two good friends, David Paterson and Craig Crawford, for their encouragement, and to Lawrence and Ruth Rath and his brother and sister for their unfailing support.

Index